P9-CKY-153

WOMANHOOD
IN AMERICA

NEW VIEWPOINTS ☆ NEW YORK, 1975
A DIVISION OF FRANKLIN WATTS

MARY P. RYAN

**WOMANHOOD
IN AMERICA**

FROM COLONIAL TIMES
TO THE PRESENT

Library of Congress Cataloging in Publication Data

Ryan, Mary P
    Womanhood in America, from colonial times to
the present.
        Includes bibliographical references.
        1. Women   in   the   United   States–History.
2. Women–History   and   condition.   3. Sex   role.
4. Sex discrimination–United States.   I. Title.
HQ1410.R9   301.41′2′0973   74-17318
ISBN 0-531-05365-2
ISBN 0-531-05568-X (pbk.)

TABLE OF CONTENTS

Acknowledgments

My work on this volume was facilitated by summer grants from the National Endowment for the Humanities and the Research Foundation of the State University of New York. Jeanette B. Cheek, former director of the Arthur and Elizabeth Schlesinger Library, Radcliffe College, was of special assistance.

I deeply appreciate the advice, support and insightful comments offered by my colleagues at the State University of New York, Elizabeth Fee and Sarah Elbert. Thanks are due to Mari Jo Buhle, Allis Rosenberg Wolfe and Milton Mankoff for reading the manuscript; to Norman Cantor for his encouragement; and to my mentor, Lynn L. Marshall. Very special thanks go to Peter Biskind for a thorough editing of my mangled prose.

This book would not have been possible without the curiosity and enthusiasm of students of women's history at SUNY.

M.P.R.
Binghamton
January, 1975

For
Marguerite Voth Ryan
Peggy Ryan

**WOMANHOOD
IN AMERICA**

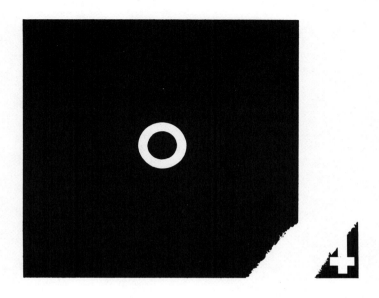

INTRODUCTION:

FROM WOMAN TO
WOMANHOOD

Yet looking around upon the world of human beings as we know it, we are hard put to say what is the natural shape of men or women, so old, so all-enveloping are the molds fitted by history and custom over their personalities.

WINIFRED HOLTBY, 1932

No history book can pretend to resurrect the life and experience of *Homo sapiens,* sex female. Such a boast presumes a magical power to exhume generations of females and to unravel the shroud of anonymity that has been the historical lot of womankind. Woman's history is both more and less than an exercise in collective biography, played out in the monotonous rhythms of the female life cycle. The aim of this volume is to describe the making of the social and cultural category, womanhood, the artificial mold into which history has persistently shaped the female sex. This investigation is inspired by the vexing question, what is woman? and is rooted in the belief that history has invested her sex with a distinctive personality that greatly exaggerates and consistently distorts her simple biological characteristics. An examination of the sundry definitions of woman that have paraded through the American past will expose the destructive impositions of culture and society upon the second sex, and thus clear away the refuse of mystique that has surrounded and suppressed the human female.

Modern science tells us with its customary certitude that the female of the human species is distinguishable from the male by but a single chromosome within a complex genetic structure. This XX pattern in the female's genetic code decrees that the human fetus develops a uterus, ovaries, and a vagina and will be equipped in adulthood to bear young. The male fetus, the geneticist tells us, develops just as the female for the first six weeks of its existence, after which its distinctive pattern of chromosomes, XY, will signal the atrophy of an embryonic uterus and trigger hormones that produce the male sex organs. Although this delicate process is subject to malfunction, it does assure that almost every child enters the world with a relatively unambiguous sexual identity, either male or female.

At the time of birth culture takes over from biology, announcing the sex of the infant with gender names, appropriate pronouns, and such quaint sexual labels as the familiar pink and blue ribbons. It may be several years, however, before a boy or girl comes to recognize the classification that will mark him or her for life. American children examined by cognitive psychologists in the last decade proved confused about sex differences for the first three years of life and did not internalize an unequivocal sex identity until the age of five or six. Once these children realized that they were permanently and definitively either male or female, sinister forces began to play upon their young minds. While the little boy quickly achieved an egotistical delight in his maleness, the girl child hesitated, and ultimately failed to accept her sexual identity with unequivocal pleasure. The girl might be ignorant of the actual anatomical differences between males and females and, of course, was unaware of the permutations of chromosomes. Yet by this tender age she had become conscious of the sexual dichotomy in the human race, and upon comparison of adult males and females, she had concluded that her own sex had been sentenced to inferiority. In the person of the adult female, whom they have clearly identified as their model, these six-year-old girls spied a disquieting projection of their life to come.

The assessment of womanhood made by these little girls was remarkably perspicacious, for, like generations of women before them, they would grow up to confront a social reality that, in one way or another, devalued them on grounds of sex. They would share the fate of women throughout time and in every culture, where the law of gender conferred inequality on females. The differences in genitalia and reproductive functions signal two categories of human beings around which are built an elaborate system for allocating the duties, privileges, and power of society. Sex, as the sociologist Harriet Holter puts it, constitutes a basic principle of social distribution, a "master status system." It is the system that creates the category womanhood and the social and cultural legacy of the girl child, which is the central concern of this book.

Despite wide cross-cultural variations in sex roles and stereotypes, the aggregation of duties, prohibitions, and traits ascribed to the female consistently relegate her to a secondary social position. Human cultures almost universally reserve positions of public authority as a male prerogative. Anthropologists have failed to uncover a single society in which male dominance has been eclipsed by matriarchal tutelage. Women's political power and status, if any, is most likely exercised in minor offices, on the periphery of the public arena, or through indirect quasi-legitimate leverage. Womanhood also translates into unequal economic relations. Not only is the matrilineal conveyance of wealth a relatively rare anthropological occurrence, but it is customarily allied with a communal system of property holdings wherein major economic decisions are determined by male leaders. The property rights granted to women in modern societies rarely provide a means to the control of economic resources and organizations. In summary, the sexual distribution of political authority and economic power tends either to place women on the bottom rungs of the status system or to exclude them entirely.

This same standard of inequity informs the economic and social roles assigned to women. While the ubiquitous division of labor by sex allows for considerable variations in male and female work, the majority of cultures accord less prestige and fewer rewards to woman's functions. Whether it be among a tribe of hunters or in a modern nation-state, the female's contribution to the material support of the group is more closely identified with meeting the immediate biological needs of her kinsmen. Conversely, she is restricted, in one degree or another, from the more public, active, wide-ranging pursuits whereby men win wealth and glory. Women's time-honored role, providing physical sustenance for a small group, carves out for her a limited space within society, more domestic than social, more sedentary than nomadic, more constrained than free, and more private than public. Accordingly, woman's roles are hidden, taken for granted, at times almost invisible in many cultures.

The sexual system of social distribution not only constricts the behavior of women but in so doing leaves a divisive imprint on the very mind and soul of humanity. With a few notable exceptions, the personal characteristics that are approved within a given culture differ for males and females. This mode of sexual differentiation falls into one predominant pattern, taking shape around the familiar poles of male forcefulness and female passivity. No less than 85 percent of the cultures examined in one anthropological survey consciously trained males to be aggressive and females to be supportive. These normative personality types neatly mesh with the prescribed behavior proper to each sex; they cultivate mental and emotional capacities conducive to worldly success in the male, and suppress the woman's urge to desert her private and inferior sphere. Because sexual differentiation deters women from ranging far afield of such fundamental functions as reproduction and nurture, her entire being is often conceptualized as an extension of biology, a kind of secondary sex characteristic. It seems at times that only the magical Y chromosome can transform a creature of sex into a full-fledged human being.

The persistent social inequality and cultural differentiation between the sexes has prompted countless intellectual excursions in search of a single biological explanation for the "eternal feminine." In the last century, scientists fastened on anything from a cubic centimeter difference in brain size to a slight curvature of the skeleton as the natural explanation of sexual inequality. Contemporary researchers look to a microscopic bit of protein, the chromosome, as the biological first cause of womanhood. Contemporary geneticists confess that beyond insuring that females will be capable of bearing and nursing children, the XX pattern has "no known direct influence on subsequent sexual or psychosexual development." Determination of the effect of prenatal hormones on the brain pathways of animals also yields an indecisive verdict for human beings, in whom these neural pathways "have not been anatomically identified." Furthermore, "the higher primates, and man especially, are more subject to the influence of postnatal biographical history." The examination of human subjects whose hormones are out of balance or whose sex identity is ambiguous also reaches minimal and tentative conclusions about the biological sources of behavioral differences between normal men and women.

The only indisputable and unambiguous natural differences between the sexes are patently obvious;

their different genital construction and reproductive systems. Beyond the roles of men and women in the acts of sexual intercourse and procreation there are no incontrovertible biological determinants of the functions of the sexes. Neither does the physiology of sex decree personality differences that inevitably create a sharp social and cultural division between male and female. Nature supplies only those sexual differences that are essential to reproduction. In so doing, however, it creates a highly visible division of the human race. This separation of the human species into blatantly dichotomous sexes provides a symbol and rubric, not a direct instrumental cause, for a long series of artificial distinctions. The ancient and obvious categories of male and female provide a convenient beginning for any functional division in society, including the distribution of economic tasks and public responsibilities and position in the social hierarchy. When these divisions are made, woman's biology has operated as a stigma, signaling inferiority in a social network designed by human beings, not decreed by nature.

Still, a perplexing question remains: Why have human cultures, unchained by the dictates of nature, recurrently interpreted femaleness as a justification for social inferiority? Anthropological literature is replete with conjectured solutions to this problem, ranging from the assertion of male domination through his superior size and strength to the functional efficiency of assigning secondary domestic roles to the necessarily more sedentary child-bearer. Contemporary feminism has given rise to more sophisticated theories, such as the hypothesis that the female's reproductive function associates her with the mysterious and often hostile forces of nature, and therefore causes her to appear as man's opponent rather than his ally in conquering the material world. Yet, each of these propositions falls short of explaining womanhood in its entirety. Each loses its cogency in advanced societies where muscular force has lost much of its primitive power, and when so much of nature, and the female reproductive system itself, has been brought within human control.

Neither biological nor anthropological paradigms, furthermore, can explain another fixture of the sexual system of social distribution: the great variety of sociosexual arrangements, as antithetical as polyandrous tribes and Victorian households, all of which culminate in female inequality. Sex roles and characteristics display the variety, adaptability, and fluidity typical of human creations; they are manufactured at the precise points in time and in the specific cultural circumstances that are the stock in trade of historians. It is to history, therefore, that we turn to observe the installation of biological woman in that matrix of specialized roles, responsibilities, and characteristics called womanhood. Removed to the plane of historical analysis, the specific origins of female inequality become more concrete. At discreet moments in time, woman's relative powerlessness is clearly visible, exposing her obvious vulnerability to an unequal share in the division of labor, power, and honor between males and females.

The investigation of womanhood leads to a unique encounter with the past, undertaken on novel premises and requiring special historical methods. This is necessary because women have been consistently shoved into the dark corners of society where their power to make history is hidden if not obliterated. The meagerly documented and largely unknown past of women invites the assertion that they are in fact without a history, are mere pawns to be maneuvered into whatever place that the male agents of social change deem appropriate. The muted role of women in history is often acknowledged in such descriptive titles as "caste," "oppressed group," "the other." The actual position of women in the system of social distribution by sex is too complex and variable to justify such rigid categories and is more contingent upon female cooperation and participation than these terms imply. By virtue of her low social status, woman confronts a web of constrictions upon individual autonomy more formidable than, but not fundamentally different from, man's predicament. Woman is merely placed at a greater disadvantage on the battleground of history as described by Karl Marx: "Men make their own history, but they do not make it just as they please; they do not make it under circumstances chosen by themselves, but under circumstances directly encountered, given, and transmitted from the past." The term womanhood is meant to convey the special handicaps with which women enter history. These constraints weave together like a finely meshed but not impenetrable cage imposed upon half the world's population.

The elemental task of woman's history is to describe how this peculiar cage is constructed, remodeled, dismantled, or rebuilt so as to consistently place women in the position of the second sex. The making of womanhood, unlike such supposedly discrete events as wars, revolutions, and elections, however, cannot be dissected into a series of facts, arranged in chronological order, weighed, labeled, and explained by a formula drawn from natural science. Neither can a single human hand, simply personified by the male sex, nor an isolated "force" be found manipulating the levers of woman's history. It is particularly difficult to discern a single explanation for the persistently secondary position of women in the United States of America. Once the European settlers of the North American continent had stilled the native population, they were left with only transatlantic memories to guide their design of sexual relations in the raw and open wilderness. The freedom of the first frontier, swiftly followed by the autonomy derived from preeminence in the world economy, enabled Americans to create their own history with little interference. The American system of social distribution by sex is so intertwined with the totality of the nation's history and so fundamental to social organization that its "causes" cannot be finely isolated. At best, the historian can trace and put in order the evolution of American womanhood and draw attention to the general societal conditions that made a particular set of sex types gel and cohere at a given time.

The making of womanhood in America has proven to be a relentless national occupation, productive of a dizzying variety of feminine images and female roles, which seem to wax and wane as if by chance. Upon closer scrutiny, however, this apparent multiplicity falls into a coherent historical pattern, taking a shape consonant with broad stages of American development. The most readily apparent patterns in the history of womanhood are foun .n the annals of cultural history, where different ideal types of femininity have marked America's growth from peasant to a "post-industrial" society. The rchetypal female images that emanated from seventeenth-century sermons or yesterday's television programs signify distinct stages of woman's history as they inculcate "true womanhood.'' These traces of womanhood left in cultural history must not be confused, however, with the actual life experience of women, more often revealed by such social data as fertility rates and the sex composition of the labor force. These two varieties of documentation can be pieced together, however, and refashioned into a particularly revealing historical composite. Popular images not only provide inducements to behave within socially acceptable limits but also expose in the process the social and economic functions of gender differentiation. This hybrid of social and cultural history is particularly appropriate to the study of American women, who have been subject to the most excessive amounts and extreme forms of normative instructions, all of which have sought to escort them into roles that provide vital services to the social order.

The following pages will identify three systems of adjusting society and sex roles, each accompanied by appropriate images of femininity. In no way should they be taken as rigid molds that gave one-dimensional shape to every woman's life. Neither do these historical constructions succeed in erasing class, ethnic, racial or regional differences in womanhood. They are presented, however, as sexual norms that exerted considerable pressure on American women, and which few segments of American society could escape entirely. The model of womanhood created by the first adventurous colonists in North America took shape in a subsistence agrarian economy, organized on the dual social principles of community and hierarchy. Compelled to toil for survival and the common good, the women of the seventeenth century acquired numerous and crucial economic responsibilities and a rugged personality along with a secondary social status and political invisibility. The coexistence of woman's central economic and social function with her constant subordination to the patriarchal male is aptly captured by the biblical symbol that heralded colonial femininity: "Adam's Rib."

This prosaic cage of womanhood did not crumble until the eighteenth century when the subsistence economy and its simple sexual division of labor dissolved in a febrile commercial spirit. Production and distribution for profit, be it on the farm or in a bustling seaport town, splintered womanhood into a chaotic array of alternatives, including such novel situations as fashionable idleness, independent enterprise, or incarceration in an almshouse.

American womanhood remained in amorphous disrepair until that point in the nineteenth century when industrial capital assumed hegemony over national production. The new order dictated that economic production be removed once and for all from the household unit. Whether the women of industrial society remained ever secluded in the home or spent a few years in the lowest ranks of the work force, their sex was identified primarily with specialized domestic functions, supplying the immediate physical and emotional needs of husbands and children. The quintessential standard of femininity became nurturance, first of individual families and through them of all America. Nineteenth-century industrial society for the first time deemed "work" as a male prerogative and in turn glorified woman as the "Mother of Civilization." The construction of this prototype of womanhood entailed major revisions in the American system of sexual distribution: the stark spatial separation of male and female into public and private spheres, a schizoid division of human personality into the feminine and the masculine, and the incessant bombardment of popular culture with sex stereotypes.

The American woman's attempted escape from her richly gilded Victorian cell was a particularly heroic feat. In the late nineteenth and early twentieth centuries women grasped for control of their own history with unprecedented force and self-consciousness, only a particle of which is embodied in the suffrage movement. Yet even the Herculean energies and acumen of this generation proved insufficient to check the historical momentum of womanhood that provided but a new cage for women born into the twentieth century.

The most recent epoch of woman's history eludes simple typologies. Its chronology is particularly difficult, spanning alternate decades of war and peace, depression and prosperity, and bifurcated by a world war that marked a basic shift in the patterns of female employment. Yet this fractured pattern itself can be seen as a defining characteristic of twentieth-century womanhood, jarred like the fragments of a kaleidoscope from one configuration of roles and images into another. On one hand, the legacy of nineteenth-century womanhood has not been entirely erased from American culture. Indeed, its domestic tenets were invoked with renewed enthusiasm after World War II. Yet these remnants of the cult of the "Mother of Civilization" had been refashioned into a new paradigm of womanhood and combined with novel female roles adapted to the social and economic organization of the twentieth century. By the 1920s woman's place had been inalterably transformed by an expanding market for consumer goods, which despite the interruptions of depression and war offered women the role of America's number one shopper. An economy geared for the production of consumer goods and services also provided increasing numbers of low-paying jobs for women to juggle along with their traditional duties as wives and mothers, and the important new occupation of consumer. The agile creature who was expected to play all these roles paraded across the pages of popular culture, and especially advertising copy, in a novelly erotic posture, signaling a new symbol of womanhood, the "sexy saleslady." Despite the variety of female roles in advanced capitalism, each one remained secondary to those of the male. It is through the intricate bars of this latest and perhaps most complicated cage that contemporary feminists peer out in search of a final escape from the bondage of sex.

The cages encountered by American women from the era of "Adam's Rib" to the reign of the "Sexy Saleslady" do not invite a progressive interpretation of woman's history. Each incarnation of womanhood served primarily to reorder rather than to dismantle the sexual barriers placed in the path of human freedom. Each was cemented in place by a combination of subtle conditioning, categorical prohibitions, and grotesque cajolery. Although the successive cages of womanhood might be invisible to the untrained eye, disguised by inviting draperies, perhaps even lined with little rewards and comforts, they were cages nonetheless, trapping women beneath man's world and in the backstage of human history. Any preoccupation with sexual differences is likely to work to the detriment of women whose legacy of inferiority and lengthy isolation from centers of power makes them especially vulnerable to being assigned onerous roles and lesser rewards. The history of American women is stocked with evidence of the mischief bred by undue attention to sex differences. Therefore, the major standard of liberation that lurks within this volume is the Utopian hope that sex differences will themselves be incarcerated within their legitimate and limited sphere, reproductive biology, and thus release men and women to develop and exercise the individuality that typifies humanity rather than sex.

Although the history of American women has not advanced steadily toward this objective, woman's aspirations in this direction can be discovered just beneath the surface of the past. Conscious feminism, as well as disguised rebellions, shrewd manipulations, and covert reprisals litter the history of womanhood, giving unremittent testimony to the disquietude of the captives of sex. Woman's rage against her imprisonment is in fact a fixture of womanhood. It records the high cost of sexism to man and to society and highlights the capacity of American women to pry free of their cages and directly affect history. Accordingly, the broad social and cultural sweep of this chronicle will be interrupted by illustrations of the personal and collective acts whereby women came to grips with their historical predicaments.

It is perhaps audacious to attempt to fill this historical bill at a time when the excavations of woman's past have only begun. Merely a rough and tentative sketch of American womanhood can be pieced together from successive generations of pioneering woman's scholarship, the raw records of the census bureau, and the decaying remains of images of "true womanhood." This work in no way encompasses the breadth of America's female population; whole groups and sections fail to make even a fleeting appearance (native Americans, southerners, frontierswomen, Lesbians, socialites, sundry ethnic groups, and notable American women, to name but a few). Numerous substantive aspects and analytic dimensions of womanhood have been neglected as well. The images of femininity described in the following pages are often stripped for the sake of brevity of their intricate qualities and complicated context. The social and economic data cited is not subjected to refined statistical analysis and often appears in the distorted form of either national averages or local case studies. The aim throughout has been to provide a framework in which to explore the making of American womanhood whose bold outline is instructive and provocative, rather than to provide a microscopic analysis of the myriad complexities of woman's situation in past time. Therefore, most of what follows should be read in a speculative and tentative tone with the recurrent qualifications which have been omitted to allow for a smooth narrative.

And then, nearly every judgment that remains requires correction and elaboration from the army of scholars now mobilized to recapture woman's past and whose insights and discoveries touch every page that follows. As the skeleton of American woman's history is given flesh, more attention must be given to the courage, strength, and mutual support of the women who lived within the cages I have attempted to describe—to the individuals who inhabited these social roles and interpreted these cultural images. Yet undue delays in the work of woman's history may facilitate the construction of yet another cage around the clamorous and adventurous women of the 1970s. Thus, this volume is offered as an incentive to further work in the field of woman's history and in hope of being some assistance in the continuing feminist struggle.

ADAM'S RIB:

WOMEN IN
AGRARIAN SOCIETY

When an American clergyman mounted his pulpit in the early eighteenth century he was apt to survey a sober and orderly congregation, each member securely settled in one of the precise social stations that composed the agrarian community. The wilderness had been tamed into a stable social order, and at its core stood clearly defined male and female roles. The pastor might articulate the ideal sex roles much as did the Reverend William Secker whose wedding sermon was published in Boston in 1750. Secker began in an unremarkable fashion, citing the familiar biblical passage "and the Lord God said, it is not good that the man should be alone. I will give him an Help-meet for him." The word help-meet rung through the sermon reminding the colonial woman of her single, immutable role: "She must be so much, and no less, and so much and no more." Secker placed a peculiar interpretation on another biblical image of woman, however, that of Adam's Rib: "Our ribs were not Ordained to be our ruler; they are not made of the Head to claim superiority, but out of the side to be content with Equality." [1] An eighteenth-century sermon seems a most unlikely place in which to find such an allusion to sexual equality. Certainly, if that concept was meant to imply equal access to political power, intellectual leadership, and the highest social and economic status, then William Secker's postulates completely contradicted the actual position of women in colonial America. Secker's use of the term equality seems patently illogical to the contemporary mind. A help-meet, symbolized by a lowly portion of another's skeleton, can hardly be judged autonomous and therefore equipped for equality.

Still, that phrase "out of the side to be content

with equality" aptly described the unique position of women in early America. Men and women were on equal terms in at least one essential: the value and degree of their participation in the social and economic development of the American colonies. This "equality" of woman was not conferred by pastoral decree, but necessitated by the arduous task that faced the American settler, that of planting a society in the wilderness. No man, no woman, could be exempted from this toilsome undertaking. Woman's central place alongside man in economic production and social organization granted her a basic and integral role in the community, not altogether unlike the function of the ribs in the human skeleton. Although women performed functions equal and similar to those of men, their status still ensued "out the side" of males, the husbands and fathers who alone held independent and powerful positions in colonial society. Adam's Rib might hold equality but only Adam himself could assume command of the operations of the household. Only the patriarch of the family could rise to leadership in the political, cultural, and religious affairs of the community. The tension built into this symbolism, the contradiction between equality of function and dependency of status, marked every aspect of early American womanhood.

Similarly complicated blueprints for the ordering of the sexes could be found in the baggage of the very first immigrants to the New World. First of all, clear sex labels were not affixed to those remnants of feudalism that were transported to proprietary colonies such as a Maryland. Here the female offshoots of important English families, women like Margaret and Mary Brent, were granted manorial rights over thousands of acres. Likewise the bustling commercial centers of Holland sent women like the Widow Margaret Hardenbrook Philipse to New Amsterdam where she converted her land resources into a merchant fortune and organized the first regular ship passages across the Atlantic. The Pilgrims added some equalitarian ideas to the multifarious conventions of early America, including John Robinson's assertion that any man, "yea, or any woman either, may as truly, and effectively loose and bind, both in heaven and earth, as all ministers in the world." [2] Similar sentiments impelled the likes of Mistress Anne Hutchinson to become the center of religious controversy in Massachusetts Bay. Seventeenth-century Europe, ripped apart by social change, opened many avenues for women, including removal to the open spaces of America.

Few of those who found their way to the colonies shared the lofty status and expectations of Margaret Brent, Widow Philipse, and Mistress Hutchinson. Three-quarters of the English population from which America's first settlers were recruited were simple farmers, tied for generations to the same small plots of land or common fields, tended by men and women alike. The early years of the peasant woman's life of toil might be spent in servitude before she entered her own rugged home upon her marriage in her mid to late twenties. The female side of her later life derived primarily from her reproductive function, recurrent child-bearing with its incumbent risks of death and infant mortality.[3] As the seventeenth century advanced, however, this timeless pattern of survival was fractured by the enclosure of peasant fields and the advances of a more complicated cash economy. Faced with the possibility of landlessness, or awakened by ambition for economic betterment, uprooted English farmers might venture as far afield as the shores of North America.

The ships that made the Atlantic passage carried principally these classes of English men and women: propertyless husbandmen, yeoman farmers, and common laborers. One in three of the passengers disembarking in Virginia were women, the majority of them indentured servants, pledging years of labor for the promise of access to land and property.[4] Single Dutch women often hired themselves out to merchants and planters in New Netherlands to pay their passage into the New World.[5] New England immigrants came more often in family units, two of every three members of which were likely to be women. Passenger lists on New England bound vessels consisted of groups such as John Carver's entourage, including "Kathrine, his wife; Desire Minter; two men servants . . . ; a boy . . . ; a maidservant and a child that was put to him . . ."[6]

Whether they came indentured to a Virginia planter, in the hire of a New Amsterdam merchant, or sheltered in New England families, women were eagerly awaited in the colonies. A petition put before the Virginia House of Burgesses in 1619 surmised that "in a newe plantation it is not known whether man or woman be most necessary."[7] The petitioners made this assertion in order to induce the Assembly to grant land to their wives as well as themselves. In Virginia and throughout the colonies the fate of women would hinge upon the distribution of this basic commodity of the seventeenth-century economy, the land. For a fleeting historical moment the inhabitants of the New

World considered holding this life source of the community in common. The Pilgrims set down in Plymouth with the radical intention of laboring in one communal field and sharing its fruits each according to his or her need. Yet William Bradford recounts the swift demise of this experiment. "For the young men, that were the most able and fit for labor and service, did repine that they should spend their time and strength to work for other men's wives and children without any recompense . . . and for men's wives to be commanded to do service to other men . . . they deemed it a kind of slavery, neither could many husbands well brook with it." [8] Thus private property based in the family quietly embedded its tenacious roots in American soil, and soon that plant would bear fruit in sexual inequity.

Occasionally a village or colony would allocate land to women. The town of Salem set out small maid lots, and Pennsylvania generously offered 75 acres to all women above the age of fourteen.[9] Within a few short years, however, each village and every colony had eliminated these tenuously held rights of women to acquire land independently. The women who were given any consideration in matters of land distribution fell into the category of wives and served only to convey property into the hands of their husbands. For example, Lord Baltimore calculated the family allowances of Maryland in the following manner: 100 acres for an adult male, 100 acres for his wife, 50 acres for his child, 100 acres for a manservant, and 60 acres for a womanservant.[10] The town meeting of Sudbury, Massachusetts, contemplated distributing its land in a similar manner (in fact, setting aside a half acre more for wives than for husbands) but decided instead to determine the size of land grants by the social status of the male head of the household.[11] Most early American communities founded their economic structure on the latter principle. When the settlers of Jamaica, New York, set down the economic order of the town in 1656 they promised a plot of land "to all who troubled to settle." Not a single woman appeared on the lists of allocations that followed.[12] Neither did communities founded late in the seventeenth century, like Worcester, Massachusetts, leave any trace of land titles allotted to women. The first, most crucial act of colonial settlement, the division of the land, simply denied the independent economic existence of women.

The subsequent day-to-day exchanges of landed property also tended to exclude women, in accordance with that provision of English common law which regarded marriage as the civil death of the wife. Married or single the colonial woman would pass most of her life under the family system of private property, which allowed only male heads of households the privileges of owning and exchanging land. Colonial statutes recognized women not as owners but as a species of property themselves; the Massachusetts Body of Liberties lumped women with goods and estates in proclaiming that "no man shall be deprived of his wife or children." The Massachusetts legal code did include a section entitled "the liberties of women," which granted wives the right to be provided for in their husbands' wills.[13] A colonial widow was assured of receiving at least one-third of her deceased husband's estate. It was primarily through widowhood that women received an economic identity of their own. By the late seventeenth century a widowed woman was listed among the top three landowners of Dedham, Massachusetts;

more than a dozen women appeared in the top tax bracket of Jamaica, New York, at the turn of the century; and as the first generation of settlers grew to maturity, the female heirs assumed the direction of sizable estates in towns throughout the colonies.[14]

The special status of the widow was, however, perfectly consistent with the concept of Adam's Rib: "It is between a man and his wife in the House as it is between the Sun and the Moon in the heavens, when the great light goes down, the lesser light gets up. When the one ends in setting, the other begins in shining. The wife may be sovereign in her husband's absence, but she must be subject in his presence." [15] The rise of the widow to the direction and command of her late husband's estate did not elevate the female sex per se, but registered the colonists' determination to keep private property in family units, in order that it might descend intact from fathers to sons. The Massachusetts Body of Liberties included this section on the inheritance rights of daughters: "When parents die intestate having no male heirs of their bodies their daughters shall inherit as co-partners, unless the General Court upon just reason shall rule otherwise." [16] The fact that women could obtain property only through death or default did not diminish the energy and efficiency with which they entered into land dealings. The loophole of inheritance freed women to engage wholeheartedly in the exchange of land and other property. One Virginia widow, Elizabeth Caursley, not only sold a piece of land, but with her capital purchased two menservants. The Widow Caursley illustrated the possibilities of totally reversing the sexual order of property ownership under the colonial system.[17]

Seventeenth-century probate records reveal that

women encroached further into the property sphere than the limits of the law recognized. First of all, daughters were seldom forgotten in their fathers' wills. If the family had prospered, sizable goods and estates could be bequeathed to females. One New England father could afford to make a special grant to his Daughter's Daughters "because Mary and Susanna theyr husbands have lands to Give theyr Sons." Others, such as William Carpenter of Providence, made provision for his married daughter in clear contravention of the postulates of common law. Carpenter's legacy to his daughter was written as follows: ". . . both for herself and who so ever shee shall make her heirs, Executors and administrators to assign to have and to hold as her proper lawful right and inheritance forever without any condition." This father went to exorbitant lengths of verbiage to guarantee his daughter's ownership independent of her husband.[18] Widows also found a means of maintaining their own property upon remarriage. The procedure was a legally binding premarital contract, such as a Plymouth document dated 1667 guaranteeing the bride's right to "enjoy all her house and lands, goods and cattle that she is now possessed of, to her own proper use to dispose of them at her own free will from time to time and at any time as she shall see cause."[19]

The routine legal practices of the colonies granted other concessions to women. Numerous deeds were not only signed by wives as well as husbands but were studded with such clauses as "with the full and free consent of my wife" or the "free and voluntary consent of my wife." Married women also retained control of the dowries with which they entered their husbands' household, and courts were careful to investigate any transaction made by husbands that might abrogate this right. In some colonies women were "privately examined" to insure that they had not been coerced into surrendering dower. In the town of New Amsterdam married women broke all the rules of propriety by bombarding the court with suits involving every possible economic matter. Occasionally a local magistrate would order an aggressive woman to "exhibit authority from her husband and then institute her action in writing." But this caveat did not deter countless bold women from undertaking suits in their own names or even in behalf of their spouses. The economic consequence of the New Amsterdam wife was acknowledged by many men in the community who called women to court to account for the debts incurred by their husbands. When one Aaltje Albers was held to account for the debt of her husband, Jacob Hay, she retorted that she "had no knowledge of her husband's affairs, and he may speak to her husband." [20]

Frenzied economic activity and liberal Dutch mores in New Amsterdam only magnified the economic concessions granted women in other colonies. In the simpler agrarian economies typical of most villages, woman's economic importance was routinely acknowledged in deeds and wills. These generous concessions and bequests to women cannot be dismissed as the gestures of southern gentlemen or loving Puritan fathers. Rather, they were the self-interested acts of farm managers who were cognizant of the economic prowess of their wives and daughters. As we shall see, every farmer knew full well that he would not prosper without the ready cooperation of the females in his household. These little rewards and acts of recognition were necessary to insure the continuous assistance of the female help-meet.

Any immigrant to the New World (whatever his foreseeable occupation) was wisely advised to acquire a female economic partner. Even advertisements for hired employment on a southern plantation were addressed to "a right good Overseer, having a wife." [21] In the first days and months of settlement, woman's contribution was even more elementary. As soon as the Pilgrims landed, by William Bradford's account, "The women now went willingly into the fields and took their little ones with them to set corn." At this initial stage of settlement, when the home existed only as a primitive hut or cavern dug from the earth, no woman's work could be confined to the niceties of housekeeping. Once the first crop had been harvested, however, women were exempted from most field labor and employed around the newly built cabin. Then custom decreed that only "those wenches that are not fit to be so employed were put into the ground." [22] These "wenches" included female immigrants from Africa whose exile to the fields signaled their swift descent from servitude to slavery.

Confinement to the household, on the other hand, was no mere courtesy to white womanhood. This demarcation of the separate spheres of the two sexes constituted a utilitarian division of labor into equal parcels of essential duties and responsibilities. The economic places of men and women were contiguous, one largely out of doors and in the fields, the other in the home plot and the house. These two imprecise divisions converged in one integral economic unit, the self-sufficient agrarian household where male and female labor commingled in the single productive enterprise that insured survival. It might be said that the male's duty was to procure the family's sustenance, while the female's charge was to prepare these supplies for household use, yet neither sex could be excluded from the process of "work," "providing," or "support." The household economy of the seventeenth century, at a time when 90 percent of the colonial population was employed in agricultural pursuits, would have been crippled without the labor of women. It was this basic economic law of preindustrial America that conferred women's tenuous property rights as well as her title Adam's Rib.

The woman's side of the economic partnership included but transcended the obligation to maintain the home. The single task of feeding the family entailed not only cooking, but also the cultivation, processing and manufacture of food products. It was the wife's duty, with the assistance of daughters and women servants, to plant the vegetable garden, breed the poultry, and care for the dairy cattle. She transformed milk into cream, butter, and cheese, and butchered livestock as well as cooked the meals. Along with her daily chores the husbandwoman salted, pickled, preserved, and manufactured enough beer and cider to see the family through the winter.

Still, the woman's work was hardly done. To clothe the colonial population, women not only plied the needle, but operated wool carders and spinning wheels—participated in the manufacture of thread, yarn, and cloth as well as apparel. Her handwrought candles lit the house; medicines of her own manufacture restored her family to health; her homemade soap cleansed her home and family. Wives of artisans and small merchants assumed these same responsibilities in the homes, garden plots, and dairies of towns and villages. Rare was the woman who could disengage herself from these productive enterprises. Even Mrs. Philip Schuyler, mistress of a New Netherlands manor, could be found in her dairy and poultry house or sewing garments for her extensive family and many servants.[23] Wives of southern planters were not ladies of leisure but the administrators and suppliers of the slave household. Prospective female settlers in the American colonies could contemplate the active life described in a Pennsylvania advertisement of the eighteenth century: "raising small stock, dairying, marketing, combing, carding, spinning, knitting, sewing, pickling, preserving, etc." [24] The women on seventeenth-century farms not only kept house but practiced a score of trades in a household economy.

These economic responsibilities constituted more than a sum of menial chores. Rather they created the office of female household manager. The mistress of the household organized and supervised an economic system, allocating labor to children and servants, overseeing the home production that supplied the basic needs of the colonial population. On occasion women could receive reimbursement for social services performed within the home, among them, the housing of boarders or caring for the sick, orphaned, and poor of the town.

No unit of economic production, however, can be perfectly self-sufficient. The early American home economy was not an ironclad fortress, for there were times when every farm family was forced to procure a few necessities from outsiders. When, for example, the home factory produced an excess of soap and was undersupplied with eggs, an exchange with another houshold was in order. In such situations the colonial woman would routinely barter the products of her labor on the neighborhood market. These simple exchanges find illustration even in the letters written to Margaret Winthrop, a governor's wife: "By Mrs. Pestor I beged garlick and sage and to borrow a gander, I have three gooses and not a husband for them, which lost me at least 40 egs last year." [25] These commonplace domestic details suggest the female roles of manager, producer, and trader, which regularly took women outside the home into the sphere of economic distribution. The women traders of New Amsterdam bartered at a frenzied pace, exchanging a seemingly inexhaustible supply of commodities— pens, tubs, brandy, garments, cows—incurring debts, and producing conflicts at almost every turn. Without the walls of the household, women peddled their skills as well as their products. An active colonial economist named Susan Helline is found suing for lack of payment for twelve hens as well as "her paynes and tyme in looking to John Major's wife tyme she did lay in child brith." The Virginia court swiftly awarded the midwife a settlement.[26]

The colonial woman's proclivity for economic dealing was second nature to Mrs. Mary Rowlandson. Not even Indian captivity could suppress her trading instinct, as she bartered well-knit stockings and her supply of tobacco for religious privileges and domestic amenities. Mrs. Rowlandson saw her release from captivity as a beneficent act of God. "As he wounded me with one hand so he healed me with the other." The irreverent modern observer, nonetheless, cannot help but attribute her survival in part to the acumen of the trading woman of the seventeenth century.[27]

Not all the female enterprises of the era transpired under the supervision of husbands and fathers. Many New England girls served an economic apprenticeship as indentured servants, bound out until the age of eighteen when their labors were rewarded with a few acres, some clothes, or a few coins. Some women acquired a trade in the course of servitude as well. Susan Warner of Providence, for one, was promised such training in "the art and mistery of a tailor whereby she might attain to the knowledge of that trade so as to do and perform it." [28] Although colonial practice frowned upon the unmarried, and commonly placed bachelors and spinsters within a patriarchal household, it did not restrain single women from gainful employment. The Massachusetts law regulating single persons stipulated that "This act shall not be construed to the extent to hinder any single woman of good repute from the exercise of any lawful trade, employment for a livelihood hereunto and it shall have the allowance and approbation of the selectmen . . . any law, usage or custom to the contrary not withstanding." The selectmen of Massachusetts had many occasions to make this clause operative. In 1690, for example, town officers of Boston consented to the request of more than thirty women, married and single, to saw lumber and manufacture potash. Elsewhere in New England women collectively removed such labors as slaughtering and flour processing from the household.[29] At least one New England woman fled the Puritan commonwealth entirely in pursuit of economic independence. Called before the court of New Amsterdam and asked "has she a husband and where?'' Elizabeth Kay replied ''Yes She has a husband at Boston being a Barber and she left him because it was more economic to do so. Her husband's hand shakes so he cannot follow his trade.'' [30] The economic independence that resonated in Elizabeth Kay's speech before the court testifies to the capacity of colonial women to separate themselves from husbands and fathers and stand alone, detached from Adam.

Still, such women were exceptional. The infrequent appearances of female names in the records of colonial economic transactions were only minor blemishes on the overall pattern of male dominance. Even the raucous female traders of New Amsterdam performed in the shadow of superior male enterprise. The women who intruded into the probate courts were predominantly widows, heiresses of great estates, exceptional spinsters, or eccentric troublemakers. Such rare women, nonetheless, demonstrated the potentiality of countless nameless women, whose economic power remained eclipsed but not annihilated by the patriarchal dominance of husbands and fathers. Most women would live out their lives as junior partners in the household economy, productively active, essential to survival, and free to barter their surplus goods, but denied ultimate control of the basic commodity of preindustrial society, the land. Yet colonial daughters, mothers, and wives were unlikely to feel useless or alienated from their labors. The subsistence economy did not eviscerate the female personality by inhibiting women from dealing directly with the material world and battling with nature to serve human needs. The capable widows who obtained direction of the household economy bear witness to the economic significance of wives and daughters everywhere.

This basic practical value of female labor served as the economic foundation for the seventeenth-century image of woman. It was acknowledged in every major treatise on womanhood in early America. Benjamin Wadsworth's advice for the Well-Ordered Family plotted this sexual division of labor: "The husband should endeavor that his wife may have food and raiment suitable for her. He should contrive prudently and work diligently that his family and his wife particularly may be well provided for. The wife also in her place should do what she can that the man has a comfortable support." [31] Cotton Mather scolded all Puritans with the reminder that "sloth and idleness in husband or wife are sinful and shameful." When Mather's theology veered dangerously close to the capitalist ethic his doctrine embraced women as well as men. He typed the virtuous woman as one "who takes a most laudable course for her own temporal prosperity. She is to be praised as a woman that effectively layes up for herself a competent and convenient portion of wordly comfort." [32] In the sphere of economics, these colonial spokesmen defined sex roles that hardly differentiated men from women and approximated equality. Wadsworth foisted the role of help-meet on men as well as women, and William Secker went so far as to inform his male parishioners that "the woman is a parallel Line drawn equal with him." [33] The few early Americans who had the time and capacity to make cultural pronouncements on the relations of the sexes simply articulated economic roles already rooted in the primitive economic organization of the New World.

This is not to say that American colonists were pawns of economic necessity nor intent upon the crass and single-minded pursuit of material gain. The economic activities of colonial Americans transpired within a dense social context, full of personal satisfaction, and constantly mediated by the values of the community. Economic behavior was scrutinized by both the church and town meeting and production was contained within the social institution of the family. In the seventeenth-century scheme of social organization, church, town, and colony were no more than congregates of family households. The colonial population collected in scattered household nuclei to practice religion, implement political decisions, and maintain social order. It was within these "Little Commonwealths," as John Demos has maintained, that the colonial society took form. Without the participation of the female sex, needless to say, the construction of this all-important social and economic unit was impossible.

Colonial leaders had these social imperatives in mind as they hectically recruited female immigrants. Lord Baltimore of His Majesties Council for Virginia requested a supply of women to be sent to the New World for "when the plantation grows to strength, then it is time to plant with women as well as with men; that the plantation may spread into generations, and not ever be pierced from without." Sir Edwin Sandys implemented this policy in Virginia when in 1619 he ordered one hundred women from England and offered them to prospective husbands along with the additional matrimonial incentive of 120 pounds of the best leaf tobacco. Sandys reasoned that the presence of women in Virginia "would make the men more settled and less moveable, who by defect therof as it is credibly reported, stay there but to get something and then return to England." [34] The calculations of Lord Baltimore and Governor Sandys rested on more than the procreative powers of women or simple clichés about the conservative essence of femininity. They recruited women in order to foster the family organization that alone would firmly attach settlers to the colony and provide the social stability in which colonial civilization could take root. The Dutch General Court and Council of New Netherlands also took pains to corral its population into legitimate families, ruling that "no male and female shall be allowed to keep house together like man and wife before they have legally been married under a fine of 100 florins or as much or more or less than their position admits." [35] New England bachelors and spinsters were swiftly placed within an established household by order of the local courts, and Massachusetts went so far as to organize unmarried arrivals into makeshift family units. Thus men and women alike were promptly placed in the nexus of social life, the colonial family.

Once situated at the center of colonial society women were delegated a whole panoply of social functions in great excess of their private services to husbands and children. Woman's parental duties, first of all, extended to servants and apprentices in perhaps one-third of all colonial families. Husbands and wives were advised "always remember, that my servants are in some sort my children. In a care, that they may want nothing that be good for them, I would make them as my children. And, as for the methods of instilling piety which I use with my children, may be properly and prudently used with them." [36] The mistress of the household was hereby employed in an extensive task of socialization, conducting the training, disciplining, education, and acculturation of the next generation, her servants as well as her own offspring. Should the marital partnership be broken by the death of her husband, the colonial woman would be sole custodian of this enterprise and would be held to account for her performance of these duties by the community. Widows were often brought to court for breach of indenture contracts, for failing to instill morality and religion in their charges, or to pay fines for the antisocial acts of their servants.

Within the microcosmic society of the colonial household women did service as welfare workers as well as socializers. Town officers, vestrymen, and justices of the peace sent widows, orphans, the poor, and even criminals into respectable homes for care and rehabilitation, thereby conferring on many colonial dames the roles of custodian, caretaker, and jailor. The town records of Worcester, Massachusetts, are replete with examples of these female functions. In 1779, for example, Catharine Segar was acknowledged to have nursed "a mulatto child, one of the poor of the town"; Lydia Taylor nursed and boarded an entire family. Another woman of Worcester named Martha Wiley cared for a poor sick woman for a period of years and received more than 100 pounds from the town purse for her efforts.[37]

The far-reaching social obligations of colonial women undoubtedly left their mark on her personality. Although woman's position at the center of the little commonwealth rendered privacy and the luxury of solitude almost impossible, it also banished loneliness, claustrophobia, and insulation from the essential operations of society, with all their attendant psychological debilitation. In the social sphere as well as in matters of economics, the women of the seventeenth century enjoyed the comfort of integral participation in community life.

Despite her basic role and functions, however, the social *status* of woman, her power and prestige in the community, derived from and was inferior to the patriarchal head of her household. Woman's vow to obey her spouse was repeatedly underscored by colonial writers and preachers. She owed her mate "reverent subjection" and was obliged to submit to his superior judgment in all things. The male's authority was termed a "government" that the female must accept as "law." Not only must woman scrupulously abide by the lawful commands of the patriarch, but she was "still subject even to those who are sinful and unkind." [38] This terminology should not be construed as a simple license for male tyranny or as a categorical endorsement of patriarchal domination. This rhetoric cannot be detached from its larger ideological context, which viewed the whole of society as an intricate series of ranks, a profusion of finely graded positions of authority and subordination, which neither male nor female could circumvent. No individual, of either sex, could presume to be one among equals in the seventeenth-century community. The enforcement of inequality extended even to stipulation of the appropriate apparel for members of different social strata. At best colonial Americans could hope for occasional opportunities to excel as well as defer, to dictate as well as submit. Within the church, all parishioners were subservient to the minister and found their destined places somewhere within the hierarchy of elders, deacons, and the general congregation whose pews were assigned according to their relative wealth and godliness. Outside the church this hierarchy was dismantled, only to be replaced by yet another clearly defined scale of authority and subordination. In civil affairs the minister might be reduced to submission before magistrates and selectmen, while all the members of community were again arranged into precise ranks according to their property and prestige. This complex status system prompted seventeenth-century Americans to speak not of equality but of relative inequality. The word relatives was used by the American colonists to designate these multiple scales of authority of which the family order was but one example. Within the household, the ranks descended from the patriarchal father to his wife, the mistress of the household, and on to children and then to servants and any other non-kinsmen who resided in the home. Thus woman's social place varied with her position in the family. Should she be the mistress of the household, her relative inequality would dictate submission to the husband and authority over her offspring and servants. Were she a widow, she took possession of ultimate power within the little commonwealth. Within this hierarchical *Weltanschauung* of the seventeenth century, inequality was not the peculiar stigma of womanhood, but rather a social expectation for both sexes.

Fearful of the devastating consequences of social chaos among the independent residents of a frontier society, American colonists held tenaciously to this system of order. The clear lines of authority were held essential to the efficient operation of the colonial household, a hub of crucial social and economic activities that sheltered a large number of individuals. The submission of wife to husband was designed to ward off internecine household conflict. It was said that in the home "differences will arise and be seen so the one must give way and apply to the other; this God and nature layeth upon the women rather than upon the men." [39] Although the sexual distribution of household authority was an arbitrary choice, attributed to God and nature, the obligation of submission in itself was rational and intelligible within the seventeenth-century social context.

Seventeenth-century rationality further surmised that a tyrannical interpretation of the household hierarchy was not in the best interest of social stability. Every treatise on household organization cautioned against dictatorial male rule. While Benjamin Wadsworth acknowledged the husband was "the Head on whom the chief respect and honor is to be put," he quickly added, "and as wives should honor and reverence their Husbands; so husbands should put respect upon their Wives too. Though the wife is the weaker vessel, yet honor is to be upon her in her station." Cotton Mather explained the expedience of this deference to inferiors: "For husbands owe mutual duties to their wives and parents to their children. Now if husbands and parents violate their obligations, if parents conduct themselves with discouraging severity and fastidious moroseness toward their children whom they are forbidden to provoke to wrath, if husbands vex and despise their wives, whom they are commanded to love and to spare as the weaker vessels; does it not follow, children shall be less obedient to their parents and wives will rebel against their husbands?" The majority of American fathers and husbands, including those far beyond the hearing of Cotton Mather, were most likely shrewd enough to mitigate their authority in their daily dealings with those female partners whose cooperation was so essential to the well-being of the household.

Should the colonial man be so foolhardy as to deal brutally with his wife, daughters, or female servants, the colonial court, the ultimate arbiter of social order, would interfere in woman's behalf. Massachusetts law stipulated that "evere marreyed woman shall be free from bodily correction or stripes by her husband unless it be his own defense upon her assault. If there be any just cause of correction, complaint shall be made to authorities assembled in some court from which only she shall receive it." Throughout the colonies women took frequent advantage of this recourse, appearing before the court to complain of their husbands' abuses. The repeated mistreatment of a New Amsterdam woman prompted the court to bar her husband from the home entirely. The judges summarily announced that this disreputable spouse was to deliver the hay to his wife's house and "not to presume to come molest her in any way." [40] Female children were also allowed access to the court to escape the abuses of their fathers. Such a case in Virginia read as follows: "Elizabeth Campbell complains of her father William Campbell, that he does not provide for her and the other children—to be summoned." [41] Women-servants made use of this same privilege, appearing before the local courts to ask remedy for the misconduct of their masters or demanding fulfillment of the codiciles of their indenture contracts. In Virginia orphaned women, some as young as fourteen, were granted the right to select their own guardians, that is, to choose for themselves a congenial patriarch.[42]

In addition to these constraints upon male authority, colonial women were often advised against lapsing into a passive sense of inferiority. Puritan leaders sternly admonished the New England wife never to make an idol of her male superior: "while she looks upon [her husband] as her guide by the constitution of God, she will not scrupple with Sarah to call him the Lord, and though she does not fear his blows she does fear his frowns, being loathe in anything to grieve him." [43] Furthermore, since woman's obligation to honor and comfort her husband was clearly designed to insure order in the social unit of the family, it emanated more from practical social necessity than from a belief in the innate inferiority of women per se. For example, Benjamin Wadsworth could write as follows: "Yea, 'tho possibly thou hast greater abilities of mind than he has, art of some high birth, and he of a more mean extract, or didst bring more Estate at Marriage than he did; yet since he is thy Husband God has made him thy head and set him above thee and made it thy duty to love and reverence him." [44] Any male or female in Wadsworth's congregation was instructed to accept such orders of an arbitrary God with little question and without detriment to his or her self-esteem. At any rate a woman's sense of self-worth found solid confirmation day in and day out as her labors contributed to the prosperity of her family and the good order of society. The congregation of male and female within the single crucial sphere of colonial society, the household, disallowed a sharp dichotomy between male and female roles, and acquits colonial history from an unambiguous blanket charge of sexual oppression.

The exclusively female side of colonial civilization was narrowly and imprecisely defined, and exhibited itself only in the private lives of mothers, wives, and daughters. This domestic experience of colonial women is almost inaccessible to the historian and leaves a trace primarily in the prescriptive literature penned by a few spokesmen for colonial culture, almost all of them Puritan ministers. As these men were responsible for the few formal postulates on the order of the sexes that colonial men and women would chance to hear, they are worth analyzing. Furthermore, the tenets circulated by New England ministers were designed to suit the everyday social and economic roles of colonial women, and hence they reflect, however obliquely, the actual practice of the mistresses of well-ordered families.

Most literature written in early America rarely and indistinctly disassociated female or domestic themes from the larger universe of thought and attitudes. Therefore, few starkly feminine characteristics can be extracted from the family histories of the seventeenth century. Cotton Mather directed his Puritan flock to rejoice in the birth of children of either sex as the generous gift of God. Colonial parents did not resort to pink or blue ribbons to announce the sex of the newborn. Indeed, it was not until children reached the age of five or six that they discarded infant gowns to don the pantaloons and skirts of the respective sexes. At this tender age the female child would take her place alongside her mother and sisters as an apprentice in home economy. According to Cotton Mather, the girl's training would include, in addition to the practice of housewifery, needlework, and cooking, such accomplishments relating to household business as arithmetic and bookkeeping.

While the girl was trained for the economic specialties of woman, she was not necessarily socialized to femininity. The rare colonial library was not stocked with books exclusively for women. The rare treatise on women and for women, such as Cotton Mather's *Ornaments of the Daughters of Zion,* held in disrepute those traits of character that are all too often characterized as feminine. At the outset, Mather announced that "Favor is deceitful and Beauty is Vain." He went on to describe the physical attributes of the beautiful woman in the most rudimentary terms, "proportion and symmetry of the parts, skin well varnished. . . . Harmoniousness of Countenance." This meager catalogue of female attractions did not offer the colonial woman much opportunity for the scrutiny and cultivation of her appearance. Puritan culture forbade any artificial embellishment of her features and colonial sumptuary laws denied most women even such simple adornments as a wedding band and a bit of lace on their Sunday dresses. Furthermore, any attire that encumbered the operations of the home economy was patently offensive: "For a woman to put herself into a Fashion that shall prejudice either her Health or her Work is to break all the commandments." [45] Those segments of the colonial population who succumbed to the corrupting influence of English fashion were not composed purely of women. Ministers in thriving seaboard towns lamented "the manifest pride openly appearing among us in that long hair like women's hair is worn by some, nor even their own hair made into periwigs and by some women wearing bodies of hair and then the cutting, curling and laying on of hair." [46] Both sexes should beware of the vanities of beauty and fashion and women in particular should refrain from using such wiles to captivate the gullible male. The Daughters of Zion were cautioned against deceiving "unwary men into those amours which beguiling looks and smiles do often betray the children of men." [47]

Colonial culture granted little expression to the "feminine" preoccupations of beauty, fashion, and flirtation, as might be expected in a social system where such frivolities had no functional purpose. Women, even with a well-stocked arsenal of endearing looks and manners, could not single-handedly capture a husband. The New England girl was repeatedly discouraged from musing about her marital future. Cotton Mather advised the American girl that if God ordained her to be a spinster, "she makes the *Single State* a *Blessed One* by improving her leisures from the Encumbrances of a family in caring for the things of the Lord." [48] Although such an eventuality was to be lamented ("For a Woman to be Praised is for her to be Married"), young women were not to presume to take the selection of a spouse into their own hands. Their marriages were subject not only to the approval of parents but also to the vicissitudes of the colonial economy. Only when the local pool of land resources could provide sustenance for a new family could the young men turn their attention to courtship. Even then the woman's parents would conduct the economic negotiations pursuant to matrimony, and the amount of dower they could offer a prospective bridegroom would weigh heavily in the outcome.

Young men would of course allow their personal preferences some play in the selection of their specific spouse. Yet they were advised to "choose by Ears, as well as Eyes," [49] paying particular attention to a woman's potential for practical household service. Her orderliness, sobriety, manufacturing skills should overshadow the soft graces of feminine appearance and decorum. The proper emotional tie between the affianced was described as a tendency to affection and sympathy, which was likely to blossom into conjugal love after their marriage. Accordingly, the young women of New England were not encouraged to cultivate the general sentiment of heterosexual love. Even after the colonial woman had soberly manuevered through the complicated procedures of courtship, she might have her choice of a marriage partner overruled by the court. Such was the fate of Abigail Silbey of Providence, barred from marrying one Thomas Cooper who, according to the town fathers, had already "forsaken a sober wife, and may do the same to this one." [50]

The thoughts of the woman who traversed the maze of courtship are by and large irretrievable from the colonial past. We get a brief look at one woman's reaction to her suitor in the diary of Samuel Sewell, however. Sewell plied a widow named Winthrop with such sweet talk as the declaration that her "kisses were to me better than the best canary." When she remained opposed to the match he tried another tack, telling her "I loved her and was fond to think that she loved me and she might do some good to help support me." Still Mrs. Winthrop preferred her independence and refused to "leave her house, children, neighbors and business." [51] The prosperous widow proved a very difficult catch indeed. A New York woman was similarly insensitive to the nuances of courtship: "I am sick of all this choosing If a man is healthy and does not drink and has a good little handful of stock and a good temper and is a good Christian what difference can it make to a woman which man she takes. There is not so much difference between one man and another." The New York *Post* observed a less calculating attitude toward marriage among the lower classes of the city, who "couple from a hearty good liking and oftenest with a mutual good disposition in all things." [52] Even this is a relatively dispassionate attachment between a bride and groom. Such sparse evidence as this suggests that young women of the colonial era devoted little of their psychic energies to falling in love. Certainly they had neither the time, the incentive, nor the socialization to cultivate the extravagant sentiments of romance. Yet another stereotypical trait of the eternal feminine is belied by colonial history.

Colonial women, young and old, married and single, did, however, exhibit sex in its specific erotic expression. Female sexuality is on full display in the town records of every colony. No daughter lodged in the crowded quarters of the colonial household, where every available space became a collective bedroom, could remain ignorant of the facts of life. Female servants were particularly prone to indulge in sexual intercourse with their male cohabitants of the little commonwealth. Many a young woman came to court suing her master for support of her bastard child or accusing a fellow servant of seduction. The commonest evidence of premarital sexual activity, however, is the prevalence of "early births." In some towns, by the eighteenth century, as many as one-third of first births to young couples occurred less than nine months after the marriage ceremony. In one New England town the Great Awakening brought sixteen couples into the church, nine of whom confessed to the act of sexual intercourse before their wedding. Most of these infractions against the Seventh Commandment took place before the formal wedding ceremony but after the announcement of the couples' banns. These early babies, then, were conceived in somewhat illicit unions but born into wedlock and therefore incurred less censure. In fact, one Puritan minister had to write a tract to demonstrate that such a practice was sinful. These early births also demonstrate the sexual restraint of colonial women, who waited until their engagement, long after puberty, before they succumbed to the weakness of the flesh.

Still, nearly every town held within it at least one woman who gave testimony to a more defiant and irrepressible female sex drive. One New Amsterdam woman allegedly "ran along the road with a can of wine one evening" and took a strange man as her sexual prey.[53] A Virginia woman seduced her partner in an open field with such delightful consequences that she pledged she "would give him as much cloth as would make him a sheet." (Here we have yet another use made of woman's skill at manufacture and barter.)[54] Yet women also appear, and probably more frequently, as the victims of predatory males. Elizabeth Dickerson of Middlesex, Massachusetts, suffered such abuse by her master, Thomas Hawes. "After forcing her to be naught with him," Hawes told Sally Dickerson that "if she told her dame; what car-

riag he did show to her shee had as good be hanged."
Another resident of Middlesex County displayed the
crassest form of male sexuality: "he flung the mayd
downe in the street and got atop her." Not even the
godly commonwealth of Massachusetts Bay could
eradicate the crime of rape.[55]

Another servant woman reported that her master
"caught me by the wrist and pulled me on side of my
bed," resulting in the birth of a bastard child.[56]
Women would pay the greater price for such illicit
sex—pregnancy and childbirth. Colonial society re-
doubled her burden by heaping shame and punishment upon the unwed mother. For simple fornication,
male and female commonly were awarded equal fines
and an equivalent number of lashes and dunkings.
Occasionally a local court would take into consideration special factors in its distribution of punishment.
Such an example is the case of John Littell, made to
"lay neck and hyels close for three hours" and fined
five shillings, for fornication with Ellen Muce, who,
"not approvinge the same," was only whipped.[57] Fornication itself was equally offensive in male and female, but when biology fated the woman to bear a
bastard child the scales of justice lost their balance. In
Worcester, where both parties to the act of fornication
were fined fifty shillings, the charge of giving birth to
a bastard child brought a five pound fine and ten
stripes.[58] Although the father of the child was obliged
to support his offspring and share in the mother's
punishment, he often escaped the court's notice.
Even the gruesome custom of browbeating a woman
in labor to reveal the name of the child's father often
failed to establish the bastard's lineage. Thus women
often stood alone before colonial courts suffering the

lash in solitude, carrying the full burden of community disapproval, and supporting a child without the aid of an economic partner.

Under threat of such dire consequences, most colonial women deferred sexual gratification until after marriage, an event which most likely occurred in her early to mid twenties. Marriage would occasion only a brief celebration and then, without benefit of a honeymoon, the bride would assume the direction of her own household economy. The exclusively private and domestic function of the colonial wife cannot be easily separated from the more wide-ranging economic and social duties performed within her household. Still the rudiments of bourgeois ideology had crossed the Atlantic with the colonists and thus transmitted to the New World the Puritan's heightened respect not only for private property, but also for the conjugal relationship that enclosed it. Colonial culture paid special regard to the bonds of matrimony and their incumbent responsibilities, the first of which was to dwell together as husband and wife and to exclude all others from their sexual union. Puritans readily acknowledged the sexual needs of women, whose "intemperate longings" the husband was duty-bound to gratify. When a husband failed to meet his wife's sexual needs, be it because of impotence or willful denial, a marriage could be dissolved. When one resident of Middlesex County refused to engage in intercourse with his wife for a period of two years he was excommunicated from the church.[59] The husbands and wives of colonial America did not record for posterity those methods they employed to give one another sexual pleasure. The ideal sexual practice is intimated by Benjamin Wadsworth, however.

"The wife hath not power of her body, but the husband. And likewise also the husband hath not power of his body but the wife; defraud not the other that Satan tempt you to inconstancy." [60] The sense of mutuality built into the content and the syntax of this quotation, the reciprocal clauses addressed to men and then to women, seem to preclude the sexual politics of dominance and submission.

The Puritans, lest they be confused with the Victorians, celebrated the satisfaction of "burning lusts" and the delights of sexuality within the institution of marriage. Benjamin Wadsworth invited his flock to "rejoice with the wife of thy youth. Let her breasts satisfy thee at all time. And be always ravished with her love, and why will thou my son be ravished with a strange woman and embrace the bosoms of a stranger." [61] Copulation with a "stranger," on the other hand, called forth the sternest reprisals from the colonial community. Adultery was punishable by death, a penalty that was exacted perhaps a half a dozen times in the history of the American colonies. More commonly, the offending couple was subjected merely to fines, lashes, or the pillory. Whatever the sanction employed, extramarital sex was in practice deemed more offensive in women than in men. Adultery was defined as sexual congress with a married woman. The married man who committed indiscretions with single women was charged with the lesser offense of fornication. This legal sophistry is understandable if allowance is made for the extensive disruption that would ensue from the birth of another man's child within the sacrosanct institution of the colonial family. Still, the onus of marital infidelity clearly fell on the female sex.

Women fared better in other domestic exchanges, particularly in the understanding that husbands and wives "have a very quiet and tender love and affection to another." [62] The Puritans in their veneration of the family elevated conjugal love to a lofty status and assigned it as a duty to husbands and wives alike. Benjamin Wadsworth told the marital couple that "the duty of love is mutual, it should be performed by each to each of them." This sexually balanced conception of love never tilted in the direction of the woman. Love was never accounted one of the peculiar virtues or characteristics of the female sex. If anything, the more loving nature was attributed to colonial men. According to one Puritan divine, "Man is an affectionate creature. Now the woman should be such towards the man as to require his affections by increasing his delectation. That the new blosomed love may not be blasted as soon as it blosomed, a spouse should carry herself to her husband as not to disturb his love by her contention nor to destroy his love by her alienation." [63]

Whatever degrees of emotional attachment husband or wife felt for one another, the duty of love served to undercut the hierarchical structure of the colonial household. Benjamin Wadsworth articulated this phenomenon in this description of the ideal love of a man for his wife, "though he governs her, he must not treat her as a servant, but as his own flesh, he must love her as himself." Cotton Mather employed such phrases as "One Mind in Two Bodies" to describe the temperamental unity between husband and wife, while William Secker resorted to such glowing images as "two Flowers in one nosegay" and "two candels burning together which makes the house more lightsome." [64] These mystical metaphors of love, designating a conjugal unity that merges the self in the other, actually served a very practical social function. For in the absence of loving intercourse between husbands and wives, the household might erupt in "civil war" or become the "most miserable [relation] of any in the world." [65] Maintenance of the little commonwealth required the constant and wholehearted cooperation of husband and wife, without it the prosperity and stability of colonial society were doomed. The Puritan writers designed the loving communion of husband and wife for this prosaic purpose.

A woman's love for her husband, and his in return, became, as a consequence, a "duty," a "performance" not a rarified emotion. In Wadsworth's "Well-Ordered Family" love took the form of a routine of kindnesses; "delight in each other's company," "be helpful to each other," "bear one another's burdens," "Unite prudent consuls," "be patient one towards another." Couples who "contend, quarrel, and disagree, they do the Devil's work." Those who exchange loving gestures, on the other hand, "render each other's life easy and quiet and comfortable." The resultant orderly household was "the first link of Human society to which all the rest are formed," the boon of the community.[66] The only restriction on conjugal love was that it not supersede love of God nor diminish love for one's neighbors.

Several New England couples surely achieved the intensity of conjugal love that Puritan writers revered. John and Margaret Winthrop's affections were so tightly drawn together that when the Atlantic parted them, they dedicated an hour during each week of separation to the pure contemplation of one another. The Massachusetts governor closed his letters to his wife with such testimonials of love as this, "I will take thee now and my sweet children in mine arms and kiss and embrace you all, and so leave you with my God." [67] The sublimity of wifely communion with the spouse is recorded in the poetry of Anne Bradstreet, whose muse sung these familiar lines to her "Dear and Loving Husband": "If ever two were one than surely we/ If ever man were lov'd by wife than thee/ If ever wife was happy in a man/ Compare with me ye women if you can." [68] Although few colonial men and women could verbalize their feelings with the sensitivity of Anne Bradstreet, they left abundant evidence of their conjugal affections in such simple phrases as "to my beloved wife," which prefaced their generous legacies. Such testaments of domestic respect surpass by far the records of desertion, brutality, and conflict within the households of colonial America.

In summary, when early Americans spoke of love they were not withdrawing into a female byway of human experience. Domestic affection, like sex and economics, were androgynous entities. Woman's love was expressed in active interchange with her marital partner. It did not precede marriage but grew out of the day to day cooperation, sharing, and closeness of the subsistence home economy. The reciprocal ideal of conjugal love and its restrained but heartfelt expressions could only thrive in the common social and economic sphere where men and women were integrally, mutually, and enduringly associated. Conjugal affection was intertwined with the persistent obligations of the household partnership.

Only one segment of colonial domestic life was

reserved purely and exclusively for women, the bearing of children. The reproductive powers of women were cause for boasting in the New World: "Our land free, our men honest and our women fruitful." [69] The Atlantic passage did seem to fructify the wombs of seventeenth-century women, whose fertility far surpassed that of English women. Colonial mothers replenished America with settlers at an annual rate of 50 to 57 births per 1,000 population. In the course of her married life the American wife bore an average of eight children, and thereby doubled the colonial population every twenty years.[70] This accomplishment is conceded to women without question and often with a bit of manly praise, but seldom with recognition of its impact on women's lives. Consider the typical experience of Sarah Stearns wed to Peter Place of Providence in December 1685. Sarah Place gave birth to her first child on November 12, 1686; in 1706 she was still engaged in reproduction, bearing an eighth child in June of that year.[71] Like many a colonial wife Mrs. Place suffered the pains of childbirth eight times and carried a child within her body for six years all told. A child suckled at her breast for eight of these years in the prime of her life. As the doctrines of Puritans were minutely debated, colonies formed, charters suspended, rebellions suppressed, and wars fought, America's women gave their time, their stamina, and their lifeblood to populate the New World. In the first trying century of settlement, when human laborers were desperately needed, the reproductive energies of women assured the survival of the colonies and generated American history.

Childbirth was an act of great womanly courage in fledgling settlements like Plymouth, where it was likely to end the mother's life in one in every thirty cases and cause one-fifth of all maternal deaths.[72] Early Americans could not ignore the threatening implications of maternity, which they called a "sentence," a "curse," the "travail of woman." Cotton Mather felt called upon to exhort the colonial woman to submit to the dangers of childbirth: "It will be a very blameable Indecency and Indiscretion in you to be dissatisfied at your state of Pregnancy. . . . It will indeed look too unnatural in you to complain of a state whereunto the Laws of Nature, established by God have brought you." Mather did not see fit to camouflage the dangers of pregnancy by celebrations of the joys of maternity: "The griefs which you are now suffering in your Body are the Fruits of Sin"; "For ought you to know your Death has entered into you."[73] Colonial ministers, in full cognizance of the temptation to abort, recurrently reminded their parishioners that "to purposefully destroy the fruit of the womb is murder."[74] Still women continued to devise primitive abortion techniques.

The high rate of population growth in seventeenth-century America indicates that most women submitted to the dictates of nature and embraced the magnanimous fertility conferred upon the New World. While Cotton Mather cheered the expectant mother through her hour of travail with the pious observation that "It is a Child of God that you now have within you. What a Consolation!" she found a more palpable support in the skilled midwife and the women of her village who retired with her into the inner chamber of her house and remained with her to celebrate a healthy birth. All returned to visit the female sanctum during the mother's brief respite from household chores that followed childbirth. The conscientious mother would suckle the infant, for to employ a wet nurse was judged "very criminal and blame worthy" as well as extravagant when she held a "bottle in her breasts." [75]

Carrying the fetus, enduring parturition, and suckling the infant commanded women's attention for large portions of their life-span. These functions decreed by woman's anatomy did not, however, confer upon her a peculiarly feminine nature and temperament. No mystique of motherhood lay concealed in the time-consuming and oft-repeated physical ordeal of motherhood. The biological intimacy of mother and child did not ordain an instinctive emotional attachment between the two. The first act of a devout mother symbolized detachment from the fruit of the womb. "Give up your New-born Child unto the Lord." [76] A woman of Puritan upbringing could not vainly presume that a child was her private creation and personal possession. Neither was any colonial woman likely to merge her identity with a child torn from her by the pain of parturition and in great danger of infant mortality. Cotton Mather spoke directly to the colonial mother's experience when he asserted that "Children are mere Loans from God which He may call for when He pleases; and [the mother] quietly submits." [77] Puritan preaching and woman's experience united to inhibit the growth of excessive maternal affection.

After infancy, in what was termed the second stage of childhood, defined by Isaac Ambrose as the period "from the time [the child] begins to be of any direction, till it be fit to be placed forth," [78] a woman relinquished her special ties and exclusive obligations to her progeny. Hereafter all directives regarding child-rearing were addressed to parents, not to mothers. Parents were called to the cooperative enterprises of catechising, training, and laying up property for their offspring. Together they were to "nourish and bring them up," "carefully provide for their outward supply and comfort." [79] The physical care and supervision of the young child might also be placed in the custody of his or her older siblings, rather than the mother, while vocational training would be directed by the parent of the child's own sex or take place outside the family entirely. A child might be judged "fit to be placed forth" as early as six years of age. The father as legal guardian could decide the time and conditions of his children's apprenticeship, but most often mothers were parties to these negotiations as well. In the service of the master, the child was removed entirely from any detrimental maternal or paternal indulgence.

Mothers as well as fathers, furthermore, could be called before the courts if their child care fell short of community standards. A Virginia widow, Martha Ryan, was summoned for "not bringing up her children in a Christian-like manner." [80] On occasion the court would decide to take a child away from a disreputable mother and place him or her in a more respectable home. Colonial husbands might also specify such a procedure in their wills. Samuel Taylor, for example, bequeathed his land to his wife but stipulated that "my children be put out to learn trades with people who will take care of them." Customarily, however, colonial patriarchs strove to bind their households together after their deaths, as did John Smith of Providence. He willed his land and mill in equal shares to his wife and his eldest son. John Junior's legacy was granted on the condition that "he fayle not to be helpe full to his mother to bring up the rest of his brothers and sisters, some of them being very young." Here an elder son was charged with parental duties, again illustrating the tight-knit social fabric of the colonial household of which motherhood was one integral part, not a single strand.[81]

Colonial daughters, wives, and mothers passed their lives within this dense and active circle, and if they escaped death by childbirth, they survived to a ripe old age. The death of a worthy matron brought forth community recognition of her life of service. Thomas Sheffield eulogized his wife as follows. "She was a woman of incomparable meekness of spirit, toward my self especially, and very loving, of great prudence to take care for and order my family affairs, being neither too lavish nor sordid in anything, so that I knew not what was under her hand. She had an excellency to reprove for sin, and discern the evil of me. She loved God's people dearly and was studious to profit by their fellowship and therefore loved their company." [82] The eulogies that followed the deaths of the wives of other prominent colonists, such as Margaret Winthrop, reverberated with simple accolades such as "she was a woman of singular virtue, modesty and piety, and specially loved and honored of the country." [83] Such testimonials were remarkably free from sentimentality and largely incognizant of the delicate virtues of femininity. While women were praised for meekness, they were acclaimed for discerning the weaknesses of their spouses and reproving them for their failures. Although woman's worth encompassed modesty and piety, it rested primarily on the capacity to manage a household economy. She was praised for her love of family but equally honored for loving her neighbors. The well-deserved gratitude of colonial men was placed at the feet of an industrious, productive partner and an efficient mistress of the household.

As the colonial woman functioned alongside the more authoritative male at the heart of the colonial social and economic order, she had little need or opportunity for acquiring and exhibiting a peculiarly feminine personality. Consequently, colonial culture did not parcel out a whole series of temperamental attributes according to sex. Women were not equipped with such now familiar traits as maternal instincts, sexual purity, passivity, tranquility, or submissiveness. Colonial writers did take note of some peculiarly female characteristics, but these were too sparse and muted to constitute a full-fledged feminine stereotype. It was often said that women were the "weaker vessels," of lesser mental and physical endowment than men. Yet every discourse on family order granted women the intellectual capacity to judge her husband's actions and to guide the will of the patriarch. Cotton Mather openly defended women against assaults upon her intelligence. "If any men are so wicked (and some sects of men have been so) as to deny your being rational creatures, the best means to confute them will be proving yourselves religious ones." [84] Mather offered as evidence several models of female genius, leadership, and piety: Hebrew prophets, ancient queens, and contemporary writers. Elsewhere Mather dramatized the fact that women could also be stronger vessels than men in the physical sense, citing as evidence the case of a woman who carried a wounded husband on her back for 300 miles. A casual observer of the colonial household could attest to the strength of women as they routinely lifted heavy caldrons from the fireplace. Accordingly, colonial culture did not delight in calling attention to the delicate frame and petite stature of its women. Womanly meekness and modesty held larger sway in the colonial image of woman. These retiring qualities had religious origins in the virtue of fear of the Lord: "Favor is deceitful and Beauty is Vain, but a woman that Fears the Lord, she is that shall be praised." [85] The injunction to humbly prostrate oneself before the Almighty and his earthly emissaries in the church, state, and family was basic to social order. Timidity and squeamishness, on the other hand, were inappropriate to the temporal concerns of frontier women, who braved the Atlantic, Indian raids, and hostile forests.

All these ascribed sexual distinctions regarding character, furthermore, were differences of degree not kind. Meekness was but a species of the general virtue of humility prescribed for both sexes; craving for a fashionable dress was but a female symptom of that vice, vanity in personal appearance; the seductiveness of Eve was a sinful weakness that she shared with the lustful Adam. Human strength and failing were conceived of as virtues or as vices, never as instincts, which God, nature, or hormones had distributed inequitably among the sexes. Colonial men and women were held to a single standard of good behavior and equipped with a will free to perfect the temporal manifestations of their character. Therefore, unlike their progeny, early Americans rarely wrote or spoke of the "nature of woman" as opposed to the "nature of man." The concepts of masculinity and femininity remained ill-defined in agrarian America.

The Christian theology that flourished there celebrated a contrary tenet of scripture: "There is neither Jew nor Greek, Bond nor Free, Male nor Female, for ye all are one in Christ Jesus." [86] Colonial Americans inherited a social and economic structure that was uniquely hospitable to certain aspects of the sexual equality implied by this Christian concept. The agrarian frontier economy kept the sexual division of labor simple and primitive, while the household system of social organization precluded the isolation of women in a private and undervalued sphere. These factors in turn inhibited the cultural gestation of sexual stereotypes.

Outside the social and economic unit of the household, however, this sexual balance disappeared. Benjamin Wadsworth interpreted the phrase "All are one in Christ Jesus" to the effect that "it does not dissolve the Relations between Husbands and Wives, Parents and Children, Masters and Servants, Rulers and Subjects." [87] Within the family, women might on occasion usurp or share the superior relationship, but all the positions of power outside it were open only to males. In the public centers of power, the ministry, the colonial assemblies, the town meetings, men alone could take up the role of "Rulers."

Women did not appear at those town meetings and legislative assemblies that presumably cradled American democracy. Certainly many men were barred from political participation by failing to meet the property qualifications necessary to vote and hold office in the colonies. The exclusion of women, however, was categorical sexual discrimination. Margaret Brent made a concerted attempt to win admission to the Maryland Assembly, denying "all precedings in the present assembly unless she may be present and have a vote." Mistress Brent came armed with sizable property holdings, lofty social status, connections with the proprietor, and a widely acknowledged administrative ability. Still her petition was denied as simply "beyond her sex." [88] Even as colonial towns became progressively more lenient in granting the vote to men of little property, they adamantly refused citizenship to women with large holdings of taxable land and a major stake in the ordering of society. In Jamaica, New York, at a time when more and more women appeared on the tax lists, town orders were issued with the flagrantly patriarchal salutation "Know all men."

It might be argued that this practice worked to the benefit of colonial women, freeing them from the time-consuming and burdensome duties that colonial citizenship entailed. Yet woman's political losses clearly outweighed her gains. Nearly every colonial male who took the time to appear regularly at town meetings was granted some office, be it selectman, constable, or the humble fence viewer. Only by diligently performing in this political position could a colonist achieve the community prestige that might lead to a higher office and a larger grant in the next distribution of town land. When women as apolitical beings were freed from the obligation to work periodically on the town road, or to assist in the construction of the meetinghouse, they also lost the wholesome opportunity to engage in communal labor. Once denied access to the political arena, women not only lost opportunities for social mobility and cooperative social action, but also for education in the procedures of public debate and the orderly resolution of conflict. Women made no direct contribution to the political consensus so sacred to the peasant village.

The political deliberation of the townsmen could, however, have a profound impact on women themselves. Town officers ruled on their most private concerns and basic well-being, their land, their taxes, their family affairs. Women appeared regularly before the local courts as plaintiffs and defendants, but never sat as judges or jurors or indisputable witnesses. When one woman was brought to trial for murder in Virginia, female witnesses were accompanied by their sons and husbands who "recognized that they appear in court." [89] Women summoned to court for domestic and sexual offenses would confront a body composed of husbands, fathers, and sons. The precarious position of female family heads caused them to make more than their share of appearances before magistrates. Many came begging the courts advice and assistance. Mary Walling is a good example of the women whose families' futures rested in the hands of the town court. Her husband, Thomas, had "departed the town," leaving her to address the city fathers, humbly desiring them "to take charge of a boy put out to her, the said Mary being unable any longer to take care of him." The judges took this occasion not only to grant her specific request but to assign one of their number as Mary Walling's guardian, dismantle her property, and lay claim to her livestock.[90] Such were the hazards to which women were liable when they placed their fate in the hands of an all-male political structure.

Single women, and especially those with children, were particularly vulnerable to summons from the courts, for without male partners they were presumed to be in precarious economic circumstances and prone to becoming "chargeable to the town."

One Johanna Harrad was called before the deputies of Providence "to see what securitye may be put to clear the Town of what Charges may arise from her. And if none will be put in sufficient Securitye. Then to send her back again to Boston." Johanna Harrad was one of many strangers—men, women, and families—who were asked to post bond before they were granted the right to settle in a town. Local courts were particularly suspicious of strange women and doubly so if they entered the town with children but unaccompanied by a husband. Such women would have great difficulty disputing the magistrates' prejudgment of their indigency or immorality. Mrs. Hannah Hayman bore the full brunt of such prejudice. She confessed to the Providence deputies that her husband had gone off to sea six months earlier, leaving her to wander from Boston to Dorchester, Dedham, Reston, and finally to Providence in search of a home. The last town proved no more hospitable than the others. The decision of the court read as follows: "we are willing for our own securetye and for ye safety of the woman to take the way as the law directs that shee may be sent from constable to constable to the place of her abode." [91]

The cruel practice of community ostracism was designed to maintain the order and uniformity of the close-knit agrarian community, not to punish the female sex. Yet women were more likely to suffer the direct consequences of this and many other procedures of the town, further exacerbating their political alienation. Although never a barrister, selectman, or even a swine-keeper, a woman could expect to become the supplicant, ward, or outcast of the town. At best she was the passive beneficiary of town benevolence, sharing perhaps in a legacy like the one bequeathed to the town of Jamaica to be distributed to the "poor, viz., poor widows and children, persons blind or lame or aged that are unable to get their living." [92] Lumped together with the lame, the aged, and children as a town charge, or carefully scrutinized and controlled by the court and town meeting, the political condition of poor, husbandless, and fatherless women was not altogether unlike that of the cows and pigs that strayed through the village. Certainly women and livestock received about equal notice in the records of public discourse of colonial America.

Set apart from the political center of authority but an equally important public arena in the American colonies was the church. Here too women were excluded from full participation and high office. Many American colonists shared in the religious heritage of English dissenting sects from which had sprung such radical dogmas as the equality of the sexes. The English Levellers, for example, pronounced that women "by birth have as much natural freedom as any other, and therefore ought not to loose their liberty without their consent." [93] Quaker immigrants to America imbibed this heritage to the extent that they invited women to participate fully in the egalitarian practices of their congregations. New England Puritans accorded women a moral status equivalent to men and an equal opportunity for salvation, but little more. In Puritan meetinghouses and Anglican churches the hierarchy of the sexes remained intact. Even the offertory procession filed by in a precisely ranked order of the sexes: "The magistrates, and chiefe gentlemen first, and the Elders and all the congregation of men, and most of them that are not of the church, all single persons, widows and women in the absence of their husbands, came up one after another."[94] If not granted a higher status by association with a venerable spouse, women were relegated to the last place in the religious hierarchy.

The ritual of an offertory procession might be construed merely as an archaic custom, but the systematic exclusion of women from positions of clerical authority had far-reaching consequences. The colonial ministry was the seat of cultural power as well as religious influence. Clerics were responsible for most of the reading materials published in the American colonies. They alone had the privilege of rising before the public in Sunday sermons and weekly lectures to bespeak, inculcate, and propagate community values. There was no female input into this colonial cultural network. Women had no direct say in the attitudes toward her sex that pastors circulated throughout the colonies, no opportunity to publicly rebut the accusations of a Cotton Mather or Benjamin Wadsworth nor of John Winthrop. Denied admission to the training grounds of the colonial ministry—Harvard, Yale, Oxford, and Cambridge—women were seldom equipped to argue the fine points of theology with their pastors. They were customarily taught only to read the Bible and passively accept its tenets as interpreted by the male clerical elite.

The secular education of women was also meager. The New England colonies took considerable pains to educate American youth, but their enthusiasm flagged when it came to women. Females were banned from institutions of higher learning and were commonly admitted to the public schoolhouse only during those hours and seasons when boys were occupied with other affairs or were needed in the fields. The burden of educating colonial children was not placed upon the school, however, but on the household. Parents and masters were charged with teaching the basic skills of reading and writing to girls and boys alike. Despite the fact that woman's right to read and write was often written into indenture contracts and colonial laws, the vast majority of females signed colonial documents with a crude mark, indicating a rate of literacy substantially lower than that of men.

It is not surprising, therefore, that few colonial women won acclaim for their intellectual acumen. Those determined women who did succeed in wresting an education from a hostile culture were severely castigated. One woman who dared to write a theological treatise was rudely rebuffed by her brother: "Your printing of a book is beyond your sex and doth rankly smell." John Winthrop maintained that such intellectual exertion could rot the female mind itself. He attributed the madness of Ann Hopkins, wife of the Connecticut governor, to her intellectual curiosity. "If she had attended her household affairs and such things as belong to women, and not gone out of her way to meddle in such things as are proper for men, she'd have kept her wits and might have improved them usefully." [95] Anne Bradstreet, the first major American poet, responded to such arrogant insults to her sex with these ironic lines: "Let Greeks be Greeks, and women what they are/ Men have precedency and still excell/ it is but vain unjustly to wage war?/ Men can do best and women know it well/ preeminence in all and each is yours/ Yet grant some small acknowledgement of ours." [96]

A few colonial women objected to the limitations placed upon them with stronger protests than Anne Bradstreet's mild-mannered verse. These rugged and resourceful dames could not politely turn away as the doors of meetinghouses, rectories, colleges, and libraries were slammed in their faces. While Margaret Brent fought on the political front with her challenge to the Maryland Assembly, Anne Hutchinson assaulted the citadel of the Puritan church. Mistress Hutchinson was fully versed in Puritan theology including those tenets that promised an elevated status for women. She found in the covenant of grace confirmation of the special powers of individuals predestined for salvation, including women, to divine the will of God. Assured of her sanctification, Anne Hutchinson deemed it proper to articulate her own antinomian theology and, by inference, to criticize the patriarchal ministers and magistrates who held it heresy. She also dared to conduct religious conversations with the women of Boston, a practice for which she also had a theological justification: "I conceive there lyes a clear rule in Titus, that the elder women should instruct the younger." Mistress Anne Hutchinson had touched upon a basic contradiction in the Puritan doctrine of woman's place. Yet the Winthrops and the Cottons held to their perilous ground and exiled her not only as a heretic but for "acting the part" rather of "a husband than a wife" and for conducting herself in a manner "not fitting for your sex." Still, Anne Hutchinson exacted a price from the Massachusetts fathers for their arbitrary treatment of women, a controversy that wreaked havoc in Boston, rocked the colony, and embarrassed its governor. At the very outset of the colonial experiment, the cost of repressing women was made clear.[97]

Other religious women proved nearly as troublesome as Anne Hutchinson, particularly those well versed in the liberating doctrines of the Society of Friends. The next thorn to be lodged in John

Winthrop's side was Mary Dyer, banished three times from the Puritan colony and thrice returned. Only a hanging could silence this bold Quaker. But before she died, Mary Dyer stood before the authorities of Massachusetts Bay to demand religious tolerance. "I say I am a living testimony for [the Quakers] and the Lord, that he hath blest them and sent them unto you: therfore be not found fighting against God, but let my council and request be accepted with you to repeal all such laws that the Truth and Servants of the Lord may have free passage among you." Mary Dyer, inspired by the Quaker belief in the inner light of godly wisdom that resided in all men and women, presumed to judge and dramatize the errors of male leaders. Yet, rather than challenging the legitimacy of male leadership, she closed her protest "In Love and in the Spirit of Meekness." [98] Anne Hutchinson also accepted the legitimacy of a political and religious elite composed entirely of men. She submitted to the magistrates' decisions with the compliant utterance "I will freely let you for I am subject to your authority." [99] Neither of these courageous women were self-conscious feminists. Almost by accident they stumbled upon the sexual contradictions of colonial America. Encouraged by the half promises of sexual equality made by religious sects, they tested the outermost barriers to female freedom in their own time but never assaulted the fortress by sexual inequality itself.

The fact remains that discontented women caused their share of trouble in the American colonies. Not all the rebellious women were of the stature of Hutchinson and Dyer. Their protests, although most often oblique and unconscious, nevertheless underscored the sexual contradictions of colonial society. Many minor social conflicts were nourished by the contradictory elements of woman's economic role. Woman's functions as manufacturer and trader, first of all, proved the source of controversy as well as economic utility. The economic conflicts in which men were likely to get embroiled largely stemmed from dealings in landed property, the value and ownership of which could be legally determined by reference to deeds, contracts, and wills. If need be, men could debate and resolve their differences before the public in the town meeting. Women's economic exchanges, on the other hand, were conducted in private in an unsystematized and unpredictable fashion. In New Amsterdam women's economic enterprises created pandemonium. The many appearances of one Geertje Teunis before the Council of New Amsterdam illustrate the special pitfalls of female business. On one occasion the court was asked to rule upon the equity of a single transaction in which the following items were exchanged: a stocking, six sleeves, some seawart, several quarters of brandy, a tub, and assorted coins. Such complicated exchanges and the quibbling that arose from them led women like Geertje Teunis into vitriolic personal quarrels. One of her creditors charged that this epitome of the women of trade called him a "drunken rogue and a knave." Geertje countercharged that the plaintiff "abused her first for a whore and beast wherto she said I hold you for a rogue and knave, till you have proved that I am a whore and I'm from beast stock." [100] Off in the Puritan enclave of Boston, where social tranquility was almost an obsession, Mistress Ann Hibbens was wreaking similar havoc. The imbroglio began when Mistress Hibbens became dissatisfied with the workmanship of some carpenters she had employed within her household. First, she complained to her husband, then consulted her minister about the alleged swindle, and finally sought retribution from the secular authorities. When no one proved sympathetic to the economic difficulties of the mistress of the household, Ann Hibbens made a general nuisance of herself, gossiping, grumbling, and blanketing the town with slander.[101] Woman's utility and aptitudes in the home economy could boomerang into social disorder when her powers were checked outside the household.

The aggressive temperament of colonial women often expressed itself in physical terms. One Anne Brown confronted the highest authorities of Augusta County, Virginia, with her belligerence. When summoned to the court for abusing the local sheriff, she vented her rage against the judge himself, threatening "that on his coming off the Bench she would give it to him with the Devil." [102] The households and tribunals of every town lived in fear of such troublesome and militant females. In one North Carolina village a man named James Warden fell victim of a woman named Margaret Briggs, who "with force and arms . . . did make and him beat wounded and evilly entreated and other Enormities to him." [103] Other colonial men met violent death at the hands of such worthy opponents. All human passions were manifested in both sexes, and the colonial community was required to inculcate pacific behavior and restrain hostility in men and women alike.

Whether the culprits were men or women, accusations of sexual misconduct and perversion repeatedly disrupted the communications network of the agrarian village. Women assaulted one another as "common hoares" and "salte Bitches." Their tongues lashed out at the men of the town in such favorite epithets as knave, rogue, and cuckhold. Two women of Virginia took direct aim at the virility of their neighbor: "Came to the cow pen and there did in a jeering manner abuse Grace Waltham saying that John Waltham, husband of the said Grace, had his Mounthly Courses as Women have, and that the said Anne Stephens should say that John Waltham was not able to gett a child." [104] The perpetrators of this slander, Anne Wilkinson and Anne Stephens, were ducked in the town pond. Although New England town clerks seldom were disposed to record episodes like this in such lurid detail, numerous incidents of slander, insinuations of dishonesty, drunkenness, and fornications indicated women's subversive effect on the town tranquility.

Although much of this squabbling can be laid to town gossip, it cannot be simply dismissed as a feminine foible. First of all, gossip served as a method of transmitting personal information of considerable significance to women: the moral failings, eccentricities, and general misbehavior of the men whom they were charged to obey. Informal verbal accounts were the only channels of such information open to women who were barred from such public forums as the meetinghouse and the pulpit. Woman's household work, however, brought her into frequent contact with neighbors and servants and her trade took her into taverns, fields, and other homes. These associations among women undoubtedly provoked many opportunities for mutual support, sharing labor, and transmitting skills. The casual and disjointed conversations that ensued could, however, acquire the volatile, shrill, and cantankerous characteristics of gossip. Many a village controversy began when a group of women just happened to assemble along a village path. The frustration endemic to the contradictory nature of woman's place in agrarian society—invested with essential social and economic responsibilities but denied the right to pursue her self-interest and exercise power in public forums—led naturally to slander, character assassination, and gossip. The social disorder that issued from this contradiction ate away at the tight-knit bonds of self-sufficient agrarian communities and sabotaged the Utopian hopes for building a peaceable kingdom in the New World.

Thus it is not surprising that women played a major role in the most dramatic example of seventeenth-century community disintegration, the witchcraft hysteria that plagued the village of Salem in 1692. Till then, American colonists had prudently refrained from conjuring up the old demonic powers that had raged across Europe in the sixteenth century, and only a few isolated charges of witchcraft were made in the early years of American settlement. Still most of those accused were women: Ann Hibbens of Boston, Anne Cole of Hartford, and Elizabeth Knight of Groton, Massachusetts, being the prime examples. It was not until the last decade of the seventeenth century, in the tiny agricultural village of Salem, that witchcraft became a widespread social menace. Before the witchcraft controversy had taken its full course in Salem nearly every element of the community had become involved, rich and poor, male and female alike. Nonetheless, the first to be accused, the major accusers, and the majority of those hanged for the offense of practicing witchcraft were of the female sex. In the deadly spotlight of a community racked by tales of witchcraft, women enacted the drama of their difficult social position, playing their complicated roles as victims, assailants, rebels, and conformists.

The fact that the majority of those accused of being agents of the devil were women invites the blunt charge that the male authorities of Salem used the terror of witchcraft to exorcise unruly women from the community. Certainly some women were cruelly victimized by the trials before male judges, and many of them had been careless of keeping in woman's place. Mistress Hibbens' economic dealings in Boston had brought her excommunication for "usurping authority over him whom God had made her head and husband." Once an outcast, she developed an uncanny power of discerning the hidden import of social discourse. This womanly astuteness was judged the work of the devil, and Mistress Hibbens was executed as a witch. As one observer put it, she was hanged "only for having more wit than her neighbors . . . having . . . unhappily guessed that two of her persecutors who she saw talking in the street were talking of her." [105] The first women accused in Salem were also town eyesores. Tituba, a West Indian slave, had indeed practiced the black arts; a trail of court cases and debts followed the accused Sarah Good, who was renowned as a village tramp and often chargeable to the town; Sarah Osbourne's relationships with her two husbands were the cause of town gossip, as was her irregular church attendance. The reputation of Bridget Bishop was also scandalous: she wore a red bodice, behaved seductively toward the young men of the town, and conducted rowdy entertainments in her home. At one time or another all these women became involved in economic squabbles with their neighbors. Rebecca Nurse, on the other hand, an aged and honorable mother, whose only eccentricity was deafness, was an unlikely candidate for witchcraft allegations. Rebecca and her husband, Francis, were parvenus in Salem, encroaching on the economic and social status of the powerful Putnam family, who played such an important role in conducting the trials. Perhaps even the prosperity reaped with the aid of an exemplary spouse could invoke community wrath amid the confusion and contagion of witchcraft trials. Yet, whatever the social transgressions of these women, witch trials were a circuitous and suicidal method of retribution, since the social turmoil and the curtailment of agricultural production left in its wake were hardly welcomed by the males of Salem.[106]

In fact the role of woman in colonial witchcraft was far more complicated than that of innocent victim. This is clearly demonstrated by the fact that the first accusing fingers in the Salem trials were pointed by a band of young, single women. The testimony of these girls, afflicted by a hysteria that they attributed to agents of the devil, was the crucial evidence that sent members of their own sex to the gallows. Only rarely did the young accusers seem to be carrying out a vendetta against the opposite sex. The offenses that singled out George Burroughs, for example, included the suspicious deaths of his wives, from whom he had exacted a pledge to secrecy regarding his affairs. This wizard had denied women that important privilege, the opportunity to gossip. More often, however, the afflicted girls acted in the interest of their fathers and masters. Three of the most active accusers resided in the home of Thomas Putnam, Jr., a village patriarch and an opponent of many of the accused, including George Burroughs during his tenure as the local minister. Two other afflicted girls lived in the household of Samuel Parris, Burroughs' successor in the Salem pastorate. These daughters and servants of Salem most likely learned the names of those vulnerable to charges of witchcraft from the rumors and grumblings that circulated through the households of the small town elite. They were well versed enough in the social skills of sheltered women to select as victims individuals against whom their household patriarchs bore a grudge. The social predicament and skills of women allowed them to be subtly manipulated into the vanguard of a witch-hunt.[107]

The implications of the afflicted girls' behavior can be carried one step further, for they also illustrate the psychological burdens of conforming to standards of womanhood in the seventeenth century. The young accusers suffered palpable pain, the tortured symptoms of psychological disturbance. Their hideous fits, complete with swoons, contortions of the limbs, constriction of the muscles, and the recurrent sensation of being pricked, spread like an epidemic among Salem's daughters. The disease itself was often called the "suffocation of the mother." This terminology, coupled with the fact that the afflicted often attributed their hysteria to witches of approximately their mothers' ages, has prompted the observation that witchcraft fantasies were products of repressive weaning and oral fixations.[108] But why then were there no afflicted boys? Motherhood, it would seem, had a very special meaning for girls; it might symbolize the suffocating social position they would shortly assume.

The first outbreak of hysteria in Salem occurred when Elizabeth Parris and Abigail Williams had employed Tituba's assistance in evoking supernatural power to divine their futures. According to one report, "one of the afflicted persons who (as I am credibly informed) did try with an egg and glass to find her future husband's calling [i.e. occupation] till there came up a coffin." [109] The New England girl whose future course in life was dependent on marriage and the stature of her husband might well be haunted by the possibility that lingered in that specter of a coffin, of being a widow or an old maid. The delirious conversations between Mercy Short and the devil give further evidence of the peculiar anxieties of young women in the seventeenth century. "Fine promises! You'l bestow an Husband upon mee, if I'l bee your Servant. A Husband! What? a Devil! I shall then bee finely fitted with an Husband: No I hope the Blessed Lord Jesus Christ will marry my Soul to Himself yett before Hee has done with me, as poor a wretch as I am! Fine Clothes! What? Such as your Friend Sarah Good had, who hardly had Rags to cover her! Pray, why did you not provide better for her Then?" [110] When the afflicted girls lashed out at poor outcasts like Sarah Good they projected the fearful possibility that through the accident of marriage they would meet a similar fate. The afflicted girls who resided in the Putnam household were granted special insight into the precarious status of women. Thomas Putnam, Jr., was beginning a long litigation regarding the conditions of his father's will in hopes of wrenching property from his stepmother.[111] Understandable premonitions of an adult life rife with uncertainty might have helped to drive the girls of Salem to hysterical fits and accusations of witchcraft.

Their actions were also a disguised form of rebellion. For a few frantic months eleven young women held an entire town in their power, making all of New England, even governors and their ladies, squirm. They received a degree of attention that children, as they were called, and women were seldom accorded by the assembled townspeople. Yet their glory was short-lived. The witchcraft hysteria was soon brought under control and within a few years the town repented, repudiating the whole bloody affair, leaving the once afflicted girls to make their way through the same old labyrinth of difficult and constricting female roles. Mercy Warren, whose master had tried to beat her out of her hysterical fits, never recovered her sanity. These girls could not extricate themselves from the frustrating contradictions of woman's place even with the aid of demonic powers.

One more conjecture can be drawn from the debacle of Salem village witchcraft: the suggestion that the agrarian town and the sex roles built into it were in the process of transformation. In days past, a girl's future had been somewhat predictable if not ideal. In 1692, however, young, single women might have had particular cause for anxiety. They were part of a large generation coming into maturity at a time when the arable land in and around the colonial town was slowly being eaten away by settlement. The possibility loomed that the young men and women of New England would not be able to obtain farmland on which to settle and raise a family. Could it be that the witchcraft hysteria was inspired by what the future held in store—spinsterhood, the poverty of insufficient land, or migration to some distant frontier settlement? At some point the residents of the agricultural villages of the New World would have to confront these premonitions, which bespoke a new social and economic order and a new alignment of the sexes.

CHANGING ROLES, NEW RISKS:

WOMEN IN COMMERCIAL AMERICA

In the annals of American history the years between
1750 and 1820 appear under the halo of independence and republicanism, and therefore prompt a
simple forthright question in the history of women:
Did the female sex demand independence in 1776 and
secure the full liberties of United States citizens soon
thereafter? The rights and privileges of Americans
could not be kept secret from the nation's women.
Abigail Adams was well aware of the ideological currents circulating through the Continental Congress
when she taunted her spouse with the declaration
that "If particular care and attention is not paid to the
ladies, we are determined to instigate a rebellion, and
will not hold ourselves bound by any laws in which we
have no voice or representation." [1] In the new nation
a few female taxpayers, fortified by the principles of
representative democracy, appeared and cast their
ballots at the voting places of New Jersey. The catholic republican spirit of the new nation was even hospitable to Mary Wollstonecraft's *Vindication of the
Rights of Women,* which went through several editions in the United States in the last decade of the
eighteenth century. The rights of women even found
their way into ladies' magazines, where they were put
to verse to be sung to the music of "My Country 'tis of
Thee." [2] This liberation theme in the history of American women cannot be pursued much further, however, for despite all the expansive talk of democracy,
women found no larger a place in the politics of the
new nation than they had under the British Empire.
Their names still remained absent from the ledger of
voters and the lists of officeholders. Neither the Declaration of Independence nor the Constitution of the
United States elevated women to the status of politi-

cal beings. If participation in public affairs were the only means of being admitted to the history of the United States, the female sex would again be denied a past.

Yet women's history was not held in abeyance while the founding fathers disengaged the colonies from British rule, designed constitutions, and squared off as Federalists and Republicans. On the social and cultural fronts, the position of women was undergoing a series of crucial changes. Although the course of women's history was uncertain and seemed often to move at cross-purposes, by the mid-eighteenth century one thing was clear: the traditional role of economic partner and mistress of the household was in jeopardy. A commercial spirit was intruding into villages and towns across the land, manifesting itself in an accelerating pace of money exchanges and the proliferation of bustling shops stored with varied goods. The principle of production for sale, not survival, disrupted the self-sufficient households in which women had played their central, though subordinate, roles. The enlargement of the commercial sector of the economy and the consequent complication of the division of labor portended a variety of new economic possibilities for women. On the one hand, it opened up to her new business opportunities, new outlets for her trading skills, which might foster a sense of enterprise, acquisitiveness, and self-improvement. On the other hand, a commercial economy made possible a disassociation of home and work, which might open a chasm between male and female spheres. As the sole fully legitimate property owners, American husbands had a head start toward commercial investment, and should they prosper in farms, shops, shipping firms, and manufactories, they would be able to acquire by purchase the products and services once supplied by female economic partners. The upsurge of individualistic ambition would exaggerate economic inequity among men as well as between the sexes, as the more privileged, talented, or avaricious wrenched from their fellows greater quantities of land and commercial wealth. Accordingly, by the late eighteenth century American women, either through their own enterprise or by dint of the status conferred upon them by marriage, went their separate ways into rudimentary classes designated by such colloquialisms as the "better," "middling" and "lower sort." The years between 1750 and 1820, then, left a decided, but ambiguous and multifaceted, imprint of change on the history of American women.

The transformation of the economic role and status of women became apparent even in the heartland of the subsistence economy, rural New England. By the mid-eighteenth century the original land grants had been parceled out and the old town practice of distributing fields and meadows gratis was discontinued. The farmland along the Eastern seaboard now became prey to private enterprise, to be won or lost according to the relative purchasing power of the townsmen. Economic power accrued to those who raised surplus crops for a regional market and used their profits to expand their landholdings, their output, and their wealth. This development had progressed sufficiently by 1760 in commercial farming centers like Chester, Pennsylvania, to transform a homogeneous farming community into a rudimentary class society, where the top 10 percent of the population controlled nearly half the local wealth.[3] The increasing numbers of landless individuals would now find employment as hirelings of prosperous farmers or in the artisan shops and retail establishments that served them. Others might heed the cry of cheap land in the frontier outposts of Vermont. By the early nineteenth century this second frontier produced a third, as Vermonters, taken with "Genesee Fever," went off to the fertile valley of New York in pursuit of bumper crops and upward economic mobility.[4] Simultaneously, the lands and opportunities of Tennessee, Kentucky, or Georgia lured southern farmers from their eastern homes. Money and movement supplanted subsistence and stability as the American economy left the agrarian age behind.

On occasion, women were invited to join the enterprising spirit of the era. A pamphlet printed in a New England village proclaimed that "a virtuous woman is a good economist. She not only labors with her hands to obtain the necessaries and conveniences of life; but she is provident and saving of her earnings." [5] One New England minister picked up on this refrain and built around it an oratorio of female entrepreneurship. In 1793 the Reverend John Ogden of Portsmith, New Hampshire, lamented that "in so wise and civilized an age and country as we live in . . . young females have not partook of a greater share of the cares and prosperity of the community." To remedy this unfortunate state of affairs, Ogden advised the New England daughter to expand her household enterprise into a commercial operation; her homespun clothing, for example, could become "a means to open a merchandizer, which gives her the production of distant regions." Then Ogden planted even more grandiose ambitions in the young woman's mind. "She does not totally confine her cares to merchandise, but knowing the value of real property, the quality of land, and the importance of agriculture, she considereth a field and buyeth it." Thereafter the female economist should strive to "improve all opportunities of increasing her wealth." John Ogden did not foresee that the stellar virtue of emergent American capitalism, individualistic economic achievement, would be recommended to males only: "So far from being masculine and improper for the delicate sex, it gives her health." [6]

Off in South Carolina Eliza Lucas arrived at these principles of commercial economy independently. Left in charge of her father's plantation at the age of seventeen, Eliza speedily embraced the spirit of economic betterment. She wrote to a friend as follows: "I have planted a figg orchard with design to dry them and export them. I have reckoned my expenses and the profit to arise from the figgs, but was I to tell you how great an estate I am to make this way and how 'tis to be laid out you would think me far gone in romance." Eliza Lucas' subsequent marriage to Charles Pinckney did not curb her enterprising spirit but carried her further into the sphere of commercial agriculture as she pioneered in the American indigo trade.[7]

Yet Eliza Lucas Pinckney by no means spoke for all American women. The advancement of the commercial economy in Worcester, Massachusetts, portended quite a different fate for Millicent Goulding. In 1785 she petitioned the court as follows: "Gentlemen, I am in needy Circumstances, destitute of an house or Home to shelter me, but thank god am in a good degree of health and by my industry am able at present to support myself if, I had a Room provided for me—I am loathe to put the town to any expense for my support and maintenance but necessity obliges me." Although the court granted Millicent Goulding's request for shelter, this did not assure her economic independence. Two years later she returned to the court, swallowing her pride and surrendering her hopes of self-support. "I am now Destitute of house or home or Decent clothing and Daily suffering for the Necessaries of Life." She begged the town to "support me during my natural life." [8] The intrusion of commercialism into American farming could bode well or ill for the American woman, but it seldom left her old roles unchanged.

Many American wives could be found between the extremes of success and failure illustrated by Eliza Pinckney and Millicent Goulding. Like Abigail Adams, they might find that their traditional economic responsibilities had increased in volume but yet remained fundamentally unchanged by the forces of revolution and nation-building. When called away from the homestead by public business, John Adams wrote his spouse: "I intreat you to rouse your whole attention to the family, the stock, the farm, the dairy. Let every article of expense which can be spared be retrenched; keep the hands attentive to there business and the most prudent measures of every kind be adopted." Mrs. Adams took this advice to heart, hoping "in time to have the reputation of being as good a *farmeress* as my partner has of being a good statesman." She fulfilled the office of husbandman most admirably, not only in managing the farm but also in manufacturing soap and saltpeter and in sewing blankets for the troops of the Revolution.[9] American women were summoned again and again to redouble their efforts in home manufacturing, impelled by the interruptions of English trade through wars and boycotts and inspired by the goal of American economic independence. In 1768, for example, when the colonists non-importation pact was in effect, the New York *Journal* referred their readers to the "glorious example" of a woman and her daughter in Newport who "have spun fully sixty yards of good fine linen cloth nearly a yard wide, since the first of March, besides taking care of a large family." [10]

The political incentives to female manufacturing, however, were counteracted by the competition of rising commercialism. While the household remained the major seat of American manufacturing as of 1820, the female manufacturers of cloth, soap, and candles saw some of their home duties ebbing away. After 1810 many of America's farms not only had access to the shops of the town and village, but also were hounded by itinerant weavers, tailors, and peddlers. Soon the products of fledgling factories would also find their way into the American woman's farmhouse.[11] Regardless of a farm wife's domestic occupations, however, her economic role was beginning to pale beside the enterprises of producing and marketing a single cash crop, be it vegetables, cotton, or wheat. This entire process, from land purchase through the cultivation, transport, and sale of farm commodities, entailed an expansion of the sphere of men rather than of women. For the time being, however, the role of the rural woman, still representative of the vast majority of the nation's female population remained that of "Adam's Rib."

Still, the eighteenth century displaced at least

some farmers' daughters from the countryside and drove them into America's cities where the forces of commercialism held sway. In the seventeenth century the towns of the Northeast were hardly urban. Boston's six thousand residents, for example, were scattered along cowpaths in homes surrounded by garden plots and foraging livestock. A century later, however, Boston began to look and operate like a city; its population of twelve thousand settled along marked-out streets and traveled to a commercial hub to exchange their specialized products and skills for coin and currency. New York eclipsed Boston as an urban center in the eighteenth century, and its population had increased no less than 500 percent by 1825. Although less than 10 percent of America's population resided in these bustling towns, it was here that women acted to the fullest their role in a commercial economy.

One index of the commercial energies of the northeastern towns was the local press with its advertisements for nearly every imaginable product. Some of these notices were placed by females and read like this Philadelphia advertisement: "Elizabeth Perkins has for sale in her shop . . ." glassware in every style and shape. The vast majority of Elizabeth Perkins' competitors were male. The city of Boston harbored the greatest number of she-merchants, but even there only 10 percent of the local advertisers were female and most of them were widows who were carrying on businesses established by their husbands. Nevertheless, those women who gave notice of their business enterprises in the city newspapers testified to the commercial skills of which their sex was capable. These women did more than barter their homemade goods. They managed a wide network of economic relationships that included purchasing and displaying and selling goods from the Continent and the American hinterland. The range of economic experiences open to women is illustrated by a notice in a Philadelphia paper: "All persons who are indebted to Anne Jones at the Plume and Feather in Second Street in Philadelphia are desired to come and settle the same. . . . she designing to go for England in a short time." One Mary Jackson was a producer as well as a merchandiser: "The said Mary makes and sells Tea-Kettles and Coffe-Pots. . . ." A widow named Anne Page also combined the roles of artisan and merchant, selling tools and engaging in carpentry simultaneously.[12]

Newspaper advertisements cannot reveal, however, the extensive participation of wives and daughters in commercial enterprises owned by men. It is only in her husband's words, for example, that we learn of the contributions of Mrs. Alexander in New York: "The next day after my wife brought to bed of a daughter she sold goods to above thirty pounds value." [13] As a child, Sarah Ripley of Greenfield, Massachusetts, casually noted her economic duties in her journal: "My father and sister Lydia departed for Boston—I am left with the care of the store, I hope I shall fulfill the duties incumbent on me in an acceptable manner." [14] Like Sarah's father, Benjamin Franklin did not climb the ladder to success alone, but with the aid of a wife, who "proved a good and faithful helpmate, assisted me much by attending the shop." [15] With Ben off with his kites and philandering in France, Mrs. Franklin's responsibilities must have exceeded simple assistance. Women also became the senior partners of their sons. For example, "Mary Jackson and Sons" advertised regularly before the firm came under the exclusive management of her male heirs. Other she-merchants consolidated their skills and capital in "co-partnerships" or "companies" with other men and women.[16] Whether as lone entrepreneurs, partners, widows or the wives and daughters of shopkeepers these retained economic centrality in early American commerce.

The commercial towns also offered women a larger range in which to practice their skills for monetary profit. The traditional services of a midwife or a nurse became paying occupations in the commercial towns where women solicited clients in the press. More exotic specialties could also be practiced in the cosmopolitan setting. For example, one woman announced that she "makes grave Clothes and lays out the dead." Other women turned to teaching. A Miss Rodes, "newly arrived in Philadelphia," offered to teach French, reading, writing, drawing, and embroidery to city girls "in homes or at her place of residence." By 1757 even the town of Dedham could employ eight women as teachers in the same schools where young men were prepared for higher education. As commerce flourished and towns grew into cities, a whole panoply of new enterprises opened to women. Female economic life was enlivened with the possibilities of profit, diversity, and social exchange with customers and middlemen as well as with their families and neighbors.[17]

The liveliest of all commercial enterprises, rural or urban, was the tavern, and there women found many opportunities for employment. As early as 1690, twenty-four of Boston's fifty-four taverns were run by women. One Mary Ballard opened a tavern "For the entertainment of gentlemen and the benefit of commerce," where "all the newspapers of the Continent are regularly taken in and several English Prints and Magazines." The illegal activities of an enterprising tavernkeeper were much more extensive than the sale of liquor and literature. One proprietor of a tavern, Alice Thomas, was brought to court for receiving stolen goods, selling liquor without a license, entertaining children and servants unseasonably, profaning the Lord's Day, and giving "frequent secret and unseasonable entertainment in her house to Lewd, Lascivious and notorious persons of both Sexes, giving them opportunity to commit carnal wickedness, and that by common fame is a common baud." Alice Thomas taxed the liberality of commercial towns in 1672 and was rewarded with thirty-seven stripes, threefold retribution, and imprisonment at the pleasure of the court.[18]

When towns grew beyond the capacity of the Puritan magistrate to oversee public morality, tavernkeepers and dealers in "carnal wickedness" were allowed freer reign. An eighteenth-century British observer spoke of a woman in Newport who kept "a house of pleasure and has done so for a great many years past in a more decent and reputable manner than common, and is spoke of by everybody in town in a favoreable manner for one of her Profession." [19] New York City authorities estimated that between 1,200 and 7,000 prostitutes roamed the city streets early in the nineteenth century.[20] Likewise, Ben Franklin found no scarcity of prostitutes in Philadelphia. He contended that streets were filled with women "who by throwing their heads to the right or the left of everyone who passed by them, I concluded came out with no other Design than to revive the spirit of love in Disappointed Batchelors and expose themselves to sale at the highest bidder." Franklin also had a good word for the economic and social contributions of prostitutes. In addition to contributing to the "health and satisfaction" of young men, streetwalkers stimulated the local economy by their exorbitant expenditures on shoeleather.[21] Within Franklin's whimsical observation lies the recognition of a new economic order, a network of specialized enterprises, linked by monetary exchanges, expanding through private profit, and engaging men and women alike. This system permitted marketing even the bodies of the second sex like saleable commodities. Most American women did not peddle their bodies on the city streets, but she-merchants sold almost every other commodity and thus partook of the boom of a commercial economy.

Moreover, the merchants who broke away from the subsistence economy created new economic roles for the whole community. A commodity sold was a commodity purchased—one shopkeeper created many buyers. As the eighteenth century drew to a close the economic activity of shopping appeared more and more frequently in personal accounts of how American women spent their days. The diary of Mrs. Mary Holyoke for the years 1760 to 1800 found her busily employed salting hogs weighing up to 188 pounds and making butter in quantities of nearly 90 pounds as well as manufacturing candles and soap. As time went on, however, this wife of an eminent doctor had more and more opportunities for visiting "the shops" and purchasing stockings, mantuas, fashionable shoes, spices, coffee, and other imports. The diaries of Mrs. Holyoke's daughters, Mary and Susanna, plot the subsequent eclipse of home production by such exertions of purchasing power.[22] In the same era Mrs. John Amory, the wife of a wealthy merchant, experienced shopping as a time-consuming avocation. For example, she spent the entire morning of September 16, 1775, "in going to the shops,"[23] the only memorable event of the day. Eunice Callender, a less affluent young lady, spent May 27, 1808, in a similar fashion: "Caroline and myself called on Mrs. Henry in the forenoon and went a shopping in the afternoon."[24] These women were the clientele for many of the she-merchants of the seaboard towns, but they themselves embraced a role that was for the first time peripheral to production, a more passive contribution to the distributive sector of the economy.

As of 1820, few Americans, male or female, had the wealth, opportunity, or inclination to while away their time examining imported luxuries in fashionable shops. The commercial economy had, however, produced a small class of very wealthy merchants capable of just such an expenditure of time and money. The merchants who conducted America's foreign trade were the major component of that upper class in northeastern port towns. The sea captains and the scions of old mercantile houses were all males and were well enough off to dispense with the female economic partner in the conduct of their business affairs. In the 1690s a handful of women appeared among the stockholders of Boston's shipping fleet, but as a few wealthy families came to monopolize the import business in the early eighteenth century, the female presence among the city's merchant elite was entirely erased.[24a] The wives and daughters of these business leaders played only indirect and symbolic roles in the making and maintaining of the family fortune. The female's most important service was to consolidate her family's wealth and power through a well-calculated marriage. The merchant elite of Salem, for example, was an exceedingly inbred circle, with no less than forty-two cross-cousin marriages in a single generation. The merchants' daughters carried into marriage the name, trade connections, and capital of the patriarch, thereby attaching great economic consequence to their matches.[25]

In wedlock these women served, like the Georgian mansions with their costly furnishings, as an objectification of their husbands' wealth and status. The merchant wife exhibited the social and economic status of her family by the conspicuous display of personal adornment and social graces. These could be very exhausting duties. The upkeep of her appearance, for example, might involve preparation of the cosmetic base Aqua Vitae, a potion requiring thirty ingredients, two months' cultivation, and an impossible final step: "shake the bottle incessantly for ten to twelve hours." [26] This variety of home manufacturing is a frivolous perversion of the economic production of a seventeenth-century mistress of the household, yet a day in the life of the wealthiest woman might be empty of any more direct economic activity. As early as 1721 Mrs. Van Rensselaer described the daily routine of New York society women in which all household chores were completed by 11 A.M. and the rest of the day was devoted to reading, dressing, visiting, and entertaining.[27] Two generations later Mrs. John Amory devoted most of her time to social events. Entries in her journal typically played on a single theme: "At home with Company," "dined out," "a large company at home." [28] The social obligations of the wife of the rich man were undoubtedly very demanding, but they still left time to pursue a fashionable ladies' magazine, designed as "an amusing companion in some vacant hour." [29] The wives of merchants and planters who basked in the opulence of the late eighteenth century constituted the first approximation of an American leisure class.

When women of the upper classes spoke of their work they were most likely referring to embroidery or ornamental sewing. When John Gregory recommended this accomplishment to the young women of the upper class he was careful to remove all connotations of productive labor. "The intention of your being taught needlework, knitting and such like is not on account of the intrinsic values you can do with your hands, which is trifling, but to enable you to judge more perfectly of that kind of work and the execution of others." [30] In other words, the wife merely directed the work necessary to operate an upper-class household, delegating actual physical labor to servants.

The growth of the commercial economy and a stratified society also opened to women the novel occupation of domestic service, that is paid employment in the homes of the upper class rather than the earlier practices of indenture and the putting out of children. Very quickly laments over the scarcity of good servants rang through the fashionable social circles. An English observer in 1710 described the American "help" problem this way. "All women's work is very dear there, which proceeds from the smallness of the number and the scarcity of the workers, for even the meanest single women marry there, and being without want are above work." In 1748 supply and demand did not seem so favorable to female servants in Philadelphia, whose standard wages were only eight to ten pounds annually in excess of room and board. This wage, furthermore, was only 50 percent of what a male servant might expect to earn.[31] Female servants had a potent foretaste of the sexual discrimination that would continue to mark woman's participation in the labor market.

By 1800 sizable numbers of women were unable to find any position whatsoever. The expanding economy unceremoniously deposited them in the class of paupers, simply judging them incapable of earning a living. By 1811 the town of Worcester allotted thousands of dollars a year "For the support of the poor (they have greatly increased in number and expense)."[32] New York City administrators estimated the number of dependent poor in 1816 at fifteen thousand. The majority of the city's relief baskets were reserved for women with such notations as these: "husband in prison," "husband has broken his leg," "husband bad fellow," "her husband abandoned her and she has broke her arm," "husband at sea."[33] Disruption of the family and its distressing economic consequences for women were particularly frequent in port towns which sent men off to sea and often to untimely death. The seaboard town of Marblehead, for example, listed 459 widows and 869 orphans (500 of them females) on the relief rolls of 1790. Sailors were also wont to leave unwed mothers in American ports. One of Marblehead's unwed mothers was renowned for her exemplary "neatness, prudence, and love of her children." Yet the chances for a single woman or a widow to support her family in such dignity were few, and as Marblehead swarmed with unemployable persons, the city fathers grew intolerant of the poor of either sex. By 1815 they were grumbling that "the women are lazy and of consequence dirty creatures" and opining that "nothing but a characteristic want of economy, even in the worst state of the fishery, can be the cause of such suffering." [34]

The onslaught of the supposedly undeserving poor overtaxed the old welfare system and compromised the community spirit of stewardship. At the turn of the century New York City deported as many as one thousand paupers a year to avoid a staggering charge to the town and a heavy burden on its families. Towns throughout the colonies were pressed to devise new methods of dealing with the pauper. One Margaret Page was summarily ushered into the new social shelter for the poor, the Boston jail, where she was identified "as a lazy, idle, loytering person" and ordered "to work for a living." [35] Soon specialized institutions were constructed for the incarceration of the town's paupers. New York established its first almshouse in 1736 and in 1816 constructed the massive walled edifice of Bellevue to house its teeming population of indigents.[36] By the early nineteenth century even Worcester, Massachusetts, was setting aside the bulk of the community tax monies for a "House for the reception and employment of such persons as are or may become Chargeable to the town." [37] The almshouse served a dual purpose, removing the poor from public view and forcing them to contribute to their own support. More than 60 percent of Bellevue's inmates were women in 1821, and they were put to work at traditional female tasks: cleaning, sewing, spinning, cooking, and nursing. The men at Bellevue were employed at such skilled tasks as carpentry and shoemaking as well as common manual labor.[38] Private citizens also designed institutions to employ the poor. In Boston, for example, a society for encouraging industry and employing the poor gathered idle women and children in a clothmaking workshop that was organized by local merchants.[39]

Calvinists and capitalists alike chafed at the sight of idleness in men, women, or children. To the proponents of American manufacturing, like Alexander Hamilton and Tench Coxe, moreover, unemployed women were transformed into a potential industrial labor force. These men calculated that poor women, as well as wives and daughters with time on their hands, could be employed in manufactories and workshops without disrupting the agricultural production of the nation. According to Hamilton, women, "doomed to idleness and its attendant vices . . . are rendered more useful by manufacturing establishments." Tench Coxe added "that the portions of time of housewives and young women which were not occupied with family affairs could be profitably filled up" by periodic stints in the manufactory. George Washington observed the female employees of a textile workshop with satisfaction: "They are the daughters of decayed families and are girls of character—none other are admitted." [40]

In the early years of American industry the employment of women meshed neatly with the changing parameters of a basically agricultural home economy, taking up the excess labor power of widows, indigents, the old, and the young. In the first stage of this symbiotic relationship between manufacturing and the household, merchants simply solicited woman's home production, her yarn and cloth, for sale in their shops. Later they would delegate specific steps in the manufacturing process to home-bound women. Artisan manufacturers, such as shoemakers, followed a similar practice, bringing the shoes bound in their shops to their wives and daughters for finishing. Occasionally females organized their own collective workshop. In the fluid era of burgeoning industry American women also played independent and inventive roles. A twelve-year-old girl devised a method of making straw braid for bonnets in 1798 and generated an industry that employed hundreds of women in her hometown of Dedham. As late as 1821 a Connecticut woman won a London Society of the Arts award for her inventive method of bleaching straw and went on to organize another primitive American industry. All such manufacturing was an unsophisticated operation, the simple collection of workers manually plying a trade under one roof. It merely transported women's manufacturing skills outside the home into more efficient and specialized economic institutions. This subtle but seminal transformation kept the female role of economist intact, and in effect declared that woman's place was not necessarily in the home but wherever she could be of economic service.[41]

By the end of the eighteenth century, however, American factories were becoming more mechanized and capable of achieving total autonomy from the household economy. The Rhode Island textile firm of Samuel Slater was the first to utilize machinery on a scale that demanded a large, permanent labor force. Slater recruited families as his labor supply, removing entire households from farm to factory. Once the family had been transported to the factory, its inner hierarchy became translated into a wage scale. A Massachusetts father contracted with Slater under the following terms: $5 a week for himself, $2.33 for his sister, $2 for his sixteen-year-old son, $1.50 for his son and his nephew, both thirteen years old, $1.25 for a twelve-year-old daughter, 83 cents and 75 cents for two girls, ten and eight years old respectively.[42]

When the contributions of each man, woman, and child to the sustenance of the household were translated into specific monetary terms, the labor of the family was proven to be divisible into individual shares—portending dire consequences for females. The advances of technology exacerbated this process, as Tench Coxe observed in 1814. "Women, relieved to a considerable degree from their former employments as carders, spinners and feeders by hand occasionally turn to the occupation of weaver." In this textile factory women usurped the role customarily occupied by the male. Yet within the textile plant weaving was a simple machine operation, which did not confer an elevated status or a larger wage on women. Rather, as Coxe went on to demonstrate, it freed men for more highly skilled and rewarding occupations. With "improved machinery and implements the male weavers employ themselves in superintendence, instruction, supervision or other superior operations and promote their health by occasional attentions to gardening, agriculture and the clearing and improvement of their farms." As the new nation's factories grew more sophisticated and more numerous, the distinction between superior and inferior, male and female, jobs became more and more blatant. As the operation of factory equipment became simpler, it commanded lower wages and was increasingly delegated to women and children. An 1816 report on the United States cotton industry listed 66,000 women operatives, 24,000 boys, and only 10,000 adult men. A similar breakdown of employees by sex prevailed in the Waltham, Massachusetts, mill in 1821. Here a common mill worker, usually a female, received $2 to $2.50 a week in wages, while a foreman, almost always a male, received $12 a week.[43]

The Waltham system, as designed by Francis Cabot Lowell, was founded on the principles of cheap female labor. Although Lowell and his associates recruited young women workers independently of their families, they nevertheless built remnants of patriarchy into the mill town. The factory owners strove to recreate artificially a household atmosphere in the mills, complete with such paternalistic inventions as tidy boardinghouses, patriarchal regulations, and the superintending presence of housemothers. When Mathew Carey surveyed the New England textile mills in 1831 he hailed the contributions of the mill girls to their own families as well as the national economy. "Daughters are now emphatically a blessing to the farmer. Many instances have occurred . . . in which the earnings of a daughter have been scrupulously hoarded to enable them to pay off mortgages on the parental farms."[44] The New England cotton industry afforded young women yet another opportunity to smooth the transition between the subsistence economy and commercial agriculture, using their wages to meet the demands of that newfangled procedure of farm finance, the mortgage. Thus the women who entered the industrial work force early in the nineteenth century did not relinquish all ties to the old economic order of the farm household. They now tread a treacherous path between domestic utility and economic exploitation.[45]

The integral totality of woman's place in the little commonwealth had, however, been shattered. Between 1750 and 1820 the role of the mistress of the household splintered away, leaving little more than a core of private domestic responsibilities. This disintegration of woman's social role was further advanced in the uppermost regions of the American leisure class, among those southern ladies and the wives of wealthy merchants who could devote themselves to displaying the wealth and status of their husbands. The anchorless and distended quality of social life for these women is illustrated by the fact that they took their cues for public and private behavior from abroad, from etiquette books written by foreigners or American publications that parroted the mores of the fashionable classes of Europe. When the upper-class woman picked up these volumes and magazines from her dressing table, she was greeted with a foreign language of femininity. "Give ear oh daughter of beauty, attend to the voice of your sister. . . . My father was brother of tenderness, my mother was sister of love." That the authors of such lines were men impersonating women would not disturb the reading lady, for she was wooed with the most extravagant compliments. "The Whiteness of her bosom transcendeth the Lily, her smile is more delicious than a garden of roses, the innocence of her eye is like that of the turtle, the kisses of her mouth are sweeter than honey. The perfumes of Arabia breathe from her lips." [46]

A farmer's help-meet or a she-merchant would

most likely respond to such a ludicrous mode of address with a quizzical guffaw. Such sentiments were offered to the American lady, however, as adulation to her sex. John Gregory outlined the elevation of women to civilized status in his American publication dated 1775. "I have not considered your sex as a domestic drudge, not the slave of our pleasures, but as our companions and equals as designed to soften our hearts and polish our manners." [47] Household utility was reduced to drudgery and in its stead the American lady was offered the narrow role of polishing male manners. The exponents of the new femininity also made use of the rhetoric of the age of reason: "Remember thou art man's reasonable companion, not the slave of his passions, the end of thy being is not merely to gratify his loose desire, but to assist in the toils of life, to soothe him with tenderness and recompense his care with soft endearments." [48] Women were rhetorically equipped with reason and equality but summoned to employ them only in soothing, civilizing, and comforting men. An insidious formulation of sexual stereotypes underlay the paean to the white bosomed, sweet lipped American daughter of beauty.

American publishers moved haltingly at first to insinuate the new femininity into the culture of the new nation. The United States publication of the *Lady's Pocket Library* in 1792 was prefaced by a polite apology. The author hoped that her American readers "will not be offended if she has occasionally pointed out certain qualities and suggested certain tempers and dispositions as peculiarly feminine, and hazarded some observations which naturally arose from the subject, on the different characters which mark the sexes. And here again she takes the liberty to repeat that these distinctions cannot be nicely maintained." [49] By the turn of the century, however, the American lady's library was littered with ecstatic endorsements of distinctly and exclusively feminine characteristics. In addition to beauty of face and form, upper-class women were flattered by celebrations of their modesty, innocence, sweetness, softness of manner, and gentleness of voice—a whole catalogue of refinements, which could be summarized in the simple aphorism "submission and obedience are the lessons of her life, and peace and happiness are her reward." [50] The natural tendency toward submission was now regarded as integral to the personality of woman and adjudged the source of her personal happiness and her self-fulfillment.

Still, additional incentives were required to seduce women into the new femininity. The fashionable writers of the eighteenth century employed a now familiar device for this purpose: the flattering assurance that a woman's differences from men were the source of her superiority. A French author whose treatise was published in America late in the eighteenth century displayed the basic principle of this casuistry: "many of them [women] rival us in the endowments of the mind and in the qualities of the heart they generally surpass us." [51] The celebrated qualities of the feminine heart included an overabundance of love, a refined sensibility, a timidity that prompted frequent blushes—and a heightened moral sense. The latter characteristic was defined as a "great innate sense within, more than a conscience—a certain instant faithful monitor which holds a residence in the female breast." [52] All these feminine qualities neatly complemented the newly designed concept of masculinity:

"Man is destined for deeds of strength and courage, has a toughness in his temper, which women alone can soften." [53] Within the libraries of the upper class, humanity was vivisected into male and female parts and then patched together again in a symbiotic union.

It should be clear that the female member of the fashionable couple was more severely crippled by this operation. Women were endowed only with the capacity to quietly cultivate their accommodating personalities, not to accompany men into the world, to acquire, achieve, and produce. Within the private sphere, the passive woman became the humble servant, and the active man became her grateful master. Female identity came as an afterthought to masculine endeavor, designed to solace, please, and refresh the worldweary male. The need to please, it was said, was lodged deep in the nature of woman. While the male half of the sexual pair might survive very well without the blandishments of femininity, his female counterpart was helpless apart from her stronger partner. She would languish without male company, support, and earnings.

As a consequence of this unbalanced arrangement, some hectic maneuvering was required to bring the two maimed sexes together again. In the fashionable social circles, the drawing rooms and ballrooms of the wealthy provided the arena for this process. The writers of the era often posed as distraught young men who rushed to balls, teas, and salons to find repose in the salubrious company of females. Women were to take up their stations there in order to "tame the young man's wildness," "civilize him" and exert their "instinctive conscience." Coincidentally, the young gallants might feast upon the physical beauty of the opposite sex as well. "Now view the maid, the love-inspiring maid/ with virtue and with modesty array'd/ Survey her matchless form . . . Survey and Resurvey from feet to head." The author of these lines, James Bowdoin, poetically traversed the entire female body, lingering with a special awe over her "tempting breasts." [54]

While the fashionable woman might amply expose her body, she was advised to be more niggardly in the display of certain attributes of her mind. John Gregory, for example, instructed American girls "if you happen to have any learning, keep it a profound secret, especially from the men, who generally look with a jealous and malignant eye on a woman of great parts and cultivated understanding." [55] The female protagonist of Charles Brockden Brown's *Alcuin* refrained from political discourse on the principle that such topics were beyond the propriety and capacity of women. When a relentless young dandy continued to invite her opinions, he unleashed an acid tide of feminism. The prescriptive literature of the period, however, repeatedly advised women to suppress such outbursts as well as the intelligence that underlay them. They must move gingerly through the social circle, exerting their civilizing influence on the assembled men without giving the slightest appearance of manipulation. The French author of *Essays on the Character of Women* put it this way. "The woman in society by being continually upon the look-out, from the double motives of curiosity and of policy, must have a perfect knowledge of men. . . . They must know how far one may direct without appearing to be interested. How far one may presume upon that art, even after it is known; in what estimation they are held by those with whom they live, and to what degree it is necessary to serve them, that they may govern them." [56]

Such duplicity, intrinsic to the maintenance of artificial sexual differences, transformed the fashionable social circle into a hot-bed of suspicion and intrigue, amply illustrated in the fashionable literature of the era. American publishers gave generous circulation to a treatise entitled *Female Policy Detected,* wherein "the art of the designing woman is laid out." The author of this humorous diatribe against women, and many others like him, alerted the young Boston bachelors to the peculiar stratagems of harlots, widows, husband-hunters. Even those females who wished no more than a sexual liaison were to be distrusted: "He that serves the lust of a woman makes himself her monkey, for she admires him no longer than while he is playing with his taile." [57] English literature of the eighteenth century abounded with references to the nearly insatiable sexual appetites of women. One Englishman warned that "the sensibilities of woman are not limited as ours. . . . Truly women do not feel themselves exhausted, even if they suffer the amourous attacks of a multitude of men successively." [58] This awareness of female sexuality merely compounded male suspicion of the opposite sex.

Women writers had some suspicions of their own. The most popular American novel of the era, Susanna Rowson's *Charlotte Temple,* was built around the innocent maiden's liability to seduction and abandonment by the predatory males of the upper class. As Rowson made clear in the following lines from another work, perfect female innocence was suicidal in the fashionable coterie. "No sooner did the tyrant see woman from every blemish free,/ Than heedless of his guardian part/ He strove by mean seductive art/ To rob her of her brightest charms." [59] One character in an American short story did not mince words in confronting a male predator: "You are a man, . . . and I dare not trust you." [60] Women were also advised to be on the alert for the chicanery of their own sex. Popular tales of seduction customarily portrayed jaded females as accomplices to the acts of a lecherous villain. Didactic books and magazine articles directed young women of the upper classes to choose their female friends with care and to share the secrets of their hearts only with their mothers.

Yet the fashionable woman must enter this circle of intrigue and distrust in order to retrieve a mate. Her very nature, it was said, necessitated her matrimony. "That Providence designed women for a state of dependence and consequently of submission I cannot doubt when I consider their timidity of temper, their tenderness of make, the many comforts and necessities of life which they are unable to procure without our aid. Their evident want of our protection upon a thousand occasions impels us to help and protect them." [61] Woman's happiness as well as her survival were now proclaimed to be contingent upon marriage: "Her family is the source of all her joy." [62] Matrimony, furthermore, consigned her to a private and dependent and isolated sphere: "The proper spheres of the sexes are distinctly different." While the upper-class husband took up his position in "the widely differing professions and employments into which private advantage and public good require that men should be distributed," his wife was relegated to the "care of the family." [63]

The wife of a wealthy businessman or landed aristocrat would still find many occasions to make her fashionable way through a large social circle. At the same time, however, a special woman's place was being set apart from this wider social sphere. The role of wife, pure and simple, gained new significance. The exclusively wifely function was described as follows: "When ruffled with the busy cares and scenes of the world [the husband] flies to his home, where the engaging smiles of the friend of his heart dispel the gloom and restore the ease and comfort of his heart." [64] At the rarefied apex of the American social order a novel and ominous concept of woman's place began slowly to take form. The home appeared, albeit indistinctly, as a private refuge set apart from society and the economy from which women dispensed domestic comforts to husbands whose major activities transpired outside its boundaries.

The routine absence of the husband from this domicile undercut the mutuality upon which earlier and more down-to-earth concepts of conjugal affection rested. The sentiment of love lost its equilibrium in the fashionable literature of the eighteenth century as the balance of conjugal affection tilted awkwardly toward the female. "Love is without dispute the passion which women feel the strongest and they express the best. . . . It is their soul." [65] Supposedly, love not only occupied a larger place in the female psyche, but consumed her entire being: "For a woman of delicate sentiments to bestow her heart is properly to give up her whole self." Put another way, "Love in one sex is

Conquest, in the other a Sacrifice." [66] Needless to say women were cast in the sacrifical role of this scenario of love among the upper classes. In order to play it adequately, married women were instructed to render unto their spouses their entire stock of love, warmth, and solace.

In point of fact, members of the female leisure class did run the risk of considerable personal sacrifice, for the wife who failed to meet her marital obligations could be easily dispensed with by a rich and powerful husband. The town records of Newport tell of one woman who suffered this fate, the wife of Timothy Dexter, merchant. "Whereas Elizabeth my wife has become an intemperate, quarrelsome and troublesome woman, inasmuch that it is impossible to live with her in peace and decency I am therefore determined not to cohabit with her any longer, while she continues her present evil courses." The local press put a different construction on this event: "Timothy [Dexter of Newport] has now parted from his wife because she is old, upon a contract paid of 2,000 pounds [sterling] and the horse and chaise and is looking out for a young wife." [67] Those men who rose to the pinnacle of power and wealth in the American commercial economy had the wherewithal to divorce a spouse who was not to their liking and support another. Their wives furthermore lacked the power inherent to practical economic partnership that might deter their mates from dissolving a marriage. Accordingly, the social role of the upper-class wife could be narrow, subordinate, and precarious as well.

The comforts of wealth and leisure, moreover, were counterbalanced by the wife's subjection to the insidious influences of fashionable training in womanhood. Nancy Shippen, daughter of a prosperous Philadelphia merchant, was fated to translate the new literature of womanhood into a real-life melodrama. In 1777 Nancy's father sent her to Miss Rogers' School with instructions to educate herself for the upperclass social circle, "in holding your head and shoulders, in making a curtsy, in going out or coming into a room, in giving and receiving, holding your knife and fork, walking and setting. These things contribute so much to a good appearance that they are of great consequence." Miss Shippen learned her lessons well, and upon entrance into Philadelphia society quickly won many suitors, including Henry Livingston, a scion of New York aristocracy. When, against Nancy's romantic predilections, a marriage was arranged by the two lofty families, Nancy's mother sent her to the altar with this piece of advice: "Never forget that it should be your first care to please and make your husband happy." [68]

Nancy Shippen Livingston had little time in which to practice these wifely virtues. Her husband turned out to be an utter fop and a compulsive philanderer. They separated within two years. Henry Livingston was vindictive as well, refused his wife a divorce, and repeatedly barred her from seeing her daughter. The belle of Philadelphia society had no other recourse but to return to her parents' home and immerse herself once again in the diversions of the fashionable coterie. Her days often went like this:

> This morning I gave orders to the servants as usual for the business of the day, then took a little work in my hands and set down before the fire to think how I should dispose of myself in the eve-

ning. The morning I generally devote to working and reading, and I concluded to go to the concert. Then I considered what I would dress in, and having determined this important part, I felt light and easy.[69]

The rest of her days typically entailed a round of social engagements interspersed with attention to her toilet.

Before the dissolution of her marriage Mrs. Livingston had one additional avocation, attention to her daughter. "Dress'd my Angel Child, kiss'd her a hundred times, thought her the most beautiful Child in the world and sent her to be admir'd by Miss Tilghman who said a thousand things in her favor in which I perfectly agreed." The devoted mother seemed intent upon transmitting the vanities of femininity unto another generation. Her ecstasies of maternal delight met with approval from some spokesmen for fashionable womanhood. One treatise assured American women in 1788 that "maternal affection was inherent in the nature of woman." [70] Other writers saw fit to take no chances and actively inculcated this supposed attribute of feminine nature: "Art thou a mother, let thy children be the darlings of thy affection, let the fruit of thy womb at the first partake of thy tenderness." [71] Such references to maternal qualities were relatively infrequent in the literature of femininity, however, merely brief footnotes to the virtues required of the status symbol and the wife. The practical duties of motherhood were given even shorter notice, limited to occasional injunctions to suckle the infant and mold its mind in the early stages of its growth. Most upper-class women could delegate the physical care and education of their offspring to wet nurses, servants, governesses, and schools. Motherhood remained a poorly articulated and ambiguous role for upper-class women, for American ladies were still advised: "Dote not on the idol of thy womb, for the extreme fondness of a mother is as dangerous as the violence of her hate." [72]

Doting upon any of these elements of upper-class womanhood was out of the question for the vast majority of Americans—the middling and the lower sort. Reverend Ogden, for one, regarded the fashionable construction of femininity as a contagious English disease, as odious as the court of King George. Of the removal of women from productive activity, he said, "the American heart revolts at the idea." [73] Other homespun authors made the fashionable feminine the butt of their satire. Mason Locke Weems concocted a humorous brew of American backwoods manners and English pretensions entitled *The Lover's Almanac*. Its subtitle reduced the sublimities of romance to the ridiculous. "A very seasonable and savory dissertation on love, courtship, and marriage— with a most enchanting flourish on beauty, admirably calculated to disclose those two most delectable and desirable of all secrets, how the homely may become handsome and the handsome angelic." The female characters in Weems' little farce displayed the American's severely retarded sense of gentility. One was renowned for "picking her teeth with her fork, snuffing up her nose, picking it with her fingers, blowing it and looking in her hankerchief." The more refined heroine of the piece was nonetheless a very down-to-earth young lady. "From the time she was ten years old, she took the keys and became her mother's little housekeeper. The dairy, the manufactory, the garden, her books and harpsichord are continually visited by the dear angelic bee." [74] Indigenous genres of American writing, like this Virginia Almanac or the Yankee sermon, were not in the business of manufacturing paragons of femininity. The best they could manage was the occasional creation of an awkward, almost schizoid image like "the dear angelic bee."

Even among the lower strata of American society, however, the social position of women was subtly changing. The incipient transformation was manifest in the growing numbers of women who escaped patriarchal surveillance in the cities of the new nation. A New York matron observed:

> I know this age has so great a contempt for the former, that 'tis but a matter of scorn to allege any of their customs. Else I should say the liberties that are now taken would then have been startled at. They that then should have seen a young maid rambling abroad without her mother or some other prudent persons would have looked at her as a stray and thought it but a neighborly office to have brought her home, whereas now 'tis a rarity to see them in any company graver than themselves and she that goes with her parent thinks she does but walk around with her jailor. [75]

Such observations cannot be dismissed as the perennial complaints of an older generation, for the commercial era actually expanded the social freedom of women in a variety of ways. For one thing, advertisements in city newspapers often recruited female workers independently of their parents. One such notice offered employment to a woman between eighteen and twenty-three, resourceful, attractive, and "possessed of 3 or 400 pounds entirely at her own Disposal, and where there will be no necessity of going through the tiresome Talk of addressing Parents or Guardians for their consent." [76] Young men and women circumvented the authority of the patriarch in matters of matrimony as well as employment. As farmland diminished and fathers lost the sanctions of dower and bequest, as new varieties of employment beckoned, young couples could plot their futures alone. By the late eighteenth century, accordingly, the age at marriage became less standard and typically younger in the villages and towns of the Northeast, suggesting a lessening of parental control over the marital decisions of sons and daughters.[77] Eighteenth-century wives also found more occasions to undermine the authority of their husbands. A Newburyport woman, for example, had "privately undertaken to buy sundry merchandize unknown to her husband" and proceeded to offer them for sale. Promptly her spouse gave public notice that he would not be held responsible for any of the debts incurred by this wayward merchandising wife.[78] Throughout the United States other distraught husbands and fathers offered rewards for the return of runaway wives and eloped daughters.

Women nestled securely within the family unit, furthermore, found their social obligations steadily reduced as the eighteenth century gave way to the nineteenth. The proliferation of prisons, almshouses, orphan asylums, and hospitals absorbed the social services once performed by the mistress of the household. These specialized institutions were supervised by salaried male commissioners, not by women who were remunerated by the town. Simultaneously, schools usurped the educational functions of women, and hired day laborers supplanted the indentured servants women once trained and supervised. Servants, the poor, put-out children, the sick, and the criminal were evicted from the household and American women were left with only their husbands and children to care for.

Even here woman's social universe was shrinking. The downturn in the nation's birth rate coincided with the dismantling of the subsistence economy. This demographic transformation, which began in agricultural New England in the late eighteenth century, was linked to the diminishing land supply. Philip Greven has charted the stages of this population implosion in the Massachusetts village of Andover. By 1764 Andover had grown from a settlement of a few young families to a town of almost 2,500 residents. The rapid rate of growth continued into the next decade, when in 1776 Andover's population peaked at almost 3,000. Then, by 1790, the number of Andover residents actually declined to less than 2,800 persons. This watershed coincided with the exhaustion of Andover's land supply. While part of the decline in population was due to the emigration of young men and women to the more lucrative frontier, the major factor in the reduction of population growth was the constriction of the birth rate. By the last half of the eighteenth century the women of Andover were bearing on the average two fewer offspring than did their grandmothers, five to six rather than seven to eight children.[79]

Other New England towns faced this demographic crisis at times appropriate to their own economic history. In Hingham, Massachusetts, for example, the number of children per married woman began to fall significantly before 1700. The depression of the fishing industry in the town of Ipswich produced a similar drop in the birth rate before 1750. A study of comfortable Quaker families in Philadelphia, New York, and Salem revealed that the fertility of women in the Society of Friends declined by an average of 1.4 offspring in the era of the American Revolution.[80] In short, women in such diverse segments of the commercial economy as urban shops and New England farms and fishing villages saw the size of the family decline significantly by the late eighteenth century.

Furthermore, there are strong indications that in at least some instances, the curtailment of family size was a purposive act on the part of married couples. Among the Quakers studied, for example, women were not marrying less or later or dying earlier in the post-revolutionary era. Such factors did not cause the drop in the birth rate. Women who married late in life bore approximately the same number of children as young mothers whose childbearing was curtailed long before they reached menopause. This pattern clearly suggests that American men and women had determined an ideal family size, substantially lower than that of their parents. They might implement this ideal size through the ancient practice of coitus interruptus, simple sexual abstinence, or perhaps induced abortion. But whatever the means they used, select groups of American parents had determined that a large family was a liability rather than an asset. In the burgeoning commercial economy and particularly in those rural towns that had reached the saturation point for farm population, the value of unchecked fertility came into question and woman's reproductive labors slowly began to diminish.

The reduced size and functions of such American households called into question the value of the family unit itself. In 1752, the Reverend Thomas Humphrey of Dreffield felt called to write and publish a sermon entitled "Marriage as an Honorable Estate." He was prompted to do so by the fact that the institution of matrimony "hath in the last century more than in any precedent age, been deprecated and villify'd by the scrurrilous inventions of ludicrous and pretending wits, and been made the common subject of railery and ridicule." [81] Edward Ward's treatises certainly fit into this category, vilifying those "millions two by two that fall into misery by matrimony and are deadly wounded by the plague of poverty for want of virtuous preceding in themselves." [82] Ward and other writers on the subject implied that marriage could be a hindrance to a young man's rise to wealth in a commercial economy. The skeptics regarding marriage were many and well-placed. Matrimony was one of Ben Franklin's favorite targets for satire. He went so low as to advise young men to conduct liaisons with elderly women if their inclinations or finances deterred a wedding. Even worse, he honored Miss Polly Baker for the patriotic service of supplying the new nation with five children without going through the formality of acquiring a husband.[83] Of course such comedies at the expense of marriage did not deal a fatal blow to the time-honored institution. This literary leitmotiv did, however, indicate that the meaning of marriage was changing and with it the social role of American women.

The cosmopolitan writers of the new nation adopted a new language in their discourses on family affairs. First of all the terms patriarch and household gave way to a concept of marriage in which increasing importance was attached to the marital pair as detached from the larger household unit. Couples, furthermore, were less frequently portrayed as the building blocks of society or the "first links of Human Society to which all the rest are formed," as William Secker once put it. When the conservative New England minister Timothy Dwight rose to defend marriage against the assaults of advocates of divorce, for example, he described the family as merely the *"source* of all subordination and government and consequently of all peace and safety in the world" (italics mine). The American family was now hailed as the fountainhead of social order, not a microcosmic society in itself. Marriage, according to Dwight and many of his contemporaries, was now valued as the seat of private and personal services. It fostered the "comfort" and the "happiness" of the couple.[84]

These American writers, members of the comfortable middle class, seldom bathed the concept of marital happiness in sentimental and romantic euphoria. More often, they couched their endorsement of marriage in the language of the age of reason. One widely circulated treatise on courtship and marriage portrayed the ideal match as "a union of mind, and a sympathy of mutual esteem and friendship for each other." [85] "Rational friendship" and "mutual respect" were the touchstones of marital propriety in the urbane literature of the new nation. The duties and manners incumbent upon the female parties to such alliances were trumpeted as far west as the Tennessee frontier where a Nashville paper exclaimed in 1811: "What is more agreeable than the conversation of an intelligent, amiable and interesting friend? But who more intelligent than a well educated female?" [86]

Many enlightened men and women of the American Republic joined in the call for female education. Benjamin Rush's blueprint for the education of women commingled old and new ideas regarding the household obligations of wives. American women still needed to be trained, he thought, to become the "stewards and guardians of their husbands' property." But Rush also added the less prosaic skill of music to the curriculum of woman's education. This accomplishment, he maintained, would equip women to perform at public worship and to "soothe the cares of domestic life." In addition to providing domestic comfort for her husband, the educated woman would be better prepared to serve her sons. Instruction in history, geography, politics, and religion would assist American mothers to populate the republic with wise leaders and patriotic citizens.[87] Women were urged to socialize their offspring in the spirit of the Enlightenment. One sermon of 1800 instructed mothers that "as soon as the blosoming flowers of reason begin to shoot forth, while yet in the bud, the opportunity to form them to virtue is seized upon with avidity and improved with care." [88] In the education of her children a woman was to employ the methods of the American rationalist.

Motherhood also came to connote certain parental duties predating the blossoming of the child's reason. The infant became the topic of the first child-rearing manual to be published in America, portentously entitled *The Maternal Physician* and written by an upper-middle-class Boston woman who was well versed in European literature on her subject. This brief volume injected the spirit of science into woman's customary roles of nurse, midwife, and overseer of household health. The anonymous author of *The Maternal Physician* informed women about the latest methods of diagnosing and treating childhood diseases and providing for the general health and well-being of the young. Simultaneously she clothed these instructions in an emotionally evocative rhetoric heretofore unheard of in the annals of American motherhood.

> And believe me, my fair friends, this is not a labour. What can so sweetly relieve the tedium of three or four weeks of confinement to a sick room as to watch with unremitting care, and mark with enraptured eyes, the opening beauties of the dear innocent cause of such confinement. Or what can equal a mother's ecstacy when she catches the first emanations of mind in the mantling smile of her babe?

The Maternal Physician went on to celebrate "the thousand raptures" that thrill a mother's bosom "before a tooth is formed." [89]

Two new principles have been introduced into the maternal role, both of which, if put into practice, would greatly expand the purely domestic functions of American women. First of all, this scenario of motherhood called for a great expenditure of woman's time devoted to the constant observation of the infant's health and the incessant supply of his comfort. In addition, *The Maternal Physician* summoned prodigious emotional energy from the infant's mother. Although it was acknowledged that the child would require "comparatively less attention" after the age of two, this intense relationship between a mother and her babe left a lasting imprint on the character of woman. Its import was fully elaborated by the *Ladies' Literary Cabinet.*

Is there a feeling that activates the human heart so powerful as that of maternal affection? Who but woman can feel the tender sensation so strong? The father, indeed may press his lovely infant to his manly heart, but does it thrill with those feelings which irresistibly overcome the mother? [90]

By 1822 when these words were printed the American woman was being invited to accept a specialized domestic function, one that not only was labeled "woman's work," but a function that also distinguished between maternal feelings and "the manly heart." This expanded concept of maternity, although far removed from the sober, largely asexual colonial idea of parenthood, was but a rare and subdued hint of the extravagant celebration of motherhood to come.

Even those privileged females who entered the domain of higher education during the American enlightenment succeeded only in buying time before domesticity inundated their sex. The students who enrolled at the Young Ladies Academy of Philadelphia, for example, were promised that they would no longer be excluded "from the discussion of subjects calculated to strengthen and expand the mind." The academy's graduates in 1794 stood before an audience that included the first lady of the new nation and several congressmen to exhibit the results of their initiation into the intellectual regimen previously reserved for men. The salutatorian oratorically proclaimed that "In the age of reason . . . we are not surprised if women have taken advantage of the small degree of liberty that they still possess, and converted their talents into public utility." Then, without a stammer, the young scholar announced, "In opposition to your immortal Paine we will exalt our Wollstonecraft." Yet this graduate of the female academy did not intend to apply her intellect nor her pride of sex in the way an educated man would. She registered her compliance with the fact that "custom and nature teach the propriety of [the sexes] being suitable to the different situations and employments of life to which they are allotted." [91]

These customs decreed that men could engage in war, politics, business—all the "more active scenes of life"—and that women, no matter how well-educated, were not to desert their stations in the home. Thus, when the valedictorian of the Young Ladies Academy of Philadelphia rose before the assembled dignitaries she delivered an epitaph for the educated women of her generation: "Anticipating soon to be called upon to fill their various domestic stations in society, [the students] will, it is probable, never more be required, or never more have opportunity of delivering their sentiments in public." [92] Even the beneficiaries of the best that the American enlightenment offered to women were escorted only within eyeshot of equality and then were ushered swiftly into private life. Their education would be applied to the direction of their servants, the care of children, intelligent conversation with husbands and friends. The economic and social transformation that brought prosperity and position to middle-class men proffered a dubious leisure and luxury to their wives.

Although the women of the new nation were barred from the countinghouse, the council chamber, and the militia, they were by no means incarcerated in their homes. The doors to the church and their neighbors' parlors were still open to them, and when these forums proved too narrow, women created new avenues to social activity. Between 1800 and 1830 women organized themselves into benevolent societies throughout the United States. They formed religious associations like the Female Missionary Society, whose chapter in western New York State was active in at least forty-six different towns as of 1818. New York City's Society for the Relief of Poor Widows with Small Children was founded by Isabella Graham in 1797, and in the next three decades similar female associations for the assistance of the needy proliferated through the eastern United States and all along the pioneer trail. One band of Boston women aided more than ten thousand families and distributed more than $22,000 in the thirty years after its founding in 1812. Women were also active in establishing new social institutions: orphan asylums, charity schools, and homes for the indigent.[93]

This feverish congregation of women in extrafamilial groups served several purposes. First of all, benevolent associations allowed women to perform some of their traditional social welfare functions outside of the home. Secondly, they provided women with company, simple access to more lively social intercourse than was available in the less populous households of commercial society. Once women went outside the family unit for social action and companionship, furthermore, they were able to master some of the procedures of commercial economy. Women could collect large sums of money, chair business meetings, and cultivate a far-reaching organizational network, all for the cause of religion and charity. Finally, the female members of benevolent societies served notice that they would not let the course of history pass them by as it portended the removal of economic and social activity from the home.

Whatever diverse directions women pursued between 1750 and 1820 toward almshouses, mansions, or commercial farms, they did not lead to the pinnacles of power and fame that capture the attention of traditional historians. Few of them even left private records of their daily activities in journals or diaries. The writing of a journal required education, a modicum of leisure, and a predilection for self-scrutiny. Therefore, only middle- or upper-class women, initiated into the individualistic consciousness typical of a commercial economy, were likely to keep diaries. Such a woman was Sarah Ripley, the daughter of a moderately prosperous storekeeper in Greenfield, Massachusetts. The early entries in Sarah's diary chronicled an active but leisurely social life, consisting of constant visiting, country walks, boat trips, and shopping sprees, often in mixed company. Her parents sent her to boarding school, where her social activities became more formal—balls and assemblies and "many of those amusements of which young people are fond." Upon the completion of her education, Sarah returned to her home where she assumed the economic responsibility of assisting in her father's shop. In busy mercantile seasons, she had little time or incentive to consult her diary, for she confessed that "time passes on in the same dull round of domestic occupations and I seldom go out or see company, consequently the incidents of my life at present afford but few materials to commit to writing." If Sarah engaged in any mode of home manufacturing she did not feel this was noteworthy enough to mention either.

The private journal of Sarah Ripley contains few references to courtship, almost none to romance. The young woman occasionally alluded to a "friend," the focal point of mysterious difficulties too delicate or painful to detail. Then in 1812 she announced without warning, "I gave my hand in marriage to Mr. Charles Stearns of Shelburn and accompanied him immediately home—I have now acquitted the abode of my youth, left the protection of my parents and given up the name I have always borne to enter upon a new and untried scene. May the grace of God enable me to fulfill with prudence and piety the great and important duties which now dissolve on me." Thus ended the troublesome courtship, which had been drawn out for five years and yet left hardly a trace in the repository of a young woman's deepest thoughts, her private diary. Once settled in what she called the "still and peaceful scenes of domestic tranquility," Mrs. Stearns seems to have contracted a slight case of ennui. Why else would she quote at great length from the memoirs of one Hannah Hodges, a shopkeeper who retired at age eighty-five only to complain that "I have not so much comfort not even in religion as when I was bustling half the day behind the counter. I need more variety than I now get. I become stiffled for want of something to rouse me."

Mrs. Stearns herself was not to rest idle for long. Within four years of marriage she had given birth to three children. With the birth of her first child, a daughter, she resolved to take "assiduous care" to cultivate her "infant reason." She assumed the same responsibilities for her subsequent offspring as well as for two children, one poor and another orphaned, whom she took into her home to raise. Now Sarah Stearns was busy enough but not altogether content. She acknowledged to her diary that "I have little time for working on serious reflections with my little family." She was, however, summoned to extensive reflection upon her own soul when the town of Shelburn was struck by revivalism in the 1810s. Sarah Stearns' religious fervor did not dissipate itself in personal introspection but drove her into more frenetic social action. She formed her neighbors into a "little band of associated females" and spurred them on to such projects as a maternal association, a school society, and a juvenile institution. Her proudest creation was the local female charity association: "Our Benevolent Society is in a flourishing state, many destitute children have been assisted and taught many things. I can truly say it affords me one of my chief sources of pleasure." Sarah Stearns, for one, was not about to relinquish the broad social contacts and extensive social responsibilities of the old-fashioned mistress of the household.

Yet Mrs. Stearns' diary also recorded a very new-fangled concern on the part of its author: a sharpened consciousness of personal feelings and emotional ties. This acute emotional sensibility engulfed the pages of Sarah's journal whenever the idea of death entered her consciousness. While in her teens, Sarah was moved to poetry by a newspaper account of the untimely demise of a stranger. "But Death's cold hands the hopeful youth destroys." When her infant brother died shortly thereafter, her elegy included the consoling observation that he had gone to "happier scenes" where they would be reunited. Sarah's musings about death amounted to more than a religious preoccupation with the afterlife. They also occasioned a heightened consciousness of her own earthly bonds. Sarah poured out her innermost feelings when a young friend died in 1808. "I can scarcely bring it home to my imagination that my Rachel is gone forever, and that I shall no more behold her loved countenance, meeting me with the smile of welcome no more to hear her soft voice, or soothing gentle accents, speaking from the feelings of her heart and assuring me of a good reception—but it is too true!!!"

Sarah Ripley Stearns was to experience many other painful separations: her brother's move to the West, her departure from her parents' village, the uprooting of her family three times in the course of her married life. The final blow came in 1818 with the death of her husband. Prior to this event Mrs. Stearns had not recounted her feelings toward her husband in any detail. Now she devoted nine full pages of her journal to this theme. She confided: "I did love him alas but too tenderly. We lived together in such terms as man and wife ought to live, placing perfect confidence in one another, bearing one another's burdens and making due allowances for human imperfection." The bereaved woman's diary ends on this note of utter loneliness: "I am now a widow, I have no bosom friend to go to in seasons of perplexity for advice, no one with whom I can unreservedly share all my griefs and sorrows, all my joys and pleasures." Sarah Stearns' reactions to her husband's death and to death in general seem to suggest an intensification of domestic affection and dependence among the women of her generation.[94]

It is unlikely that American women of this era experienced deaths in the family more frequently than did their mothers and grandmothers. They did, however, inhabit a more unstable social environment. The community and the little commonwealth were splintering into individual fragments; young men sought more lucrative frontiers; young women married away from the parental homestead; economic production fled the household; trade moved out into the commercial marketplace; social services were lodged in specialized institutions. The family and close friends were the primary buoys in a sea of social change, and the sundering of these ties by death took on added significance. Simultaneously, women were placed at a greater distance from the central processes of social and economic life, and left in the relative solitude of home with time to cultivate their emotional responses.

This process did not affect all American women in the early nineteenth century. But it did touch the lives of women like Sarah Stearns, located in the middle-class center of the commercial economy. The diaries of such New England women are peppered with maudlin descriptions of death. Sarah Ripley Stearns' friend Eunice Callender left a private journal steeped full of sentimental visions of death, touching her family, friends, and even total strangers. The most devastating emotional breach for Miss Callender was the death of her mother: "From this bleeding heart a Mother! A parent—the Author of my being . . . dearer to me than my own existence." [95] Catharine Maria Sedgwick, another Boston spinster, also filled her journal with the anguish of separation. Every object on which she fixed her affection—parents, siblings, nieces, and nephews—ultimately departed, leaving her to grieve in later life, as she had from the tenderest age, "who can see the dreaming that brings tears to my eyes from a world of memories and mourning." [96]

These preoccupations with personal feelings and emotional attachments were not unique to New England women. Neither was their sentimental expression. Westward, in the town of Montrose, Pennsylvania, a local poetress wrote graveyard verses: "Not for the dead but for the woe of sever'd bliss, these sorrows flow;/ For sleep the good on sweeter bed,/ Than this world's love can ever spread." [97] Off on the Tennessee frontier the newspapers harbored the same genre of poetry, devoted to such themes as "The Dead Twins" ("Within a little coffin lay, helpless babes as sweet as May," etc.).[98] Such sentimental preoccupations quickly seeped out of diaries into newsprint and little gilt volumes. By 1820, Lydia Huntley Sigourney of Hartford, Connecticut, had made a national reputation on paeans to dead children and their weeping mothers.

This curious blossoming of sentimentality must be added to the myriad nuances of womanhood whose appearance coincided with the rise of commercial capitalism. While the glamorized parasitism ascribed to the fashionable lady was perhaps the most dramatic innovation of the era, it was practicable for only a few American women before 1820. Meanwhile, other women plummeted to poverty and exploitation in the almshouses and the factories of the new nation. At the same time, the openings for she-merchants, as well as the duties of help-meets, slowly dwindled as men took the reins of a more complicated economic system. The middle-class wives of commercial farmers, shopkeepers, and professionals were stranded in narrower households, where sentimental predilections might flourish and perhaps be molded into a new femininity. For the time being, the female role and image had not congealed into a cohesive and convincing standard of womanhood, but remained battered by social changes, fragmented by class, uprooted from the old home economy.

**MOTHERS OF
CIVILIZATION:**

THE COMMON WOMAN,
1830-1860

The vagueness and diversity that characterized images of woman at the turn of the century was to be short-lived. By mid-century woman had once again been put in her place, a place neither better nor worse than that of her foremothers, carved out still by the arbitrary dictates of sex, merely updated by social-historical change. The question of woman's role seemed decisively settled by 1860. She was the guardian of the home fires, nestled by the hearth, while the great common man conquered the West, built railways, and championed American democracy. The American democrat, however, was loath to call the female sex unequal or designate her sphere as inferior, subordinate, or servile. Woman's place was only different, as she was. Hers, in fact, was a far better place than the rough and tumble world of work, war, and politics, and woman's superior nature—pure, pious, and gentle—entitled her to reign there. It was between 1830 and 1860 that this familiar set of stereotypes was first adopted in America. By 1860 sex had cut a bold gash across all of society and culture, bluntly dividing American life and character into two inviolate spheres labeled male and female. The egalitarian and individualistic ethic of Jacksonian America was blighted from the first, tarnished by the sex bias of its central myth, the common man.

One might expect this sexual barrier to be corroded by the celebrated common denominator of nineteenth-century experience, the frontier. Women did follow close on the tracks of Daniel Boone, wrestling alongside men to tame the wilderness and acquiring some of the rugged characteristics of the pioneer in the process. The history of the American West is replete with anecdotes of women who discarded the pretense of femininity. Kate White, for one, exchanged her Virginia refinements for a six-shooter and saddle and won a reputation for being "as big and broad and capable as a strong man." Women routinely abdicated gentility in the West, sleeping wall to wall in mixed company, bathing publicly, and donning deerskin garments. Pioneer women had little time for such domestic amenities as romantic love and maternal affection. Kate White married without much thought or enthusiasm and lived with her spouse in a "cheerful combination" rather than true love. Neither Mr. nor Mrs. White took much time away from their chores to dote over their children. Even Mrs. Anne Coleman, who was called a "Victorian Lady on the Texas Frontier," was kept busy breeding five hundred chickens while her husband tended the cattle.[1]

Expansion to the Pacific seems at first glance to have prolonged the historical life of Adam's Rib, perpetuating a sexual partnership in the labors for survival that minimized female domesticity and feminine manners. Yet the nineteenth century could not be escaped so easily. First of all, the pioneers themselves carried westward many new attitudes that had germinated in their eastern homes. Westbound women had acquired the sentimental perceptions of Sarah Stearns and Lydia Sigourney, and at times exaggerated them in proportion to their distance from beloved homes to the east and in response to the loneliness of the sparsely settled frontier. At any rate the women of the West penned tearful letters to mothers and sisters back home and littered the wilderness with graveyard poems dedicated to "Rose of a Western Bower" or "Fair Flowers of the West." Mrs. Eliza Farnham's account of her sojourn in Illinois was besplattered with images of dying infants and consumptive mothers and was sidetracked by lengthy and detailed accounts of the death of a sister and her own child. "Who shall ever tell the bitter, the agonizing pangs, that rend the very bonds of life, when a mother stands by the cold clay of her only child." Mrs. Farnham and countless other writers told this tale over and over again, gilding the western woman's experience with newly feminine conventions.[2]

Many other women braved the frontier for the specific purpose of carrying domesticity across the continent. As women roamed across the prairies, the appetite was whetted for "Ah the luxury of a house, a house." One woman explained her participation in western settlement by saying, "Wherever he [her husband] goes, that is my home." Another young mother wrote to her sister in the east urgently requesting the latest mothers' magazines that she might enlighten herself and her neighbors. Eastern residents also dispatched schoolmarms and female agents of benevolent societies to the West, instructed to "reclaim the waste places and conquer uncivilized man."[3]

This mission was well underway once the forest was cleared and the first crop planted. Within a few years of settlement frontier towns had re-created the family pattern of the East, nuclear in structure, housing only a couple and their offspring and marked by the lowered birth rate of the nineteenth century. Trempealeau County, Wisconsin, was hardly wrenched from the Indians before maternal associations, ladies' aid societies, and female authors cropped up. Soon the women of Trempealeau were gathering to read Shakespeare and discuss the writings of Margaret Fuller. The rugged western town of

Chicago had blossomed with such feminine amenities as "ladies' fairs" and temperance crusades as early as the 1830s. The ardors of pioneering were but a brief episode in the life of the typical western woman. Like Kate White, "when the time came" she was "able once more to enjoy the refinements and comforts of girlhood." [4]

The ties between East and West were more substantial than girlhood memories, however. The West was linked to the rapidly changing eastern economy by turnpikes, canals, and soon railroads. This transportation network sent books, magazines, and newspapers, all steeped in a new femininity, to the doors of western cabins. Within the popular literature manufactured in northeastern centers, western women could find this role proscribed: "the companion of the restless rover on his westward march in order that the secret craving of his soul may be satisfied in that home of happiness and rest, which woman alone can form." The transcontinental communication of ideas regarding women also moved from West to East. Writers like Alice and Phoebe Carey from Michigan vied with Lydia Sigourney for the honor of being America's preeminent female poet. Western essayists and novelists Eliza Farnham, Caroline Gilman, and Margaret Coxe pronounced upon the life and role of women with as much authority as their counterparts in the East. Western writing might give greater play to homespun humor and rustic details, but it shared the basic premise of the role assigned woman by antebellum culture: creating the "home of happiness." [5]

This widespread conformity to a single model of womanhood was made possible by an epic event in American history: the development, between 1830 and 1860, of a national cultural industry capable of transmitting common ideas throughout the United States under the expert direction of a few powerful publishing firms situated in the cities of the Northeast.

The mainstay of the American publishing industry, which mushroomed after the invention of inexpensive printing machinery in 1830, was literature by, for, and about women. For the first time in American cultural history, womanhood was a distinct and popular topic of discourse. Furthermore, new and more subtly addictive literary genres carried the doctrines of womanhood to the American reading public. By the 1850s female readers were imbibing directives in femininity through the vicarious experience provided by sentimental novels. The so-called "scribbling women," Mrs. E. D. E. N. Southworth, Augusta Jane Evans, Maria Cummins, and an army of popular female novelists, turned out books at a frantic rate and sold them in editions of one hundred thousand. The prime medium of woman's culture in the 1830s and 1840s was the ladies' magazine, most illustriously represented by *Godey's Lady's Book*. Under the editorship of Sarah Josepha Hale, a New England widow, *Godey's* consolidated all the diverse elements of the new female roles, functions, and sentiments into an integral self-image for American women.

Godey's eschewed the fashionable aristocrat as decadent and celebrated instead the wholesome American woman dedicated to the service of her family. This ideal woman was not rendered in prosaic simplicity, however, but in regal hyperbole. *Godey's* presented Queen Victoria as the archetype of femininity. "Victoria we consider as the representative of the moral and the intellectual influence which woman by her nature is formed to exercise." The moral and intellectual qualities that the English monarch typified included "all that is majestic, all that is soft and soothing, all that is bright, all that expresses the one universal voice of love in creation." Invested with love and gentleness, not power and energy, women were suited to reign only in the domestic circle, on "the throne of the heart." They could usurp the patriarch in the family unit, guide their husbands, and direct their child subjects, but little more. From their little kingdoms, however, women were assured that they could dictate national morality. A marriage manual of the 1850s described the circuitous route of "woman's influence" as follows: "The great current of society is created by those thousands of little streams, which are pure or impure according to the character of our homes. To purify them or to keep them pure, is chiefly woman's work, and if truly done, the current would roll on pure as a mountain stream to the ethereal region." Similar convolutions of social theory lead Ralph Waldo Emerson to conclude that woman was the "civilizer of mankind." [6]

By the middle of the nineteenth century womanhood had become a distinct ontological category and a highly glorified one as well. The majesty of being female, however, was merely gloss upon a stereotype. The veneration of feminine characteristics—love, purity, softness—arose with the desiccation of those attributes that were now deemed masculine: ambition, courage, forcefulness. The heralded influence of woman, moreover, was contingent upon her confinement to a narrow social habitat, a household stripped of productive economic activity. Her virtues would be expressed primarily in private psychological service, dispensing warmth, cheer, solace, and purity in the home. Whether she supplied her husband or her children with this emotional support, her role was primarily nurture, nourishment, and mothering. The mother's task was to guard the national soul and strengthen the moral fiber of America. Laboring far away from the fields of economics, social organization, and politics, she set the tone of "civilization." In short, ante-bellum culture placed women on a pedestal labeled "mother of civilization."

The cult of motherhood was set in opposition to larger and more unseemly social realities. Margaret Coxe enumerated the salient features of a man's world in the Jacksonian era: "fluctuating state of our population, the alternations in commercial affairs to which the country has been especially subjected, the sudden and unexpected reverses in fortune which have been witnessed in every section of the union, by the mania for land speculation." The world outside woman's tranquil home was unstable, impersonal, and rugged. It was rife with "snares and temptations"—taverns, brothels, gambling houses—the reverse of feminine purity. The ambience within which the businessman operated was particularly viperous, steeped in greed, dishonesty, and cutthroat competition.[7]

This ante-bellum paranoia was symptomatic of large-scale economic and social change, commonly labeled urbanization, industrialization, and modernization. Between 1830 and 1860 nonagricultural production, urban residence, and modern methods of social control increased at unprecedented rates, all under the aegis of laissez-faire capitalism. These impersonal historical forces plunged American men and women into a series of devastating economic panics and left them prey to the vicissitudes of the free market. In eastern cities and on western frontiers the population was repeatedly uprooted; Bostonians and Iowa farmers could see all their neighbors come and go within a decade. City residents became obsessed with crime rates and westerners longed for law and order. To women like Catharine Esther Beecher, a major architect of the cult of motherhood, it appeared that a "revolution," a social "earthquake" was in the offing.

It was this collision between the peaceful home and a society bent on disaster that generated the idea of the mother of civilization. In this opposition domestic femininity found its meaning and its social function. The truncated personality proscribed for women was an antidote to a world gone mad with change, acquisitiveness, and individualism. Her conservatism would tame the economic ambitions of men. Her warmth would assuage the pain of failure; her gentleness would mollify the ruthlessness of the successful. The women of the West would secure "home calm" for those "restless rovers" prone to land speculation. Woman's maternal purity would instill morality and social probity in generations to come. Catharine Beecher spied "signs of disease in the body politic," abolitionism, crooked electioneering, unbridled democracy, which could be best allayed by the "subordination taught in the family through her agency to whom is committed the moulding of the whole mass of mind in its first formation." While New England's daughter, Catharine Beecher, implored "American women! Will You Save Your Country?" Margaret Coxe summoned her western sisters to become "national conservatives in the largest sense." [8]

Mother of civilization was, then, a prescribed social role as well as an honorific title. It evolved with industrial capitalism and served as a method of maintaining social order after the patriarchal social system had been dismantled. The amorphous egalitarianism suggested by Jacksonian rhetoric threatened anarchy. The competitive individualism now expected of the American male portended both personal insecurity and interpersonal conflict. Internal restraints rather than the dictates of social hierarchy were employed to subdue the common man. These restraints were anchored in the institution of the family, where women, half the population, deterred their husbands from antisocial behavior and instilled law, order, and love in their offspring. Countless tracts summoned women to this task, enveloped in the most exuberant language: "The influence of woman is not circumscribed by the narrow limits of the domestic circle. She controls the destiny of every community. The character of society depends as much on the fiat of woman as the temperature of the country on the influence of the sun." The banishment of women to the fireside did not render her useless. Rather, it made her the chief agent of a matrifocal system of social order.[9]

It was a diffuse and decentralized system. It could function only if masses of women, scattered in isolated homes across America, embraced the social role incumbent upon a mother of civilization. Accordingly, the task of the American culture industry between 1830 and 1860 was to recruit the emotional energies of masses of women for a civilizing mission. The campaign to reconstruct the female personality began with the early socialization of girls. This project was already under way in 1830 when Lydia Maria Child expressed alarm about the precocious femininity of America's daughters. "The greatest and most prevailing error in education consists in making love a subject of such engrossing and disproportionate interest in the minds of young girls. As soon as they can walk alone they are called 'little sweetheart' and little wife and as they grow older the boyish liking of a neighbor or schoolmate becomes a favorite jest." Mrs. Child was bucking not only folk mores but a concerted cultural movement. Lydia Sigourney directed her feminine propaganda to girls in books "designed to combine with the accomplishment of reading sentiments that are feminine in their character, and knowledge that enters into the element of woman's duties." Catharine Sedgwick joined the new literary enterprise of writing girls' books. Sedgwick, a lifelong spinster, advised her young readers that "God has appointed marriage. He has designed you for it. It is the great circumstance of your lives." Sigourney chimed in with the platitude: "A happy wife and mother is undoubtedly the happiest of all womankind." [10]

The young girl's acculturation not only dictated marriage and motherhood but also inculcated the specific virtues that these roles entailed. Stories for girls pictured model little ladies, "so quiet and so affectionate and looked so much like a dove." The girl's literary universe was cluttered with flowers, kittens, and, of course, dolls. The latter invention was designed to give little girls a playful apprenticeship in the adult female role. "The dressing of dolls is a useful as well as a pleasant employment for little girls. If they are careful about small gowns, caps, and spencers, it will tend to make them ingenious about their own dress when they are older." More importantly, playing with dolls was practice for motherhood. "When little girls are alone, dolls may serve for company. They can be scolded, advised and kissed, and taught to read and sung to sleep, and anything else the fancy of the owner may devise." "Playing house," complete with toy tubs, brooms, and cookware, was also a creation of ante-bellum culture.[11]

Games for girls were carefully differentiated from boys' amusements. A girl might play with a hoop or swing gently, but the "ruder and more daring gymnastics of boys" were outlawed. Competitive play, even with members of her own sex, was also anathema: "little girls should never be ambitious to swing higher than her other companions." Children's board games afforded another insidious method of inculcating masculinity and femininity. On a boys' gameboard the player moved in an upward spiral, past temptations, obstacles, and reverses until the winner reached a pinnacle of health and prosperity. A girls' playful enactment of her course in life moved via a circular, ever-inward path to "the mansion of happiness," a pastel tableau of mother and child. The dice of popular culture were loaded for both sexes, and weighted with domesticity for little women.[12]

As the American girl neared her late teens, preparation for her adult role became more pressing. If she attended a female academy she would probably be taught the principles of housekeeping and child-care. Simultaneously, the inculcation of feminine personality traits would be stepped up. According to John Todd, the regimen of a girls' school would approximate the domestic sphere, where "you can't expect every day to do some great thing, but you can do a courtesy." Women were put in training for the private service of others: "Make it a part of your duty to please," "Cultivate the habit of making others happy daily." Female education was preparatory to altruism rather than personal achievement. Teacher training emphasized the same genteel practices. In a journal account of life at a normal school, one young woman transcribed bits of advice such as this: "As it is desirable that everything that is presented to children should be beautiful . . . we should be careful about our personal appearance." [13]

Yet the professional femininity of the schoolteacher was peripheral to a young woman's major obligation in these years, the selection of a husband. She was given abundant incentive but imprecise instructions as to how to proceed in this crucial undertaking. Mrs. Margaret Graves, in a book entitled *Girlhood and Womanhood,* alerted her readers to all the pitfalls of mate-selection, the snares of drunkards, gigolos, and the overly ambitious. To avoid them and to escape the odium of being an old maid, young women were advised to present themselves in society as warm, self-controlled, and chaste ("No man not even the most dissipated and reckless would choose" a flirtatious woman "as the wife of his bosom and future mother of his children"). The principal instruction for the eligible woman was simple but vague: marry not for money, status, or parental approval but for "love." The exact meaning of this injunction was a mystery. No female essayist or schoolteacher succeeded in defining heterosexual love. They left its elaboration to the novelists. [14]

A character in *Clarence,* a novel by Catharine Sedgwick dated 1830, presented the be-all-and-end-all of courtship this way: "Ever since I first thought of it at all, though I can't remember when that was, I have always said I would never marry any man that I was not willing to die for.'' In this instance love appeared as an aspiration rooted deep in childhood and so intense that a woman would give up her life for it. The object of this extreme passion was not just a kind, sympathetic, reliable person of the opposite sex. The heroine of *Clarence* was courted by such a man but rejected him, saying, "I feel for you . . . the sentiments of a sister." The Victorian heroine was not referring to the absence of sexual attraction. Whatever it was that catalyzed friendship into love was mysterious, fated, so elusive that it can only be labeled romantic.[15]

The social factors that underpinned the ante-bellum notion of romantic love can be read between the lines of novels. First of all, romantic love had its temporal parameters, it predated marriage. Love waxed ecstastic during the quest for a mate, not in the course of married life. This is what propelled the sentimental heroine through two lengthy volumes or a score of chapters in a magazine serial. For example, an epic love story, Mrs. E. D. E. N. Southworth's *The Curse of Clifton,* introduced the fated lovers in the first few pages but took four hundred more to securely unite them in connubial bliss. The novels of the 1850s put women in the central role of the lover, awaiting, nurturing, or begging reciprocation from the hero. Women were most richly endowed with, and more sensitive to, the emotion of love. As Sigourney put it, "A woman's nature feeds on love. Love is its life."[16]

This urgent quest of the ante-bellum ingenue, the search for romantic love, culminated in the pairing of opposite temperaments, the stereotypical traits of heroine and hero. The sexual distribution of love was obvious:

> The characteristic endowments of women, are not of a commanding and imposing nature, such as man may boast of, and which enable him to contend with difficulties and dangers, to which both personally and mentally, he is liable. They consist in purity of mind, simplicity and frankness of heart, benevolence, prompting to active charity, warm affection, inducing a habit of forbearance and self denial, which the comfort or good of their human ties may demand.

These were the basic raw materials from which popular novelists molded their favorite characters: worldly, courageous heroes and timid, loving heroines.[17]

This sexual imbalance was built into the romantic union. The difference between man and woman could be disguised as a symbiotic and protective alliance. "Man, possessing reasoning faculties, muscular power, and the courage to employ it, is qualified for being a protector; the woman . . . requires protection. Under such circumstances the man naturally governs; the woman naturally obeys." *The Curse of Clifton* ended in such a protective alliance, with the hero patting his wife on the head and uttering "my child, my child." Romantic euphoria also camouflaged the power structure of nineteenth-century love. Ante-bellum heroes articulated their love in metaphors of control and ownership. "I feel a sort of unratified right of property in her," "I wish to control her destiny." When the heroine of Marion Harland's *Alone* was asked to describe her dream of love, she answered "to have my woman's will bent in glad humility before a stronger mind." [18]

Not every heroine was quite this meek. Beulah Benton, the major character in Augusta Jane Evans' *Beulah,* was a recalcitrant heroine, intent on winning independence, self-sufficiency, and fame as a writer. Augusta Evans, like other female authors, displayed awareness and oblique disapproval of nineteenth-century sexual politics. Still, the romance must go on and the author of *Beulah* bombarded the heroine with the platitude that love alone could bring woman happiness. She constructed a hero of gigantic proportions to subdue the obstinate Beulah. Guy Hartwell was not only older, wiser, and stronger, but Beulah's former guardian as well. To make Beulah submit, love had cast off all its romantic pretensions and exposed itself as tyranny. The "happy ending" reads as follows:

> "Beulah Benton, do you belong to the tyrant ambition or do you belong to that tyrant Guy Hartwell? Quick child, decide."
> "Well if I am to have a tyrant I believe I prefer belonging to you."
> "Beulah I don't want a grateful wife. Do you understand me?"
> "Yes Sir." [19]

When young women were convinced that marriage was the central fact of their existence, and romantic love would guide them to that goal, they were led into another snare of inequality, and often by writers of their own sex. Nonetheless, romantic love had a certain logic as a method of female socialization. This emotional extravagance, first of all, might bridge the ever-widening gap between the sexes. The euphoric leaps to romantic love could transcend the gulf between worldly men and retiring girls. The fragile, over-specialized female, furthermore, was helpless without a man to support her and accept her emotional riches in return. Romantic love conveyed the urgency of her search for a spouse. Intense heterosexual attraction also helped to wrench a young woman away from the maternal home where she had been thoroughly protected and dearly loved. Finally, a glorified and overpowering sentiment like romantic love could disguise the inequitable relationship a bride was about to accept. She was asked to serve a husband faithfully in the backstage of American life, without power, status, or achievement of her own. The hope of "being paramount in one heart" was a major consolation. All these reasons help to explain the rise of romantic love as the official rationale for nineteenth-century marriage.

The ante-bellum woman was not expected to retain her romantic euphoria after marriage. She should be prepared to descend from "the tropic to the temporal zones," "from adoration to friendship." Romantic love, no longer fed by the anxiety of winning a spouse, gave way to "the affections of one, on whose truth and virtue I may repose without fear of any change." The refined emotional sensitivity that preceded a love match had, nonetheless, prepared women for the services expected of them after marriage. Secure in matrimony, a wife's emotional perceptivity helped her to ascertain and supply the affective needs of her spouse. A popular male writer, Donald Mitchell, articulated the domestic fantasy that a wife was to fulfill: "Your wants are all anticipated:

the fire is burning brightly; the clean hearth flashes under the joyous blaze; the old elbow chair is in its place. . . . If trouble comes upon you, she knows that her voice, beguiling you into cheerfulness, will lay aside your fears." This now hackneyed image of the woman who tends the home fires was emblematic of the novel role of the ante-bellum wife, her domestic ministry to the psychological needs of the American breadwinner.[20]

The stores of love with which a female was fortified in early socialization, and which were replenished by the reading of novels and ladies' magazines, were to be dispensed as antidotes to the coldness her husband met in the marketplace. Timothy Shay Arthur, once an apprentice without a job and subsequently an entrepreneur in the booming publishing industry, could speak with authority on the value of a wife. A husband in one of Arthur's many domestic parables begged his wife to "be a true woman! Stand generously by your husband and sustain him in his struggle for eminence, and you shall share his reward. Strengthen his hands and I will press onward with pride, and obtain high places; oppose me and I may sink into oblivion." Similar evocations of woman's indirect economic function echoed throughout ante-bellum fiction. Day in and day out the good wife soothed the weary male on his return from work, refreshed him, and sent him back to his job with renewed vigor. The comfort of his wife and children would be both a man's incentive and his emotional reward as he endured whatever tension-ridden occupation the free labor market had granted him.[21]

In addition, the model wife would insure that her husband fulfilled his economic responsibilities with honesty and sobriety. "If all is well at home we need not watch him at the market. One will work cheerfully for small profits if he be rich in the love and society of the home." A good woman would steer her husband away from "the vanities of worldly ambition," teach him that "true wisdom consists in being contented with the station that providence has allotted them." In other words, ideal wives would modulate the economic aspirations of the male labor force, keeping their husbands' noses to the grindstone in routine, middle-level occupations. They would also deter men from the counterproductive diversions of taverns, game-rooms, and political agitation.[22]

The manual labor of the wife now centered around personal services to the sole male breadwinner. By 1860 household manufacturing was a significant woman's activity only in the most remote outposts of the frontier and was almost negligible as a component of the national product. Women continued to cultivate and process large portions of the family food supply as of 1860, and garden plots and livestock could still be found on the northern tip of Manhattan at the turn of the century. Yet this food production, and the abundant physical labor still required of the homemakers, was designed primarily for the daily sustenance of her family; it was peripheral to the family's economic status and thus often taken for granted. Woman's most honored labor in the home served quite another purpose; it answered this question: "How is the head of the household to be made comfortable when he returns from those toils by which the household is maintained?"[23]

The common woman was a housewife, not a mistress of the household. The housekeeping "profession," as nineteenth-century writers liked to call woman's domestic labor, entailed much more than clothing, feeding, and nursing members of her family. The model homemaker was charged with creating a shrine of domesticity, a total environment of connubial bliss. The husband purchased and planned the ideal edifice, and if at all possible, chose a rural or suburban site for its construction. The blueprint of domesticity was an intimate cottage, carved up into private spaces in which strong home associations could be kindled. But this was only the skeleton of home charm. A woman "whose genius delights in decorating life with manners, with propriety, with order and grace" was required to adorn the structure with symbols of domesticity—curtains, knickknacks, and flowers.[24]

The housekeeping routine was an obsession to Mrs. Eliza Farnham, who was compelled to transform every enclosed space into a home. Within a few hours she created a domestic shrine out of a few feet in a frontier cabin. She scoured and polished, assembled quilts and flowers and carpets, and then rested in "anticipation of Mr. F's surprize when he should come in and find such a snug little home grown up since morning." Mrs. Farnham judged other women according to her own standards of housekeeping, scrutinizing the cleanliness, culinary skills, and decorative faculties of every woman she met in the West. Homes like Mrs. Farnham's, it was said, would seduce men away from all the dangers and temptations of the man's world.[25]

The model woman combined homemaking abilities with the acute psychological perception, which was hers by definition of her feminine nature, in such a way as to create a foolproof method for civilizing her spouse. She would never coerce, argue, or nag, but win him by love. The preferred practice was demonstrated by one of T. S. Arthur's model wives. Confronted with the task of preventing her husband from rendezvousing with some nefarious businessmen in a local tavern, Mrs. Penrose playfully announced, " 'You are my prisoner. I will not let you go.' And Mrs. Penrose twined her arms around his forehead. As she desired it so it was." Another writer described the ritual of wifely service to the breadwinner as follows: "When wearied with the turmoil of life, or wounded in spirit, he can open to you his whole soul, unbosoming his sorrow as on a mother's breast, assured of encouragement and sympathy. Then indeed you are happy. You have attained the highest aspiration of the faithful wife." The good wife was essentially a mother, her womanly bosom the panacea of social and economic ills.[26]

Fashion plates, corset advertisements, and mammarial balms all testify that an ample bosom was the glory of womanhood in the nineteenth century. Marriage manuals and gynecological texts endorsed these commercial fads, designating the large-busted woman as the best candidate for marriage and the healthiest of her sex. At the same time a woman was advised to "guard her bosom well," that is, to regard it as the receptacle for conjugal affection and her infant's nourishment, never reducing it to an object of sexual attraction.

Even the sexual relations of husbands and wives were suspect. Woman's duty was to subdue male passions, not kindle them. Nineteenth-century sexual theory decreed that sexual release and ejaculation expelled the vital energies concentrated in a man's semen. Excessive intercourse was sheer profligacy, destructive to a man's health, offensive to bourgeois frugality, and detrimental to the national economy. Accordingly, marriage manuals were very niggardly in their prescription of the recommended frequency of sexual intercourse; once a month, ninety times in a lifetime, abstinence for twenty-one months, were recommended formulas.[27]

Victorian women were asked to play a central role in this sexual economy, and equipped with a special power to control the destructive passions of men. According to most nineteenth-century physiologists, the normal woman had no sex drive per se, only the generosity to submit to intercourse out of love for her husband. Female sexuality was subsumed under woman's affections and her spirit of self-sacrifice; "When a delicate, exhausted woman lies on the bosom of a strong man with his loving arms around her a new life is instilled in her." Even a prostitute was presumed untarnished by lust; presumably it was only her boundless love that led her to the brothel, betrayed by a man who had won her heart. Purity, like the other ascribed characteristics of the female sex, served a social purpose and conferred a dubious power. "It is the part of the woman to accept or repulse, to grant or to refuse. It is her right to reign a passional queen." The winning of this right was a pyrrhic victory, to say the least, since women had officially been robbed of sexual passion.[28]

The biology of woman resisted this larceny. Well into the nineteenth century medical books paid awestruck homage to the clitoris, "exquisitely sensible, being as it is supposed the principal seat of pleasure"; the origin of "the most vivid excitement of pleasure." As late as the 1860s some physiologists still maintained that female orgasm was essential to reproduction. Other physicians, however, came to see female sexuality as a perversion of nature, a disease which must be systematically rooted out. A woman with an enlarged clitoris was subject to "madness which irresistibly impels the individual to seek gratification regardless of consequences." The offending organ could be treated medicinally, or, if need be, surgically. Dr. Frederick Hollick contended that the clitoris "can readily be amputated more or less . . . and its excitability reduced." He added, "This operation I have frequently performed with great success." [29]

Inundation with the value of female purity, combined with these brutal medical procedures, was certainly calculated to undermine the sex drive of upper-middle-class women. Actual sexual practice might then deal a near fatal blow to female sexuality. The Victorian woman, denied knowledge of her own body, sheltered from such animal functions as the sex act, cloistered from the man's world, and unversed in virile manners would understandably approach her marriage bed with apprehension. The behavior of a husband, who had been advised that women had little desire or capacity for sexual pleasure, was unlikely to dispel a wife's fears. As one woman put it, at the turn of the century, sex with her husband consisted of "slambang" intromission and ejaculation, which left her sensually unmoved and sexually ungratified. Accordingly, women themselves could supply gynecologists with evidence of female disgust for the marital bed, "place of secret assassination where no mercy is shown to the victim." Mary Gore Nichols, a convert to the doctrine of "free love," recounted a history of sexual torture. "I have had my life drained away by uterine hemorrhage and worse than all, I have had the canker of utter loathing and abhorrence forever eating in my heart and for one who like the frogs of Egypt sharing my bedroom and spoiling my food." The possibilities of becoming pregnant, or contracting venereal disease from husbands who habituated brothels, were likely to exacerbate a woman's distaste for sexual intercourse.[30]

Once active sexual desire, and the organ of sexual pleasure, the clitoris, had been all but eradicated from female physiology, the nineteenth-century gynecologist proceeded to elevate a woman's reproductive system to the position of biological hegemony. Experts on female anatomy presumed to speak with authority on every aspect of woman's life, "for both her particular organization and temperament are made subservient to the important part she is destined to perform in conception, gestation, delivery and suckling." According to nineteenth-century gynecologists, a woman's reproductive organs destined her for a primitive role in life: "The employment of the mind in investigations remote from life—from procreation, gestation, delivery, nursing and care of children, cooking and cleaning, appear to be limitedly allowed to women." The tyranny of female anatomy was centered in the womb. One professor of medicine surmised in wonderment that it was "as if the almighty in creating the female sex had taken the uterus and built a woman around it." The uterus, a "simply passive and accommodating" organ, provided an appropriate symbol for ante-bellum femininity, and a convenient rationale for the domestic confinement of women.[31]

The possession of a womb seemed to inevitably doom women to weakness, fragility, and chronic disease. Almost every minor discomfort and major illness to which a woman fell prey was traced to the menacing power of the womb. Treatises on female disease were little more than catalogues of uterine disorders: routine infections, the ubiquitous fallen womb, and such exotic maladies as "uterus dropsey," "cauliflower excrescence of the uterus," and "uterus madness." This diagnostic system made a woman patient vulnerable to repeated examination and brutal treatment of her womb, the application of leeches, harsh douches, burning surgical implements. Being female came to be seen as a form of invalidism.

The pathology of the uterus, however, was merely the underside of the positive function of the hallowed organ. The womb, after all, was the biological origin of the most glorified role of the nineteenth-century woman, motherhood. The actual physical process of giving birth was a relatively minor aspect of Victorian womanhood, however, for the fertility of the common woman continued to plummet throughout the nineteenth century. By 1860 native white women were bearing an average of five children and by 1890 four or less. By mid-century a falling birth rate was characteristic of eastern and western, rural and urban areas. In isolated middle-class districts of cities like Detroit and Chicago, women were typically bearing fewer than four children by the 1870s. Smaller family size was linked to urban residence and nonagricultural employment as well as the exhaustion of farmland by midcentury.[32]

The nineteenth-century decline in the birth rate was achieved without any notable advance in contraceptive knowledge. Even those few eccentrics who advocated conscious birth control did not offer any techniques more efficient than withdrawal, exotic recipes for douche solutions, and an ill-advised rhythm method. William Alcott, for example, assured women that if they abstained from intercourse in the first ten days of the menstrual cycle, pregnancy would never ensue. Should unwanted conception occur, which was extremely likely given these primitive methods of contraception, induced abortion remained a feasible but difficult and dangerous means of limiting family size. Although states began to declare abortion illegal in the 1830s, newspapers continued to accept advertisements from practitioners of this shady occupation. A New York paper could still get the abortionists' message across in the 1860s: "Sure Cure for Ladies in Trouble. No injurious medicines or instruments used. Consultation and advice free." The safety and effectiveness of these services was dubious, however, and hardly inspired mass usage. Abortionists and contraceptive vendors cannot claim sole responsibility for the falling birth rate of the nineteenth century. The lowered fertility of the common woman, it seems, was relatively independent of contraception or abortion, achieved not through these unseemly devices but through the pure instrumentality of sexual abstinence.[33]

Extrapolating from the birth rate, it would then appear that some American women abstained from intercourse for months and years. To the nineteenth-century gynecologist this was a healthy regimen. According to one doctor, two years of celibacy was a prudent routine, compelled by pregnancy and lactation. During pregnancy, the mother must shield the fetus from disruptive passion and the father was obliged to comply. "Who is he that would shake roughly or in any way agitate the soil in which the young embryo plant was forcing its way to life?" Sexual intercourse during lactation would inhibit the flow of a mother's milk to the suckling babe, and "what father would deprive the child, a helpless infant, of his rightful property, real and personal?" The medical proponents of the sacred obligations of motherhood sought to free conception itself from unseemly passions, declaring that a child conceived in fits of lust was subject to all sorts of character disorders, especially the solitary vice of masturbation. In short, the suppression of the female sex drive and the use of abstinence as a mode of family limitation were additional by-products of the cult of motherhood. The female's sexuality was reduced to a reproductive instinct, her insatiable desire to bear children.[34]

Early in the nineteenth century, both men and women were frequently reminded of the somber responsibilities of parents. Sermons, family manuals, and even an occasional "father's book" delineated the methods of training and educating the young. After 1830, however, child-care became designated as woman's work, with the usual flourish of adulation. Countless mothers' books and mothers' magazines informed women "What a delightful office the creator has made for the female. What love and tenderness can equal that existing in the mother for her offspring." Motherhood was proclaimed the essence of femininity, woman's "one duty and function . . . that alone for which she was created." Expectant mothers were forewarned that this female role would absorb the bulk of their time and energy: "It truly requires all the affection of even a fond mother to administer dutifully to the numerous wants of a young child." Lest ante-bellum women should find their maternal obligations onerous, they were assured of the bliss of maternity by Mrs. Lydia Sigourney herself. This writer, the most revered of female authors, introduced her *Letters to Mothers* by posing with a newborn child cradled in her arms and announcing: "I have never been so happy before. Have you?" [35]

Both the rigor and the bliss attached to maternity stemmed from a novel interpretation of child-rearing. *Godey's Lady's Book* defined mothers as "those builders of the human temple who lay the foundation for an eternity of glory or of shame." The mother encroached upon the Almighty's power to dictate salvation and create human beings. She was in fact granted "entire, perfect dominion over the unformed character of [her] infant." The "empire of the mother," as defined by nineteenth-century writers, was more than a feminine mystique. It conferred upon women the function of socialization, transforming infant human animals into adult personalities suitable to the culture and society into which they were born. Parents could not fully articulate this process in the preindustrial era when childhood was brief and enmeshed in the routine practice of adult roles. In the nineteenth century, however, middle-class, and particularly urban, children were removed from the nexus of social and economic activity and left with only vague notions of the occupational and social situations in which they would find themselves as adults. In the intervening years parents had time to deliberate about a child's future. If they could not dictate the life course of the next generation they could at least strive to instill in their own offspring those general traits of character deemed conducive to success in the bourgeois world: propriety, diligence, conscientiousness. The task of implanting these virtues in human minds while they were young and malleable was allocated to mothers, conveniently cloistered with children in the ante-bellum home. America's female agents of socialization collectively molded "the whole mass of mind in its first formation." This was the preeminent social function of the mother of civilization.[36]

Mothers were initiated into this role by a long list of highly detailed instructions in infant care: feeding schedules, balanced diets, cleansing rituals, complicated wardrobes and equipment. The mother's manual also attuned women to such childhood crises as teething, constipation, and masturbation. This regimen of physical care, however, was secondary to the task of socialization. Each maternal gesture toward the child, no matter how trivial it seemed, conveyed a moral message. This hybrid of physical care and moral training was termed "gentle nurture" and constituted a total system of child-rearing. Its goal was primarily negative, to suppress all the immoral and antisocial passions of the infant. Its first injunction was to begin early, with the first spark of human consciousness. Its principal vehicle was the emotional exchange between mother and child, out of which was woven an environment of perfect trust, untarnished purity, and complete tranquility. In essence, gentle nurture merged mother and child in one morally antiseptic and love-saturated unit, deemed the cradle of national health and social order.

The first crèche of socialization was the mother's body. Pregnant women were advised to furnish the environment of the fetus with all the salubrious qualities of femininity—no lust, anger, aggression, mental or physical overexertion should disturb the embryo's nest in her womb. Carrying a child ordained living a stereotype. A pregnant woman was not expected merely to imitate the plastic feminine icon but to mold her whole being to its contours, donning a cheerful, composed, and altruistic nature. The biological bond between a mother and a suckling child prolonged this self-abnegation another year; "her passions, calm, her being serene and full of peace and hope and happiness," she breast-fed her babe. Nursing an infant was one of the most hallowed and inviolate episodes in a woman's life. "She must not delegate to any being the sacred and delightful task of suckling her child." Breast-feeding was sanctified as "one of the most important duties of female life," "one of peculiar, inexpressible felicity," and the "sole occupation and pleasure" of a new mother.[37]

This occupation entailed more than nourishing the infant, for a mother's milk and the warmth with which she offered it also conveyed the child's first moral lessons. Nineteenth-century child-rearing experts assured mothers that a four- to six-month-old infant was morally cognizant, as evidenced by his or her ability to mimic the smiles and frowns of others. This was the opening wedge of social control: "While the tenderest affection beams from her own eye and plays upon every feature of her countenance she contrives by the soft and winning tones of her voice to over-come the resistance of the child, too young indeed to know why it yields but not too young to feel the power by which its heart is so sweetly captivated." The infant marionette of a mother's moods would not only be a good-natured child but would be inextricably bound to the values she represented. All a mother's actions should be calculated to draw the reigns of her "invisible control" ever tighter. "As the infant advances in strength its religion should be love. Teach it to love by your own accents, your whole deportment." Once the child's physical and psychological well-being had been intertwined with a mother's love, it was said that her disapproving reaction to misbehavior would trigger pangs of guilt and genuine pain in the youngster. Therefore, the favored punishment of the nineteenth-century child-rearing manual was the withdrawal of love, evidenced in the curtailment of a mother's smiles and kisses or ostracism from the warmth of the family circle. The penitent child would be quickly restored to his mother's good graces, embraced once more by loving intimacy.[38]

If the mechanics of love were securely established during infancy, assiduously nurtured in childhood, and later reinforced by female school-teachers, they were expected to retain control for a lifetime. The most crucial test of gentle nurture would come just as young men and women took leave of the parental home. Child-rearing literature assured mothers that a well-bred adolescent would be shielded from every temptation by his mother's loving image in his heart and her gentle instructions in his ears. Literature addressed to young men and women assisted mothers in exerting this uncanny power. One parable for adolescents pictured a broken-hearted mother consigning her daughter to a house of correction. The moral of the tale was this: "Her own daughter was the serpent which had stung her bosom. Such is the grief which children may bring upon themselves and their parents. You probably have not thought of this very much." The pious young reader was advised: "Soon you will leave home and will sit down and weep as you think of parents and home far away. Oh how cold will seem the love of others compared with a mother's love." Mother's abiding love would steer young men clear of brothels, saloons, gambling tables, shady business enterprises, and disruptive social and political causes. If gentle nurture was even half as effective as its exponents guaranteed, the domestic machinations of mother love had substantial social consequences.[39]

Ante-bellum theories of child-rearing also left a deep imprint on the American woman. By incessantly penetrating the mysteries of her child's psyche, the model mother developed an almost preternatural acuteness in divining human emotions. It is here, in the nineteenth-century child-rearing regimen, that the curious doctrine of "female intuition" took root. Lydia Sigourney inculcated and defined woman's intuition at one and the same time. A mother's title to a child's "first love, her intuitive discernment of its desires and impulses, her tact in discovering the minutest shades of temperament, her skill in forming the heart to her purpose, are proof both of her prerogative and the divine source whence it emanates." [40] Although this "intuitive discernment" (currently labeled woman's "expressive function" in the sphere of "interpersonal relations") might have been serviceable in the private home, it also cut women off from the larger world, where men related to machines, to products, and to one another in impersonal, rationalized terms. Outside the home men dealt in financial calculations, wielded technology, competed in acquiring wealth, commanded political machines, and staffed bureaucratic social organizations. The regimen of motherhood tended to cripple women for such economic, social, and political action and, in the process, seemed to sanction the sterile masculinization of these activities.

Motherhood, furthermore, for all the honor heaped upon it, brought with it a very precarious sense of accomplishment, for to presume to create and possess human beings is an inherently problematical aspiration. A mother's products seldom turn out quite as planned and inevitably obtain some degree of self-actualization. Children change and grow away from the "author of their being." Ante-bellum female authors were obliquely aware of this internal contradiction of the cult of motherhood. It was the emotional force that inspired Sigourney's *The Faded Hope,* an account of the life and death of the author's young son. The American mothers who wept over Mrs. Sigourney's tragedy were offered some consolation. First of all, the young man's fatal illness brought him home to his mother; "scarcely without grateful tears could his mother perceive that everything from her hand was accepted with the docility of a child." Secondly, Andrew Sigourney's death made him the immutable possession of his mother, confirmed by a portrait of his corpse and his mother's exhilarating exclamation, "A youth forever! He is there. The parting hour hath not changed him. Time scattereth on us the hoary frost, but on him it shall never fall." Another spokesman for the cult of motherhood, Mary Mann, watched the kindergarten students whom she had gently nurtured march to their deaths in the Civil War. Her reaction was also bittersweet: ". . . having died martyrs' deaths for human freedom in the desolating war that now ravages our beloved country—angels in heaven." The meaning of the omnipresent poetic images of dead children may have been more complicated than their sentimental surface. Death at least preserved women from terrestrial separation from their young, the act with which time would inevitably crown their life's work.[41]

It would be a gross fallacy as well as an insult to female intelligence to conclude that ante-bellum women led lives perfectly congruent with all these dictates of ladies' magazines, domestic novels, and child-rearing manuals. Real women were hardly that gullible. As a child growing up in Canandaigua, New York, Caroline Richards was self-willed enough to resist the guilt-inducing methods of books, teachers, and parents. When she and her sister overheard their grandmother say that she would rather die than to see her grandchildren sin, Caroline reasoned: "I didn't believe we would be as good as that, so we kissed each other and went to sleep." Similarly the common woman was not so foolish as to fly into marriage on wings of romantic love without stopping to calculate the status, wealth, and reliability of her suitor. Even an observant habitué of southern ballrooms, Mary Boykin Chestnut, could recall "not a half dozen" cases of true love amid a circle devoted to the "pleasant but very foolish game" of romantic flirtation. Neither was Elizabeth Cady Stanton, for one, convinced by gynecological expertise on female sexuality: "A healthy woman has as much passion as a man . . . she needs nothing stronger than the law of attraction to draw her to the male." Many mothers employed the time-honored child-rearing method, the rod, without qualms. One Montana woman nonchalantly tied her infant to a high-chair and went about her own business.[42]

The contradictions of the feminine role-model were, in fact, built into the emphatic core of sentimental literature, the threatened estrangement, departure, or death of loved ones. One of the most popular ante-bellum editions of domesticity, *Fern Leaves from Fanny's Portfolio,* toyed mercilessly with sentimental sensitivities by sketching maudlin scenes of infants dying from parental neglect, wives driven mad by infidelities, and mothers betrayed by criminal offspring. The author of these tales soon grew impatient with this careful disguise of the tensions inherent to womanhood, however. Halfway through the filigreed volume "Fanny Fern" dropped her genteel mask and broke into acid satire. Sarah Payson Willis now called on sage and salty-tongued women to dub their mates "pussycats" ("There is nothing manly about you except your whiskers") or offer advice on "How to Manage Your Husband" ("Give him a twitch backwards, when you want him to go forwards"). Countless ante-bellum women were no doubt equally shrewd, capable both of manipulating stereotypes to their own benefit and of vying for power within their domestic cages. Yet they still remained constrained by a marital role that another of Willis' sardonic characters described as "the hardest way on earth of getting a living." [43]

This female role, created by industrial society's sexual division of labor, was itself well nigh inescapable. The fact that economic production had fled the household, and that it was very rare for a middle-class married woman to work outside the home, turned woman's attention more intently toward such domestic occupations as child-rearing, housekeeping, and wifely solicitude and made her more susceptible to the blandishments of sentimental womanhood. Even the faithful reader of women's literature, however, would blend its instructions with her common sense and adjust them to her own experience. The result would be at best a fractured, imprecise, and humanized rendition of the gospel of mother of civilization. The brief diary of Mrs. Eliza Rogers of Old Town, Maine, illustrates the prosaic life of the common woman. As of 1860 Mrs. Rogers was occasionally employed canning fruit and spinning yarn. Yet her diary more often recorded her payments to outsiders for such services as sewing, weaving, painting her pantry, or carpeting her living room. In addition, she commented on the weather and noted births, deaths, and marriages in her neighborhood. The social sphere of this New England wife had receded from the center of the community, for the accounts of goings-on around town that appeared in Eliza Rogers' diary most often came from indirect and impersonal sources, such as the local newspaper or the limited view from her kitchen window. Social life and worldly affairs, it seemed, could be gleaned only partially and passively from the interstices of modern woman's domestic cage.

The social and economic vacuum that had grown up in Mrs. Rogers' life was filled with anxiety about her children. She devoted her journal entry for one day to this topic. "My heart yearns for the welfare of each member of my dear family, for their prospects. My dear son Charles Emery this day is 21. Well do I recollect the emotion of my heart at his beloved birth—a blessing from God!—How often have I desired that he might prove to be such." The dutiful mother resolved to continue "to labor and pray" for her adult son. "May he be kept from temptation and that he may set his standard high and live for a noble purpose." Two months later Eliza Rogers had cause to commemorate the second epic event in a woman's life, her marriage twenty-three years earlier. Her recollection of wedded life was not altogether satisfying. "I have lived for his [her husband's] little daughter who was four years old and our additional ones now numbering four. Not for my family alone have I endeavored to live tho' I feel that I have done very little good." Even a woman in Eliza Rogers' situation, rooted in the old piety and community traditions of rural New England, had reluctantly adopted a private child-centered role by 1860. As she bowed to the new womanhood, however, Mrs. Rogers had the perspicacity to observe that her sphere was not ideal; it was not entirely gratifying to live just for one's family.[44]

Few women could circumvent all the obligations incumbent upon a mother of civilization. This paradigm of womanhood was not only a pervasive cultural value, but also an entrenched system of distributing social function to the sexes. To escape its power entirely a woman would have to do battle with American industrial society. Consequently, the women who most successfully avoided the strictures of the cult of motherhood inhabited a distinct social system, detached from mainstream America. The opportunity could be grasped in the hundreds of Utopian societies and religious communities that grew up in the United States before the Civil War. Two of these, the Society of Shakers and the Oneida Community, survived and prospered for more than a half century without benefit of mothers of civilization. In essence, these ante-bellum Utopians succeeded in constructing an economy and social structure reminiscent of the seventeenth-century village and household. In the process, the specialized duties of mother and housewife either became obsolete or were absorbed by the community as a whole. Women reclaimed a central and integral place in community life.

The economies of Oneida and the Society of Shakers were based on the production of a variety of commodities—foodstuffs, medicines, silverware, brooms, furniture, traps—often on a mass scale in efficient workshops. What distinguished these mini-economics was their communal organization; goods were manufactured and profits shared by all, men and women alike. Men and women worked side by side in the Oneida workshops, and while the work sites of the Shakers were sexually segregated, women were never excused from economic production. The personal needs of the members of these communities were also attended to communally. The middle-class role of housewife was eradicated by both the Oneidans and the Shakers. The Society of Shakers harbored a vestigial specimen of the housewife in the Shaker sisters, who made the beds, mended the clothes, and tidied the rooms of their assigned brothers. This was a minor function, however, and left Shaker women free to spend most of each workday in the shop or the fields. At Oneida, males and females shared in the essential domestic labors; chores were rotated among the membership and performed in groups. Again, the occupation of housewife was abolished. "Home" and "work," woman's sphere and man's world, were never detached from one another by the ante-bellum communists.

Since women were tightly integrated into these enclosed and self-sufficient communities they had little time or incentive to develop the symptoms of ante-bellum femininity. They certainly disdained its outward accoutrements—the Shakers in their simple gowns and chaste caps, Oneidans with their pantaloons and clipped tresses. Romantic love was irrelevant and a mite ridiculous to Shaker women who vowed to be celibate. One young Shaker dismissed the love match as a "day-dream of the mind." The members of Oneida Community, who practiced a regulated form of promiscuity called complex marriage, did not reject heterosexual love itself, only its customary exclusiveness. An Oneida woman named Sarah Bradley praised complex marriage for rooting out "idolatry and exclusiveness," while Fanny Leonard said Oneida's sexual practice "is like fire which purifies and refines." Oneida Community outlawed monogamy but not romance. While the Shakers annihilated the roles of husband and wife by decreeing celibacy, John Humphrey Noyes, the architect of Oneida, dissolved the traditional roles in diffuse and temporary sexual partnerships: "The marriage supper of the Lamb is a feast at which every dish is free to every guest, exclusiveness, jealousy, quarreling have no place there." [45]

Noyes' unconventional sexual theories were particularly beneficial to women. He devised a method of birth control, male continence, or coitus reservatus, in deference to his wife, who had suffered five painful pregnancies in six years of marriage. While the practice of male continence demanded that the male sacrifice orgasm, it reputedly enhanced sexual pleasure for woman. Noyes reported "that my wife's experience was very satisfying, as it had never been before, and . . . we escaped the horrors of involuntary pregnancy." The first converts to complex marriage, Noyes' neighbors in Putney, Vermont, resorted to this practice after a religious revival when "a great trouble fell upon the district, a trouble which was felt in every house; and the only comfort to many distressed husbands [was] a strong conviction that the world would shortly pass away." The wives of Putney had in fact demanded the right to celibacy and compromised on complex marriage and male continence. Consequently, neither Victorian purity nor its concomitant sacrificial female sexuality could take root at Oneida Community.[46]

The bulwark of ante-bellum femininity, motherhood, was also undermined by Utopian communism. The few children who resided in the Shaker commune were completely isolated from their parents and reared by caretakers of both sexes. Young Oneidans were cared for in a similar manner. Noyes reported that the separation of mother and child

made occasion for some melodramatic scenes; but the wounds of philoprogenitiveness soon healed and the mother soon learned to value her own freedom and opportunity of education more than the luxury of sickly maternal tendencies and then the periodical visits of the mother to the nursery and of the children to the mansion house were found to be the occasion of more genuine pleasure than would ever derive from constant personal attention.

Both mothers and children seemed to thrive without benefit of the supposedly instinctual intimacy between the two.[47]

Both the Oneida Community and the Society of Shakers explicitly courted the favor of women. Noyes' proposal of complex marriage promised woman "not to monopolize or enslave her heart or my own, but to enlarge and establish both in free fellowship of God's universal family." Oneida publications continually asserted that all rights of women were upheld by the community. The Shakers claimed the same honored place in the history of nineteenth-century women: "the first to disenthrall women from the condition of vassalage, to secure her the just and equal rights with men that by her similarity in organization and faculties both God and nature would seem to demand." The Shakers could even boast of a female founder and prophet, Ann Lee, and the fact that "the sisterhood is entirely governed by its own sex." While Oneida was dominated by the patriarchal John Humphrey Noyes, sex was no bar to participation in the lower levels of decision-making and social participation. Both these communities could promise and provide a more balanced relation between the sexes because they had constructed a social order that destroyed private property and banished competitive capitalism from their midst. In a noncompetitive economy and communal social system, the specialized duties and feminine characteristics of the mother of civilization were unnecessary. The ultimate affront to laissez-faire capitalism was that these societies, with their primitive sexual division of labor, were among the most prosperous and efficient economic enterprises of ante-bellum America.[48]

Other communitarians, with the highest ideals and best of intentions, who failed to steer clear of the ubiquitous tenets of the cult of motherhood were not so successful. Although American disciples of Charles Fourier officially rejected the domestic confinement of women, they could not keep elements of the mother of civilization from creeping into their publications and their communities. The *Harbinger,* organ of the American Fourierists, described the place of women in the Phalanx in a way that almost perfectly harmonized with that ideal: "Her intelligence will quicken and stimulate the intellect of man, her intuitive wisdom, refined by all the influences of a true education, will be a perpetual refreshment to his spirit and the purity of her nature, fortified by the power of a well-developed understanding, will guarantee the purity of society." With such a commitment to the stereotypical feminine role, communities like Brook Farm and the North American Phalanx were not about to toy with its social base, the middle-class family. Fourierist communities were seldom more than congregations of conventional homes. As such they were hopelessly fragile and disintegrated within a decade. The men of Brook Farm courted women into private cottages where they might find "a home feeling," "a sense of perfect seclusion," and a wife whom they could claim as a "possession forever." The ephemeral life of communities like Brook

Farm was due, at least in part, to the corrosive influence of the doctrine of mother of civilization.[49]

Once the cult of motherhood had been established it became very difficult for middle-class women to avoid installment in its bastion, the isolated home. These women relied heavily on the informal associations within a female circle for social intercourse and support—the enduring ties between mother, daughters and sisters, the neighborly exchanges along the housewives' circuit. The inner dialectics of that home, however, propelled many women to transgress its official boundaries, especially in the 1830s when the immature cult of motherhood remained contaminated by memories of woman's larger social role. Ante-bellum women not only continued to form benevolent societies, but they also impressed them into their own domestic service rather than in the distant causes of religion and philanthropy. In maternal associations women collectively assaulted the difficulties and tensions of child-rearing. Through Female Moral Reform Societies they not only attacked prostitution, but also the men who frequented brothels. Female temperance associations also assisted women in controlling the vices of fathers, husbands, and sons. In all these societies women congregated outside the home, the better to uphold motherhood, purity, and sobriety.

The female's domestic concerns, combined with the doctrine of woman's influence, could also foment a crusading zeal that encompassed much more than her own husband and children. By the 1830s the maternal vigilance of some women extended even to the slave families of the South. The fiery compassion of women in the antislavery movement was fueled by the cult of motherhood. The antislavery poet Elizabeth Margaret Chandler used the same literary devices as did Lydia Sigourney, the deaths of babies and the tears of mothers, with the added spectacle of the slave master's carnal assaults on women and children. Each of Chandler's poems, however, ended in a call to social action: "Shall we behold unheeding/ Life's holiest feelings crushed/ When woman's heart is bleeding/ Shall woman's voice be hushed?" [50]

Elizabeth Chandler heeded the cries of black women and children by becoming a writer for William Lloyd Garrison's *The Liberator.* Female antislavery societies like the one in Boston were organized so that "all true friends of the cause should enjoy the benefits of cooperation and natural sympathy, the power of association, the faculties of mutual understanding, and division of labor." In other words, women discovered in the antislavery cause the emotional bonds that could transcend their isolated homes and an incentive to form more complex social organization, complete with a division of labor. The bulk of the activities of female antislavery societies were within the range of female propriety, like raising funds through bake sales and bazaars, teaching their children to abhor slavery, praying for slaves and slaveholders alike. Elizabeth Margaret Chandler channeled her outrage into the narrow housewife role, urging women to boycott goods produced in the South. Sarah Grimké suggested that they embroider antislavery slogans and images on domestic artifacts—"May the point of our needles prick the slave owner's conscience." [51]

Although ante-bellum women did not have direct access to the levers of political power, they were acquainted with the doctrine of "woman's influence," their moral hegemony over the males in their families. The female abolitionists proceeded to test this doctrine: "Let them embody themselves in societies and send petitions to their different legislatures, entreating their husbands, fathers, brothers, and sons to abolish the institution of slavery, no longer to tear husbands from wives, children from their parents." In short, antislavery women consolidated their domestic consciences into a public protest and overstepped the boundaries of woman's place. When the Grimké sisters were so bold as to voice their protest from the public podium, before an audience of men as well as women, they had gone too far.[52]

In 1837 Nehemiah Adams, writing for the Associated Clergymen of Massachusetts, advised these renegade mothers of the limits of their moral power. Woman's proper influence was "private and unobtrusive," confined within her own home, and conducive to public peace. Speaking out in public, particularly on such incendiary issues as slavery, was a dangerous perversion of femininity. Catharine Beecher also chided female abolitionists. She reminded them that "Heaven has appointed to the one sex the superior, to the other the subordinate station." Although this "divine economy" did not imply that female "influence should be any the less important, or all-pervading," it did ordain that women always serve the cause of social peace. Therefore, during the abolitionist crisis, which "shakes this nation like an earthquake," females should exert a "saving influence" and awaken their natural pacificity and gentleness to temper the political passions of men.[53]

Angelina Grimké saw through this sophistry immediately. She wrote Beecher: "Indeed! Did our holy Redeemer preach the doctrine of peace to one sex only?" These paeans to the civilizing power of women were "silly ineptitudes," used by man "ever since he laid down the whip as a means to make woman his subject. He respects her body but the war he has waged against her mind, her heart and her soul has been no less destructive to her as a moral being." [54]

The dialectic of nineteenth-century womanhood, catalyzed by antislavery, led women like the Grimké sisters to shun the delicacies of femininity and demand simple sexual equality. Sarah Grimké moved swiftly from a defense of female antislavery to a stalwart feminism. "I ask no favor for my sex. I surrender not our claim to equality. All I ask our brethren is that they will take their heels from our necks and permit us to stand upright on that ground which God designed us to occupy." The Boston Female Anti-Slavery Society supported this forceful stance, asserting that in all human rights and responsibilities men and women "are alike bound to the free and strenuous exercise of such faculties as God has given them." These daughters of New England, many of them Quakers, were sustained by a sense of woman's past, the religious equality and practical equivalence of the sexes, which had not been entirely effaced from their memories as of the 1830s. They combined this with the egalitarian ethic of the Jacksonian era to create a genuinely feminist ideology.[55]

These doctrines were far too radical for most Americans. Even the antislavery movement was wary of feminism. While Garrison championed the cause of sexual equality, the bulk of the antislavery forces balked; they broke off to form the Foreign and American Anti-Slavery Society, which barred female membership. The World Anti-Slavery Convention, which met in London in 1840, banished all women to the galleries. Not all the ousted women left London in abject submission, however. Eight years later two of them, Lucretia Mott and Elizabeth Cady Stanton, organized the first women's rights convention. They assembled more than one hundred men and women in Seneca Falls, New York, and placed the American women's rights movement on a broad and sturdy foundation. The Seneca Falls Declaration was both adamant and comprehensive, demanding political, social, religious, and economic equality for women. The protest was modeled on the Declaration of Independence and infused with the principle of a uniform, asexual moral code. The women's movement was mounted on an ideological base that was available long before 1830.

The formulations of womanhood subsequent to 1830, moral superiority and domestic power, were not so congenial to feminism. The strength of the women's movement was systematically undercut by the doctrine of the mother of civilization. Most feminists came to accept the doctrine of home nurture uncritically. Occasionally they contended that men as well as women should practice this crucial and honored occupation. More frequently, however, feminists used the cult of motherhood as a rationale for reform: guardianship of children would make women better mothers, education would enhance the services of a wife, property rights would allow the widow to keep her children in their hallowed nest. Ultimately, some women's rights advocates swallowed the ideology of mother of civilization entirely. By the 1850s, *The Lily,* a

temperance and women's rights periodical, was proclaiming that a "home mother is the greatest acco-
lade a woman can ever receive." Even Sarah Grimké
surrendered in the end to the seductive pronouncements of woman's moral superiority. In 1856 she
claimed "the great moral power of the world is in
woman" and celebrated the "beautiful difference" between the sexes as "so many levers to lift each other
to the great levels of virtue and wisdom." The insidious feminine stereotype and the sex role it entailed had eaten away at the foundation of American
feminism, leading Sarah Grimké to confess, "I feel no
haste, no anxiety to see my sex invested with their
rights." [56]

By 1860 the women's movement was too weak to
disturb the common woman in her isolated home and
too eviscerated to contradict the ladies' magazines
and domestic novels she read. American culture fed
the domesticated woman a steady diet of rich and
evocative domestic images: dying children, doomed
romances, marital crises. In the 1850s hundreds of
thousands of American women wept in unison with
Harriet Beecher Stowe's fully orchestrated domestic
melodrama, *Uncle Tom's Cabin*. It was Catharine Beecher's own sister who brought the divisive issue of
slavery to the attention of masses of women. Unlike
the public podium of the 1830s, however, the novel
was a proper avenue through which to communicate
female moral sensibility, and Mrs. Stowe proclaimed
herself an emissary of sectional peace and understanding. To qualify for roles in the sentimental novel,
slaves were transformed into beings in whom the domestic affections were peculiarly strong. Black men
became child-like Christian Uncle Toms; the women,

delicate, fair-skinned, devoted mothers like Eliza. To provide the novel with dramatic force, the system of slavery was portrayed as the stage of incessant domestic crises; the threat that Eliza's son would be sold away and Legree's lecherous assaults on Cassie and Emmeline provided the linchpin of the plot.

Mrs. Stowe assumed correctly that femininity and domesticity were not held sacred by slave owners. Such amenities were outlawed by a system of forced labor, where men, women, and children were considered agricultural machinery, valued primarily for their muscle, endurance, and productive capacity. The sexual division of labor was of necessity very primitive under slavery. A few black women were employed as cooks, nurses, mammies, and domestic servants, but most were relegated to arduous physical labor in cotton fields or farmyards. The only exclusively female function was to reproduce the slave labor force. The slave population doubled twice between 1790 and 1850, primarily because of the high fertility of black women, who typically bore seven or eight children in a lifetime.[57]

Aside from procreation, black women were assigned few exclusively female roles. Wifely service remained rudimentary in a system where marriage was officially outlawed and the patriarchal master had usurped the husband's role by supplying the mass of slaves with most of their food, shelter, and clothing. Motherhood might be reduced to giving birth, interrupting work in the field to nurse the infant, and perhaps cooking frugal meals for the young. On the large plantations where almost half of America's slaves resided, children could be housed in special quarters and then quickly put to field labor without benefit of maternal socialization. The slave master, therefore, felt few compunctions to model the black family after the cult of domesticity.

The operation of the slave system by no means annihilated family institutions, nonetheless. The self-interest of planters and the resilience of Afro-Americans combined to create a relatively stable domestic environment. Many black women nurtured strong family loyalties, so strong that they escaped northward to be reunited with their mates or struggled and saved to buy their children's freedom. A few house slaves even mimicked the mother of civilization. One slave woman, Hannah Valentine, wrote to her children, "It is all my thought for fear you not conduct yourselves as Genteel as I would wish you to do." She elaborated her maternal instruction, saying, "take Good care of Master and Mistress, knowing they are the Best friends . . . in this world." Hannah Valentine also pledged her own loyalty and affection to her mistress: "Oh Miss Virginia my heart is so full I know not what to say . . . Oh Master! Oh Mistress! . . . My heart is large enough to hold you all." Some house servants at least pretended to assimilate the sentimentality of their mistresses. Even here, however, their domestic affections were apparently tied to the master's family as securely as to their own husbands and children.[58]

Although the private feelings and family practices of slaves remain shrouded in historical anonymity, it remains unlikely that the domestic relations of ante-bellum blacks corresponded with Harriet Beecher Stowe's fantasy. Frederick Douglass, for example, hardly remembered his mother. He escaped to Baltimore at age seven or eight and "found no severe trial in . . . departure. My home was charmless; it was no home to me; on parting from it I could not feel that I was leaving anything which I could have enjoyed by staying." When another former slave was asked about her marriage, she responded, "Wedding? Uh uh, we just stepped over the broom and we's married. HA. HA. HA." Under such circumstances the affections of black men and women, rather than concentrating exclusively on husbands and children, might have extended to a large group of kinsmen and numerous adopted uncles, aunts, brothers, and sisters. A Georgia slave named Phoebe, for example, sent greetings to a multitude of friends and relatives:

> Clarissa your affectionate mother and Father sends a heap of love to you and your Husband and my Grand Child Phoeba Mag and Cloe. John. Judy. Sue. My aunt Aufy sinena and Minton and Little Plaska. Charles Nega. Fillis and all of their children. Cash. Prime. Lafitte. Rick Tonia sends their love to you all. Give our Love to Cashes Brother Porter and his wife Patience. Victoria gives her love to her Cousin Beck and Miley.

Neither sentimental white women nor the domestic novel could comprehend such diffuse, extensive extrafamiliar affections. Certainly the human ties of black women were at times brutally severed by the slave system; it was a mistake, however, to view this black experience through the distorted domestic sentiments of white middle-class mothers.[59]

The sentimental version of slavery also failed to recognize the peculiar strength of black women. To survive at all within the slave system, women had to develop a strong sense of self-preservation. This characteristic is exemplified by one slave woman's second thoughts after returning a blow from her mistress: "I guess I just clear lost my head cause I knowed better than to fight her if I knowed anything at all. But I start to fight her and the driver he come in and he grabs me and starts beating me till I fall to the floor nearly dead." In order to withstand the blows of the master and mistress, and driver, and to systematically circumvent their wrath, slave women, like slave men, developed toughness, cunning, and cynicism, not fragility, love, and piety. Another woman venerated her slave mother for traits quite unbecoming to a Victorian woman. "My mother was the smartest Black woman in Edes . . . she would do anything. She made as good a field hand as she did a cook. She was a demon, loud and boisterous, high-spirited and independent. I tell you she was a captain." This slave mother did not gently instill ladylike virtues in her daughter. Quite the contrary, she warned, "I'll kill you gal if you don't stand up for your self, Fight. If you can't fight, kick, if you can't kick then bite. I can't tolerate you if you ain't got no backbone." Such were the traits of character that prepared slave women to regard freedom as more than the right to coddle children and care for husbands, and which equipped some to fight like demons for that goal. Like Harriet Tubman, they could resolve, "No man should take me alive. I should fight for my liberty as long as my strength lasted." [60]

Literature like *Uncle Tom's Cabin,* however, reduced black women to such a state of weakness and delicacy that they could be driven to resist slavery only in the event of domestic emergency and only by escaping to the North. To sentimental authors, slaves were mere children to be emancipated by the paternalistic decree of white men. Furthermore, myopic focus on the domestic evils of slavery blinded sentimental authors to the economic and social changes necessary if black emancipation were to be meaningful. It distracted them from the plight of free blacks in northern cities, including their own female servants. Nonetheless, slavery, thus construed as an insult to the cult of motherhood, engendered bitter conflict between the North and South and precipitated a literary war that predated the Civil War by several years. Southern writers countercharged that northern industrial conditions were more offensive to true womanhood than was slavery. As politicians and clergymen picked up the domestic arguments for and against slavery, the mothers of civilization fanned the flames of sectional hatred.

American mothers also trained the soldiers who would fight the Civil War. The easy compliance and conformity instilled by gentle nurture prepared a generation of middle-class sons to march docilely into battle and follow orders without complaint. And as they fought they sang of mothers back home, such ballads as "It Was My Mother's Voice," "Mother, I'll Come Home Tonight," and "Shall I Never See My Mother." When a Union solider was found in a Civil War hospital, drenched in tears with a letter clutched in his hand, a nurse surmised the cause. A letter from his mother had gently rebuked him for drunkenness and foul language. "I have no doubt that she spoke of the Sabbath school, the church, and prayer he used to say when a little fellow at home, when his mother tucked him in bed. He instantly made for the blankets . . . the poor fellow is there sobbing his heart out."

American males and American politics were not left unscathed by this gentle mother.[61]

The system of sexual differences that was established between 1830 and 1860 was surely implicated in the confluence of events and conditions that culminated in the Civil War. When mothers of civilization released their pent-up domestic powers into the slavery debate, rather than insuring social peace they incited a national outbreak of bloodshed and destruction. At the very moment when the intricate scaffolding of a sexual division of labor, roles, and temperaments was finally completed, its dangerous imbalance was exposed. In 1860 the women of America served notice that they would not be flawless servants of the social order, that they would find ways to manipulate man's world from their secondary social positions.

WORKERS, IMMIGRANTS, SOCIAL HOUSEKEEPERS:

WOMEN AND THE INDUSTRIAL MACHINE, 1860-1920

In 1889 the icon of domesticity was installed in a new citadel of popular culture, the *Ladies' Home Journal.* The founder of the magazine, Edward Bok, wrote from the "Editorial Desk" in the February issue of 1890 his observations on "Woman's Equality with Man." His pronouncements could have easily emanated from Sarah Hale's "Editorial Table" at *Godey's* a half-century earlier. Bok still defined woman's "equality" as an outgrowth of her domestic service to her husband and sons: "Man in the outer world is her emissary, carrying out the ideas she early implants in his mind." The *Ladies' Home Journal* held fast to the doctrine that the American woman's home was the "fountainhead" whence all "civilizing" forces flowed forth to replenish a male world. In the same issue, however, an article entitled "Annoyances of Woman's Life" exposed some tarnish on the ideal of the home mother. It recited a long list of domestic complaints, including unruly children, spoiled pudding, gossiping neighbors, and the little heartbreaks that reportedly made one-half of America's housewives victims of nervous disorders. Two other items in this same issue, "Experiments in Wage-Earning" and "Side Talks With Girls," offered advice to women who were contemplating leaving the home to enter the work force. By 1890, signs of restlessness among America's mothers of civilization were cropping up even in a genteel ladies' magazine.[1]

It was quite obvious long before 1890 that many American women had neither the pretense nor the possibility of conforming to the middle-class model of womanhood. The class cleavage of American womanhood was already apparent during the Civil War when the rowdy Irish women of Boston's slums broke ranks with sentimental and patriotic ladies to hurl the first stones in the anti-draft riots. The more than thirty million immigrants who entered America between 1820 and 1920 were more likely to take up residence in tenements and sweatshops than in vine-covered cottages. Immigrant women flocked to the female work force, which numbered five million by 1900, and approximately one fourth of these labored in the very bowels of industrial society, the factory. The mothers of civilization would not have been accorded their genteel retreat from the industrial job market in the first place if ample numbers of workers, male and female, had not been recruited from abroad. The American rate of female employment lagged well behind industrialized Europe throughout the era of frenetic immigration. The immigrant woman and the working-class daughter, however, had, from the first, greater difficulty in evading the clutches of the factory and seldom retreated farther from the industrial quagmire than into a fetid slum.

Neither middle-class mothers nor immigrant workers rested complacently in their assigned places for long after 1890. By 1920, eight million American women were engaged in gainful employment outside the home, and thousands of them had taken to union meetings and picket lines. Middle- and upper-class mothers had simultaneously mobilized into a great army of clubwomen, reformers, and, of course, suffragists. Some daughters of the ante-bellum tradition took up residence in settlement houses, others headed bureaus of statistics and government commissions, becoming housekeepers to the nation rather than the private servants of husbands and children. Other audacious young women entered the male professions and dared to remain single by choice. By the turn of the century the ideal of the home-mother itself came under attack as a few free-thinking women demanded practical equality for themselves and for all classes of American women. The late nineteenth and early twentieth century brought into sharp focus the inherent contradictions and inevitable exceptions to the cult of domestic womanhood. Female employment outside the home was only one relatively simple manifestation of the myriad changes that evolved out of the cult of motherhood.

Not even in the heyday of the mother of civilization were women entirely absent from the work force. The vast majority of women workers at mid-century were still in nonindustrial and traditionally female occupations, however, agricultural labor, and domestic service. By 1890, when the rate of female employment stood at slightly more than 20 percent of women of working age, the Census Bureau counted 1.5 million domestics, which accounted for nearly 60 percent of America's working women. These women, who entered the work force at a very primitive level, were confined to homes nearly twenty-four hours a day and awarded only minuscule wages beyond their room and board. More than 30 percent of these servants were foreign-born, and in heavily immigrant states like Massachusetts the figure rose to more than 60 percent.[2]

Domestic service remained an easily accessible job for recent immigrants well into the twentieth century. One maid-servant wrote home to her family in Poland that "I do well. I have fine food only I must work from 6 o'clock in the morning to 10 o'clock at night and I earn $13 a month." This Polish girl, Aleksandra Rembienski by name, quickly moved to more lucrative posts. Her second job paid $16 a month, for which she and another woman cleaned eighteen rooms, cooked all meals, washed three hundred pieces of linen a week, and ironed for periods of up to four days. Shortly Aleksandra earned a wage of $22 a month in return for which she single-handedly cleaned sixteen rooms and cooked for a large family. Such meager wages in exchange for exhausting services were coupled with the particular discomforts of servant status: constant attendance, limited free time, isolation from family and friends, and residence with strangers who often spoke a foreign tongue. Consequently, the average tenure of a servant in one job was very short, and those women obliged to earn their own living gravitated to other occupations.[3]

By 1900 the second most common place of work for females was a manufacturing or mechanical establishment. A large percentage of these were time-honored employers of young women, the textile factories, which New England daughters laid claim to as a place of woman's work early in the nineteenth century. The boardinghouse and paternalistic conditions of factories like those in Lowell shielded the first mill girls from the full strain and stigma of industrial wage labor. The Lowell girls in the 1830s did not conceive of themselves as common workers, banished from the mainstream of femininity. They usually worked for a few years, saving their earnings to help their farm families or to purchase a genteel education or to provide a trousseau. In the pages of the company magazine, the *Lowell Offering,* the mill operators projected a romantic, pious, and domesticated self-image that would not be out of place in *Godey's Lady's Book.*

Soon, however, the ineluctable power of the American industrial machine captured even the Lowell girls in its iron grasp. Improved technology dictated a swifter work pace, more monotonous tasks, and a nerve-racking working environment. The capitalist commanded more and more production and coveted a high margin of profit. Accordingly, by the 1840s, the Lowell operatives were tending more machines, for longer hours, at the same or even lower wages than a decade earlier. Simultaneously, the showcase boardinghouses began to decay and became overcrowded and unsanitary as industrialization ran roughshod over the feminine sensibilities of native American girls. The Lowell workers did not passively comply with the dictates of the capitalist machine. Operatives like Sarah Bagley dispensed with deference to the factory patriarchs, mere "drivelling cotton lords," a "mushroom aristocracy." Bagley enrolled New England daughters in the Female Labor Reform Association and led them, thousands strong, on strikes, which could last for months. When these stalwart protests failed, however, the New England girls gradually deserted the mills. They moved west, took up more genteel occupations such as schoolteaching, married into middle-class homes, and bequeathed the factory to the immigrants.[4]

By 1860 the majority of the Lowell operatives were foreign-born, the bulk of them recent immigrants from Ireland. In other mill towns such as Warren, Rhode Island, Irish and French-Canadian women were the major component of the work force by mid-century. Immigrant women flocked to Warren for at least three decades for the express purpose of finding work in the mills. By 1885 there were only 64.1 men in Warren for every 100 women. As late as 1890 only one-third of the foreign-born women under twenty-five years of age were married, and the married women were such reluctant mothers that they failed to even replace the immigrant population by natural growth. In Warren in the last half of the nineteenth century women were first and foremost industrial workers.[5]

The women who crossed the Atlantic to replace the New England farmers' daughters at Lowell factories might be in the company of her husband and children, but she was hardly ensconced in domesticity. The immigrant labor force dwelt not in boarding-houses but in shacks and cellars densely and haphazardly clustered around the mills. Small, squalid rooms sometimes housed eight to ten persons of both sexes and from different families. The labor of men, women, and children was all welcome at the factory, each according to the lowest wage for which he or she could be bought. Female labor in the cotton mills at mid-century was evaluated at about half that of a man's, or under $3 for up to seventy-five hours of work a week. The advent of the immigrant worker marked the entry of women into the open labor market free of fathers and husbands where their sex would only specify the cheapest pool of workers.

As the nineteenth century wore on, more and more industries took advantage of this labor supply. By 1890 all but nine of the 369 industries listed by the U.S. Census Bureau employed women.[6] Many of these were particularly eager to hire "greenhorns," women just off the immigrant vessels, eager for work and unversed in the ways of industry. From 1890 to 1920 these vulnerable women came from southern and eastern Europe in great waves, courted by promises that "for girls there is work in America, but not for men." Although men far outnumbered women in the immigrant steerage, millions of women landed in America, alone, penniless, and begging for work. Between 1912 and 1917, for example, 500,000 women under thirty disembarked on America's shores.[7] Two-fifths of the immigrant women workers in the industrial districts of Pennsylvania had traveled to the United States alone, without their families, and three-fifths of them were under eighteen at the time.[8] Work was not a novel experience to these women, but in Europe they had been employed in agriculture, or alongside their husbands and brothers in construction or handicraft. In America they sought and found work almost immediately and most often in factories. The European peasant girls were swiftly deposited in the midst of the nineteenth-century industrial society.

These "green" women entered a segment of the industrial work force that was clearly labeled female. Although a great variety of industries employed them, their status, wages, and working conditions were designated for women only. The division of labor in the cigar factories of Pittsburgh at the turn of the century illustrates the opportunities available to immigrant women. Many of the recent arrivals had skill and experience in rolling cigars, traditionally a woman's task in Slavic countries. In America, however, the well-paying job of hand-rolling expensive cigars had become a male monopoly. The second echelon of the cigar industry, machine rolling, was reserved for men and women of American birth or long experience in the United States. The raw immigrant women were exiled to the damp and putrid basement rooms to strip tobacco. One Pittsburgh shop employed 523 strippers, including eighteen men, 4 of them black, 2 feeble-minded, 3 boys, and the remainder aged. The remaining occupants of this most odious post in the factory were immigrant women, largely Polish. One Slavic woman acknowledged this pattern of discrimination with the simple phrase, "Greenie not wanted in nice clean places." [9]

Women could find work in a variety of industries in the late nineteenth century. They swarmed into the garment industry, food processing plants, laundries, cigar factories, and even the metal trades. But whatever their place of work, the pattern of sexual segregation was the same. The first principle of the sexual division of factory work decreed that women would be relegated to unskilled tasks. In the garment factory this meant that men would cut out and usually press, while women finished garments, sewed on buttons, or worked with inferior materials. In the National Biscuit Company's Pittsburgh plant in 1906 the baking was done by men, while 1,100 women packaged and frosted cakes. The sexual division of labor was not necessarily based on relative muscular power. In the Pittsburgh metal trades, for example, women carried sand cores (devices to reduce the bulk of molded steel) weighing ten to fifty pounds through dusty shops to fuming ovens. Men in the same factory worked only with more intricate sand cores, after being apprenticed to acquire the necessary skill. [10] In the printing industry as well women were excluded from apprenticeship and denied the acquisition of skilled jobs. As early as 1856 a Boston union ruled that "this society discountenances any member working in any office that employs female compositors and that any member found doing so be discharged from the society." [11] Whether the result of custom or of the jealousy of male craftsmen, the exclusion of women from skilled employment worked to the benefit of the factory owner, assuring him of a large pool of female workers consigned to the monotonous repetition of simple tasks.

Of course, such labor also came cheaper, as indicated by the wage scale in Pittsburgh factories in the first decade of the twentieth century. Tobacco strippers, usually recent immigrants of the female sex, seldom earned more than $5 per week, while the operators of rolling machines, more likely to be either men or women of native parentage or longer tenure in the United States, took home up to $10 per week. The garment cutter received $16 a week, the average female needle worker $6 to $7. Master bakers were awarded salaries of up to $100 a month, the female packager averaged $22 a month. In the Pittsburgh metalworks, male core carriers made $3.50 a day on a union scale, while the nonunionized and unskilled female core carrier made $1.25.[12]

Women, furthermore, were most often in those segments of American industry, where earnings were determined by the piece rate rather than a standard wage. Piecework proved a convenient method of accelerating woman's output, which involved the repetition of a simple manual process in which speed was at a premium. Women workers, well aware of the few pennies earned with each collar stitched, each bottle scrubbed, or each tobacco leaf stripped, sped on relentlessly to earn a living wage. Only speed possibly could win them economic betterment. Sarah Cohen, a seasoned worker who was allowed to roll cigars, worked her way up to making $12 a week with her deft hands by the age of sixteen. The nervous strain, however, became too much, and at twenty-one she had descended to the stripping room, where she made a mere $4.20 a week. When a female core maker's Herculean efforts brought her wage up to $2 a day, in another Pittsburgh factory, she and her peers were punished by a reduction in the piece rate.[13] Upward economic mobility was as elusive and frustrating for women workers as was the labor of Sisyphus.

Women's hours were also subject to the iron will of the employer. One immigrant woman reported this procedure: The boss would say, "Rosy, are you doing anything tonight?" When she replied in the negative, he would respond with the politely phrased order: "I guess you can work until half past six." [14] Commonly, the boss or foreman did not resort to such formalities. In the busy season women workers would be expected to work late into the evening and through the weekend or forfeit their jobs. When the season was slack, on the other hand, desperately needy workers would be summarily informed that no work and no wage would be forthcoming for days on end. Elizabeth Hasanovitch, an immigrant dressmaker, held no less than fourteen jobs in her first four years in America. She reeled from "that eternal repetition —slack, busy; busy, slack! My head grew overburdened with heaping up broken thoughts." [15] Tattered nerves and unrelenting anxiety were part and parcel of female industrial labor, inherent in seasonal unemployment, piecework, and unskilled jobs.

The greenhorn worker was subject to special manipulation of her paycheck. It was common to initiate the unskilled worker into the sweatshop routine with nominal or nonexistent wages. In 1905 one eager young girl worked two months without pay for the privilege of learning to operate a power sewing machine. Countless women like her, unfamiliar with industrial practice and often ignorant of the language of the boss, were ill-prepared to question this practice. Others, without basic arithmetic skills, were vulnerable to the bosses' chiseling on the weekly wage checks. It took one Philadelphia worker a year to summon the courage to resist the conniving boss: "Last year I was shy, too, and I never fuss for anything under $1, but now I get tired telling him all about 25 cents. I copy in my book all the amounts on the work slip before I take them back to the factory, so I know what I due just like a bookkeeper." [16] It took shrewdness and vigilance to bind the industrial employer to even such a pathetically low wage agreement.

Some sweatshop managers carried this routine exploitation to the extreme of outright theft of a woman's labor power. An Italian girl, a greenhorn in the garment industry, sewed coats for three weeks and accrued a debt from the shop owner of more than $30. Her boss kept saying, "I pay next week"; "I pay after Sunday," until she returned to work one morning only to find the shop locked, the machines removed, and the boss absconded. Her wages were never recovered and she was deep in debt and without the carfare to look for another job. "Then what I do? I get married. He want me; he help me pay my ship card. I help him buy nice things." [17]

The women workers who were spared such utterly callous treatment were just as ill-equipped to be self-supporting. Studies of working girls in industrial cities from the 1880s to 1920 revealed that a woman's wage was rarely a living wage. In Pittsburgh, for example, 60 percent of female workers made less than the $7 a week essential for subsistence in 1906–07.[18] The Boston working girls were in a similar predicament in 1885.[19] Elizabeth Hasanovitch budgeted her greenhorn's wage of $2.55 a week as follows: $1 for rent, 60 cents for carfare, 6 cents for the newspaper, a variable sum for her diet of sugar, bread, milk, butter, and beans, and saved the remainder, toward bringing her family to America. After nine weeks in the United States she spent New Year's day clutching $2 in her pocket, in despair and bewilderment. "Does it pay to live, after all. Work, work and never earning enough for a living! Eternal worry how to make ends meet." [20] The immigrant woman's work was not only alienating itself, but it failed even to earn her a decent living. Still, she had no choice but to struggle on. As one tobacco stripper expressed it, "I must live. What I eat, if I not work?" [21]

The exploitative industrial use of female labor reduced immigrant workers to individual atoms denied economic self-sufficiency. The surest means of survival in this impossible predicament was to pool their wages in family units. Three out of five of the working women of Boston lived with families in 1885.[22] The majority of Pittsburgh's workers two decades later did the same.[23] A survey of immigrant working women in Pennsylvania in 1925 revealed that 90 percent of them resided in families, with an average of 2.4 workers per household.[24] In essence, women's paltry wages were but one component of working-class family income.

In the first decade of the twentieth century, a Senate investigation of workers in mining and manufacturing found that a mere 38 percent of the foreign born families surveyed relied solely on the income of the male head of household.[24a] The provider role in the immigrant family was shared by parents and children of both sexes. While woman's work might be far removed from the home and her wages won as a solitary individual, her economic status, her very survival, was a function of a family income pool. Thus female immigrants were not simply workers, but women of the working class, and as such, they played out in their distinctive way woman's role, mediating between the family and industrial society.

The majority of the women in the industrial work force before 1920 related to the family unit as daughters, young, single women living with their parents. A Bureau of Labor study in 1887 revealed that three-fourths of female industrial workers in America's large cities were under twenty-five years of age and 96 percent of them were single. As late as 1920 approximately 90 percent of the entire female labor force was unmarried and the bulk of them were under twenty-five.[25] Immigrant girls customarily entered the work force at a very early age. The typical immigrant working girl entered a Pittsburgh factory in her mid-teens and retired early in her twenties.[26] A twelve-year-old immigrant from Russia, Rose Cohen, was placed in a garment shop alongside her father immediately upon her arrival in America and put to work earning passage money for her mother and siblings. Needlework was no novelty to Rose Cohen. She recalled that as a child in a Russian village, "as soon as we were able to hold a needle we were taught to sew." Within a year of her arrival in America, however, Rose was sent to a shop apart from her father and placed in the company of workers whose ways and language were foreign to her. Now she admitted, "I was eager to begin life on my own responsibility, but was also afraid." [27]

Girls like Rose Cohen braved the factory and sweatshops because their employment was vital to the support of their families. Very often their earnings represented a crucial component of family subsistence. In the cotton mill town of Cohoes, New York, four out of every five Irish women between the ages of fifteen and nineteen were employed in the textile factories. The labor of these girls was a major contributing factor to whatever modicum of comfort and security that laboring families enjoyed, reflected in savings accounts and home ownerships.[28] Elsewhere the wages of factory girls supported entire families when male workers were unemployed, disabled, or dead. At several points in her teens Rose Cohen, like her younger sister, was the only breadwinner in the family. Mary Kenney apprenticed herself to a dressmaker at fourteen and a year later became a bookbinder to support her mother after her father's death.[29] One Philadelphia girl made $8 a week in a glass factory, and this along with her little brother's weekly income of $4 sustained a family of seven for five winter months in 1907 and 1908.[30]

Not all immigrant daughters worked outside the home, however. Certain ethnic groups like the Italians rarely allowed young girls to leave the home for any reason. Furthermore, most working girls expected to spend but a few years in the labor force. As of 1890 the average tenure of women who worked outside the home was only eleven years.[31] Marriage promised retirement to most working girls, but some were disappointed. A Hungarian girl named Anna, for example, entered the cigar factory almost the minute she arrived in America in 1912 and left the factory upon marriage to a fellow worker a year later. Her spouse's wages proved insufficient; he was recurrently unemployed and Anna was forced to return to the factory. In the next ten years her working life was interrupted only by the birth of six children, several of whom she took to the factory to nurse after a brief confinement.[32] When Anna recounted her history in the work force in 1925, working women were becoming more common. Although only one in ten immigrant families contacted by the Pennsylvania study of which Anna was a part contained women workers, the bulk of these were wives and mothers. Wives began to supply the supplementary income once earned by daughters who were sent to school and barred from the factory by child labor laws. The wives resorted to the factory for familiar reasons: "Greenhorns need their wives to help them," "If woman does not help, bad for men," "Husband sick; nobody give me eat. I work." These wives and daughters were essential breadwinners to their families, but to the employer they were merely women workers, and therefore entitled to a wage well below the level of subsistence.[33]

Participation in the industrial labor force, furthermore, did not excuse females from woman's work in the home. Daughters like Rose Cohen left the factory early on Saturday in order to clean the tenement apartment. Working wives in the industrial districts of Pennsylvania, whose factory hours were often longer than those of their husbands, were given some assistance in housekeeping by their spouses and children.

The interviewers of Pennsylvania workers often found husbands and wives engaged jointly in housework. In one home the wife washed the clothes and her husband wrung them, while a brother-in-law did the dishes.[34] Rose Haggerty, the fourteen-year-old breadwinner for a family of siblings, was assisted by a five-year-old sister who did the dishes, the cleaning, the shopping, and ran errands.[35] Still, the chief responsibility for home labor fell to the wife. One factory wife described a typical day as follows: "Everything I do—wash, iron, cook, clean, sew, work in the garden, make bread, if time. Get up at 4:30, feed the chickens, make the breakfast, get ready the lunches and it is time to start work. 6 o'clock come home, make eats for the children, washing at nighttime, and make clothes for children." [36]

The responsibilities of a working mother were particularly burdensome. Few working women could afford to provide reliable care for their children while they were at the factory. They left their children under the casual supervision of husband, siblings, neighbors, or alone. One worker described her routine procedure as follows: "I give them their breakfast, put the meal on the table for them, lock the front door, and the gate in the backyard and go away." Other working mothers had to take jobs at hours when their child would be cared for or out of mischief, typically menial work, scrubbing offices and shops at night. Such unpleasant devices were necessary if working-class women were to balance their manifold roles—housewife, mother, industrial worker. Working women were the second sex in double jeopardy, at home and in the work force.[37]

Most wives and mothers would not invite twofold

oppression by entering the work force if it could possibly be avoided. Yet the economic contribution of the vast majority of married women who remained at home was not by any means negligible. A Chicago social worker at the turn of the century encountered in Mrs. Nowicki, a Polish mother, an adamant determination to bring income into the home: "She wishes help by taking in work which she can do and still care for the seven weeks' old baby." Previously, Mrs. Nowicki had milked cows, opened a home dairy, and started a grocery store in a vain attempt to support her family and remain at home. Only as a last resort did she ask "for night work providing it comes at such hours that she could be home to see the boys are not on the streets." [38] Whatever homework immigrant women acquired tended to be less profitable than selling their labor power in the industrial marketplace. Still the home mother grasped at any chance to earn a mere pittance. Immigrants soon learned that in America "nothing is to be had without paying," that they had traded a subsistence peasant community for a specialized modern economy where dollars as well as the sweat of the brow were essential to maintaining a household.

Even Italian immigrant women, sheltered by the patriarchal mores of their ethnic group, were expected to contribute a few dollars to the family coffers. Italian daughters and wives brought in wages through seasonal work in fields and canneries, by taking in boarders, and doing work in the home.[39] The homework of finishing the products of the garment industry was a commonplace of immigrant economies. Italian mothers with large families could be found busily finishing cloaks, cutting carpet rags, and stringing tags as late as 1925. The pennies awarded for each little job seldom totaled much more than $3 a week. Some women turned to their piecework only intermittently—"Whenever the baby sleeps." Others worked steadily, whirling from dawn to dusk in a dizzying cycle of piecework and housework. "So much to do can't breathe." [40]

Opening one's home to boarders was a less debilitating mode of supplementing family income and an equally important one. Polish immigrants, for example, commonly settled in groups whose meals were cooked and rooms cleaned by the wife of one of their number in exchange for a dollar or two a month. The husbands in these makeshift boardinghouses were fortunate indeed. One young man wrote his parents in Poland of his brother's good fortune: "In the beginning he did not do very well, but now every thing is going very well with him. His wife keeps eight persons boarding in his home and he earns $2.50 a day." [41] Other immigrant women managed to at least cut down their own home expenses by living in cooperative households, sharing kitchen facilities with neighbors, or doubling up with their kinsmen. When Rose Cohen's family was hit by the depression of 1893–94, they boarded with two male relatives, sharing the rent and the housekeeping labor of the womenfolk. [42]

Immigrant and working-class wives routinely played at least this economic role: stretching the income of others to make ends meet. The wives seem to have been customarily placed in charge of the household budget. Margaret Von Staden's working-class family in San Francisco is a case in point. Three male wage earners, her father, who was a longshoreman, and two brothers, who were employed by the ironworks, brought home the family income. Of her father, Margaret reported, "He drank once in a while. Most of the time he brought all of his money home to my Mother." Mrs. Von Staden then doled out the family finances in the tight-fisted manner that kept a roof over the heads of seven people. "My mother always put so much a week in a cup in the closet to save for rent. Many a time we had to do without butter when she didn't have money enough. But she would never touch that money in the blue cup." [43]

A Jewish wife recounted her singular methods of distributing family income to her husband: "I worked and worked mighty hard and have gone without food days so that he could have it and then I would maneuver different ways to pay our way so that he always should have a little change in his pocket." When this altruistic wife discovered her mate had sabotaged her budget system by failing to report his full income, she promptly left him.[44] This role was also a cherished source of woman's self-esteem in the Irish family of Mary Kenney. Even after her marriage to Jack O'Sullivan, the devoted daughter deferred to her mother in budgetary matters. "I had always given my salary to Mother. I wanted her to feel she was still running the house. After I married, Jack brought his salary to her too." [45] As fiscal agent of the family, the woman of the immigrant working class played a highly significant role: She eased the transition into a complex money economy and kept families with meager dollar-power from financial disaster.

The role of housewife in the working-class family was physically arduous as well as crucial. It was a formidable task to keep families of working-class neighborhoods alive, healthy, and fit for work. The ramshackle houses of the slums, the crowded quarters of the dumbbell tenement, neighborhoods where almost a thousand people resided on a single acre, were hardly propitious to family hygiene. Neither were the starchy, meatless diets that the workers' frugal budget allowed particularly nutritious. The most meticulous mother would be hard-pressed to keep her children clean in the New York City tenement district of the 1890s, where only 306 of 255,000 residents had access to bathtubs and only 51 of nearly 4,000 tenements had private toilets.[46] As late as 1925 only 1 in 3 immigrant homes in Bethlehem, Pennsylvania, had indoor toilets, and three-quarters of the families had no bathtubs. In the most squalid areas, whole blocks shared a solitary water hydrant.[47] An investigation of working-class homes in New York City completed in 1909 revealed that shelter, diet, clothing, and health care were repeatedly substandard. Neither "the habits of the fathers" nor "the managing ability of the mothers" were responsible for this dire situation, according to the investigators. Rather these families fought a hard but losing battle against the American system of wages and prices.[47a]

Against all these odds, the housewives of the slums managed to keep most of their children and husbands alive. The Jewish residents of the Lower East Side, as a matter of fact, succeeded in having one of the lowest mortality rates in the city of New York.[48] While philanthropists groaned about the unwashed aliens and their filthy homes, slum residents were lugging pails of water up stairways several times a day. While settlement workers set up housekeeping classes for slum dwellers, working-class women were slaving in primitive kitchens to get a frugal meal on a crowded table and devoting a day each week to washing and ironing. In the less austere immigrant community of Hannibal, Missouri, Mary Kenney's mother had a full day's work in keeping her family fed, clothed, and cleaned: "Mother made soap, boys waists and pants, my dresses and father's shirts. Every night when he had gone to bed, she would scrub the kitchen floor." [49] Mrs. Kenney's dedication to housework sustained her husband and sons who worked in Hannibal's railroad shops. The womanly labors of Mrs. Kenney also contributed to the building of the American railroad system. She left New England with her groom in the 1860s, and as they traveled westward she cooked for an entire railroad work crew ("used a barrel of flour a week!"). East and West, the wives of the immigrant working class toiled day in and day out to replenish the labor power of the husbands and children who composed the industrial work force.

Simultaneously, working-class women were reproducing the industrial labor force. Once the immigrant population had settled into a balanced sex ratio and high marriage rate, foreign-born women achieved a fertility rate substantially higher than that of the native American middle class. As of 1910, for every 1,000 married women of native parentage there were 3,396 births; the comparable figure for foreign-born women was 4,275 births.[50] The immigrant woman usually brought her offspring into the world with only the assistance of midwives and home nurses. Two women who performed these roles, Emma Goldman and Margaret Sanger, observed the fear and fatalism that surrounded birth in the working-class home. Mothers entreated them to perform abortions and supply contraceptive information.

Goldman described childbearing in the slums as follows: "Most of them lived in continual dread of conception; the great mass of the married women submitted helplessly, and when they found themselves pregnant, their alarm and worry would result in the determination to get rid of their expected offspring. It was incredible what fantastic methods despair could invent: jumping off tables, rolling on the floor, massaging the stomach, drinking nauseating concoctions, and using blunt instruments." According to Goldman, both Irish Catholics and Jewish women referred to pregnancy as "a curse of God." [51]

Rearing these heirs of poverty often became a somber and difficult task. Immigrant and working-class methods of socialization were neither fully articulated nor self-conscious. Parents bequeathed their values to children through the daily exemplification of principles of survival—hard work and frugality. The child was educated as much by practice as by instruction, through the seldom gentle nurture of joining the labor force and living in the slum streets at an early age. Still, working-class culture assigned women the larger parental role and invested females with refined maternal feelings. For example, the movies which provided distinctly working-class entertainment in 1910 specialized in portraits of selfless, long-suffering mother figures. When a settlement worker questioned one immigrant mother about her solicitude for the souls of her children, the logic and the ethic of child-rearing in the slums were revealed amid the rancor of her answer:

Who's got time to think about souls grinding away here 14 hours a day to turn out contract goods? Tain't souls that count. It's bodies, that can be driven an' half-starved an' driven still, till they drop in their tracks. I'm driving now to pay a doctor's bill for my three that went with the fever. Before that I was driving to put food into their mouths. I never owed a cent to no man. I've been honest and paid as I went and done a good turn when I could.[52]

The major objective of the lower-class mother was simply to keep her children fed and alive. Her central values were honesty, hard work, and being a good neighbor. Yet she was not optimistic about maintaining her own dignity nor that of her children. She went so far as to question the basic virtue of bourgeois maternity, purity: "If I'd chosen the other thing while I'd a pretty face of my own I'd had ease and comfort and a quick death. Such a life as this isn't worth living."

This extreme fatalism points up the quandary of parentage for the immigrant poor. Fathers and mothers hoped their children would find the good life in the promised land of America and be able to "live like folks." The gulf between the glamour of the guilded age and the gloomy environment of the immigrant, however, engendered despair and defeat. It could also tempt their children away from the arduous and austere climb up the economic ladder. Mothers of the working class could not insulate their children in cozy cottages and antiseptic classrooms nor immunize them from the contagious allure of American materialism. Throughout the nineteenth century immigrant children flocked to neighborhood theaters, where visions of romance and wealth tantalized them from the stage. Then nickelodeons and the silver screen made these fantasies even more immediate and appealing. Immigrant boys, impatient to taste the fruits advertised in America's popular culture, took to thievery and flooded the juvenile courts of industrial cities. Immigrant girls saw a short cut to glamour in prostitution.

Jane Addams told of a Chicago girl who went directly from the theater to the brothel. She had hoarded her wages for a week of melodramas and could not bear to return again to the sweatshop.[53] Margaret Von Staden told a similar story in her own words. She went off to her first job at age twelve full of excitement. "I thought all the time of the money I could make and the fine clothes I could have." The nerve-racking work of the garment factory and $3 a week in wages brutally shattered her fantasy. As she went from one menial low-paying job to another, however, she still dreamed of "classey" men, "real swells," and the fine clothes and good times they would buy her. Margaret soon found herself in a circle of devil-may-care youths and showered with presents by a devoted beau. When this flood of riches ebbed she could not return to living on $4 or $5 a week. She became a prostitute instead.[54]

Caught between class exploitation and sexual discrimination, Margaret Von Staden descended to the lowest chamber of woman's oppression, the brothel. Here she played out the contradictions of class and sex to their fullest, serving the lust of the husbands of model Victorian women. Von Staden observed that nearly all the men who visited the brothel were married; "they would not dare to even mention such practice to their wives, so they came to us." At the same time, Von Staden retained the belief that almost every prostitute was at heart a true woman, steeped in maternal instincts. Her full bitterness erupted only once, but with ferocity: "But oh, to be just once the animals [men] think us, so as to turn on our tormentors, sinking sharp, vengeful teeth in their flesh and glory in their agony as the blood is drawn." [55]

The European peasant culture, in which so many immigrant prostitutes grew up, did not nurture Victorian sexuality. The Polish immigrant Wladek Wiszniewski, for example, acquired his sex education at age twelve from an eighteen-year-old peasant girl, adept in the arts of "foolishing." [56] American industrial conditions were not hospitable to such *joie de vivre.* Polish girls in Chicago were more apt to describe their sexual experiences in the repressive language of rape: "There he knocked me down and . . . did something bad to me." [57] The sweatshop, in particular, conditioned working-class women to fear sex, as bosses and foremen promised a better wage for sexual favors, and lecherous men preyed upon the working girl on the way to and from the factory. Rose Cohen confessed that she "liked the companionship of men, but the thought of marriage often filled me with fear, even with disgust. So the sweatshop left its marks." [58]

The first years in America, when visions of a land of milk and honey often gave way to cynical recognition of what one Polish immigrant called "the great golden whore," could lead men and women to the very depths of despair. The dreams of Wladek Wiszniewski, for example, gave way to the reality of trying to survive on $3 a week earned by his wife. Then Mrs. Wiszniewski became pregnant and left her job. "I cannot even now take a walk with my wife, for she has not even shoes to put on her feet but wears my old shoes. And she must bear all this through me for I brought her to this. . . . She suffers for me like a slave and nobody pities her." [59] This Polish couple could not even afford to visit with their relatives, but clung only to one another as they were battered by the torrents of American industrialism.

Most immigrants struggled their way out of such desperate circumstances. In fact, many of them, with the help of working children and saving mothers, achieved a modicum of working-class comfort within a generation, perhaps even a house of their own in the growing working-class suburbs. Few, however, made their way swiftly into the middle class. The female members of nineteenth-century working-class families played a distinctive and pivotal role in the American proletariat. They were more likely than any other segment of the female population to enroll in the industrial labor force and to enter its most exploitative sectors. Yet this female proletariat was not excused from more womanly duties. In fact, the extreme austerity inflicted on the working class during the period of rapidly expanding industrial capitalism assigned these women perhaps the most difficult domestic burden of all, bearing, nurturing, nourishing, and solacing the industrial labor force. Demeaning attitudes toward women and a special set of sex stereotypes seeped into the working-class culture by way of patriarchal ethnic traditions, a male dominated street life, and the agencies of American popular culture. These women not only accepted factory jobs when called upon and waited in the backstage of the economy as a cheap labor pool, but also kept a domestic vigil behind nearly every male worker, creating and enhancing his power to labor.

The fracturing experience of immigration and sudden immersion in industrial society did not bode well for the development of working-class consciousness for anyone. The majority of immigrant women who labored in their homes were mired in the numbing routine of seeing their families through another grueling day. Immigrant women did enroll in numerous organizations, but these were attached to churches and synagogues to encourage religious and ethnic loyalty rather than to engender collective protest against industrial society.

The young women in the factories expected to be liberated by the *deus ex machina,* matrimony. When Elizabeth Hasanovitch complained of her plight to her fellow workers, the usual reply went something like this: "You are so young, so full of life. It's a sin to waste it. You are so pretty you would make an ideal darling wife." Hasanovitch tried in vain to dispel these visions of the working girl. "She finds [marriage] the easiest way out and she goes on breeding human stock for misery's pleasure." [60] Union organizers addressed similar arguments to Rose Cohen and her co-workers: "Don't think you'll get married, who'll want a broken down worker, and if married your husband will be in the same shape." [61]

Union organizers made little headway among women workers before 1910. The collective interests of women workers were deflected by a sense of temporary employment, fragmented by ethnic differences, atomized by an irregular wage scale, and dispersed in a multitude of small shops. Furthermore, after 1890 and the demise of the Knights of Labor, the male leaders of American unions were by no means eager to organize women. The American Federation of Labor, under Samuel Gompers, focused its energies on skilled laborers and expediently ignored the weakest links in the industrial labor force, women and blacks. AFL affiliates, such as the Bakers, Carpenters and Molders Unions, explicitly barred women from membership as late as 1918. In 1921 the national AFL was still resolving, in a halfhearted fashion, to abolish sexual discrimination. Even the International Ladies' Garment Workers Union ignored the female segments of an industry where women workers outnumbered men two to one.

The conditions in the garment industry had become impossible by the early twentieth century. The hours in New York City's shirtwaist factories were 8 to 6 Monday through Friday and 8 to 5 on Saturdays. Twenty-five percent of women workers were making $3 to $4 a week, and the average weekly wage ranged between $7 and $12. Seasonal unemployment was endemic. Petty regulations rubbed salt in these wounds: fines for breaking equipment, being late, even talking; worker purchase, at a profit to the company, of needles, electricity, chairs, and lockers. At the turn of the century there were sporadic protests against this state of affairs, and in 1909 several major strikes. The leaders of the ILGWU toyed with the idea of calling an industry-wide strike. When 2,000 workers gathered at Cooper Union to discuss the course of action, a young worker named Clara Lemlich rose and announced in Yiddish, "I am tired of listening to speakers who talk in general terms. What we are here for is to decide whether we shall or shall not strike. I offer a resolution that a general strike be declared now." The audience reportedly rose en masse, shouted their approval, and took the Jewish pledge: "If I turn traitor to the cause I now pledge, may the hand wither with the arm I now raise." The "Up-rising of the 20,000" had begun, and 80 percent of the strikers were women, 75 percent of them under twenty-five years of age.[62]

It is customary to emphasize the spontaneity of this epic event in labor history and to extole the naïve courage of the anonymous women who, like Clara Lemlich, assumed "emotional" leadership, worked unselfishly in the emergency, and then were heard no more. The strike is also remembered in condescending references to genteel participation on the part of the wives and daughters of the rich, Anne Morgan, Olive Belmont, and students at Wellesley. The Women's Garment Worker's strike of 1909–10, however, constituted far more than the visceral reaction of young workers and the noblesse oblige of upper-class ladies. Solid organizational support came from the Women's Trade Union League and its seasoned working-class organizers like Mary Kenney O'Sullivan and Leonora O'Reilly. The WTUL leadership had long included upper- and middle-class women like Margaret and Mary Dreier and Mary McDowell. Mary Dreier had not only been a relentless champion of working women, but was among the first to support the striking garment workers and one of the first to be arrested at the picket lines. By 1910 women from all classes had acquired organizational abilities and experience in the rugged ways of the male world. Something of major consequences in the history of American women had taken the mothers of civilization into such unlikely places as union halls, picket lines, and jails.

Certainly many women passed the last half of the nineteenth century secluded in middle- and upper-class American homes, oblivious to the advances and the hazards of industrialization. Some of them were collecting the symptoms of the fashionable female diseases. Alice James presented one of the most poignant examples of the destructiveness of domestic seclusion. While her equally "neurotic" brothers, William and Henry, won laurels in psychology and literature, Alice utilized her acute perceptions in bantering with her maid and recounting the foibles of mankind in her diary. Oscillating from lucidity to madness, gentility to violent fantasies, she consigned herself to "the glorious role" of standing for "sick headache to mankind." [63] So many women were in similar predicaments that this catatonic condition of the sex acquired a name all its own, neurasthenia, and legions of physicians designed cures and built sanitariums for its treatment. Charlotte Perkins Gilman was taken with this dread disease in "a charming home," with a "loving and devoted husband, an exquisite baby, healthy and intelligent and good; a highly competent mother to run things; a wholly satisfying servant—and I lay all day on the lounge and cried." The consulting physician recommended the standard cure; "have as domestic a life as possible, have your child with you at all times . . . have but two hours of intellectual life a day." Compliance with this advice merely drove her further into madness.[64]

Charlotte Perkins Gilman did not recover until she had left her small family, and then part of her recuperation occurred at Jane Addams' Hull House, a center of rehabilitation for many tormented mothers of civilization. Jane Addams herself had grown up to sentimental sensibility in Cedarville, Illinois. As a child her precocious maternal heart poured out to the poor who resided in a shantytown. She resolved: "When I grow up I should, of course, have a large house, but it would not be built among the other large houses, but in the midst of horrid little houses like these." Her compassion was nurtured by her Quaker father and his friend Abraham Lincoln. To the young Jane Addams, Lincoln represented the maternal principle of social benevolence, "content merely to dig the channels through which the moral life of his countrymen might flow." [65]

Simultaneously, many women were discovering an enlarged arena for their maternal influence in the Sanitary Commission's Civil War philanthropy. There was the nurse who "rarely rendered any service to those poor fellows that they did not assure me that I was like their mother, or wife, or sister." There were the women who sent hand-knit stockings to unknown soldiers with notes like this: "You are not my husband or son; but you are the husband or son of some woman who undoubtedly loves you as I love mine." [66] Such maternal rhetoric would suffuse female social action for a half century.

Motherhood was used to justify a multitude of extrafamilial activities. Jane Addams clothed settlement work in maternal metaphor, an expression of "the great mother breast of our common humanity." [67] Women's clubs were founded under the motto "Now show a more glorious womanhood . . . a new unit, the completed type of the mother-woman working with all as well as for all." [68] Of course, the suffrage movement resorted to maternal rhetoric, asserting that "the mother of the race, the guardian of its helpless infancy" must keep watch over the ballot box. [69] The union organizer Leonora O'Reilly surmised that "the labor movement must be purified by a woman's movement." [70] The most honored woman in the labor movement was "Mother" Jones, whose route of agitation was littered with sentimental images of the plight of angelic children. [71] Even anarchism could be rhetorically related to maternity: Emma Goldman chose *Mother Earth* as the title of her magazine, proclaiming her intention to "find an outlet for my motherliness in the love of all children." [72]

This enlargement of the promise of motherly power was recognized and tacitly approved by the pioneer social scientists of the late nineteenth century. Social Darwinism had identified sexual differences as the driving force of progressive evolution. By selecting her mate, it was said, the female of the species determined the course of future generations. Furthermore, the female, equipped with mammary glands and larger amounts of adipose tissue, was by nature the more social sex, formed to nurture and serve the race, rather than to scrap and fight for personal gain. The social Darwinist posited these sexual differences in temperament: "the male as extreme egotism or selfishness, . . . a female as altruism or care for other individuals outside of self." [73] Anthropologists such as Henry Lewis Morgan and Johann Jakob Bachofen were simultaneously describing the point in primitive history when the male sex had by animal force usurped social hegemony from women. Pioneer American sociologists Lester Ward and W. I. Thomas held this to be a retrogressive stage in sexual history, which lamentably still endured. As early as 1883, however, Ward espied with delight a new turn in the evolutionary cycle. "Even in our own times we are beginning to observe the most unmistakable signs of the eventual resumption by woman of her lost scepter and of her restoration to that empire over the emotional nature of men which the female of nearly all other animals exercises." [74]

As women emerged from their homes to enter clubrooms, settlement houses, and reform groups, they absorbed some of the spirit and techniques of the scientific era as well as the doctrine of female altruism. The women of the Sanitary Commission deployed as much tough-mindedness as sentimentality. The nurse in a Civil War hospital had to hold herself "in iron control" until she had become "habituated to the manifold shocking sights that are the outcome of the wicked business men call war." The female leaders of the Sanitary Commission, in charge of a nationwide system of collecting and distributing medical supplies, quickly developed "administrative talent" and came to value the female who was "erect and decisive, quick of comprehension and prompt in action." The exemplary personality of the Sanitary Commission, "Mother" Byderdyke, symbolized the dual personality of the new woman reformer. To the soldiers she tended, Mary Byderdyke was "more to his army than the Madonna to a Catholic," but to hospital administrators, doctors, and generals, she was "energetic, resolute and systematic." Woman's exposure to the first modern war made it clear that tearful appeals for moral reform would not serve to civilize industrial society. Lessons in executive ability, practical stamina, and rational organization would have to be assimilated by the feminine temperament.[75]

In her graduation essay at Rockford Seminary Jane Addams contended that more than feminine intuition was called for in the civilizing mission of her generation. The woman's mind must "grow strong and intelligible by the thorough study of at least one branch of physical science, for only with eyes thus accustomed to the search for truth could she detect all self-deceit and fancy in herself and learn to express herself without dogmatism." [76] As a teen-ager, Charlotte Perkins Gilman made a similar resolution to pursue the study of physics, anthropology, sociology, and history and thereby equip herself to guide the course of human evolution. The same principles of intellectual discipline had crept into institutions like Vassar, Smith, and Wellesley, originally dedicated to the cultivation of the softer feminine virtues. The fortunate woman who acquired this broad education had only begun the struggle to escape feminine confinement. The most difficult trial came after college when the young woman searched in vain for an opportunity to put her hard-won education to work. At this point Gilman was sidetracked by an unhappy marriage and Addams floundered for eight full years, "absolutely at sea so far as my moral purpose was concerned, clinging only to the desire to live in a really living world and refusing to be content with a shadowy intellectual or aesthetic reflexion of it." [77]

In 1887 seven graduates of Smith College met at a class reunion and launched a direct assault upon the real world, founding the College Settlement Association. A week after these women and their recruits set up America's first settlement house, Jane Addams and Ellen Star chose an old Chicago mansion as the site of Hull House. All these young women were driven by what Addams called "the subjective necessity of social settlement" to provide "cultivated young people with an outlet for the sentiment of universal brotherhood." At the same time, however, Addams directed prospective settlement residents to develop a "scientific patience in the accumulation of facts and the steady molding of their sympathies as one of the instruments for that accumulation." [78] By 1910, more than four hundred settlement houses had been established, and thousands of young people, three-fifths of them women, gathered there, assured of a chance to put their talents as well as their compassion to work.[79]

Within the settlement house, maternal sentiments were further sifted and leavened until they became an entirely new variety of social reform. Initially, Jane Addams and her comrades set out to civilize their immigrant neighbors through literary evenings, art classes, genteel embellishment, and kindergartens. Soon Miss Addams found herself out sweeping the slum streets, dramatizing to her neighbors that good housekeeping in the industrial city required that a woman enter the public sphere and sacrifice her gentility. The next step in Addams' industrial education took her to city hall where she won the appointment of another college-educated woman as district sanitation director. Simultaneously, another settlement house resident, Mary McDowell, left the kindergarten for the Chicago stockyard where she unionized working women. Florence Kelley went far afield of the settlement house to investigate child labor. By 1915 this extraordinary range of female reform was commonplace and quasi-legitimate: "Women by natural instincts as well as long training have become the housekeepers of the world, so it is only natural that they should in time become effective municipal housekeepers as well." [80] By this time, however, social housekeeping entailed more than wielding a broom and dust rag. For Florence Kelley it meant heading a state board of labor, compiling statistics, and lobbying with legislators. For Mary McDowell it meant organizing unions and leading strikes. For Jane Addams it meant blazing the long winding trail from the social housekeeper of Hull House all the way to national political conventions and international peace organization to become one of the most famous and honored women in American history.

A similar transformation was occurring in other segments of woman's world. The little bands of women's reading groups across the country were organized into the massive General Federation of Women's Clubs in 1890. Within a few years the GFWC leaders were asking, "Is there not room in the clubs for outlook committees, whose business it should be to investigate township affairs, educational, sanitary, reformatory." [81] By the turn of the century women's clubs were not only investigating social conditions but conducting social reforms—forming corporations to build sanitary housing in the slums, reconstructing the judicial system for juvenile offenders, and endorsing factory inspection and child labor legislation. The Women's Trade Union League founded in 1903 devoted less and less time to bringing middle-class culture to working girls and became deeply embroiled in union activities and strikes. Meanwhile, traditional women's groups had become careless of their lady-like ways. As early as the 1870s, the Women's Christian Temperance Union resorted to the vulgar antics of Carrie Nation, entering saloons and destroying the tavernkeeper's property. By the turn of the century, the WCTU had become a broad social service organization, embracing labor legislation and suffrage and prone to debate such questions as "Is housework incompatible with the higher life?" By the 1880s and '90s women were even sloughing off the outer crust of Victorian purity and joining the social purity movement where they openly discussed prostitution and sexual offenses.[82]

Whatever the specific direction upper- and middle-class women took as they emerged from domestic confinement it lead them to mass organizations headed by members of their own sex. By the second decade of the twentieth century, women had formed a veritable army composed of many well-organized divisions, strategically linked, and positioned on the outer flank of the home. By 1920 it was estimated that the General Federation of Women's Clubs had perhaps 1 million members; the Women's Christian Temperance Union 800,000; the YWCA 500,000; there were 400,000 women union members; and as many as 2 million women participated in the suffrage campaign. The seeds of the major contemporary women's organizations, from the PTA to the American Association of University Women, were planted before 1920. Organized women chaired business meetings, were nearly obsessed with writing constitutions and formulating resolutions, and traveled the country to give lectures and attend conventions. Most of the major women's groups had interlocking directorates, supported one another's pet causes, and pooled their resources for the cause of suffrage. Between 1890 and 1920 women built a rationalized organizational network that was nearly as sophisticated in its own way as the corporate business world.[83]

The avowed goals of most women's organizations remained altruistic: to serve the needy and weak rather than to conquer wealth and power for the female sex. Countless individual women, on the other hand, were pursuing their personal, educational, and professional objectives. When M. Carey Thomas was Jane Addams' age she did not weep for poor children but at the thought of being denied a college education. Thomas pursued her personal goal with as much diligence as Addams directed to her social dream. She toiled, begged, and blackmailed her way into Cornell, to a Ph.D. in Zurich, and finally to the presidency of Bryn Mawr in 1894. M. Carey Thomas strove to carry the next generation of educated women with her on her upward climb. She urged Bryn Mawr students to imitate their brothers and to disdain the self-abnegation of marriage and motherhood as detrimental to professional success.[84]

Schools like Byrn Mawr, and coeducational state universities, cleared the way to professional careers for women between 1890 and 1920. During that period the number of professional women increased 226 percent, almost triple the rate of male advancement. While the majority of professional women were teachers at the elementary school level, some women made substantial inroads into traditionally male spheres. By 1920, 5 percent of the nation's doctors were women, 1.4 percent of the lawyers and judges, and 30 percent of the college presidents, professors, and instructors. The route of social housekeeping also led women to prestigious posts. By 1920 women headed three state wage boards, five industrial commissions, and eleven children's bureaus. Florence Harriman sat as chairwoman of the U.S. Industrial Commission, Ida Tarbell headed the Tariff Commission, Julia Lathrop, the Children's Bureau, and Mary Anderson, the Women's Bureau. These were some of the hardest-won jobs in American history: Women had organized, propagandized, and lobbied to create the bureaus and commissions which they later headed.[85]

Very few of these posts, however, were outside the limited domain of social housekeeping. Despite the systematic, forceful, and innovative methods that brought women into the center of the progressive movement, they remained the social charwomen of the industrial system. They tidied up the man's world, removing the most unsightly evidence of corrupt politics, smoothing over the ugly clash between the rich and the poor and cleaned up around the slums. Jane Addams saw her role as "socializing democracy," bringing the classes into harmonious relations with one another without disturbing basic differences in wealth and power. "The dependence of the classes on each other is reciprocal, it gives a form of expression that has peculiar value." [86] The Women's Trade Union League was perfectly explicit about its program of pacifying class conflict. They reasoned that "If the whole burden of remedying unfair industrial inequalities is left to the oppressed social groups, we have the crude and primitive method of revolution." To avert the "crude and primitive" social behavior was a fitting and time-honored duty for these organized mothers of civilization. Progressive women remained guardians of social order and enemies of class conflict. Furthermore, they became so engrossed in the immediate goal of ameliorating slum and factory conditions that they lost sight of the inequities built into the capitalist industrial system. Florence Kelley was an avowed socialist and onetime friend of Frederick Engels, but once she became absorbed in the effort to ameliorate factory conditions, her Marxism was drowned in the day-to-day exigencies of social housekeeping.[87]

Most career women were also either social housekeepers or assistant professionals. Women congregated in professions of social service, public health medicine, legal aid, public-school teaching, and social work, rather than storming the citadel of financial and industrial power. As of 1920 the term businesswoman did not refer to executives and tycoons but to professional secretaries, clerks, and telephone operators. These occupations were wrenched from males but did not lead to the power at the center of the male business world. Social work had also been certified a profession by 1920, declared closed to "vaguely benevolent persons" and open to the college educated, who were specially trained for casework and social research, 62 percent of whom were women. Yet women were less likely than men to advance to high positions in the new profession. In Minneapolis, for example, more than 30 percent of the male social workers held executive positions and only 7 percent of the women. Pioneer career women were advised of the difficulties they would face in the male-dominated professions. "They will have to learn not to ask nor to expect any concessions whatever on the grounds that they are women, nor even sometimes that they are human, since any weakness is likely to be considered feminine." Yet beneath the excitement of careers for women lurked the dangers of being integrated into the man's world at endemically subordinate levels.[88]

The fate of these eager careerists and social activists was more closely intertwined with the remnants of domesticity than they realized. The traditional female home functions interacted in a complicated fashion with the extrafamilial advance of women between 1860 and 1920. On the one hand, the tradition of the mother of civilization could be a source of strength to social reformers. For the mass of the members of reform groups, rather than the leaders, middle-class motherhood could be an incentive to social activism, nourishing their humanistic impulses and leaving them reserves of talent and time for social benevolence. In fact, mothers of small families were more prone to join the ranks of social reformers and suffragists than were childless wives, single women, or more prolific mothers.[89] In addition, the Victorian age granted both dignity and incentives for social motherhood to celibate women like Jane Addams and her coworkers who could not be castigated as Lesbians or dismissed as sexually frustrated. Leaders and followers alike found in the ante-bellum doctrine of female moral influence a stimulus to serve civilization outside the home. This dialectic of motherhood propelled their movement into clubs, settlements and conventions. Single women, like Addams, sacrificed a private home life in order better to serve the entire human family.

Professional women found particular solace in

the doctrine of female purity. Carey Thomas' disgust for sex made it easy for her to discount marriage for herself and for talented Bryn Mawr graduates. Unencumbered by household responsibilities, these women could devote themselves fully to their careers. The female college graduate of the era had a low marriage rate and the married wed later in life and bore fewer children than less educated women. As of 1915, more than 42 percent of the female graduates of eastern colleges were gainfully employed, and almost 70 percent of them had spent some time in the work force. Overall, 75 percent of female professionals were single as of 1920.[90] As long as the veneration of female purity and the suppression of woman's sexual needs endured, the stigma of being unmarried was less likely to detour women from single-minded devotion to their careers. The role of the mother of civilization could be stretched in two different directions, either toward an enlarged maternal mission or to the complete rejection of the unclean state of matrimony.

Some women, in particularly opportune circumstances and possessed of extraordinary stamina, even managed to combine the roles of mother, housewife, and woman of the world. It was relatively easy for middle-class, educated young women to achieve independence and acquire broad experience before marriage. Florence Cross, for example, had her postgraduate education in a settlement house, learning how the other half lives and summoning the courage to live in a house "vulnerable at every point" to intrusion by thieves and vagabonds. After her stint among the other half, she toured Europe with some female friends and resented attempts by chivalrous men to guide and protect her. After her marriage, Florence Cross Kitchelt curtailed her activities to intermittent participation in the women's movement and the campaign for the League of Nations.[91] Florence Kelley, determined not to let marriage slacken the pace of her activism, separated from her husband and struggled to combine motherhood and reform. The task was exhausting: "Me voila! There is only a limited amount of me at best."[92]

Mary Kenney O'Sullivan, on the other hand, had the advantage of a sympathetic husband who even shared the cooking. She wrote that "Jack believed in mental equality between husband and wife. He felt that without it there was a lack of comradship. And if a mother gave all her time to unnecessary cooking and housework, she and the children were the losers." Mrs. O'Sullivan also had the benefit of a course in "the new science of motherhood," which recommended that she abstain from pampering and overprotecting her offspring. Nevertheless, she moved out of the convenient and congenial settlement neighborhood for the benefit of her children. "I owed it to the children to give them a chance to have fresh air and an opportunity for recreation and health." Furthermore, her husband's theories of marital companionship could be demanding as well as supportive. "When night came I was content to stay at home. But Jack wouldn't let me," and the exhausted wife and mother was carried off to a union meeting. Even under the best of circumstances the combination of home roles and public activities placed an excessive burden on the shoulders of the women.[93]

In 1921, when Elizabeth Kemper Adams commended "a growing number" of young couples who were "working out the problem" of a two-career household, she seemed to be compounding the difficulties of women rather than simplifying them. She maintained that a woman couldn't adequately meet "her obligations to her own children without, at the same time, meeting her obligations to other children and young people of the community, in the school, on the playground, in the home, the store, the office and the factory." [94] In the exhilaration over unfolding opportunities for the female sex, some women tried to stretch their energies to superhuman proportions in an effort to encompass both the home and the workplace. The new career woman's only options were to remain single or to assume a bevy of domestic and community responsibilities along with her professional obligations.

If a reasonable balance was to be struck between career goals and home responsibilities, the extravagant propositions of the cult of domesticity had to be drastically modified. In fact, middle-class women had been timidly questioning the cult of motherhood for some time.

As early as 1874 Julia Ward Howe rebutted the assertion that college education impaired female domesticity with the declaration that "the higher the state of civilization and refinement the more nonmarried women there are." She quickly added, however, that single women were well supplied with maternal instincts, which bore fruit in "culture, benevolence, and devotion to human improvement." A few decades later some purity crusaders and feminists hazarded the observation that perhaps not all women were instinctively propelled toward procreation, that maternity itself was not instinctive. Simultaneously, the medical profession expressed its alarm at the frequency with which middle-class women resorted to abortion.[95]

The skepticism regarding the cult of the home mother reached maturity with the publication of Charlotte Perkins Gilman's *Women and Economics* in 1898 and *The Home* in 1903. Gilman directly challenged the assumption that women were natural child-rearers. "Who but mothers," she asked, "raised our huge and growing crop of idiots, imbeciles and cripples and defectives, and degenerates, as well as the vast number of slow minded, prejudiced, and ordinary people who clog the wheels of progress." Gilman shattered the icon of domesticity, declaring that it hindered progress "by keeping woman a social idiot, by keeping the modern child under the tutelage of the primeval mother, by keeping the social conscience of the man crippled and stultified in the clinging grip of the domestic conscience of the woman." In *Women and Economics* Gilman contended that the home was an archaic vestige of preindustrial society and proposed that its essential functions be mechanized, collectivized, or surrendered to other institutions. Still Gilman couldn't entirely free herself from the seductive aspects of the maternal stereotype of woman. As late as 1911 she wrote, "The mother instinct throughout nature is one of unmixed devotion of love and service and defense, with no self interest." [96]

By this time, however, such effusive rhetoric rang a bit hollow, and the maternal image had lost its functional imperative. Gilman made note of only one field of endeavor on which the nurturers of mankind would not excel: Giving birth satisfied woman's creative urge, diminishing the energy that drove men to excellence in the plastic arts. Nonetheless, she added that after a generation had been reared without regard to sexual differences women might also conquer this last sphere. Early in the twentieth century educators began to consider socializing women for many roles other than motherhood. Mary Beard nonchalantly asked: "Why should girls not be taught the principles of machinery? Such knowledge would be useful to them in energizing as in enervating occupations. It is only a matter of getting used to the idea . . . Women swing golf clubs, hockey sticks and tennis rackets. Why shouldn't girls swing hammers?" [97] It is obvious from Beard's analogy that young women already had been introduced into activities inappropriate to the passive, fragile mother of the nineteenth century. The *Ladies' Home Journal* had been presenting its readers with models of active and athletic women for two decades. In the 1890s the *Journal* recommended a panoply of "Out-door Sports for Girls," bicycling, gymnastics, badminton, tennis, golf. The fashion pages sketched apparel for the active woman: divided skirts, sports frocks, looser corsets, and lightweight girdles. By the turn of the century the cracks in the old idol of womanhood had penetrated beyond the heroic levels represented by Jane Addams and Carey Thomas into the center of popular culture. [98]

In the 1910s the *Journal* saw fit to print a Cornell student's report on "How Can a Girl Work Her Way Through College" and a long series on two young women touring Europe alone. The *Ladies' Home Journal* endorsed an interval of independence before marriage. The editors were more ambivalent about a career in the work force. As early as 1890 they wrote of "The Aspiring Girl of To-day." "She is bright and ambitious. She looks out at the workers in the world and thinks that if she were among them she would make a great success." While the *Journal* writers did not want to "say one word to discourage young women intent on pursuing such a course," they asked the reader to consider the old-fashioned ways: "May not the life work for you be in the home?" Thereafter the *Journal's* policy toward working women fluctuated with the state of the national economy. The editors lost their qualms about working outside the home during World War I, for example. They boldly proclaimed: "Thousands of women are wanted practically at Men's Pay," and praised "Women Who Have Blazed New Trails" in law, investment, and construction.[99]

Before 1920 advertisers in the *Journal* were not particularly attentive to feminine manners. Car companies posed women behind the wheel of their own automobiles, and gun manufacturers pictured armed women capturing burglars. From the 1890s on these images of plucky, self-sufficient women competed in the *Journal's* pages with maternal symbols of an earlier era, and by 1920 it seemed clear that the newer image would triumph.

At the same time, traces of a transformation in the domestic role of woman were left in the pages of the *Ladies' Home Journal*. In the December issue of 1899, *Journal* readers found an article entitled "Let the Children Live Their Own Lives," in which mothers were advised against watching their children too closely and smothering their individuality. In the next issue one article asserted that a child "must be taught independence early," and another recommended that fathers play a larger role in the rearing of children. At the turn of the century, in short, the predominant American magazine suggested that modern motherhood was no longer an obsessive and exclusive woman's role. As late as March, 1910, the "Mother's Guide" in the *Ladies' Home Journal* reiterated that it was a sacred obligation of womanhood to breast-feed her infant. Yet on the very same page Nestlé's food was advertised as "The only substitute for Mother's Milk." Other advertisements heralded a transformation in the role of the housewife. Van Camp's Soup, for example, detailed "How a Million Housewives Have Created a Cooperative Kitchen." An increasing number of manufacturers of food products and home appliances presented themselves as the housewife's liberators, freeing women from the bondage of the home. The home role was at least slightly frayed by the turn of the century, exposing a few narrow openings through which women could escape from the strictures of nineteenth-century stereotypes.

Many of these new opportunities represented hard-fought gains won by women themselves in the lonely campaigns of social reform and professional schools. These daring women were often propelled into battle by the dialectic of motherhood, in search of expanded outlets for nurturance, surrogate homes, and foster children. Other women of the middle class seized upon the antithesis of true womanhood, rejecting domesticity entirely for a career defined in the most spartan masculine terms. Simultaneously, the social alignment of home and the marketplace was slowly changing and leaving its imprint on popular culture in the form of more various images of women, invitations to spend at least some time in the work force, and promises of mechanized households. Industrial society seemed to be outgrowing the need for mothers of civilization, causing the contrast between home and work, masculinity and femininity, to lose the stark definition characteristic of the nineteenth century. As this polarization between male and female diminished, the fundamental axis of the system of social distribution by sex became less obvious. Career women and social housekeepers did not take direct aim at the overall sexual division of labor, neither the remaining domestic responsibilities of wives and mothers nor the deep-seated advantages of husbands and fathers in the world of work.

In addition, the vanguard of middle-class women was ill-prepared to penetrate the complications of womanhood among the working class; the reformers were too enamored of the role of ameliorating conflict between the rich and the poor, and professional women were too absorbed with career advancement to transcend class barriers and in the process grapple with the social and economic structure that underplays sex roles. In the end, these self-assertive women, however heroic as individuals, were not in a position to mount a collective, ideological assault on sexual inequality.

One might expect that the larger parameters of sexual inequality would be perceived by critics of the capitalist industrial system. Yet while socialism flourished, in the early twentieth century, feminist theory did not blossom with it. The American Socialist Party admitted women, and labor organizers like Elizabeth Gurley Flynn and Mother Jones were radical heroines; but on the whole, females were very sparsely represented in policy-making bodies. Female membership in the Socialist Party never exceeded 15 percent and most of these women were shunted aside into auxiliary groups where they held fund-raising bazaars and organized socialist sabbath schools. Occasionally the party held a "Woman's Night," characterized by condescending political education for the weaker sex. Only when the suffrage movement threatened to entice females away from the movement, and pit the wives of socialists against their husbands, did the Socialist Party grant women a larger organizational role. Yet this concession was halfhearted and short-lived. By 1920 female membership had declined to around 10 percent.[100]

This token representation of women in the socialist movement did not encourage a radical analysis of sexual inequality. At its founding meeting the Socialist Party merely resolved to favor "equal civil and political rights for men and women." Socialist attitudes toward the social role of woman at times tended to be reactionary. In his preface to August Bebel's *Women and Socialism,* Daniel De Leon argued that socialism would purify monogamous marriage. He did not question woman's role in that institution. "Women—the world's mothers, wives, sisters, daughters, long sinned against through unnumbered generations, are about to be atoned to." [101] When Margaret Sanger raised the issue of sexual hygiene and contraception among socialists, she received a cool reception from her comrades, especially those who held tenaciously to nineteenth-century standards of female purity. One male socialist accused Sanger of presenting women as mere "animal beings" and feared subversion of "mother love and the exquisite loyalty of the eternal female." [102] Thus feminism and socialism were never united. No plan of action, nor even radical perspective, regarding the complicated connections between class society, sexual inequality, and the institution of the family emerged in America before 1920.

As a consequence, the principles and programs of the women's movement were clearly limited. Its fate remained tied to the dialectic of motherhood, which produced social housekeepers, a network of female organizations, a new beleaguered career women—and then stopped short of equality. It has often been noted that the American women's movement, from 1848 to 1920, gained momentum by manipulating the cult of pure motherhood. In the suffrage movement, the mothers of civilization claimed the right to exercise their purifying influence in the voting booth. The pall of corruption that hung over political machines and city bosses made this demand all the more urgent. The doctrine of female moral superiority occasionally took on the ugly garb of racism and xenophobia. Some pure white women claimed legitimacy as voters in contrast to the bestial negroes and ignorant immigrants,—"ex-slaves, illiterate and semi-barbarous" and the "Riff-Raff of Europe." [103]

The use of these arguments from the tenets of pure motherhood was not, however, simply an example of naïve sentimentality and conservatism. The organized women of the suffrage era were wise to the ways of American politics. These arguments were part of an arsenal of expedient devices suffragists used to achieve their goal. The pragmatic resourcefulness of the suffrage movement was epitomized by the National American Woman's Suffrage Association's actions during World War I. When war became imminent, Carrie Chapman Catt and her fellow leaders carefully withdrew from women's peace organizations and dispensed with rhetoric about the innate pacifism of their sex. By supporting the war effort, the NAWSA courted public opinion, President Wilson, and Congress, simultaneously installing themselves in federal offices and incurring political debts that could be repaid with the endorsement of the Nineteenth Amendment. The suffragists were not blushing Victorians but seasoned politicians who had learned how to beat the male at his own game.

The special experience of organized women also helps to explain the narrow focus of the women's movement on civil and political rights. The members of the Sanitary Commission acquired this preoccupation in the 1860s. One of the commission's leaders, Mary Livermore, was utterly shocked when a builder would not accept her check for the construction of a hospital. "Here was a revelation. We two women were able to enlist the whole Northwest in a great philanthropic money-making enterprise in the teeth of great opposition, and had the executive ability to carry it forward to a successful termination. We had money of our own in hand, twice as much as was necessary to pay the builder. But by the laws of the State in which we lived our individual names were not worth the paper they were written on." Such practical affronts to the enterprising women of the nineteenth century were not easily forgotten. Mary Livermore "registered a vow when the war was over I would take up a new work—the work of making law and justice synonymous for women." [104] By 1890 state legislatures had removed the most egregious legal bars to women's property rights, but disenfranchisement remained as a glaring insult and obstacle to female equality. The denial of the vote to women was particulary offensive to women in the progressive movement, whose reform efforts inevitably took them before city councils, state legislatures, and the U.S. Congress. It was demeaning as well as inconvenient to be rebuffed time and time again by male public officials whom the energetic reformers had no role in electing. Mary Beard put it this way: "Women who have experienced these political reverses have often become ardent suffragists because they realized that the direct way to work for sanitary municipal housekeeping is through elected officials and having been unable to influence the votes of men they have acquired the desire and determination to cast the ballots themselves." [105] The vote was not simply a panacea for sexual inequality. To the organized reformers, it constituted an immediate and practical instrument of reform, another step toward efficient participation in the man's world. By focusing on and winning equal suffrage, the women's movement succeeded in gaining the support of a wide spectrum of the population. The feminist tactics were typical of the era; electoral politics was the recourse of both Progressives and Socialists; limited and specific objectives characterized Populists and labor unions as well.

The ratification of the Nineteenth Amendment not

only testified to women's adroitness in manipulating the American political system, it finally raised the second sex to the full rights of citizenship in the United States. Official admission to the American political system, however, had some short-term liabilities. As outsiders, working from the sidelines of the system, women acquired acute social and political perceptions and built their own organizations and institutions to implement them into effective action. In their truly heroic struggles to break free of nineteenth-century constrictions, women released abounding energies and created an enlarged sphere all their own, where women could plan, organize, and lead without the interference of men. With the passage of the Nineteenth Amendment, women were invited to enter a political universe where the rules were made and the positions of power were held by the opposite sex. In 1920 women had to begin another steep upward climb, now from within the man's world.

The removal of the last blatant constitutional obstacles to the equality of the sexes could also be deceptive and demoralizing. After 1920 the practical inferiority of women could be attributed to her own failures of nerve, stamina, and capability, rather than legal fetters. Women entered politics at a very real and often obscured disadvantage, weighed down by the burdens of culture, the family, and history. So encumbered, but judged by the standards of male performance, women were prey to a new mode of inequality. The female sex seemed destined for only secondary posts in politics, the professions, and the labor force. Yet such difficulties would not seem insurmountable to the women who between 1890 and 1920 had organized millions, created a whole new social machinery, shut down industries, and stormed the constitution. The new struggle would begin at a most auspicious point in the history of American women.

**THE SEXY
SALESLADY:**

PSYCHOLOGY AND
CONSUMPTION IN THE
TWENTIETH CENTURY

Jane Addams entitled her biography for the years between 1909 and 1929 *The Second Twenty Years at Hull House.* Yet the later chapters in the pioneer reformer's career took her far afield of that enlarged home in the slums into national and international politics and a variety of benevolent projects, all pursued with the hard-nosed efficiency of a seasoned social activist. Forty years' immersion in the sordid conditions of industrial America had purged the sentimental ethics with which her career of social housekeeping had begun. Jane Addams still retained the conviction, however, that the female sex had a distinctive and segregated role in public life. In 1930 she issued a caveat against the political "masculinization" of women, that tendency to "dovetail into the political themes of men [rather] than to release the innate concerns of women, which might be equivalent to a revolutionary force." Truly feminine political values, for example, might have been an effective counterforce to World War I, as women's social conscience "rebelled against the destruction of their own children, the waste of life they had nurtured." At this point Addams' reiteration of the doctrine of social motherhood was clearly defensive and became more so as she confronted the "contrast in a Post-War Generation." She observed remorsefully that the uninhibited young women of the 1920s were too concerned with personal freedom and self-development to devote themselves to the cause of social freedom and justice for all Americans.[1]

Other social reformers of Addams' generation echoed her anxiety, admitting to a "surging despair" in the 1920s, which was well-founded in fact. Ironically, woman's official admission into the political arena seemed to retard rather than enhance the social power of women. Acting without benefit of the vote, the women's organizations of the pre-suffrage era had pressured state legislatures and the U.S. Congress into enacting literally hundreds of child labor, woman's equity, and social hygiene laws. Thereafter the women's lobby consolidated into the Joint Congressional Union and kept up the momentum of female social influence, bringing some of the most cherished projects of female reform to legislative fruition immediately after suffrage was granted. By 1925, however, this flood of social legislation had been stilled to a murmur. Even the operations of the Women's Bureau were curtailed without concerted feminine protest. Election studies revealed that women did not vote in a block, in greater numbers, or in opposition to their husbands.[2] The Republican and Democratic parties, which had scurried to recruit women members after the passage of the Nineteenth Amendment, and had written the resolutions of the League of Women Voters into their platforms in 1920, soon began to ignore women with impunity.

The organized phalanx of female reformers was no longer a force to be reckoned with. When the National American Woman's Suffrage Association reconstituted itself as the League of Women Voters its membership dropped to one-tenth of its original size. Some organizations, like the Women's Trade Union League and the Consumers League, slowly disintegrated. Others, such as the General Federation of Women's Clubs, retrenched into privatized and conservative positions. In the late '20s the GFWC mixed reformist policy with such resolutions as the recommendation that women should seek a physician's advice before going on a diet and such reactionary concerns as the rooting out of communists in American schools. The colleges of the '20s no longer sent large numbers of young women either into settlement houses or reform organizations. No one rose from the new generation to accept the mantle of Jane Addams. The only remote competitors for her title were Frances Perkins, New Deal Secretary of Labor, and Mrs. Eleanor Roosevelt, both residents of settlement houses in the waning days of social housekeeping. The typical woman politician subsequent to the 1920s did "dovetail with the schemes of men," often losing status and autonomy in the process. In the 1936 electoral campaign, for example, the most energetic woman in the Democratic Party, Mary Dewson, devoted herself to organizing sixty thousand female precinct workers for F.D.R. The fate of women blessed with the vote was to be integrated at a secondary level into the male-dominated political system. Postwar reaction, vicious red-baiting, and the obstinacy of male power combined to check the advancement of the second sex.[3]

Jane Addams added a subtler factor to the explanation of the disintegration of the women's movement. It was, she surmised, "associated in some way with the breaking down of sex taboos and with the establishment of new standards of marriage." The young, educated women of the '20s seemed to Addams to be preoccupied with sexual gratification and self-fulfillment through marriage, an observation that was confirmed by attitude surveys of college women, 90 percent of whom aspired to the role of wife above all else. Jane Addams found this emphasis on the heterosexual relationship both alarming and perplexing. She surmised that "Perhaps this astounding emphasis upon sex was less comprehensible because of the unique element in the social situation during the last half century regarding the role played by the educated unmarried woman." The centrality of sex and marriage in the new woman's consciousness also boded ill for women's advancement in the professions. Emily Greene Balch, whose last twenty years had been spent as chairman of the economics department at Wellesley, felt that the new mores would undermine single-minded devotion to careers. While Balch welcomed relief from the sexual frustration suffered by Victorian women, she could not help but feel a bit resentful of the connotations of neurosis now visited upon the spinster. She feared that the celebration of sexual fulfillment might go too far. Balch, like Addams, balked at "the reinterpretation of life, in novels, plays and psychological treatises that represent sex as practically the whole center of life." [4]

By the mid '20s, celibate careerism and social motherhood were clearly out of fashion, eclipsed by the antithetical image of the flapper. The slim figure of the new woman seemed designed for play and pleasure, energetic self-expression rather than altruistic service to mankind. The exposure of the flapper's legs rose to the knees, betokening a disdain for the purity that had once been used to justify both social action and spinsterhood. The new woman entered into the sporting world with her male chums, smoking, drinking, dancing lasciviously, and necking openly. It was old-fashioned to gather with one's own sex and pledge mutual dedication to solace the poor children of slums and factories. The flapper symbolized a solipsistic, hedonistic, and privatized femininity, a gay abandonment of social housekeeping, women's organizations, and dogged professionalism.

The flapper was only a symbol, and a very ephemeral one at that. The *Ladies' Home Journal* proclaimed the "Flapper Is Dead" as early as 1920. The celebrations of the roaring '20s (which more properly spanned the mid-teens to the late 1920s) loomed larger in the public imagination than in the everyday life of the average American. This symbol, however, effectively erased the nineteenth-century ideal of the mother of civilization. The icon of the flapper was also a more fitting representation of woman's place in twentieth-century America than the traditional portrait of Jane Addams, with immigrant children clustered around her ample form. The social mother of the period 1890 to 1920 had helped to create her own obsolescence. The female social activist was central to the construction of institutions and professions —government bureaus, urban services, organized philanthropies, and social work—which usurped and rationalized the process of social housekeeping. Simultaneously, the flight of second generation immigrants into more comfortable homes and regulated factories, followed by the federal restriction of immigration in the 1920s, depleted the social mother's supply of adoptive children. The highly specialized and bureaucratized new century had less use for creative humanitarians than for self-absorbed service workers, whom it rewarded with a paycheck. In short, flappers were preferable to social mothers.

The cherished nineteenth-century ideal of feminine purity had also outlived its usefulness. For one thing, improved technology of contraception eliminated the female role of curtailing the birth rate by enforcing sexual abstinence. The social-psychological function of the chaste female—internal control of the economic lust and antisocial tendencies of the middle-class male—was also outmoded. By the twentieth century the advantages of middle-class upbringing and career education could secure young men a predictable job and a post so highly routinized that individual passion had little destructive potential. Finally, sexual repression, operating as deference to the wishes of pure wives, had lost its economic usefulness by the 1920s. Saving semen was as inessential as hoarding pennies in banks when the intensive capital accumulation of industrialization was completed and corporate financing methods became more sophisticated.

In fact, the middle-class American was asked to play a role in the advanced stage of capitalism basically antithetical to either sexual or economic frugality. Twentieth-century industry shifted from producing iron for railroads to steel for cars, from power for factories to electricity for homes. Those industrial products were designed not to build a public transportation network or to mechanize factories but to be purchased by private individuals. This consuming, rather than saving, habit was sufficiently far-advanced by 1929 that there were more than 25 million automobile registrations in the United States and almost 70 percent of American homes were equipped with electricity to power a panoply of home appliances. American economic expansion depended on the private purchase of a growing variety of nondurable goods as well—apparel, food products, and articles of personal hygiene. By 1920 the majority of American homemakers purchased bread manufactured by large baking companies and bought ready-made clothing from mail order houses or department stores. The appropriate economic practice had become spending rather than thrift by the turn of the century, and in the '20s frugality gave way to a devil-may-care quest for material goods. The Chamber of Commerce in one Indiana town made the message patently clear: "The first responsibility of an American to his country is no longer that of a citizen, but of a consumer. Consumption is a necessity." [5]

American businessmen rushed to inform the public through the medium of advertising of the virtues of immediate material gratification. Advertising first became the colleague of big business late in the 1880s when producers used the press and magazines to announce the availability of certain goods to a nationwide audience. These early advertisements were quite matter-of-fact, simply acquainting the public with national brand names and with the functional superiority of a particular product. For example, a car manufacturer early in the twentieth century prosaically promised that "The Oldsmobile Goes." The commonsense advertisements of the Fair Soap Company even resorted to feminism, picturing Elizabeth Cady Stanton extolling the virtue of their pure, simple cleansing product, unadulterated by perfume. By the 1920s, however, businessmen had concluded that the advance of the consuming sector of the economy demanded a more extravagant advertising campaign. One executive described the function of advertising as the cultivation of a healthy "dissatisfaction with what they now have in favor of something better. The old factors of wear and tear can no longer be depended upon to create a demand. They are too slow." [6]

In the '20s, then, advertising agencies set out to create demand for consumer goods, to instill a greater and greater appetite for things. Advertising itself became a major industry, accounting for 2 to 4 percent of the national income up through the 1950s. American advertising business, which amounted to $95,000,000 in 1890, reached $1,000,000,000 annually in 1920 and by 1950 was a $6,000,000,000 enterprise. Advertising had become the handmaiden of the consumer economy, "almost the only force at work against Puritanism in consumption." [7] Clearly the sexy flapper was a more commodious emblem of the sales mania than the pure mother. The women's organizations that survived the '20s were integrated into the market network as well: The General Federation of Women's Clubs offered its members as subjects for surveys of both sexual behavior and patterns of domestic consumption. [8] Concurrently, the Consumers League, the agency through which social housekeepers like Florence Kelley had attempted to establish a self-directed and socially responsible role for women as a phalanx of purchasers, failed to attract a second generation of enthusiasts and became moribund. These events hailed the arrival of the sexy saleslady, entailing a provocative new model of femininity and symbolizing new patterns of behavior in both private relations and the public marketplace. It was to be an era in which women would be divided from one another and preyed upon by new mentors, professional psychoanalysts as well as popular advertisers, who continually updated the female image and completed some major revisions in the 1940s. Still change was built into the image of the ever-new sexy saleslady, the hallmark of at least a half century of American womanhood. This image and its most immediate behavioral manifestations—sexual practices and commodity consumption—are the theme of this chapter.

In the ebullient youth of the sexy saleslady, the 1920s, the veneration of motherhood itself was temporarily suspended, and feminists disentangled themselves from their former constrictions. Contributions to a volume entitled *Woman's Coming of Age* cast many aspersions on the cult of motherhood: "an available refuge only to the ignorant and the stubborn"; "like the glory that surrounds soldiers—pomp and noise made to distract the attention of the warriors from the agony they are called to endure." Freed of maternal inhibitions, Suzanne La Follette could place the feminist argument on a firmer foundation: "It is for the sake of humanity and not for the sake of children that women ought to have equal status with men. That children will gain enormously by the change is true; but this is beside the issue, which is justice." As the birth rate plummeted again in the 1920s, it seemed that women were prepared to mount a direct attack on sexual inequality. The new feminists embraced the flapper, one of them going so far as to prognosticate disaster "if she consents for so long a period as a single year to cover her knees." [9]

The older generation of feminists was suspicious of pinning women's equality to any part of her anatomy—breasts, wombs, *or* knees. Charlotte Perkins Gilman looked askance at the flappers, "as much the slaves of fashion as before, lifting their skirts, baring their backs, exhibiting their legs, powdering their noses, behaving as foolish as ever if not more so." Although Gilman endorsed sexual liberation, she interpreted this predilection to display female anatomy as a "backlash of primitive femininity." [10] Any image that focuses on specifically female biological attributes and distracts attention from the common humanity of men and women can be a very dangerous cultural instrument. The overt exhibition of the female body as a sexual attraction to men in the '20s proved to be particularly detrimental to sexual equality.

The destructiveness unleashed by the heightened consciousness of sex appeal is illustrated in its extremity by the biography of Mabel Dodge Luhan. Growing up in Buffalo, New York, at the turn of the century, young Mabel Ganson adopted the Victorian standard and vowed "never to concede my whole self to any man until I was married." After her marriage Mabel Dodge experienced the "pleasure of the flesh, but usually there had been a certain hidden, forbidden something in my feeling about it." She finally learned of the "possibilities of the body for 'sex expression'" in conversations with Margaret Sanger and analysis with Carl Jung. These sex theorists of the twentieth century legitimized and exacerbated Mabel Dodge's conception of herself as a pivot of sexual attraction. She unblushingly described herself in her *Intimate Memoirs* as a sex object: "sunk in furs, breathing of drooping violets, noting the glow I exhaled, noting the magnetism I exhaled like a perfume, something tangible like the musk of an animal, and irresistibly attractive to at least three of the men in my neighborhood." [11]

Once Mabel Dodge became intimately involved

with a man, her sex consciousness degenerated into self-destructiveness. Her celebrated affair with the revolutionary journalist John Reed culminated in the feeling that "nothing counted for me but Reed . . . to be close to him, and empty myself over and over, flesh against flesh." When a second love affair ended, she was utterly prostrate, "sinking down to the old depressed nothingness, which was all I was without a man. Be he ever so unsuitable a man, a man was what gave me identity I thought." Mabel Dodge was by no means as self-effacing as she pretended. She harbored a nearly insatiable craving for power, but it was directed toward personal hegemony over other persons and was exercised through sexual relationships with men and women. Amid all her love affairs Mabel Dodge had little time for social causes. She quickly shunned the invitation to become involved in the United States Industrial Commission, a post that social housekeepers would have rejoiced in obtaining. "I heartily declined to be put to the test, possibly more because I was not really imaginatively interested in the industrial crises, than because I was afraid to tackle it." Mabel Dodge craved neither social responsibility nor a career: "I felt I was made for love, not for art, not for the life of the worldly world, but for the fire of love in the body, for the great furnace of love in the flesh . . ." [12]

Mabel Dodge was sinking into this quicksand of sexual obsessions at the very time that the suffragists were mounting their successful assault on the disenfranchisement of women. Her precocious immersion in the cult of sexuality contradicted the spirit of the women's movement in every way. She delighted in intimacy with men rather than in cooperation with women; she blossomed in the privacy of the boudoir rather than in the public political arena. Rather than working and sacrificing for social or political goals, she pursued every opportunity for "experience," for immediate personal pleasure. By withdrawing from the woman's crusade to achieve self-fulfillment, furthermore, Mabel Dodge Luhan squandered the opportunity to achieve equality with men in the "worldly world" of economics, society, politics, and culture. She came perilously close to forfeiting her personal identity as well. In retreating into a private female world under the banner of sexual freedom Mabel Dodge blazed a trail that would soon open up to many women of the twentieth century and close once and for all the career of the social mother.

Already in the first decade of the twentieth century the *Ladies' Home Journal* had expressed concern about suggestive dance steps and the glamour associated with the chorus girl. By the mid-teens, the *Journal* unabashedly displayed calves, arms, and shoulders, and bobbed hair. Shortly thereafter American magazines began to voice editorial approval of relaxed sexual mores. By 1918, 23 percent of the intellectual periodicals endorsed the psychological doctrine that sexual release was healthy for both sexes. By 1928, 40 percent of the mass magazines concurred.[13] The '20s also saw the proliferation of pulp magazines like *True Story,* with a circulation of two million. Although pulp literature adhered to a Puritanical code of sex ethics, it by no means shied away from titillating themes and such titles as "The Primitive Love," "She Wanted a Casanova Husband," "What I Told My Daughter the Night Before Her Marriage."[14] Wide segments of the female reading audience had been alerted to at least the fashion of a more open sexuality by the '20s.

By 1920, furthermore, the magazine layout resembled the modern periodical, complete with glossy photographs in which the images of females took on a realistic and sensual aura. This sexual authenticity was further advanced by the development of the cinema, which brought the sexy image of woman to a larger audience than ever before. Even the greenest immigrant girl could decipher the message on the silent screen. Estimates of the size of the weekly film audience ranged from sixty to one hundred million up through the 1940s. Even in the depths of the Depression, according to a study by the Connecticut Consumers League, young working women whose wages hardly reached the subsistence level attended the movies regularly, 66 percent of them once a week or more.[15] The immediacy of sex in the movies was revealed to one sociologist by a waitress's reference to Rudolph Valentino as her "boy chum." [16] The same women aped the hairstyles, apparel, and gestures of screen heroines. The silver screen demonstrated the new priority of twentieth-century women: attracting the male through sexual allure, and very few women could escape exposure to this message.

The American movie industry was at times ambivalent about the treatment of sexual topics. Certainly its most accomplished director, D. W. Griffith, was steeped in nineteenth-century prudery. Yet many of the sweet roles in which he cast Lillian Gish betrayed the fragility of her pure, delicate ways and the vulnerability of the ethic of chastity. For example, in the 1919 production *True-Heart Susie,* Gish's values were in deadly combat with the mores of the "fast crowd." In fact, Susie lost her childhood sweetheart to the audacious Bettina, with her painted face, short skirts, and provocative walk. Only after Bettina exposed her vile cooking, discarded her make-up, courted marital infidelity, and then died of pneumonia in retribution for her sins, did True-Heart Susie win back the hero.

From the very first, innocents like Lillian Gish and Mary Pickford were rivaled at the box office by the likes of Theda Bara, whose gluttonous sexuality demonstrated the etymology of the term "vamp," and Clara Bow, whose packaged sex appeal labeled her "the 'it' girl." The odds against the nineteenth-century heroine surviving through the '20s were raised in 1919 with the release of Cecil B. De Mille's *Male and Female*. De Mille dared to show Gloria Swanson bathing and revealed her thighs and surging breasts in the shipwreck sequence. All these films employed that curious Hollywood representation of lust, the clinch. The box-office success of *Male and Female* led to relentless replication of the sexy formula for moviemaking, under such titles as *Married Flirts, Sinners in Hell, The Price She Paid, Queen of Sin*. Although the operations of the Legion of Decency and the Production Code in the '30s inhibited explicit sex on the screen, female characters continued to be presented as sex symbols and as embodiments of the standard of sexual attractiveness by which women in the audience could measure their own worth. The model of the new femininity was not Jane Addams but the latest Hollywood discovery, the star of the moment.

The official imprimatur for this image came from the new compartment of human knowledge called psychology, whose first pronouncements regarding women had some liberating implications. The first invitations to sexual gratification were issued to women at the turn of the century by America's pioneer psychologist G. Stanley Hall and his disciples at Clark University, who began to speak of "sexual fulfillment" in the 1890s. Much like Mabel Dodge, Hall had been maimed by the sexual repression of a nineteenth-century home and hesitantly began to suggest some reforms to his colleagues in the psychological profession. Simultaneously, Emma Goldman, embittered by the sexual frustrations of her Russian Jewish upbringing, became acquainted with the teachings of Sigmund Freud and took to touring America and lecturing on the merits of free love. Pioneer writers on female sexuality such as Havelock Ellis championed the "love-rights" of women, who according to his clinical observations suffered immensely from sexual frustration. In fact, in his highly select study, 55 percent of the women claimed to have strong sexual desire and nary an orgasm. Nearly one-fourth of his subjects accused their husbands of being "undersexed." Ellis urged women to assert their rights to sexual satisfaction and described a variety of sexual techniques whereby they might be fulfilled.[17] Sigmund Freud himself was sensitive to the sexual frustrations of Victorian women. He wrote plaintively to an American psychologist in 1909: "What would you have us do when a woman complains about her thwarted life, when with youth gone she notices that she has been deprived of the joy of loving for merely conventional reasons?" Freud pledged himself to help change "other social factors so that men and women shall no longer be forced into hopeless situations."[18]

Although Freud would subsequently lay the

groundwork for yet another set of hopeless conventions, the mere announcement of the legitimacy of female sexual needs did much to relieve the frustrations of women. Robert Latou Dickinson, whose gynecological practice spanned forty years, recalled that prior to the '20s his patients had been trained to repress their sexual desires by mothers who said that "No good woman ever has pleasure, passion is for the vile" or "If you love enough you can stand it." Another woman reported to Dickinson that it was only after six years of marriage, and then by masturbating, that she learned that women could reach sexual climax. By the '20s, young women in Dickinson's practice, largely upper-class college graduates, had been informed that sex was wholesome, pleasurable, and essential for health. G. Stanley Hall went so far as to say that it was "the open sesame to the deepest mysteries of life, death, religion and love." [19]

A woman's sexual enjoyment was further enhanced by the availability in the '20s and '30s of more reliable methods of birth control, among them the condom, a reasonably accurate rhythm method, and the diaphragm. Prior to these innovations, Dickinson's patients told hair-raising tales of contraceptive failure. One woman's childbearing history went like this: "The first was intended; the second was withdrawal; the third was a Lysol douche." A mother of two admitted she had eight abortions following nine failures of the douche method of birth control.[20] By the '20s, 70 to 80 percent of the upper- and upper-middle-class women surveyed used some more or less reliable means of birth control. By the 1930s approximately one-third of the lower-class women used some method of birth control, now available in

Planned Parenthood Clinics and part of the curriculum of most American medical schools. By the 1950s, rich, poor, black, and white women were regularly employing relatively reliable methods of birth control. Contraception was by no means foolproof, but it was effective enough to remove much of woman's anxiety from the act of sexual intercourse.[21]

Some writers of the 1920s were so exuberant about the awakening possibilities for sexual pleasure that in its pursuit they trampled on nearly every marital and sexual convention. V. T. Calverton concluded that marriage was a bankrupt institution; unwed mothers were courageous and proper; monogamy and the bourgeois home were obsolete.[22] Calverton's contribution to *Woman's Coming of Age* was entitled "Are Women Monogamous?" and his answer was negative. Calverton and several other writers also dismissed romantic love as an ephemeral by-product of sexual sublimation. Meanwhile, the father of American behavorism, John B. Watson, predicted with scientific assurance that monogamy would disappear in fifty years; [23] Suzanne La Follette, speaking as a feminist, did not go quite that far but did put marriage in perspective. She saw it not as a dictate of God and nature but as a deep-rooted habit that was conducive to social order and the retention of private property.[24] At any rate, many alternatives to marriage as an outlet for sexual desire were posed in the '20s: open promiscuity, divorce and remarriage, or serial monogamy, and Judge Ben Lindsay's suggestion of companionate, or trial, marriage. Even homosexual relationships were proper to some writers. Katherine B. Davis, in her survey of female sex practices, revealed a high incidence of homosexuality (one-fourth of the twelve hundred college women she questioned) without great alarm.[25] Lesbianism became a quasi-legitimate literary theme in Radclyffe Hall's *The Well of Loneliness*.

The proponents of sexual freedom in the '20s observed and applauded the sense of independence that new ethics could engender in young women. Judge Ben Lindsay in *The Revolt of Modern Youth* quoted with approval the marital philosophy of the young working woman engaging in permarital sex. "He's crazy about me. But I'm not sure I want to marry him. I haven't any too much confidence in Bill's capacity. Why, I'm earning more than he is right now." [26] The sociologist Robert Park took note of a "new type of woman evolving, a woman sophisticated, self-reliant, competent—a woman of the world." In the lives of working women, he maintained, "marriage plays a considerably less important part than it has in the past and still plays in the lives of most women who have not achieved economic independence." [27] Economic independence for these avant-garde women could also nurture sexual freedom. For example, a saleslady, who was interviewed by the sociologist Frances Donovan in one of her studies of female employment, considered a series of short affairs more convenient than marriage as a means of sexual release for the working woman.[28] V. T. Calverton judged from his observation of the mores of the roaring '20s that women had become the more liberated sex. "Men are more sentimental than women. When a woman grows up, she grows up. And she comes up simply and says to the man,—'If you feel like coming up today and spending the night, come. But tomorrow don't bother me with your heartaches. Out, don't interfere with my useful work.' " [29] The new sex mores, combined with contraceptive progress, laid open the possibility, at least, of a more satisfied, self-sufficient, and worldly-wise womanhood.

The breakdown of reticence about sex did result in a proliferation of surveys on sexual practice, which suggested that one significant upsurge in the sexual activity of women occurred around 1920. In G. I. Hamilton's sample of middle- and upper-class women, for example, 24 percent of those born before 1891 had sexual experience outside of marriage, while 61 percent of the women born after that year reported illicit sexual behavior.[30] Kinsey's massive study of nearly eight thousand subjects also indicated that the generation of women whose sexual experience began around 1920 engaged in sexual intercourse outside of marriage at about double the rate of their mothers. In the next three decades the incidence of illicit sex remained practically stable for the college-educated population subjected to the relentless barrage of sociological questionnaires. Another method of gauging the sexual practice of the population at large, and encompassing more than the upper classes, is a compilation of statistics on illegitimate births, which continued to rise in the twentieth century, most sharply after 1940. This apparent increase in the incidence of extramarital intercourse, however, does not mean that the sheer quantity of woman's sexual experience was increasing. In fact the majority of twentieth-century women followed the sexual routine of the 1890s, engaging in intercourse approximately twice weekly, a frequency governed by the predilections of their husbands.[31]

These compilations of statistics, furthermore, do

not measure the quality of a woman's sex life. Kinsey's exhaustive survey did suggest that the sexual practices of the '20s were more sophisticated than in previous decades. Prior to the '20s sex was described by Dickinson's patients as merely brief intromission without foreplay and in the standard man-on-top woman-underneath position. Understandably, few women achieved orgasm in the process. Ninety-four percent of the women born after 1900 and interviewed by Kinsey in the 1930s and '40s had explored positions other than the missionary one and saw their chances of reaching orgasm increased 10 to 15 percent. Still, these relatively minor increases in the variety and quality of woman's heterosexual experience were insufficient to satisfy most women. The majority of subjects confessed that they resorted to masturbation to assure sexual release. Furthermore, the most contented women in his survey were homosexuals, who seldom failed to reach orgasm in their sexual relations.[32]

Clearly, the promises and hopes of sexual gratification made to women by twentieth-century culture had not been fulfilled. In fact, almost as soon as the existence of female sexuality had been acknowledged, physicians and psychologists began to register alarm at the appearance of "a new and alarmingly prevalent female disease," frigidity. According to Dickinson 10 to 50 percent of his patients were affected with the malady, and by the '50s the epidemic had spread to 40 percent of the female population, according to conservative estimates.[33] In 1959 Dr. Marie Robinson exclaimed to her avid readers that "No other public health or social problem of our time even approaches this magnitude." As Marie Robinson bemoaned rampant frigidity, she celebrated the delights of orgasm all the more wildly. The be-all-and-end-all of woman's happiness was described as "A sensation of such beauty and intensity that I can hardly think of it without weeping," or in such similes as "like going over Niagara Falls in a barrel." The women who failed to obtain this ecstasy were described as abnormal, immature, and *masculine*.[34] The awakening of female sexuality had come to this: the construction of a new standard of femininity, a new norm of woman's competence, which it seemed she had considerable difficulty conforming to.

The transformation of female sexuality from simple pleasure into a mechanism of inculcating and measuring femininity was well under way in the '20s, eating away at feminism and sexual liberation simultaneously. By 1920 the *Ladies' Home Journal* had a new rationale for ushering women into homes and nurseries: not only the dictates of biology and "divine purpose" but "sex psychology" as well. The earliest sex theorists set eagerly to work, hoping to rekindle consciousness of sex differences. Havelock Ellis' work *Male and Female,* published in 1894, began with the observation that as contemporary women entered the social and economic spheres once reserved for men, "we are brought face to face with the consideration of those differences which are not artificial and which no equalization of social conditions can entirely remove, the natural character and predisposition which always inevitably influence the sexual allotment of human activities." [35] At the same time, G. Stanley Hall saw fit to recount the distinctive features of female psychology, impelled by the alarming evidence that nearly one-half of all American girls "choose male ideals or would be men." [36]

So inspired, Hall and Ellis began to scrutinize once again the biological differences between the sexes. Ellis set out to measure and compare every bone, sinew, and ligament in the male and female bodies. He concluded that "a man is a man even to his thumbs and a woman is a woman down to her little toes." Ellis' potpourri of statistical trivia provided the foundation on which schemes of mental and behavioral differences between the sexes were built. "While the man's form seems to be instinctively seeking action, the woman's falls naturally into a state of comparative repose, and seems to find satisfaction in an attitude of overthrow." After determining by a haphazard comparison of skeletons of the two sexes that women failed to rise to the completely erect stature of *Homo sapiens,* Ellis concluded that women were designed for the posture of giving birth and were similar to children in their anatomy and character. Naturally placid, formed for procreation, and childlike in temperament, women were made for motherhood. The cult of maternity was wrestled from the clutches of feminists. Ellis felt he had proven that "the realization of the woman's movement in its largest and completest phases is an enlightened motherhood in all that motherhood involves, alike the physical and the psychological." [37] G. Stanley Hall focused on the menstrual cycle and built on it a theory of woman's temperamental periodicity, which was conducive to piety, dependence, and passivity. Hall reached the same anti-feminist conclusions as did Ellis. He regarded his bio-psychology as a justification for the emancipation of women from "the man-aping fashions now just beginning to wane and will no doubt sometime be wrought out." [38]

The anti-feminist implications of the psychology of sex were abundantly clear. After reading *Male and Female,* Alice Beale Parsons felt "all I was sure about was that I was stunned by another one of those Olympian bolts that are hurled at woman every time that she is almost convinced that she is a person like man." As she wrote in 1931, however, Parsons had information to refute Ellis' "Alice-in-Wonderland science." Dr. Helen Thompson and Professor C. L. Thorndike had conducted their own review of the differences between the sexes and concluded that "individual differences within one sex so enormously outweigh the difference between the sexes in these intellectual and semi-intellectual traits that for all practical purposes the sex differences may be discarded." The concept of the statistical normality, the standard male and female as determined by the collection and averaging of data, could not withstand the test of logic and certainly did not justify the segregation of every man and every woman into two different compartments of human personality and endeavor. Sex surveys published in the 1920s further revealed that the sexual appetites of men and women were remarkably similar, differences in anatomy and reproductive functions notwithstanding. By 1931 even Havelock Ellis was somewhat chastened, convinced by simple empirical studies that there need be no distinctly feminine psychology of sex. [39]

Just as these primitive theories were being refuted, however, the path of female psychology took another devious turn. In 1918 H. W. Frink introduced a psychological text with the announcement that "the day has fortunately gone by when the far-reaching investigations associated with the name of Sigmund Freud need be introduced." Frink then proceeded to launch a new attack on feminism: "Upon analysis, this patient's violent warfare against all forms of subordination of women was revealed to be very largely a compensation for a strong but imperfectly repressed masochistic tendency." Of feminists in general he said, "A certain proportion of at least the most militant suffragists are neurotics who in some instances are compensating for masculine trends, in others, are more or less successfully sublimating sadistic and homosexual ones." [40] R. L. Dickinson attributed all sorts of feminine ills as well as unfeminine behavior, including involvement in "social and political causes," to "compensation neurosis." [41] By the 1920s social reform as well as feminism was being dismissed with the appellations "neurotic," "masochistic," "sadistic," "homosexual."

Although American experts were familiar with Freud's postulates before 1920, and the public was chanting the jargon of id and ego soon thereafter, it took several decades for a Freudian view of specifically female psychology to be fully formulated.

By the mid-twentieth century any questioning of woman's place was readily equated with neurosis by the Freudian psychologists and their popularizers. Helene Deutsch psychoanalyzed nineteenth-century anthropologists who propounded the matriarchy theory and determined that they suffered from unresolved Oedipal complexes. [42] Marynia Farnham put Mary Wollstonecraft's biography to the test and declared that it read like a case history of hysteria. [43]

Marie Robinson put Victorians, suffragists, and flappers on the couch and in one full swoop dismissed them all as hopeless neurotics. The psychoanalytic rendition of female personality was almost immune to criticism. Any argument against the sexual status quo was dismissed as a perversion of psychic normality, a malfunction of the ego, a mental illness. Psychoanalysts and Freudian-oriented psychologists proclaimed that they alone were capable of deducing the proper sexual practices and the appropriate social roles for men and women. When Kinsey's statistics conflicted with psychological theory, for example, Marie Robinson wrote them off with arrogant disdain: After all, "the great observers in the field of human sexuality in the past fifty years have been in the field of psychology." [44]

Popularizers of female psychology like Robinson invoked the holy name of Freud in order to justify their monopoly over the allocation of sex roles. Freud himself had belatedly turned his attention to the psychology of women and announced his observations with some trepidation. Nonetheless, he bequeathed to his disciples a formidable scaffolding for doctrines of woman's practical inferiority by positing the centrality of genital construction to personality development and then building up his theories around the male model. Freud nurtured a conception of woman as a castrated male destined to live out her life in homage to the awesome shadow of the male genital and hopelessly garbled female anatomy in the process. The Freudians worked out endless variations on a general scheme of female genital trauma and resultant character formation. With the first infantile observations of the penis, and upon comparing it with her small organ of pleasure, the clitoris, the female was doomed to a life of genital envy and subordination. Convinced of her anatomical inferiority, the female child would reject her sexuality in despair. When she reclaimed it as an adult, the normal woman would transfer her sexual sensitivity to the vagina, now valued as the receptacle of the enviable penis.

In the course of the '30s and '40s several of Freud's followers went to work transcribing the master's theories regarding women into an elaborate doctrine. Freud's hypothesis of the crippled sexuality of woman was taken as gospel truth. For example, Marie Bonaparte derided those women who failed to transfer their sexuality to the vagina in the most condescending fashion: They acted "as though the clitoris were not an organ forever condemned to be inadequate but, like the boy's, would continue to grow." [45] By 1959 Marie Robinson had effectively blotted out the sexual identity of the clitoris: The woman who reached orgasm via the clitoris was purely and simply frigid.[46]

The Freudian psychologists refused to modify their theories to conform to the mundane realities of biology. Ordinary physicians like Dickinson reported that the sexual feelings of his patients centered in the vulva and around the clitoris, and that he knew of very few cases of "exclusively vaginal orgasm." [47] Similarly, 84 percent of the women interviewed for the Kinsey report achieved orgasm through manual friction against the clitoris or labia minora. Furthermore, one-half of these women suffered anxiety regarding such masturbation, having been informed by the Freudians that it would diminish the proper vaginal sensitivity. Kinsey set their minds at ease, explaining that "actually the vagina in most females is quite devoid of end organs of touch. It is incapable of responding to tactile stimulation, and the areas primarily involved in the female's sensory responses during coitus are exactly those which are primarily involved in masturbation, namely the clitoris and the labia." [48] A few outspoken writers in the '40s and '50s continued to remind psychologists of this simple anatomical lesson but to little avail. It was not that the Freudians read different biological textbooks; Marie Bonaparte readily admitted that "the vaginal mucosae are almost insensitive; they barely feel heat or cold or pain. Surgery operates inside the vagina itself almost without a local anesthetic. Nevertheless, it is the vagina itself, and more or less distant from the entrance according to the individual, that for the functionally adapted and adult woman true erotic sensitivity dwells. It is from this point that in coitus terminal orgasm starts." [49] Simple, direct sexual satisfaction obviously took a back seat to the development of "normal" female personality—"true," "adult," and "functionally adapted." To achieve this primary goal decreed by Freudian convention, a very circuitous sexual route had to be pursued. Basically, the female child was obliged to deny her clitoris and sexual gratification in homage to the penis. As Bonaparte phrased it, her sexuality "sinks into slumber until such time as the hymenal forest awakens her from sleep." According to this pastoral fantasy, the first penetration of the groom's penis would activate the sexual sensations of the vagina.

This Freudian version of female sexuality proved to be an enduring and captivating maze. Karen Horney made the most concerted attempt to escape the dictums of her mentor. She took into consideration clinical experience with women as well as the social and cultural conditions that made men's roles, if not their genitals, cause for justifiable envy. Horney tried to escape the Freudian paradigm by turning it on its head, postulating that the vagina was an awesome mystery to the male; that the ability to give birth was an enviable power; that the vagina itself was sexually sensitive from childhood on. Not even Karen Horney could escape the Freudian obsession with penis and vagina. Horney's fellow rebel in the house of Freud, Clara Thompson, circumvented the destructive doctrine of penis envy by calling attention to the symbolic nature and historical origins of the theory itself, namely the oppressive patriarchal conditions to which Freud's Victorian patients were subject. Such an abdication of the biological paradigm in favor of simple common sense was deemed treasonous, and in 1941 both Horney and Thompson were ousted from the New York Institute, the bastion of American Freudian psychology.[50] Freudians continued to ask women to perform psychological magic, to deny their own physiology and create by force of will an artificial center of erotic sensitivity.

Fortunately women can reach orgasm through penetration of the vagina provided the contiguous zones of the clitoris and vulva are indirectly stimulated, but it is a convoluted and often frustrating route to pleasure. The Freudian error of postulating two distinctive erogenous zones and ranking them in terms of their legitimacy caused considerable confusion for many women, including some who carried considerable weight in intellectual circles. Anais Nin, for example, recorded in her diary a discussion of the two orgasms as she had learned of them from her analyst and from D. H. Lawrence.

How well he described the two kinds of orgasm. One in which women lay passive, acquiescent and serene. The one orgasm came out of the darkness miraculously dissolving and invading. In the other a driving force, an anxiety, a tension which made the woman grasp for it as if it would elude her, and the movement became confused and unharmonious, cross currents of forces, short circuits which brought an orgasm that did not bring calm satisfaction but depression.[51]

Anais Nin was deeply divided between an apparent vaginal orgasm associated with passive femininity and a clitoral experience which was somehow improper and anxiety-provoking. Mary McCarthy portrayed the relative virtues of the "two orgasms" in the sexual encounter between two characters in *The Group*, Dottie and Dick. Dottie's first orgasm came through intercourse, her second through manual stimulation of the clitoris. "This second orgasm . . . was different," left her "jumpy and discontented, it was something less thrilling." Dick quickly endorsed Dottie's disappointment with the "clitoral" orgasm: "A nice normal girl. Some of your sex prefer it." [52] Regardless of the differences in sexual taste and the varieties of pleasure, women were inculcated with an insidious new standard of the "normal," one which invaded their most intimate experience and played havoc with their awareness of their own bodies. Sexual pleasure itself was made a function of a schema of feminine propriety, which entailed far more than boudoir manners.

Helene Deutsch contended that sexual pleasure was healthy "only under the condition that it is experienced in a feminine, dynamic way and is not transformed into an act of erotic play or sexual equality." [53] In Deutsch's multi-volume catechism of female psychology, sexuality was dissociated from vulgar "play" and attached to the serious business of maintaining stark differences between the sexes. She wrote: "I have defined as characteristic of the feminine woman a harmonious interplay between narcissistic tenderness and masochistic readiness for painful giving and loving." [54] Marie Bonaparte described the "true woman" as "normal, vaginal, and maternal" and made frequent reference to the virtues of narcissism and masochism.[55] This new jargon merely refined the old-fashioned stereotype of the passive, retiring, home-bound woman and rewarded conformity to its tenets with promises of sexual fulfillment. It was this interpretation of the psychology of woman that penetrated most deeply into popular culture, receiving its largest circulation after World War II, when, in keeping with the "feminine mystique," it celebrated a completely domesticated version of female sexuality that was unadulterated by the emancipating qualities of the '20s.

First of all, the popular psychologists reinforced the cliché of feminine passivity with Freudian sexology. Bonaparte contended that "the role of everything female, from the ovum to the beloved, is a waiting one. The vagina must await the advent of the penis in the same passive, latent and dormant manner that the ovum awaits the sperm." [56] Post World War II popularizations of Deutsch, like Ferdinand Lundberg and Marynia Farnham's Modern Woman: The Lost Sex, gave particular attention to the passive role of woman in sexual intercourse. Lundberg and Farnham employed the ludicrous but revealing metaphors typical of sex manuals to describe woman's inaction during intercourse. "It is not as easy as rolling off a log for her. It is easier. It is as easy as being the log itself. She cannot fail to deliver a masterly performance by doing nothing whatsoever except being duly appreciative and allowing nature to take its course." [57] Despite this injunction to remain passive, women were held entirely responsible for their own frigidity, according to Marie Robinson, who disparaged either blaming the male or resorting to new sex techniques to reach orgasm. Frigidity resulted, she maintained, from the woman's refusal to accept "the passive attitude which nature demands of her in the male embrace." The only avenue of pleasure was the "power of sexual surrender," a very curious mode of potency. A woman's sexual responsiveness at the same time should be instantaneous and persistent. According to Robinson's scenario of feminine perfection, "when her husband is ready to make love our lady is nearly always willing . . . and she is always willing to forgo love-making if he is not ready." [58] The elaboration and popularization of Freudian psychology had by the 1950s reduced female sexuality to passive compliance with the needs of her husband.

Such passivity meshed nicely with other central feminine characteristics: narcissism and masochism. If woman's satisfaction came from submitting to a man's lust, she would crave his advances primarily as testimony to her own sexual desirability, a highly narcissistic mode of pleasure. Accordingly, Robinson built a high degree of personal vanity into the female personality. The normal woman was "quite a show-off and likes sexual compliments from her husband dressed or undressed." [59] In Deutsch's more sophisticated paradigm the principle of narcissism was expressed as follows: "In the sexual act her partner's elemental desire gratifies her self-love and helps her to accept masochistic pleasure without damaging her ego." [60] Having outlawed clitoral stimulation, and asked women to submit to each and every sexual request of the husband, it logically followed that Deutsch would associate female sexuality with masochism. These psychologists of sex commonly attached suggestions of violence and laceration to the penetration of the penis. Deutsch referred to the female role in intercourse as a "dangerous and painful giving." [61] Both she and Marie Bonaparte on occasion equated female sexual experience with rape. According to Bonaparte, a woman's psychic structure "impels her to welcome and to value some measure of brutality on the male's part." These apparently contradictory characteristics, narcissism and masochism, somehow transformed physical pain into psychological pleasure. This incomprehensible sophistry was described by Bonaparte as follows: "Though penetration of her body will be wounding, what matter to one who is loved. The pain she feels will become yearned for pleasure and feminine masochism then reaches its heights." [62]

The ultimate expression of feminine narcissicism and masochism was found not in sexual intercourse but in woman's reproductive role. According to the psychoanalysis of woman, the perfect narcissistic gratification came with the creation of another self in pregnancy; and the greatest masochistic test was the ordeal of childbirth. Bonaparte cavalierly dismissed the pain of parturition as she scoffed: "Childbirth will imply the peril of death? Who bothers about that in love's realm?" [63] Deutsch was so enamored of the pain of childbirth that she suspected the use of anesthetics was "a masterpiece of masculine efficiency designed to rob women of masochistic satisfaction." [64] Thus maternity became the ultimate fulfillment of female sexuality. In fact, Deutsch went so far as to reduce the woman's sexual desire to a maternal urge. "In the normal healthy woman coitus psychologically represents the first act of motherhood." [65] During the postwar baby boom popular writers on female sexuality delighted in propagating this interpretation of female sexuality. Farnham and Lundberg told women in 1947 that "In proportion as she inwardly rejects the idea of receiving the seed—that is of being impregnated—she fails to attain full sexual pleasure from the sex act." [66] Marie Robinson went on to say that the ideally adjusted woman unconsciously fantasized pregnancy with every act of coitus, and the hope of impregnation of itself kindled sexual desire.[67]

Thus, by the 1950s, by way of the Freudian psychology of sex, the female stereotype had completed another cycle. Women were directed right back to where they were a century earlier, in the captivity of the cult of motherhood. All the sophisticated involutions of clinical and popular psychoanalysis only served to direct women back to familiar roles, exiled her not only to the bedroom and the maternity ward, but to the kitchen, nursery, and dressing table. Deutsch dismissed working mothers as a "war evil," and in the course of her psychiatric practice Marie

Robinson sent doctors, lawyers, businesswomen, and academics back to the home to recapture their femininity. In addition to her domestic duties, the sex-conscious woman of the twentieth century was obliged to devote special care to physical attractiveness, to dote over her appearance and assiduously cultivate a seductive image. The psychosexual imperative only slightly updated the doctrine of separate spheres, temperaments, and roles for the sexes. The psychology of sex rendered the policy of separate and unequal as follows: "The really fundamental difference between man and woman is that he can usually give his best as a creator and she as a lover; that his nature is according to his work and hers according to her love." [68] Under the guise of achieving sexual fulfillment, women were once again sent to work molding their personalities into replicas of a stereotype.

By mid-century the psychologists' prescriptions of femininity had reached a wide middle-class audience. Deutsch's treatises had become the bible of female psychologists, and the preeminence of the vaginal orgasm had been written into basic gynecological textbooks. The general tenets of Freudian sexology reached American women through mass ladies' magazines and popular paperbacks like Marie Robinson's *The Power of Sexual Surrender,* which sold approximately a million copies. Obviously only a very select group of women was aware of the fine points of the psychology of sex, and even fewer were captured by its casuistry and willing to comply with its impossible dictates. If it were otherwise, the incidence of madness and paralysis among twentieth-century women would have reached horrific proportions. Still, the magnitude of damage caused by this ideology and the role it prescribed is suggested by the fact that in selected communities, like the suburbs of the 1950s, wives and mothers were the most frequent visitors to psychotherapists and the members of households most likely to be consigned to mental institutions.[69]

The pernicious psychology of sex itself, however, was merely one specialized and laboriously wrought reflection of the general cultural preoccupation with intimate heterosexual relations. In fact, woman's vulnerability to the sexologists was bred in this narrowing universe which channeled social relations into private pairings with the opposite sex. In the course of the twentieth century the American woman's attention was focused more and more intently upon her private interaction with men. The period of adolescence was set aside especially for this purpose, "development toward heterosexual attraction." [70] G. S. Hall was the first to classify adolescence as a period of critical psychological development. At the turn of the century Hall advised young women to devote this era of their lives to the contemplation of their motherly nature. In 1916 Caroline Wormley Latimer updated the concept of adolescence, defining it as the epoch in a woman's life that brought to the fore "the great elemental instinct, sex, which henceforth is to be one of the most powerful agencies in her life." [71] The popular enthronement of sexuality by the '20s decreed that teen-age girls move out into a circle of their peers to acquire training in heterosexual relations. As Latimer put it, "It is through a girl's intercourse with the other sex that she receives the one most valuable part of her social training, namely the knowledge of how to accept [men's] attention and also to protect herself against them when necessary to do so." [72]

The adolescent's task, making her "heterosexual adjustment," was a difficult one. She was expected to exhibit her sexual attractiveness and test her ability to charm the teen-age boy, but never to "go too far," to pass from social intercourse with men to sexual congress. By the '40s, guidebooks for teen-age girls advised them to master "the strategy of keeping the relationship within bounds." One sociologist recommended that when a boy became too familiar the girl would say, " 'No, that's not the sort of thing I do,' and turn the subject quickly with a question about the football game or anything that interests him." [73] Marie Robinson proposed that daydreams of romance were probably the safest way for a girl to exercise her heterosexual interests without risking her virginity. Adolescent fantasies of prince charming and the matinee idol were also proposed as effective mechanisms of rooting out the bisexual tendencies of childhood. Prior to adolescence, in what was called the latency period, girls sublimated sexuality in "male" achievement in schoolwork, athletic competition, and rough play. At puberty a young woman's retreat into dreams of love and motherhood, Robinson maintained, would place her on the track to the proper adult female role.[74]

The twentieth-century teen-age subculture provided girls with ample opportunities for heterosexual contacts. In the 1920s approximately 50 percent of the nation's teen-agers were attending high school, largely public coeducational institutions. Robert and Helen Lynd discovered that the high school was the nexus of modern mores in middle America. There intellectual training took a back seat to the social life of the teen-age peer group. Middletown's youth in the '20s flocked to dances, sports events, and parties. Approximately one-half of them spent less than four evenings a week at home. Admittance to the major social events of the high school was by couples only, and rumor had it that petting parties were rampant among the "in crowd." Middletown's mothers expressed alarm at the mores of their daughters: "Girls have more nerve nowadays—look at their clothes." "Girls are more aggressive today. They call the boys up and try to make dates with them." [75] By the '20s the American high school had become a fitting environment in which to begin training in heterosexual relations. Psychologists applauded the teen-age subculture: "This conformity to the manners of her own age group is the result of a wholesome impulse. For the final adjustment of the girl must be with her contemporaries and not with the older generation if she is to be successful in her adjustment to work, play and marriage." [76]

American popular culture also provided ample food for adolescent romantic and sexual fantasies. The *Ladies' Home Journal* published "girls' issues" as early as the first decade of the twentieth century, packed full of bridal fashions and wedding pictures. During and after World War II, the era of the bobby-soxers, teen-age girls were supplied with periodicals all their own, like *Seventeen* magazine. These literary depositories of girls' culture harped on the importance of heterosexual attractiveness and peer group conformity and doled out copious advice on how to deal with boys. The "Sub-Deb" column of the *Ladies'*

Home Journal, which first appeared in the '30s and endured through the '50s, dispensed such advice as this: "He Loves Me, He Loves Me Not—How to Detect" and "The Boy Watcher's Guide." [77] In short, popular culture fulfilled the instructions of the sociologists and psychologists of adolescence, teaching the "A.B.C.'s of the New Language: how to impress a certain boy or girl, how to be liked by many, and how to know when one is getting ahead with one's chosen groups." [78]

Proponents of adolescent heterosexual norms had an even more effective ally in the movies. In Middletown the majority of high school girls frequented movie houses at least once a week. [79] A study of suburban adolescents in the '30s revealed that, while girls went to movies less often than boys, they spent a larger proportion of their leisure time, 26 to 44 percent, before the silver screen, while males were out on football or baseball fields. [80] Studies of popular cinema taste, furthermore, indicated that women preferred the themes of romance and love, "the woman's picture," while males delighted in adventure films: Westerns and war stories. [81] As adolescents flocked to the neighborhood theaters they imbibed potent doses of feminine and masculine stereotypes, while the love stories nourished the romantic fantasies and heterosexual consciousness of young girls.

Evidence soon flooded in to confirm that the propaganda campaign of the new womanhood was successful. As early as the '20s girls began to write to columnists on the woman's page displaying their anxiety about popularity. One girl wrote: "Please help me out. I am not very popular and yet according to people I have met I am pretty. I am five feet eight, with short brown hair, greenish eyes, good color and inclined to be fat. I do not use cosmetics and don't talk much. It is hard for me to make friends, but I have some. How can I become popular?" [82] Young girls worried about standards of sexual behavior as well as personal attractiveness. Columns of advice to teen-agers were bombarded with questions as to whether a girl should engage in necking and petting. A survey taken in the '20s revealed that 18 percent of a sample of single college and working women thought that the willingness to pet was essential to popularity.[83] Ben Lindsay's experience in the juvenile court of Denver, Colorado, led him to project that 90 percent of the fashionable high school set engaged in at least hugging and kissing. The judge quoted one popular girl as saying "there is something wrong with boys who don't know how to love me up." [84] At the same time Frances Donovan, a participant-observer of the waitresses of Chicago, found that these young working women "always talked about men" and were "loose in their sex relations." [85]

Popularity may have imperiled virginity, but the adolescent girls and single women were hardly *loose* in their sex relations. One young waitress of Donovan's acquaintance described her devious control of sexual relations as follows: "I always keep two or three fellows on the string and I get all I can out of them. I never come through unless I have to . . . , always make them think that you intend to go the limit and when it comes to the showdown give 'em the merry ha! ha! The damn fools will stand for it over and over again." [86] From the freewheeling waitresses of the '20s to the pregnant brides of the '50s most women were highly conscious of the proper limits of premarital sexuality and attentive to the goal of matrimony. One waitress reported the reinforcement of this ethic in a movie she had seen entitled *The Reward of Virtue.* The plot of the picture moved through a series of titillating episodes and climaxed when a young single girl was about to surrender her virginity. In the moment of crisis a summons from an adjacent apartment to aid in the holy event of childbirth saved the heroine from deflowering. When she rebuffed her seducer with the moral that "the reward of virtue is motherhood," the penitent roué proposed she become the legitimate mother of his children. The young waitress judged this "the most impressive picture . . . every girl ought to see it." [87] Right up to the 1950s the majority of both the men and women polled held tenaciously to the old adage that men require that their brides be virginal.

The standard of sexual fulfillment, in fact, made marriage more imperative than ever. The single women interviewed by Katherine Davis in the '20s suffered from psychic distress as well as the social stigma attached to being unmarried. One of Davis' subjects said that "the single woman must always be bothered with questions of sex. Her life is stunted." Another took the modern disdain for sexual abstinence so seriously that she declared "I have never lived." [88] Such attitudes would consign the lives of women like Jane Addams, M. Carey Thomas, and Leonora O'Reilly to oblivion. In the '30s the indictment of celibacy was hurled at single working women by Frances Donovan. The unmarried schoolteacher, Donovan surmised, was probably too devoted to study in her youth to engage in "the childish love affairs that educate the emotions." Denied adolescent training in the techniques of winning male approval, these romantically retarded women were unlikely to ever catch a husband. Their festering sexual frustration gave rise to the sternness, tyranny, and moodiness that characterized the "queer teacher." [89] The ideal girlhood, the apprenticeship in heterosexual relations, on the other hand, led directly to the altar: "Developed to a mature heterosexuality, love will be given first place in her dreams of happiness, and she will not think of sacrificing marriage for any prize." [90]

Pursuit of the prized object of twentieth-century sex-conscious femininity put women in ruthless sexual competition with one another. When the painted girls at the drugstore flirted with the beau of *True-Heart Susie*, even the sweet countenance of Lillian Gish contorted into a squint-eyed, jealous snarl. According to Donovan, a woman must begin the husband hunt early or "she will find the matrimonial prizes have been carried off" by women who have "concentrated upon what it takes to get men to give up their liberty." The autobiographical writings of women like Mabel Dodge Luhan and Anais Nin are spiced with acute calculations of the sex powers of their opposition. The twentieth-century sexual competition among women did not, however, end with the marriage vows. Zelda Fitzgerald's autobiographical novel, *Save Me the Waltz*, reveals how the carefree sexual games of adolescence could give way to the wife's anxious vigilance to protect her sexual property. The character of Alabama, modeled after the author, exposed the wives' worries and the accompanying distrust of women. Alabama saw her husband's gaze fixate on the sleek body of a competitor—"a half-wit . . . but she's very attractive"—and heard the coquette baldly announce: "I'm in love with your husband. I thought I'd try to make him if you didn't mind—of course I'd try anyway—he's such an angel." Alabama compared herself to her rival, felt angry and "clumsy," and collapsed into tears at her husband's infidelity.[91] The ordinary wife's sexual competition was hardly as glamorous as that of Mrs. Scott Fitzgerald, but she had her own little worries. The *Ladies' Home Journal* repeatedly issued "Warnings to Wives" about the captivating girls in their husbands' offices and printed stories of spouses enticed away by younger women. Admonitions to maintain sexual attractiveness and thus her husband's interest peppered ladies' magazines, and by 1950s the anxieties of being a wife in a sex-charged culture were catered to by regular features such as the *Journal*'s "Can This Marriage Be Saved?"

The nervous energy entailed in winning and keeping a man was brilliantly captured in Clare Boothe Luce's play *The Women,* which was made into a film by George Cukor in 1939. The entirely female cast of the film exuded wit, aggressiveness, and stamina in so concentrated and intense a form that one left the theater panting for breath. All these female resources were mobilized in a "war" to win, steal, or recapture husbands. The campaign ended when a covey of acid-tongued, scheming women (bonded together by their joint trip to Reno) retrieved the former husband of the heroine from the clutches of his duplicitous second wife. The energy and highly developed skills needed to protect the heterosexual relation were seldom exercised in a collective manner, however. The comic life-blood of *The Women* was in fact cutting insults passed between the female characters, and culminating in the most vicious "cat-fights." The sexual mores of the twentieth century put women in distrustful competition with one another for the exclusive rights to one male.

This competitive sexual marketplace was not completely removed from the actual American economy. Psychology, the compartment of knowledge that nurtured the sexy woman to maturity, also provided accompaniment for the consumer economy. The first book on the *Psychology of Advertising* appeared in 1908, and in the 1920s a nephew of Freud's joined a major New York advertising agency. Once the producers of consumer goods had determined that expansion of their business depended upon the constant escalation of popular demands they looked to psychology for assistance. As one businessman put it, "I want advertising to rouse me . . . to create in me a desire to possess the thing that is advertised even though I don't need it." In order to induce such irrational behavior psychologists of advertising recommended that consumer products be associated with the gratification of more fundamental human appetites, the most basic of them being sexual. The deep-seated cravings of the female consumer were expanded to include romance, marriage, and domestic security. Subliminal promises of sexual fulfillment, love, and a happy home life—all the prizes at stake in the marriage competition—were attached to anything from automobiles to toilet paper in the hope of engendering compulsive buying habits. Advertisers readily admitted that this tactic was suitable for a public whose average intelligence approximated that of a "14-year-old human animal." [92]

The male animal was customarily enticed into the

pattern of consumption by the more undisguised sexual stimuli. Advertisements for male-oriented products—cars, liquor, cigarettes—were adorned with female bodies. Often the association between sex and purchase was made explicit, as in an automobile advertisement that pictured a woman beside an Oldsmobile above the inscription "A Man Is Known by the Car He Keeps." Well before 1920, the liquor industry had discovered its characteristic ploy, posing its product in the hands of an attractive woman with the inscription "a bottled delight." The tobacco industry followed suit, combining sexy models with such slogans as "Reach for a Lucky when you crave something sweet." Occasionally men and women were jointly informed of the sexual power of a product. For example, a perfume was advertised during World War II as follows: "He will if you wear it. She will if you give it." Relatively straightforward invitations to make major purchases were last addressed to women in the early '30s when the automobile industry occasionally recommended their latest model to career women— "Women Know Success and Know Buick." Thereafter most products and advertisements were clearly typed according to conventional sex roles.[93]

The female body was unveiled by advertisers early in the twentieth century in order to suggest to women that love and romance could be acquired by a purchase. The manufacturers of cleansing products formed the vanguard of this marketing practice. Woodbury began its pioneering advertising campaign before 1920 with the promise "You too can have the charm of a skin he loves to touch." When the *Ladies' Home Journal* announced in the 1920s the advent of "the Cosmetic Age" (and recommended that cosmetology be taught in the nation's high schools), an avalanche of new products was declared essential to sexual and romantic fulfillment. Shampoo companies insisted you "must have beautiful well-kept hair to be attractive" and a deodorant manufacturer proclaimed that a "woman's instinct tells her" that body odor will deny her romantic canoe rides in the moonlight. The Palmolive company carried the sexology of advertising a step further by displaying the testimonials of movie stars who reputedly used their facial soap and by touching the sensitive nerves of competing females with such queries as "Will others he meets outdo you in natural charm?" In the 1930s the sexual connotations of advertising grew more and more explicit. By then Woodbury ads displayed a full rear view of the nude female body.

In general, however, the Depression subdued the sexual daring of American advertisers. Rather than escalating the promises of fulfillment, the advertisements of the '30s played on women's fears of marital and financial disaster. One advertisement asked, "I love you so but how can we afford to get married?" The illogical answer was: use Lux soap. Increasing attention was given to the pathology rather than the pleasure of the body. A distraught woman in a deodorant ad asked, "What's wrong with me?" and Listerine put a warning of domestic disaster in the mouth of a little girl: "He didn't kiss mummy yesterday either." In the '30s, consuming was portrayed to women as a simple method of keeping her family healthy and intact through the crisis of the Great Depression. Bran flakes would remove the frown from the worried face of the working man; aspirin would relieve the nervousness of the mother; hot cereal would protect children from the pangs of hunger.

Neither the economic hardship of the '30s nor the mobilization of the economy for military production in World War II interrupted the consumer education of women. Ponds went on proclaiming that soft hands won fiancés, while both sleek hair and romance could be purchased in a bottle from Woodbury. The only differences in these advertisements in the war years were that the woman in the Ponds' ad announced her engagement while operating heavy machinery in an aircraft factory and the Woodbury girl's romantic hero was in uniform. In celebration of the rising marriage and birth rates, brides and babies blossomed all over the advertising copy of the '40s and '50s. The Freudian psychology of woman seeped into the advertisements of the '50s as models were photographed in the posture of sexual surrender. The Woodbury girl lay in passive ecstasy as the male loomed over her in a suffocating embrace. In grotesque mimicry of Helene Deutsch's doctrine of the equivalence of sex and maternity, mattress manufacturers placed mothers and children in bed together or posed a toddler between somnolent husband and wife. The child also became the mouthpiece of the female anxiety reflex, which advertisers exacerbated and exploited; one ad even had a child say: "Mommy, you look like a witch." In keeping with the domestic spirit of the '50s, aproned models competed with one another for the whitest wash on the block, pans that were twice as clean as one's neighbors', the healthiest kids in the suburb.

As the advertising media inculcated habits of consumption in a vast American audience, it also conveyed sex stereotypes. Not only were women portrayed as lovers, mothers, and housewives but as narcissists and masochists as well. As the female body was plastered over billboards, magazines, and then the television screen, women were conditioned to conceive of themselves as the objects of sexual desire and romantic love. In advertising as in psychology, narcissism merged into masochism. Since the self-worth of the sex object depended upon conformity to popular standards of feminine attractions, women were directed to chisel their bodies into fashionable molds. In the '20s this required that the unlucky woman bind her breasts and employ exercise machines and diets, while by the '50s padded bras, bust developers, and more diets were in order. Women were urged to take up deodorants and mouthwash to combat the natural odors of their bodies. Routine bloodletting was in order to remove unfeminine body hair. Women were also asked to fight relentlessly and vainly against the natural process of aging, aping starlets and models who never surpassed the age of twenty-five. Fashioning the female body could be a time-consuming occupation as well as a self-mutilating occupation. Not even the simplified fashions of the '20s offered relief from this regimen of self-maintenance. Advertisements for beauty aids commented on "how exacting this new simplicity can be" and reminded the flapper that "being a woman means more today than ever before. She wants more and she gets more. But she has to put more into the job." In other words, by the 1920s a new mini-role was assigned to members of the female sex, the "job" of enhancing and maintaining physical attractiveness through the purchase and application of beauty aids.

Female sexuality once again led to work and anxiety rather than the simple pleasures of the body. The twentieth-century interplay between sex and sales created yet another more substantial and expansive role for woman. The businessmen who reminded Americans of their patriotic duty to consume spoke particularly to women. They spoke with the authority given to them by the market researchers who produced evidence that two-thirds of the $70,000,000,-000 worth of consumer purchases were made by women.[94] Some said that the women of America propelled economic expansion by purchasing $1,000 worth of goods every minute.[95] Studies of shopping patterns in New York City indicated that husbands were responsible for only 12.2 percent of the family consumer decisions and were consulted on only about 23 percent more.[96] As early as 1922 American home economists introduced women to their important new role of routine extravagance. "That we want more than we have is the very foundation of progress, whether what we want is material or spiritual." [97] High school home economists in the same decade set about "equipping the girl to be an intelligent consumer." [98] When the frenzied consuming and installment buying of the '20s ended in the debacle of the stock market crash and the Great Depression, women were chastised for their profligacy and admonished to restrain their lusts for goods. Eleanor Roosevelt chastened American women to "see that they live within their incomes, that they buy as fairly as possible from the fair merchant and buy only such goods as are manufactured by fair merchants." [99] In the next decade Mrs. Roosevelt recited her message of frugality in the pages of the *Ladies' Home Journal,* whose editors shamed and cajoled women to ration and conserve for the good of the war effort. In the marketplace as in the bedroom, the appetites of the sexy saleslady were supposed to be passively responsive, turned on and shut off in keeping with the fortunes of the male-directed world as it careened from war to peace, from prosperity to depression.

At the close of World War II the economic climate changed again, and women were invited to indulge in a more extravagant shopping spree than ever. They were primed for the revival of consuming even before the end of the war, as advertisements for U.S. war bonds pictured young women dreaming of the shiny mechanized kitchen they could purchase with their savings at the close of hostilities. By the 1950s the domestic aspirations of women had become the driving force of unprecedented expansion of the consumer sector of the economy. In 1952–53, *Fortune* magazine pinned the success of American business on the fact that more "nubile females are marrying than ever before." The market researchers at *Fortune* estimated that the young wives and mothers of the '50s could be counted on to incite $10,000,-000,000 worth of home construction and expend $60,000,000,000 on food, $30,000,000,000 on family recreation, and $12,000,000,000 on home furnishings and appliances. The "age of affluence" began with a crescendoing fanfare of domesticity and sexual salesmanship. Advertisers serenaded the women of the 1950s with promises of both domestic bliss and sexual fulfillment. The alliance of home, sex, and consuming reached perhaps its most ludicrous expression in the following piece of advice on the decorating of the bedroom: "Create a good background for the nude body. Its color and texture should be designed to complement the body's modeling and softness." The possibilities of linking sex and materialism seemed limitless, and it was the American female consumer who was asked to pursue them all.

Sex and sales were so tightly conjoined with the female gender that women themselves began to resemble marketable commodities. Female bodies paraded through popular culture and advertising copy like standardized, interchangeable parts coming off an assembly line. The resemblance between the female form and a product in a display case became ritualized in the beauty pageants of the '20s, which have been annually reenacted ever since. One of the most crass and explicit presentations of women as sexual commodities was enacted on the movie screen of the '30s and '40s in Busby Berkeley's dance extravaganzas. In a single film, *Footlight Parade,* Berkeley lined up scores of female bodies to project such images as mechanical dolls wound up by male dancers, slaves of old Africa, occupants of honeymoon suites, Singapore prostitutes, and, of course, water nymphs. The waterfall number in *Footlight Parade* can hardly be rivaled as a fantasy of sex objects en masse. At one point the camera passes between a long formation of thighs, pointing up at a long line of bead-covered crotches. The *Gold Digger* musicals of the '30s attested to the marketability of these assemblages of sex objects appropriately costumed in jingling coins. Under the direction of Busby Berkeley, the image of the sexy saleslady was fully unveiled, her body titillatingly exposed, molded into one standard, infinitely replicable shape, displayed en masse, and put up for sale. Berkeley was Hollywood's Henry Ford, the master salesman of the sexy feminine.

The evolution of this image had far-reaching consequences for the woman of the twentieth century. It entitled her to sexual fulfillment and then tied her psychology to her genital construction. The saleslady promised the gratification of both sexual and consumer appetites. The preeminence of the heterosexual relation put women in competition for men and directed them to seek fulfillment in the privatized isolated sphere of the bedroom. In sum, female sexuality became the rationale for a new stereotype and a new specialization of male and female roles. Despite all this erotic imagery, however, the actual sexual experience and satisfaction of women probably changed very little over the half century. Female sexual gratification was impeded by the doctrine of the impossible vaginal orgasm, and real sensuality was obfuscated by the objectification of the body. Likewise, if advertisers and businessmen had their way, the lust for consumer goods would never climax in material contentment, but would endlessly expand demand for goods. In the last analysis, the sexy saleslady was anti-sexual. The prescription of the new feminine image tended to channel woman's energies into a hopeless quest for personal fulfillment.

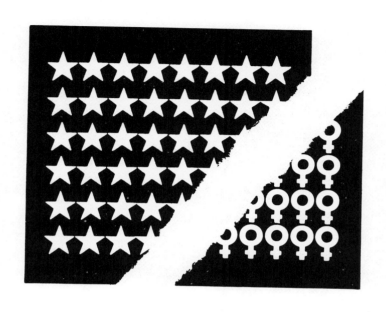

A KALEIDOSCOPE
OF ROLES:

TWENTIETH-CENTURY
WOMEN AT WORK
AND IN THE HOME

The catchphrase "sexy saleslady" encompasses more than an upsurge in heterosexual activity and shopping sprees. For hundreds of thousands of women in the twentieth century it also denoted a position in the work force. In the '20s alone, seven hundred thousand American women took up employment behind the counters of the rapidly proliferating retail stores, where they constituted 30 percent of the nation's sales personnel.[1]

Sociologist Frances Donovan, who took a job in a Chicago department store in 1928 in order to observe closely the important new area of woman's work, enthusiastically commented: "The girl who works in the department store today is no longer taken on as a decoration. She is, for the most part, selected by women and bossed by women—her sex appeal doesn't count." Yet Donovan's own report on the salesladies of the '20s was full of evidence to the contrary. A "business girls' contest," given notice in the Chicago *Tribune,* for example, clearly suggested that "sex appeal counts." Contestants were judged on their efficiency, business ideals, and poise, but 50 percent of the measure of excellence in saleswomanship was based on appearance. Furthermore, while Donovan liked to speak of the "man-sized" job of the saleslady, the vast majority of the women she encountered never rose to the positions of prestige and prosperity that men found in the retail industry. The typical saleslady sold relatively inexpensive, nondurable goods to females and left her low level job within a few years, usually upon her marriage.[2] Neither did the saleslady claim a man-sized paycheck, but rather a wage judged sufficient for a woman who was not expected to be economically independent. When one young woman complained to her boss that her salary was beneath a comfortable level of subsistence, he asked, "But haven't you a man friend to help support you?" [3] The women who took up jobs in the sales sector of the economy encountered myriad discriminatory practices based solely on sex. The saleslady was representative of the millions of women who entered the labor force in the twentieth century. Women's introduction into gainful employment outside the home, like her official invitation to political participation, and her rising expectations of sexual fulfillment, integrated her further into the male-dominated sphere, but kept her at its lowest levels. In short, only a secondary and womanly mode of employment was available to most members of the female sex.

As early as 1916, conservative writers like Caroline Latimer offered a young woman at least a brief taste of the rewards of work, advising her to pursue "some kind of definite occupation before she marries and goes to a home of her own." [4] In 1914, Ellen Key, a fervent partisan of motherhood, allowed for women's employment not only before marriage but also "after the years of their children's minority." [5] Some new feminists of the 1920s proposed changes in both the job market and the home designed to accommodate the working wife. Lorine Pruette, for example, was appalled by the waste of woman's talents that the excessive leisure of the modern housewife entailed. She called for a "readjustment within the division of social labor, a new allocation of functions." Pruette went only so far, however, as proposing that married women alternate their daily routine between household chores and part-time jobs. [6] As Mary Ross pointed out in *Woman's Coming of Age,* institutional advances in the field of childcare—"baby health stations, the kindergarten, or nursery schools, the public schools and the health clinic, the public health nurse, the gamut of specialists in the growth, behavior and needs of children"—made this readjustment of home and work roles feasible. Yet she, like most writers on the subject, shied away from the possibility that woman could enter the work force as man's equal. Mary Ross greeted with approval the demise of "self-assertive and antagonistic feminism," wherein women "worked against heavy odds and usually had to buy success at the price of marriage and children, sometimes charm and personal appearance, of being considered queer—as some of them undoubtedly were." No, the women of the twentieth century would not compete with men, nor threaten to usurp the dominant position of the husband in economic affairs. Rather, the wife would only share in the provider's role, while retaining full responsibility for child-care and housekeeping. Mary Ross looked to some Utopian future for even this "adjustment" of sex roles that "would be brilliant not only for women but also for men." [7]

As it turned out, this minor remodeling of sex roles was already under way as Ross wrote. The adjustment indeed proved brilliant for the economy and beneficial to the male chief provider; but its implications for women were far from Utopian. A woman had to scavenge for jobs, here and there, now and then, when a let-up in the demands of her home role permitted it. Her work was to be interrupted whenever overriding home responsibilities beckoned. Consequently, although women's participation in the work force more than doubled in the first six decades of the twentieth century, the economic status of the female worker never approached that of the male. Between 1900 and 1940 the percentage of women engaged in gainful employment outside the home increased 23.5 percent, and in the following two decades skyrocketed by 35.8 percent.[8] Prior to 1940 the typical working woman was young and single. Without complaint, she left her low level job for marriage. Thereafter, the largest segment of the female work force was composed of middle-aged women returning to the job market after years of exclusive attention to homemaking and child-rearing. By the '50s more than one-third of the working women were shouldering the responsibilities for a home and children of school age along with an outside job. These two roles, at work and in the home, whether separated in time or juggled simultaneously, greatly handicapped the women who entered the sphere of work, tagging along behind their husbands.[9] It contributed in many subtle ways to the fact that throughout the twentieth century the average income of full-time woman workers hovered between 50 and 60 percent of their male counterparts.

The difficulties of the twentieth-century adjustment of women's roles were clear from the start. The struggles of a trained social worker named Elisabeth Levin Stern demonstrated the tensions inherent in the dual role system. She confidently greeted the new century with the intention of surmounting the obstacles to independence that had impeded her Jewish immigrant sisters. She shunned the pattern of early menial labor and swift escape into marriage. "Many things are great besides love. There was fame, a great world outside to discover." Elisabeth Levin determined to make her way to success by becoming a professional social worker. Yet she eschewed the model of the "old women in the settlement house." "I wanted a career and love, not a career and the sacrifice of love." The idealistic young social worker soon fell in love with her boss, a fellow proponent of egalitarian companionship marriage. She had overcome, she thought, all the ancient inhibitions of her sex. "I was to be free, free with my love to enrich my freedom." [10]

The course of Mrs. Stern's married life, however, was ridden with constraints upon her freedom. First, her career as a rising social worker was interrupted by pregnancy and three years chafing at the tedium of child care. When she reembarked upon her profession she had to battle against the prejudices of employers against working mothers and against the far more painful disapproval of her husband. His endorsement of a woman's right to work, it turned out, had many qualifications attached to it. She now learned that her husband saw women's employment "not as a way of earning a living. That never entered his mind, but as something that would fulfill my life perhaps as a child would." The ideal mode of female fulfillment, he thought, would be for his wife to write feminine novels in the shelter of their home. No sooner had Elisabeth Stern surrendered to these arguments, when her husband took ill, and she, by the force of necessity, had to reenter the work force. After the second interruption in her career she found a new and more lucrative occupation as a sales manager. Mrs. Stern proved adept at this job too and was soon jubilantly announcing that she was "as successful as a man." [11]

Her exhilaration was again short-lived. Upon her spouse's recovery, he requested that she quit her job to become his assistant in a social work project at half her current pay. Again she submitted, but with full consciousness of the contradictions of her married life. "We were married, had our children, and we were doing *his* work together . . . I was a 'new woman'; I'd just read a paper at our club on the 'right of the girl child to her own personality'—and yet I was happy to lose mine for my husband's. My husband was well enough to get to work at once—today." Soon the paths of husband and wife diverged again, and for a span of a few years Elisabeth Stern forged ahead untrammeled in her career as an executive social worker. Just when her marital relationship and her work role had been accommodated to one another, however, the obligations of motherhood rose up to block her path. A doctor diagnosed her young son's fragile health as the result of insufficient home affection. Again Stern turned aside from her chosen profession to fulfill a woman's responsibilities in the home. Now she turned in her hours of domestic leisure to write an autobiographical account of the pitfalls of the dual female role.[12]

The life of Elisabeth Levin Stern illustrates in the extreme the vertigo created by the multiplying roles of women in the twentieth century. Her life was like a kaleidoscope repeatedly jarred into new configurations composed of such fragments as worker, lover, wife, mother, and homemaker. Stern, who had run the gamut of women's roles by 1926, acquired a bitter foretaste of what was in store for the generations that followed. As the century wore on, working women, wives and mothers, would not have to endure the stigma to which pioneers like Elisabeth Stern were exposed. On the other hand, the passing decades would bring the home roles into sharper relief and more intense combat with the work sphere. In fact, this battle was waged beneath the frothy surface of the feminine mystique. In 1955, the heydey of the teen-age bride and the baby boom, 46 of every 100 American women were in the labor force at some time during the twelve-month period. As marriage and motherhood became more and more highly honored, the distraction of the working woman would be intensified, her difficulties and her burdens compounded.

Despite the glorified place of women in the home, American employers had been jealously eying the labor power of women since at least the 1920s. As the economy expanded by leaps and bounds, businessmen noted with alarm that their labor needs would no longer be satisfied by a stream of immigrants. The largest single reserve of labor was composed of women. Simultaneously, an embryonic sector of the economy was flexing its muscles and crying for workers. As of 1900, the great bulk of the American work force was employed in either manufacturing or agriculture. By 1930 both these sectors of the labor force had been surpassed by the combined employment in services, trades, finance, and civilian government. This tertiary sector of the economy provided jobs for 44 percent of America's workers as of 1930. Women had a head start into these non-manual occupations; as of 1900, 81 percent of America's female workers had been freed from the primary economic sector, agriculture, while only 58 percent of the male workers were in nonfarm occupations. Women were within easy reach of the expanding tertiary occupations and began to funnel steadily into the growing number of white-collar and retail jobs.[13]

Prior to 1940 the major transformation in the pattern of female employment was a simple shift from manufacturing and domestic services into white-collar jobs. As of 1900, 28.2 percent of the nation's women workers were employed in non-manual occupations; by 1940 that proportion had risen to 45 percent. Many of these workers were recruited from the ranks of domestic servants, who constituted one-third the female work force in 1910 and only a fourth by 1930. Others transferred from the sweatshops and factories, which employed many immigrant women early in the century. The most popular new frontier for female workers was the clerical occupations. One million women had entered business affairs as clerical workers by 1920, and by 1930 females came to dominate an occupation once reserved for men. Secretarial work was the most popular female job early in the century, the most prevalent occupational choice for the high school girls of middle America. The lure of clerical work lay not in superior wages, but in its refinement and prestige relative to manual labor. The Katherine Gibbs School was established in 1911 to groom women for glamorous secretarial jobs. By 1940, more than one-fifth of all female workers were in clerical occupations.[14]

Most of the female recruits into the expanding tertiary sector of the economy in this first stage of the dual role that predated 1940 were young and single. For the first four decades of the century the highest rate of female participation in the labor force was in the age group twenty to twenty-four, and rates of employment declined steadily after the mid '20s. Moreover, right up to 1940 less than 20 percent of America's married women were in the work force. The relatively modest demand for female workers prior to World War II was met primarily by an increase in the employment rate of young women and the shift of others from older occupations into the tertiary sector of the labor force.[15] Employers continued to discriminate against older women, judging them unreliable, inefficient, and frequently neurotic. The average working man shared in this prejudice. The response to a poll of men early in the 1920s was typical: the vast majority concurred with the statement "the married woman should devote her time to the home." [16]

The ordeal of the Great Depression intensified opposition to the employment of married women. A poll in the '30s put this question to men and women: "Do you approve of a married woman earning money in business and industry if she has a husband capable of supporting her?" Eighty-two percent of the sample answered in the negative.[17] Some men incapable of supporting themselves and their families held tenaciously to their prejudice against working wives. One unemployed husband went so far as to say, "I would rather turn on the gas and put an end to the whole family than let my wife support me." [18] In the '30s, twenty-six states had laws prohibiting the employment of married women. The majority of the nation's public schools, 43 percent of public utilities, and 13 percent of American department stores enforced a curb on the hiring of wives.[19] Despite these cultural and legal bars, however, the emergency of the Depression brought a substantial increment in the gainful employment of married women. The relevant percentage rose from 11.7 to 15.2 percent. The bulk of these working wives were not only in desperate financial straits, but also were members of ethnic and racial minorities. On the other hand, the white, middle-class, educated women who pursued professional careers remained overwhelmingly single up to 1940. For middle-class women, then, the roles of worker and homemaker were still temporally separated up through the '30s.[20]

The size and characteristics of the female labor force changed dramatically during World War II. The exigencies of mobilizing for global war warranted a clear and unambiguous invitation to women to come to work. In July, 1943, when nearly all available men and single women were enrolled in the labor force, the War Manpower Commission estimated that 4 million additional workers were needed in the armed forces and munitions industries alone. Accordingly, the call for more women workers went out in clarion tones, from government, industry, and ladies' magazines alike. The call to work was no longer clothed in feminine rhetoric. Posters for the Women's Army Corps and advertisements for Camels advised women of the "man-sized" jobs that awaited them. War propaganda pictured women operating heavy machinery, and the *Ladies' Home Journal* placed a female combat pilot on the cover. The urgent need of the war economy for women workers also enabled women to exact concrete concessions from government and employers. Women's wages almost doubled in the war industries; protective legislation was suspended to allow women to work long hours; the federal government and American trade unions endorsed the principle of equal pay for equal work; and more than 2.5 million women received training for skilled jobs.[21]

As a result of all these enticements and opportunities, no less than 8 million women entered the work force during World War II. The overall participation of women in the labor force jumped from 25 to 36 percent of the adult female population. In heavy industry the numbers of women workers increased from 340,000 to more than 2 million. Females could now be found in such novel places as on the docks, in the steel mills, behind the steering wheels in cabs and buses. American airlines employed hundreds of women, not merely as stewardesses, but as pilots and mechanics.[22] Some women were metamorphosed overnight from the feminine stereotypes into hefty workmen. One beautician, for example, became a switchwoman for six hundred Long Island Railroad trains, and a onetime cosmetics sales girl operated a 1,700-ton keel binder.[23] By the end of the war popular commentators were proclaiming the ability of women to perform all sorts of "male" tasks. Dorothy Thompson, editor of the *Ladies' Home Journal,* congratulated her sex for meeting the test of masculine strength, endurance, and agility, while sociologists attested to the fact that "there are very few jobs performed by men that women cannot do with changed conditions and methods."[24]

The working women of World War II also deserved praise for their performance in the traditional female sphere. By 1944 millions of American mothers had responded to the call to double wartime duty. Seventy-five percent of the new workers were married, 60 percent of them were over thirty-five years of age, most of them were mothers of school-age children. Despite the recommendations of the Women's Bureau, precious little was done to ease the domestic burdens of these workers. The federal government appropriated only $400,000 to establish day-care centers, a sum grossly inadequate to care for the children of war workers. Federal and local day-care programs served only 10 percent of the nation's working mothers; only one in ten of the war production centers had any such facilities. Similarly, the housekeeping assistance, public kitchens, and family services that the Women's Bureau called for were never forthcoming. The tacit assumption was that women could shoulder an extra burden on behalf of their country in time of crisis.[25] This was certainly the construction that advertisers placed on woman's role during the war. A lipstick manufacturer asked, "Doing Double Duty?" while another company recommended a hand cream for women "leading a double life."

Despite the excessive responsibilities it entailed, women workers treasured their wartime furlough from the home. Surveys conducted toward the end of the war demonstrated that 75 to 90 percent of female workers hoped to remain in their jobs after the end of hostilities. Some federal officials and even the editor of the *Ladies' Home Journal* appealed to the government and industry to extend the operations of day-care centers and the employment of women into peacetime.[26] As one sociologist put it, the war worker "cannot be cast off like an old glove. To be sure, many working women will be glad to go back to their homes and to their aprons. The choice, however, will be made by them as adults, mature members of society, not for them."[27] Nonetheless, the familiar sexual limits on "free choice" quickly closed in again on American women. Two months after the end of World War II, 800,000 women had been fired by aircraft companies. International Business Machines immediately reactivated its policy against hiring married women. By 1947 women had practically disappeared from the heavy industries where they had received nearly man-sized wages during the war. The employment of women by automotive companies was reduced from 25 to 7.5 percent of their labor force, and the remaining female employees were largely in low-paying clerical positions. By November, 1946, more than 2 million women had been summarily dismissed from their jobs, and most of these were seeking new employment opportunities.[28]

Despite these reversals it soon became clear that the bulk of American women would never again revert to the low level of participation in the labor force that was maintained before the war. In fact, by 1952, 2 million more women were at work than in the peak years of World War II. By 1955, the proportion of women in the work force exceeded the highest level reached during the war, and female employment continued to expand each and every year thereafter. Postwar workers, however, seldom received the "man-sized" jobs and salaries that had been promised during the national emergency. The tertiary sector of the labor force grew by leaps and bounds in the postwar era and by 1960 employed 56.6 percent of America's working men and women. This sector of the economy now employed 75 percent of all women workers (as opposed to 49.2 percent of the males) and chiefly at the lowest levels. The single most prevalent occupation for women as of 1960 was clerical work, where 30 percent of all female workers could be found.[29]

The postwar expansion of the service and sales sector of the economy set up the conditions for a more and more precise segregation of the work force by sex. By 1960 an estimated 59 percent of working women were employed in industries and occupations where the majority of their co-workers were females. Perhaps as much as 48 percent of female workers found themselves in categories of employment where 80 percent of the employees were of their own sex. Women who constituted 38 percent of the work force accounted for 40 percent of all sales workers and two-thirds of all clerks and typists. When the levels of each occupational grouping are further refined, the sex segregation of the work force becomes even more meticulous. Within the sales sector, for example, 96 percent of the clerks in American five-and-dime stores were female. The professions were similarly sex typed, as indicated by the fact that 85 percent of American elementary-school teachers were women. This pattern of employment demonstrated the maturation of a distinctly female labor market, a feature built into the dual role of the twentieth century. Women did not enter the work force competing for male jobs, but to take up positions in sectors of the economy carved out almost exclusively for their sex.[30]

One defining characteristic of the female labor sector was the importance accorded to the heterosexual attractiveness of the applicants. One waitress articulated this job qualification even before 1920: "there ain't no chance for an old hen, they all want chickens and they want 'em slender." [31] In many sales and service occupations women were placed on display for the benefit of customers, clients, and bosses. The typical worker of the twentieth century could not indulge in the dowdiness of the housewife nor the dishevelment of the industrial worker. By the '30s, Frances Donovan was advising even elementary-school teachers to display sex appeal before their pupils: "She will never forget that she is a woman and that she owes it to her sex to be charming." [32] The archetype of the sexy feminine in the contemporary work force is the airline stewardess. One airline executive interviewed by *The New York Times* put the job prerequisites bluntly: "It boils down to whether some chicks look good in their uniform. If you have fat stewardesses, people aren't going to fly with you." [33] Statistical surveys of office managers are just as telling if not as tasteless. In one poll in 1962, 28 percent of the companies questioned openly admitted that they considered sex appeal a requirement for some office jobs. [34]

The more general attributes of the female labor market are less directly sex-linked but equally perfidious, and most of these discriminatory characteristics of female occupations were built into the largest employment category for women, clerical work. It was the lot of the occupants of this typical "woman's job" to perform monotonous, mechanical tasks, which in white-collar occupations alienated the labor of the mind as well as the body. Clerical work at times replicated the routine of a factory. Such was the case in an office of Commonwealth Edison in the 1920s, where eighty "girls" were stationed along an assembly line processing information:

> Orders are passed along by means of a belt and lights from a chief clerk to a series of checkers and typists each of whom does one operation. The girl at the head of the line interprets the orders, puts down the number and indicates the trade discount; the second girl prices the order,

takes off the discount, adds carriage charges and totals; the third girl gives the order a number and makes a daily record; the fourth girl puts this information on an alphabetical index; the fifth girl time-stamps it; it next goes along the belt to one of several typists, who makes a copy in septuplicate and puts on address labels; the seventh girl checks it and sends it to the storeroom.[35]

The twentieth-century sexual division of occupations allotted to women a regimen that routinized, compartmentalized, and expropriated the operation of the human mind, a more deadly alienation than ever.

The proliferation of bureaucracy and the mechanization of information collection sucked more and more women into this deadening round of work. By the 1950s the paperwork in the woman's office had multiplied with the increasing sophistication of data processing machinery. One insurance company employed over 500 women to sort by machine 150,000 dividend notices each week. Another increased the output of 85 employees, four-fifths of them women, to 850,000 transactions a month, with the aid of computers. The automation of the office resulted in the transfer of female workers from typewriters to key-punch machines. The key-punch operators in one office of the '50s were described as an assemblage of nervous wrecks, frozen at their places, armed with aspirins and tranquilizers. In this office the annual turnover rate for women workers was 65 percent, testifying to an assault on the woman's nervous system reminiscent of the sweatshops at the turn of the century.[36]

Not all clerical jobs reduced women to anomic captives of office machinery. The personal secretary and the receptionist, for example, were typically asked to infuse bureaucracy with the human qualities with which women were supposedly richly endowed. When one executive was asked if automation could replace the secretary his answer was an emphatic "no." "Machines are poor receptionists and can't run errands and meet the public." The feminine personality was highly valued in the business office, offering the boss his coffee with a smile, while pacifying irate clients with her charm. The woman, in short, was asked to cultivate and display an image of human concern; she was mechanically to provide human warmth for public relations purposes, all in the face of her own alienating office routine.[37] The dehumanizing regimen of such female workers has been brilliantly analyzed by Elinor Langer, who spent several months as a participant observer among women employees of the New York Telephone Company. These workers conducted two hundred telephone conversations a month in which their task was to quickly and efficiently translate customer requests into bureaucratic codes while making a convincing sales pitch for the latest models and colors in telephone apparatus. Through all this frantic activity the company representative was expected to always express interest in the case and indicate willingness to help. The dual requirements of bureaucratic efficiency and personable public relations were enforced by the department supervisors, who periodically monitored the calls of the workers. By 1970 the organization of women's work at the telephone company had become a masterpiece of alienation, ensnaring the manual, mental, and emotional labor of women workers in its bureaucratic labyrinth.[38]

Much of such women's work, furthermore, required skilled laborers. As early as 1920, applicants for clerical jobs were expected to have a high school education. The proportion of women graduating from high school early in the century exceeded men by almost 20 percent, accelerating the female take-over of clerical work. A high school diploma was by no means an irrelevant credential for office workers. Clerical work required the verbal skills and the level of literacy and self-discipline that a lengthy sentence in the American schoolroom instilled. Women who did not pass this educational regimen had considerable difficulty complying with the bureaucratic imperatives of the office. For example, two middle-aged Italian women, in the training program at the New York Telephone Company, confessed that they "never read" and as a consequence could not comprehend the company sales manual. They admitted defeat and dejectedly returned to the repair department to be manual "robots" rather than mentally programmed machines.[39] The specific skills of clerical workers, typing, stenography, filing, were acquired in the vocational programs of high schools or in specialized business courses. Entrants into the female segment of the labor force, in short, came to their jobs with considerable preparation.[40]

The skills of these women workers, unlike those of blue-collar men, were prerequisites for employment rather than the results of on-the-job training. An employer of women seldom had to invest in the training of his workers. In addition to this substantial saving, the employer awarded clerical workers salaries far lower than equivalently skilled workers in the male sector of the labor force. As of 1960, 42 percent of all women workers were in jobs that required an education but garnered wages lower than did similarly educated men.[41] In the state of California this inequitable policy operated such that a woman with a college education made on the average only $300 more annually than a man who left school after the eighth grade.[42] The segregation of the labor force allowed employers to gauge pay scales according to the sex of their employees and to discount a woman's education and training. Because women did not compete for jobs with men, their superior qualifications were ignored; different work decreed unequal pay for women. Furthermore, the few men who entered female-dominated occupations were assigned high positions and granted larger salaries. The income of women clerks in 1964 was only 44 percent of that of men in the same category of employment. Female sales workers earned 60 percent less than males in the sales sector of the labor force.[43] The pattern of sexual discrimination was also a commonplace characteristic of the female professions. In 1939, for example, the salaries of women teachers and social workers amounted to approximately 70 percent of the annual income of men in these professions.[44] Much of this inequity was a function of the superior posts granted to men within each occupational category. Still, blatant sexual discrimination, unequal pay for equal work, took a heavy toll on women's wages. In a survey of nineteen hundred office managers conducted in

1961, one-third of the respondents admitted that they routinely paid men higher salaries than women in the same positions.[45]

The sexual segregation of the labor force also inhibited the upward mobility of women workers. Even a middle-aged wife and mother was still a "girl" in the eyes of many employers. The typical female worker was consigned to permanent occupational adolescence. Secretaries and sales girls could not expect to rise to the posts of executives and managers. While young white-collar males embarked upon the systematic climb to higher posts in the firm, women remained on the plateau of female occupational status, performing the same functions and taking home the same amount of real wages year after year. Technological advances in the woman's sector of the economy did not break this cycle of stagnation. The development of typewriters and office machines at the turn of the century created a demand for more skilled workers, but once women had secured the bulk of these positions, their prestige and pay declined precipitously. The innovations in data processing in the 1950s and '60s created higher level positions in the field of programming, which in the beginning often went to women, but not at the rate of openings in the new seats of monotony and inferiority at the key-punch machine. The quantum leap in women's participation in the work force, which characterizes twentieth-century womanhood, merely occasioned a more multifaceted and widespread pattern of sexual inequality. It welcomed females into secondary jobs outside the home, where they contributed immeasurably to the expansion of the economy and enhanced the profit margin of their employers, without offering equivalent rewards to women themselves.

Simultaneously, the ranks of professional women and ambitious careerists were depleted. The avalanche of women into the professions at the turn of the century, increasing female representation by 226 percent, had subsided by 1930 and began to recede thereafter. As of 1930, women accounted for 32 percent of the nation's college administrators and professors. The figure had plummeted to 19 percent by 1960. Despite the abolition of restrictions against women in medical and law schools by the late 1940s, women's representation in these professions remained well below 10 percent. Between 1940 and 1966, when women's rate of employment skyrocketed, the proportions of women in professions declined from 45 to 38 percent.[46] Meanwhile, these female professionals remained concentrated in their traditionally segregated job classifications, as nurses, elementary-school teachers, librarians, and social workers. Ironically, as women entered the labor force in greater and greater numbers, the overall economic status of the female labor force declined. By 1960, 90 percent of all women worked outside the home at some point in their lives, and the majority of them spent twenty-five years in gainful employment. Women had become a kind of working class unto themselves, mired in the inequities of the female sector of the labor force.

The distinctive characteristics of this female proletariat were forged in the home as well as on the job. Early in the twentieth century the female labor force was an unstable congregation of young women on their way to the altar and early retirement. Then, between 1940 and 1960 the dramatic expansion of women's work roles and home responsibilities occurred simultaneously. The increased demand for workers during World War II and in the postwar economy coincided with a decreasing availability of young, single women workers. As a consequence of the low birth rate during the '20s and the Depression, the generation of women reaching working age was smaller than ever before. As if to make things even more difficult for employers, these women, encouraged by postwar prosperity, married and began to raise families earlier than before. In the 1950s, less than 20 percent of the American women fourteen years of age and over were single, clearly insufficient to meet the demand for female labor. In addition approximately 60 percent of the married women were mothers of children under eighteen.[47] The businessmen of America had no alternative but to recruit wives and mothers as workers. American women welcomed this economic opportunity; between 1940 and 1960 the number of working wives doubled and the number of working mothers quadrupled. By the late 1960s the majority of female workers were married and almost 40 percent of the mothers with children between the ages of six and seventeen held jobs. The typical working woman was over forty years of age, neither an aspiring young careerist nor an eager ingénue, but a woman whose youth had been spent in the nursery and the kitchen.[48] Her wages, no matter how paltry, became a treasured income, bringing a modicum of independence and financial leverage into her marriage. Her work, however menial, provided opportunities for wider companionship and a sense of accomplishment outside the home.

The typical working wife conceived of herself as a supplementary worker, whose assistance was urgently needed by the male breadwinner. Studies by the Women's Bureau in the '20s and '30s, when wives were still a minority among working women, demonstrated that 90 percent of these workers used their income to sustain their families. The comparable statistics for the postwar era were within the range of 70 to 90 percent.[49] Nearly half of the working wives of Middletown in 1925 went to work because their husbands were temporarily unemployed. The bulk of the remainder used their wages to supply the essential needs of their families or to provide educational advantages for their offspring. Up through the 1940s, the highest rate of employment for married women occurred at those income levels where a husband's income could not keep the family comfortably and reliably above the poverty level. The meager wages of female workers were essential to keep these families out of poverty and provide a modicum of comfort. As such, a woman's wage provided benefits for her family that disguised their insufficiency for women who aspired to be, or were by necessity, economically independent.

Most wives, when asked why they worked outside the home, responded "for the money and for my family." [50] Yet the money that a wife deposited in the family coffers could enhance the family's life-style in a variety of ways. For a significant number of families it could be used to fulfill the expanding artificial needs created by the consumer economy. One of the working wives of Middletown had fully internalized the consumer ethic by 1925. After her wages helped to pay off the family mortgage and refurbish the home, she went on to purchase a washing machine, electric iron, and vacuum cleaner. "I don't even have to ask my husband any more because I buy these things with my own money. I bought an icebox last year—a big one that holds 125 pounds; but most of the time I don't fill it, but we have our folks visit from back east and then I do." This working wife's growing appetite for material goods also led to the purchase of a car, which she described with the acumen of a seasoned consumer, minutely detailing its model, color, and accessories.[51]

The escalation of the consumer sector of the economy in the 1950s and '60s brought more and more women into the labor force where they might increase the purchasing power of their families. After mid-century the working wife was the source of affluence in many a household. Among families whose income exceeded $10,000 a year the proportion of working wives rose as high as 60 percent by the late 1960s. For the first time college-educated women were more likely to assist in the financial support of their families than were high school graduates. These middle-class two-worker households expended significantly more on consumer goods than did families with a single male breadwinner. Although the working wives of the 1950s and '60s contributed on the average only 15 to 25 percent of the family income, they added a garnish of luxury to middle-class family life, which had far-reaching consequences for "the affluent society" and was acknowledged by market researchers as a major source of that "discretionary income" on which the consumer economy rests.[52] Thus, women went to work in sex labeled jobs to increase the purchasing power of their families and to gratify consumer lusts, manifesting yet another facet of the archetype of the sexy saleslady.

The circle of family, work, and consumption closed in on women in yet another way. The spurious fulfillment of consumerism served to accommodate women to the monotony and depersonalization of the female work force. The purchase of clothes and cosmetics, for example, could give the overworked and underpaid service workers of the 1920s a semblance of social status. According to Frances Donovan's observations in 1920, waitresses were "pretty good imitators of their sisters whom we call 'society girls,' wanted only the smartest clothes and bought them on $20 a week." [53] Clothes were also a major element in the individuality and self-esteem of the salesladies whom Donovan investigated nine years later. The department store clerks ranked one another and asserted superiority over their wealthier customers by critical evaluation of styles of dress and skill in grooming.[54] Likewise, the working wives whom Elinor Langer encountered at the telephone company in 1970 found relief from the regimentation of their work and a sense of individuality by adorning their persons. "Most women have several wigs and are in some cases unrecognizable from day to day, creating the effect of a continually changing work force. The result of wiggery is escapism. The kaleidoscopic transformation of one's self while everything else remains the same." [55] A change in appearance, purchased at the going market price, could generate an ersatz sense of identity, which woman's work rarely supplied. The consumer ethic, in short, provided an escape valve for the pressures built up in the female labor force, release by way of purchase from the monotony of dead-end jobs.

Adjustment to the tensions intrinsic to the female labor force was also fostered by the deflection of the worker's identity away from the job and into the home. Working girls and working wives rarely conceived of themselves primarily as workers. This refracted consciousness of women was evidenced early in the twentieth century. A poll cited by Lorine Pruette in 1924 revealed that the majority of teen-age girls, almost all of whom expected to work at some point in their lives, viewed their future through the rosy fantasy of a happy home life. When asked what would prompt them to enter the work force, 32 percent checked the response: to succeed personally, 15 percent to help one's children to succeed, and 46 percent to help one's mate succeed.[56] Polls conducted regularly for the next three decades conveyed the same expectations of women, both to work and to maintain a home, while resting one's identity on the latter. By the mid '50s only 20 to 25 percent of college women had any intention of molding their work experience into a career. The roles of wife and mother were so predominant in the aspirations of the co-eds of the '50s, and that phrase so frequently in use, that it was shortened to the acronym "wam." Yet 54 percent of these college-educated women eventually found themselves in the work force, having arrived there without the forethought and singlemindedness to overcome discriminatory wages, low status and monotonous chores. The kaleidoscopic roles of women, perceived through this domestic consciousness, worked to accommodate women to these inequitable positions.

From the perspective of the working man, on the other hand, the lowly place of women outside the home prevented undue alarm about job competition and the breakdown of sex roles. Changes in popular attitudes regarding woman's work did not always keep pace with the movement of wives and mothers into the labor force. A 1960 poll by the Michigan Survey Research Center revealed that only 34 percent of all the husbands questioned approved of wives working, at a point when 38 percent of the wives in the survey had earned some outside income in the last year. The vast majority of those husbands who did endorse their wives' entry into the work force justified their opinions by reference to supplementary family income earned by working wives. An earlier poll of husbands got to the heart of the male response to working wives. The ideal was this: a wife could work and thereby enhance the economic power of the family as long as she achieved only "moderate success," that is, did not challenge the superiority of the male breadwinner.[57] The frequent interruption of women's work by pregnancy and child care helped to bring a husband's dreams to fruition. The commonest varieties of female employment, clerical and sales work, had the additional advantage of being readily available to women whenever it became appropriate for them to reenter the work force, or wherever the family might move to enhance the husband's career. The wives' employers eagerly cooperated with American husbands in this conspiracy against women's success. As late as 1960, 68 percent of the office managers polled chafed at the idea of placing women in supervisory or management positions. A woman's co-workers, of either sex, also resented being put under the direction of women.[58] The attitudes of employers, fellow workers, and husbands, as well as the domestic sensibilities of women themselves, all conspired to keep the female sex in its segregated and inequitable place in the labor force.

The underlying tension between women's two roles assumed almost schizophrenic proportions in the postwar world when the women in the work force were serenaded with a chorus of praise for the vocation of housewife and mother so ear-splitting that it could have drowned out even the nineteenth-century cult of domesticity. American culture simultaneously charged women with working outside the home and creating bigger and better families. The pattern was already set in World War II, when a writer in the *Ladies' Home Journal* advised women of the nation's "most important postwar job . . . to make it cheaper, safer, easier, and more emotionally rewarding for most married women to have three babies apiece." Women were charged "to correct the mistakes of the 1920s and '30s" and supply the world with an exploding population of freedom-loving and patriotic Americans.[59] During and after the war the ladies' magazines and Hollywood films were besplattered with images of cuddly babies. On the Broadway stage the cast of one musical sang and danced to the joyous theme "We're Having a Baby." The television media was inaugurated in the same spirit of domesticity and bizarre showmanship. In 1953 two-thirds of American television sets were tuned in to watch the comedy of pregnancy on "I Love Lucy." Then, uncannily, in the same week that the long-awaited birth was celebrated on national television, Lucille Ball brought her first child into the world.[60] The rites of motherhood were everywhere as women marched off to their jobs.

The partisans of domesticity had to surmount many obstacles before they won cultural hegemony after World War II. The twentieth century had begun with cries of alarm that the home was in peril and iconoclastic assertions that "home is but a place to dine and die in." Social commentators in the 1920s took note of the rising divorce rate and wondered if monogamous marriage was a viable institution in the modern world. Sociologists catalogued a long list of social and economic functions that could now be performed outside the home: economic production, early childhood education, the recreation of family members, the inculcation of national values. Yet in the face of this skepticism, social scientists set to work to pick up the pieces of the nineteenth-century family and build a "finer, more plastic form, one which will respond more fully to the sensitive and imperative needs of the modern human being." [61]

By the 1940s their success was emblazoned across textbooks on the sociology of the family: **"MARRIAGE IS A FUNDAMENTAL HUMAN NEED."** [62] This need was tersely defined for high school readers: "The family will always be necessary to give emotional stability, care and social acceptance to the child. It is the only group in which can be developed love, kindness and the enduring relations of life." [63] A young woman interviewed by the *Ladies' Home Journal* attempted to explain this growing identification between the family and all that was warm, secure, and human; "the depression or something, somehow, made human relations important again," and the war illustrated that "the only security I can count on now is emotional security." [64] The legacy of insecurity left by the Depression and World War II undoubtedly encouraged a grasping toward the family for personal support and stability. Yet the American home was also responsive to the larger sweep of social history, at a time when change had become commonplace and when public services, social needs, culture, and recreation, as well as economic relations were all funneled into cold and rigid channels. The twentieth century accelerated and extended beyond the middle class the process of privatization that compounded the psychological functions if not the social tasks of the family. A new definition of the family was constructed out of an absorption of all emotional satisfaction into the home, leaving the rest of society etiolated, and impersonal.

The line between home and society was most tautly drawn in the social theory of Talcott Parsons.[65] According to Parsons, the family was merely a "subsystem of society" whose social strength was in its smallness and isolation. The essential function performed within the narrow, insulated sphere of the nuclear family, he maintained, was the socialization of children and the control of tension for adults. The domestic unit was an emotional refuge in a bureaucratized and routinized society. In short, the family was defined by opposition to modern societal organization, further removed from the outside world than ever before. By contrast, the nineteenth-century concept of the family allowed for the overflow of domestic values into society at large, and, in fact, many women disguised as social mothers succeeded in escaping the home via that outward bound emotional current. Parsons, in contrast, defined the twentieth-century family as a completely privatized social unit, whose specialized functions served society only by remaining cloistered from it.

This influential theory, regardless of its accuracy as a description of actual family life in postwar America, provided the foundation for another stark dichotomy between male and female roles. It decreed that it was man's role to represent the family in society and woman's to direct the emotional and psychological functions of the home. Man's function was "instrumental"; it required the ability to earn a living, compete with other men, deal efficiently and rationally with people and things. Woman's home function was "expressive" in nature; it called forth her aptitude for divining personal needs, supplying emotional support, and monitoring interpersonal relationships. The new family system dictated that women socialize children but leave their education to schools and soothe weary husbands but never interfere in their business affairs. The prescribed female role was more rarefied than ever, an unadulterated emotional and psychological emanation.

This twentieth-century sociological paradigm, and the popular conceptions it both incorporated and sustained, instructed women to seek in marriage the only outlet for personal fulfillment. "The family has become an end in itself and one that is essentially the development and satisfaction of personality. If success is realized, it has to be by at least partial fulfillment of the individual's union with the other self. The woman has become less a helpmate and more a comrade in an adventure which proves hopeless, unless it is a reciprocity not so much in services as in responses." [66] Marriage, in other words, was an intensive communion of male and female personalities, unalloyed by such practical factors as exchange of economic and social services. This heterosexual unity was given the hallowed title "intimacy." Women, more than men, were exposed to this new marital ideal, expounded in high school home economics textbooks and college courses on marriage and the family. As the wife supervised the "expressive" home functions, it was expected that she would be more attuned to the demands of intimacy. Furthermore, women were assumed to have greater needs for intense human relationships than men. Readers of one textbook on the family were told that "the companionship of her husband was not enough to feed [a woman's] craving for intimate response," which would ineluctably propel her to bear and rear children. [67]

The teen-age girl who studied Paul Landis' paean to family intimacy was alerted to another sexual imbalance in the modern marriage. With careful deliberation Landis planted some statistical warnings in the mind of the high school girl. He cited a series of surveys which suggested that the intelligent and accomplished girl might have some difficulties in finding a husband; only 11 percent of high school boys would think of marrying a girl who surpassed them in intelligence, while 76 percent of college men were happy to wed their intellectual inferiors. Landis considered it common knowledge that "a man desires a woman who is femininely attractive and emotionally satisfying, as well as intelligent. The intellectual woman must cultivate these traits if she is to be successful in courtship." [68] With such ideas in vogue, it is not surprising that the percentage of women who attended college fell precipitously between 1940 and 1960, and two-thirds of all college women in the '50s failed to receive their B.A.'s. Co-eds intent on getting married, furthermore, were not above disguising their intellectual abilities while in the company of prospective husbands. One poll taken on a western campus indicated that 65 percent of college women thought high intelligence was a liability in the marriage market. Forty percent of the girls questioned at Barnard College in the '50s confessed that they "played dumb" to bolster their dates' sense of superiority.[69] Landis congratulated the girl who employed such wily methods. "It does, however, require a woman of considerable intelligence to flatter such a male ego." [70] In short, women were encouraged to embark upon marriage in a spirit of duplicity that seemed to contradict the idea of intimacy.

The sex roles prescribed by the twentieth-century concept of the family—the polarization of male and female into "instrumental" and "expressive" functions—also undercut the intimacy of the married couple. They decreed that the wife would commune with her spouse only in fleeting moments stolen from the periphery of his career. The wife would assist the breadwinner only indirectly and in keeping with her expressive skills. The wife's specialized role was defined as early as the '20s by Dorothy Dix in her syndicated newspaper column.

A man's wife is the show window where he exhibits the measure of his achievement. . . . The biggest deals are put across over luncheon tables; . . . we meet at dinner the people who can push our fortunes. . . . The woman who cultivates a circle of worthwhile people, who belongs to clubs, who makes herself interesting and agreeable is a help to her husband.[71]

Robert and Helen Lynd found in the 1920s that the wives of the business class in Middletown often conformed to these prescriptions, playing the roles of "show window" and socialite to enhance their husband's careers. The upper-class wives in the suburbs of the postwar era discovered that the exercise of their expressive function often decreed almost a complete abdication of marital intimacy. A doctor's wife described her function as follows:

> My influence is this: if he has a complicated life at home, his mind is not at ease. The wife has the obligation to leave his mind at ease so that he can give his best to work. Added with help in social contacts she should not pester him at the office to bellyache. She must give him a chance to get together with fellows to exchange ideas [medical colleagues]; give them the right to spend time as they want.[72]

In actuality, the woman's supposed craving for deep marital union and intense emotional response was forfeited to the demands of her husband's instrumental role in earning the family living.

The flight of families to the suburbs, the largest single residential area in America by 1960, sheltering more than 30 percent of America's population, drastically reduced the practical possibilities of marital companionship.[73] A study of Westchester County,

New York, in the 1930s illustrated the effect that commuter living was to have on conjugal unity. The wives of Westchester not only spent their working hours in the home but 56 to 65 percent of their leisure time as well. The typical husband, meanwhile, with more leisure time than his wife, spent only one half of it at home.[74] After World War II, males who made daytime excursions into the suburbs for sociological research were such a minority that they provoked nervous jokes about harems. When a researcher succeeded in finding a husband to interview, the ensuant conversation would not be rich in domestic detail: "I'm home so little, I only see the kids for an hour in the evening, that is if I'm not going off to a meeting." [75] The ladies' magazines of the '50s read the weak pulse of family intimacy with alarm. *McCall's* inaugurated a campaign for togetherness, and the *Ladies' Home Journal* provided a regular feature to remind its readers that "There's a Man in the House." Families were urged to devote weekends to remedial programs in family recreation and ritual enactments of fatherhood like the backyard barbecue. Helen Lopata's investigations at the end of decade, however, revealed that most wives had simply discarded the goal of marital intimacy. The women she interviewed seldom spoke spontaneously of their husbands, and when asked to rank their most gratifying roles only 8 percent attested that they found the most satisfaction in their relationship with their husbands.[76]

In terms of the expenditure of a wife's time, she was more intimate with pots, pans, and appliances than with the man she married. In fact, despite the heralded preeminence of "human relationships" in the modern family, the suburban housewife had little intercourse with people. Lopata found that only 2 to 4 percent of the women she contacted ranked such things as community and religious organizations or friendship among their more important activities. Even the coffee klatch, it turned out, was a minor source of human contact: only 16 percent of the housewives reported seeing a friend in their homes during a typical day.[77] The bulk of woman's time, never less than fifty hours a week, was devoted to housework and child care, and when young children demanded attention, the mother's workweek often surpassed one hundred hours of labor. One young mother described her working day to Mirra Komarovsky in exhausting detail:

> I get up at 6 A.M. and put on coffee and cereal for breakfast and go down to the basement to put clothes into the washing machine. When I come up I dress Teddy (1½) and put him in his chair. Then I dress Jim (3½) and serve breakfast to him and to my husband and feed Teddy.

> While my husband looks after the children I go down to get the clothes out of the machine and hang them on the line. Then I come up and have my own breakfast after my husband leaves. From then on the day is as follows: Breakfast dishes, clean up kitchen. Make beds, clean the apartment. Wipe up bathroom and kitchen floor. Get lunch vegetable ready and put potatoes on to bake for lunch. Dress both children in outdoor clothes. Do my food shopping and stay out with children til 12. Return and undress children, wash them up for lunch, prepare lunch, feed Teddy and put him to nap. Make own lunch, wash dishes,

straighten up kitchen. Put Jim to rest. Between 1 and 2:30, depending on the day of the week, ironing (I do my husband's shirts home and, of course, all the children's and my own clothes), thorough cleaning of one room, weekend cooking and baking, etc.; 3 P.M., give children juice or milk, put outdoor clothes on. Out to park; 4:30 back. Give children their baths. Prepare their supper. Husband usually home to play with them a little after supper and help put them to bed. Make dinner for husband and myself. After dinner, dishes and cleaning up. After 8 P.M. often more ironing, especially on the days when I cleaned in the afternoon. There is mending to be done; 9 P.M., fall asleep in the living room over a newspaper or listening to the sound of the radio; 10 P.M., have a snack of something with my husband and go to bed.

I read this account to my husband and he said that it sounded too peaceful, that the children seem to keep out of the way too much. I haven't conveyed to you at all the strain of being constantly with the children for twelve hours a day, day in day out.

This harassed housewife spent most of her time interacting with food, dirt, appliances, and children. The latter provoked more irritation than enriching human contact, much less a deep quaff of "intimate response." [78]
The inundation of the home with automatic gadgets, miracle cleaning potions, and instant food products, only served to clutter up the household and compounded woman's chores. In fact, as Betty Frie-

dan discovered, the packaged foods of the '50s were advertised as methods of making cooking more elaborate and demanding, rather than simplifying the homemaker's job. Cake mixes were to be used "creatively," given a "personal touch," and required effort to expiate the "underlying guilt" of the housewife who cut corners.[79] Cooking could, and should, be made into a complicated art, according to Lynn White, president of Mills College. White maintained that college women should be exposed to the intellectual rigors of gourmet cooking rather than such irrelevancies as philosophy and science: "Why not study the theory and preparation of a Basque paella, of a well-marinated shish kebab, lamb kidney sautéed in sherry, an authoritative curry?"[80] In 1961 *The New York Times* looked forward to the development of computerized homemaking, but not because it would liberate women from housework. On the contrary, "the computer would free a woman to spend her day preparing an exotic evening meal at which many foods would be tasted and consumed over a three-hour period."[81] In the face of advancing domestic technology the women of the postwar era turned to primitive woman's labor in the name of creativity, cooking gourmet food and sewing the family wardrobe.

These soaring standards of homemaking, however, were only peripheral demands on the housewife's time. The stellar image in the kaleidoscope of woman's roles was maternal. By the 1950s, the ladies' magazines were proclaiming "motherhood is a way of life." The women interviewed by Helen Lopata ranked motherhood as their most important role; one of them confessed "it's been my whole life."[82]

Motherhood, like the family, had weathered the attacks of feminists, flappers, and social theorists early in the twentieth century. The boldest assault on motherhood was made by the behavioral psychologist John B. Watson in the '20s. Watson seriously questioned whether "there should be individual homes for children or even whether children should know their parents." [83] This sacrilegious nihilism had been brewing for some time. Freudian psychology, particularly the concept of the Oedipal complex, placed unpleasant, incestuous connotations on the hitherto sacrosanct ties between mother and son. Even the *Ladies' Home Journal* was prompted to tell mothers to keep a polite distance from their male offspring. Progressive thinkers suspected that doting mothers retarded the advances of the younger generation, encumbering them with archaic values and conservative ties to the home. The child, it was said, belonged to the future, and, therefore, "parents should never expect their own highest ideals to become the ideals of their children." [84]

Despite the negative implications of parental power, no one expected that the private family would be supplanted as the nursery of human development. Even Watson conceded that "the home we have with us . . . the behaviorist has to accept the home and make the best of it." The first necessary reform, if the home were to become the seat of scientific child-rearing, according to Watson, was the eradication of obsessive maternal affection. Intense emotional ties between a mother and son created weakly "mama's boys," incapable of becoming self-reliant and efficient within the impersonal and grueling system of modern life. Therefore, Watson advised: "Let your behavior always be kindly firm. Never hug and kiss them, never let them sit on your lap. If you must kiss, kiss them once on the forehead when they say goodnight. Shake hands with them in the morning." Cuddling and coddling would give way to rigid conditioning and exposure to life's hard knocks in the socialization of the "problem-solving child" of the twentieth century.[85] The new theory of child-rearing called for major revisions in the physical treatment of infants. The behaviorial methods included bottle feeding, rigid schedules, early toilet training, exposure to heat, cold, and pain. Elements of this regimen had appeared in child-rearing manuals as early as the 1890s, and the behaviorist's methods were widely popularized in the 1920s and '30s. The major objective of this theory, to foster the child's independence and individualism, required that mothers send their offspring to preschools, kindergartens, summer camps, and a panoply of extrafamilial institutions to be "emotionally weaned." [86]

The child's newly won independence did not, however, necessarily liberate the mother. Ellen Key told mothers that "our soul is to be filled with the child, just as the mind of the scientist is possessed by his investigation and the artist by his work. . . . This devotion much more than the hours immediately given to one's children is the absorbing thing; the occupation which makes an earnest mother always go to any external activity with divided soul and dissipated energy." [87] The mothers of the business class in Middletown illustrated how time-consuming the encouragement of a child's independence could be. One mother said: "I accommodate my whole life to my little girl," which entailed chauffeuring children to school, music and dancing lessons, being at home when they returned from school, and voraciously reading the latest literature on child psychology and nutrition.[88] The attempt to develop independence in infants was particularly productive of nervous exhaustion, entailing as it did the pressure to toilet train an infant by three months of age; feed the child precisely on schedule; and endure the childish tantrums and long bouts of screeching that were deemed healthy. The ordeal of behaviorist motherhood was minutely and painfully detailed in Mary McCarthy's *The Group*. It was the fate of one character, Priss, to wed a pediatrician who imposed this spartan regimen on her and their child, reducing the mother to a nervous, stuttering wreck. The advances of child-rearing theory held yet another disaster in store for Priss, one, which like so many of the incidents in the novel, must have fallen upon many real women as well. After years of dedication to her task she was informed that her method of child-rearing was outmoded, "a fossil relic of behaviorism." [89]

By 1940 Dr. Arnold Gesell had revamped child-rearing theory, contradicted John Watson, and laid the groundwork for Benjamin Spock. During the throes of the Depression and World War II, Gesell and his disciples became convinced that the human personality needed an atmosphere of warmth, intimacy, and trust in which to develop. The mother, of course, was called upon to provide this environment for the young child. Breast-feeding was once again in vogue, invoked in order to "strengthen the bonds between mother and child." In order to establish the child's sense of trust, the mother was required to be immediately responsive to the child's cry for nourishment.

Feeding according to the child's demands replaced the schedule imposed by behaviorists; the infant was now the dictator of the mother's routine.[90] Helene Deutsch interpreted demand feeding so as to discourage mothers from working outside the home. She knew, she said, of working mothers who arranged somehow or other to be "ready exactly at the minute to give suck to their babies. But these modern sucklings! They do not like punctuality and at the mother's slightest gesture of impatience, her furtive glance at the clock for instance, they react as if she were as wicked as a she-wolf." [91] The mother's undivided loving attention was considered absolutely essential in infancy in order to create the sense of emotional security on which a healthy personality could be built.

After infancy, however, the child's development proceeded to the stages often labeled autonomy and initiative. The mother's task from this point on was to gradually release the child to the world. Gesell advised an hour a day at nursery school for an eighteen-month-old child. From the ages of three to five the mother should take particular care to encourage the child's independence and see him past the crises of the Oedipal stage. Excessive maternal attention from this point on suggested overprotectiveness and a domineering mother. Still, a mother must always be there as a reliable source of warmth and love for the growing child. The expert mother was asked to walk a fine line between coldness and excessive warmth, between negligence and possessiveness.

The mother of the postwar era, reeling from the change from behaviorist to the developmental scheme of child care, and dizzy from conveying trust and encouraging independence at one and the same time, found a sympathetic guide in Dr. Benjamin Spock. His tome on baby care, which was first issued in 1946, and eventually sold more than twenty million copies, opened with fatherly reassurance. "Don't be afraid to trust your own common sense. Bringing up your child won't be a complicated job if you take it easy, trust your instincts and follow the directions your doctor gives you." Spock then went on to celebrate the central feature of the postwar child-rearing ideology, mother love: "We know for a fact that the natural loving care that kindly parents give their children is a thousand times more valuable than their knowing how to pin a diaper on just right or how to make a formula expertly." [92]

Spock's use of the word "parents" in his introduction is deceptive. His actual instructions on the loving care of children were addressed to mothers. Only a few paragraphs in more than six hundred pages spoke of the duties of fathers. He went only so far as to say that the father might "occasionally" give the baby a bottle or change its diapers. Then he added this proviso: "Some fathers get gooseflesh at the very idea of helping to take care of a baby and there is no good to be gained by trying to force them. Most of them come around to enjoying the children later, *when they're more like real people*" [93] (italics mine). One inference to be drawn from Spock's words is that the mother's role, like her most intimate companion, was somehow juvenile and subhuman.

Arnold Gesell had set the stage for this reduction of the mother to the child's level. The ideal mother he said, "instead of striving for executive efficiency . . . aims first of all to be perceptive of and sensitive to the child's behavior. Thus she becomes a true complement to him, alertly responsive to his needs." [94] Spock expressed this maternal duty in more homely phrases: "Don't be afraid to love him and enjoy him. Every baby needs to be smiled at, talked to, played with, fondled—gently and lovingly." The developmental approach required that a mother participate in the mental life of her child, indulge in baby talk, play childhood games, and perform the most menial tasks with childlike zest. Spock quoted one woman who seemed to have accomplished this remarkable feat. She triumphantly reported that she had toilet-trained her child and "it seems to have brought us closer together. It's as if we'd found a new trust in each other." [95]

Benjamin Spock was very much aware that motherhood entailed more than a series of such edifying episodes. He told mothers to expect postnatal depression, periods of nervousness, and frequent physical exhaustion. When the strain of motherhood became overwhelming, Dr. Spock prescribed a properly feminine cure: "Go to a movie or to the beauty parlor, or to get a new hat or dress." Taking a job outside the home, on the other hand, was not advisable. Spock allowed that some mothers could not be deterred from seeking a job, but he made sure that they would leave the home with a guilty conscience: "If a mother realizes clearly how vital [her love and care] is to a small child, it may make it easier to decide that the extra money she might earn, or the satisfaction she might receive from an outside job, is not so important after all." After the child reached school age, the prohibitions against working mothers were relaxed, provided she could be at home when her offspring returned from school. [96] Thus the directives of the child-rearing theorists neatly meshed with the demands of the female labor market. They encouraged women to seek employment outside the home after the interruption of child-rearing, when women were preoccupied with family affairs and consequently well suited for and satisfied with low paying, low status part-time jobs.

Furthermore, the length of the interruption in the typical woman's working life was prolonged to at least a decade during the baby boom, which began in World War II and extended up to 1960. In this era, middle-class white women were bearing typically three to four children and had achieved a fertility rate higher than this segment of population had reached for almost a century. Some commentators urged women to be even more prolific. Helene Deutsch was afraid that once her children left home a woman's narcissistic psyche would be irreparably damaged. In order to prevent this disaster she opined that "probably the path traced by nature is the most successful: having many children is the best protection against this tragic loss." [97] Farnham and Lundberg placed no maximum limit on the number of children women should bear, and in fact urged the federal government to award prizes to women for the birth of every child beyond her first. The consequences of such fecundity, a population explosion, was a problem that "would have to be solved by some future generation." [98]

Child-rearing experts like Dr. Spock were more concerned that future generations would perpetuate the appropriate sex roles. Spock's use of the pronoun "he" to designate all children was quite apt, for the goal of developmental child-rearing, the production of adults who were "systematic," "independent," and trained to "orderly ways of doing business" was designed for males. The girl child received attention only on those occasions when Spock expounded on the importance of inculcating sex roles at an early age. He hoped that the female child would "realize that it is her destiny to be a woman" at least by age three and urged that a boy who continued to play with dolls much beyond that age should be sent to a psychiatrist. Both mothers and fathers were admonished to present themselves as stereotypical models of masculinity and femininity for their children to imitate. In order to prepare the preschool girl "for her adult role in life," a father was told to "compliment her on her dress or hairdo or the cookies she made." The little girl's relationship with her father would determine "the way she makes friendships with boys and men later on, the kind of man she eventually falls in love with." Meanwhile, a boy's adoration of his perfectly feminine mother will lead him to "protect, please, and idolize" his wife someday. The constant and exclusive exposure of the young child to two role models, representing the sharp dichotomy between male and female roles, masculine and feminine character, was carefully designed to propagate another generation of sexual stereotypes.[99]

The prescribed womanhood of twentieth-century America, like its many predecessors, was widely disseminated, neatly integrated with social and economic structure, and tightly woven in its internal logic. As always, the prescriptive literature on sex roles and popular images of femininity interacted with the realities of woman's life in a complex and unpredictable fashion. Women were puppets neither of

Freud, Spock, General Motors, nor Madison Avenue. They shaped their kaleidoscopic personal histories, however, within the options, directives, and alternatives provided by American society. The journals of Margaret Fowler Dunaway from the years 1926 to 1960 give private testimony to the way at least one woman built a life within the shadow of the twentieth-century stereotypes. Margaret Dunaway submitted her diaries to the Radcliffe Woman's Archives in 1953 with "a blush of shame. . . . I write painfully, acknowledging . . . to have been a Nobody all these years." In her youth three decades earlier Margaret Dunaway was not given to such self-abnegation. She had been a charter member of the League of Women Voters and harbored strong personal ambitions. Later, she recalled "the desire for marriage and a career, coming from different directions, streets, and at about the same time, and the whirlwind of conflict can never be erased from my memory. I chose, as most, I imagine, both, but took marriage first." In the 1920s she surrendered her aspirations for personal achievement to dedication to the welfare of her husband and three children, but not without second thoughts. "My office as a Mother seems to take all my time but it should not. I am an individual outside of that." Occasionally she expressed her restlessness in verse: "So goes the morning/ So go my days/ So go the years/ Why, Why, do I long for achievement?" [100]

Still, Mrs. Dunaway set out in search of personal satisfaction rather than public achievement. She sought fulfillment, first of all, in conjugal intimacy, "longing for the perfect marriage—the uniting and flowing together in one large and powerful stream of life." In her case the pursuit of this goal met with more than the usual obstacles. Not only was Mr. Dunaway preoccupied with his career, in some vague business that his wife seemed to know little about, but the difficulties of the Depression took him to jobs a half continent away from his family. For years on end Mrs. Dunaway saw her husband only on holidays and during vacations. As her elder children left home, more and more of her family relations were conducted through letters—"so necessary to keep the sense of unity alive." Margaret Dunaway grasped at every ephemeral chance to make family intimacy transcend physical distance. One reunion with her husband and children in 1936 prompted this comment: "the wonderful family we have . . . united—though thousands of miles apart, the members [illegible] confident of each other's success, of the others' right to achieve, to progress." [101]

While her husband and older children were off achieving, Mrs. Dunaway devoted herself to her youngest daughter, Joan. She devised new plans of character development, joined in her daughter's games and school projects, deliberated over her education, and speculated on her future—in short, she lived vicariously through her child. At the same time Mrs. Dunaway disdained maternal possessiveness: "Your children are not your children. They are the sons and daughters of life's longing for itself. . . . They come through you, but not from you. And they are with you yet they belong not to you." When her youngest child graduated from high school, Margaret Dunaway observed: "Mothering, a wonderful profession! But it leaves one always looking for someone to clutch on to, to mother. Now I shall subdue the mother instinct and perhaps be an individual for a few years." With her children grown and scattered around the world, Mrs. Dunaway's journals changed little, were still the repository of family details, now interspersed with comments on current events—chiefly nervous murmurings about the advances of Communism and the threat of atomic holocaust.[102]

Margaret Dunaway had no regrets about the course her life had taken. She found abundant satisfaction in the success of her three children and contentment in the company of her spouse finally retired. Her journal of the 1950s did not echo with the malaise of her youth. She no longer lamented the fact that the prose, poetry, and religious theory of her journal were never made public, that she had to settle for being a "nobody." She was content with "the office of Mother and of Wife—and now of Grandmotherly joy—still bring me into the current of supreme satisfaction." Still, the life of Margaret Dunaway was hedged in by the conventions of womanhood, invisibly constrained within the narrow set of alternatives for the female sex. One comment in her diary of 1928 suggests, albeit obliquely, that Margaret Dunaway dimly recognized the subtle strictures of woman's role. "I saw today a little bride entering her bright new home on the arm of her elderly husband. Why did I think of a little bird entering a shiny new cage?" Was Mrs. Dunaway merely reacting with distaste to the couple's age differences? Or did that metaphor convey her own sense of claustrophobia in woman's place? At any rate, the configuration of roles proffered to women in the twentieth century did resemble just another in a long series of "shiny new cages."[103]

Margaret Dunaway's account of the lives of her daughters also provides a brief glimpse at the slightly renovated cages of the generation of women who came of age in the 1930s and 1940s. Her oldest daughter, Dorothy, left home in the mid '30s and found herself in a position typical of her generation, a low-paying, dead-end office job. She realized, according to her mother, "you have gone as far as you can. Unless you get into a new field of thought and work you stagnate." Dorothy was "so tired of the dead, dull routine of the law office" that she escaped into marriage. Her younger sister, Joan, also devoted her youth to marriage. It was only in 1959, more than twenty years after she graduated from high school, that Joan decided to go to college and get a teaching credential. "I have debated so long this . . . I am at last really excited at the prospect of preparing to do something useful." Only in middle-age did she even prepare to move out of the home and undertake a role that she considered "useful." Dorothy also reentered the work force late in life, finding a job in the admissions office of the University of Chicago. Mrs. Dunaway was unable to find much of interest in the work of her daughters. Her son and son-in-law, on the other hand, had truly notable careers, one with the Atomic Energy Commission, the other as a Standard Oil executive, occupations whose "usefulness" was rarely open to question in the American value system.

Although a woman's work, and often her self-worth paled by comparison, the wives of these successful men shared in and contributed to the family status. Joan and Dorothy provided expressive support to their struggling husbands, and later contributed their hard-won earning as well. The wife of Don Carlos Dunaway played the classic role of the executive wife, right down to wining and dining his business contacts. In 1960 Mary Dunaway's indirect contribution to America's international oil interests entailed, among other things, entertaining thirty-two Arabs—"I cooked two entire days." [104]

Mrs. Dunaway's daughter-in-law illustrated a widespread middle- and upper-class phenomenon, the two-person career. Like the scholar's private typist, editor, and critic; the professional's patient, undemanding, and supportive mate; and the politician's ceremonial companion, the executive's wife devoted her time and energy to promoting the family's status. When worldly success came to such a couple, it would be acclaimed as the husband's achievement, and his helpmate would be left with only the lowly title "housewife." Mrs. Dunaway's daughters demonstrated a more typical life pattern for women in the postwar era, the kaleidoscopic dual role. They devoted their youth and consigned their identity to marriage and motherhood. When they reentered the labor force, it was with rusty skills, if any, and with their attention distracted by domestic responsibilities. These women were ideal recruits for the discriminatory female labor force. When a woman assisted in performing the breadwinner role, her husband did not reciprocate by taking on an equal share of home chores. At best, the male might lighten the working wife's load by drying the dishes and taking out the garbage, leaving her to fill, if not two, at least one and three-quarter jobs. This dual role was in fact a double burden, which helps to explain the low female representation in the twentieth-century annals of the famous and successful.

Those married women who did make names for themselves displayed extraordinary drive and energy, were, in short, superwomen. The Herculean stamina of these women is epitomized by Sylvia Plath, who galvanized the tensions of woman's kaleidoscopic roles into poetry of extraordinary power. Sylvia Plath, like many talented young women, fervidly pursued academic achievement. "All my life," she recalled in her autobiographical novel, *The Bell Jar,* "I'd told myself studying and reading and writing and working like mad was what I wanted to do, and it actually seemed to be true. I did everything well enough and got all A's, and by the time I made it to college nobody could stop me." Sylvia Plath toiled onward to achieve academic and literary success right up through her junior year at Smith College.[105]

In the summer of 1952, however, her march to fame was diverted into an epicycle of self-doubt. As a guest editor of the college issue of *Mademoiselle* magazine, she was bombarded with the seductions of the feminine mystique: the latest fashions, cosmetics, and techniques of man-hunting. Under the bright light of fashionable woman's culture her intellectual and artistic goals seemed flimsy. She fantasized retreat into the undemanding role of the wife of a mechanic with a "big cowey family." Then, again she observed, "this seemed a dreary and wasted life for a girl with fifteen years of straight A's." Sylvia Plath's role conflicts fermented into images of sexual mutilation and eviscerating childbirth. Soon the "Bell Jar" of madness closed over her, and she plotted her escape through suicide.[106]

Were it not for the accidental discovery of her unconscious body, Sylvia Plath would have died before reaching the age of twenty-one, her life rent apart by the conflict between devotion to the home and personal achievement. Slowly she crawled out of the Bell Jar and became strong and self-confident enough to take up both a literary career and the role of wife. Briefly, Sylvia Plath's muse was eclipsed by the rising reputation of her poet-husband for whom she performed all the traditional services of wife and mother. The marriage soon ended in divorce, however, leaving Sylvia alone to care for an infant and a two-year-old child. She stole time for art whenever the respite from housework and child care permitted. Her peak of creativity was "at three in the morning, that still blue, almost eternal hour before the baby's cry, before the glassy music of the milkman, setting his bottles." [107]

Her friend the critic Alfred Alvarez contended that Plath's "drab domestic life fused with her imagination richly and without hesitation." The images of home that emanated from her experience, however, were most often tinged with blood and pain; cuts, burns, fevers, and hemorrhaging. Among Sylvia Plath's most violent poetic themes was the memory of her father who had died when she was eight years old.

If I've killed one man, I've killed two
The vampire who said he was you
and drank my blood for a year,
Seven years, if you want to know.
Daddy, you can lie back now.
There's a stake in your fat black heart . . .[108]

The vividness of these images indicates something more than the poet's fixation on her father's death or the determination to conquer immortality through art. The violence and self-destructive force in Sylvia Plath's poetry were so often attached to domestic themes and intimate images of femininity that it must have been, at least in part, a product of the feverish imagination of a woman trying to shoulder the double burden conferred upon her sex. The onus of womanhood in the mid-twentieth century must have also played a part in Sylvia Plath's death by suicide in 1963, ten years after her first attempt. In one of her last and most moving poems, "Edge," she presented death as the act of putting womanhood to its final rest.

> The woman is perfected.
> Her dead
>
> Her bare
>
> Feet seem to be saying:
> We have come so far, it is over.
>
> Each dead child coiled, a white serpent,
> One at each little
>
> Pitcher of milk, now empty.
> She has folded
>
> Them back into her body as petals
> Of a rose close when the garden
>
> Stiffens and odors bleed
> From the sweet, deep throats of the night
> flowers.[109]

Needless to say, neither the sensational nature of Sylvia Plath's life and death nor the explosive force of her confrontation between the domestic role and the individual woman's aspirations were typical of her generation. The middle-class women of the '50s, by and large, suppressed their desires for personal achievement, sought their identities in motherhood, and retained only enough residual ambition to fill arduous but unrewarding roles in the work force. The ordinary working wife of the '50s balanced home and job to her own satisfaction, tempered her desire for personal achievement with domestic priorities, and created her identity out of myriad responsibilities and piecemeal rewards. At the same time, women of the lower classes, ethnic minorities, the poor, and racial outcasts, hoisted uniquely onerous burdens of sexual oppression. The experience of these classes of women will be explored when this account moves on to the late 1960s and early 1970s when the kaleidoscope of womanhood was jarred again and gave shape to a new feminism.

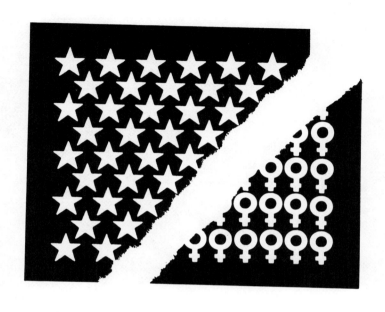

THE CURRENT SNARES OF SEXISM:

INEQUALITY IN ANY CLASS

In the 1970s the veil of secrecy that shrouded the inner sanctums of the American ruling class began to unravel, and in the year 1973 the clandestine operations of the powerful were being exposed in every quarter: the corporate empire, the Pentagon, the White House. Investigations of International Telephone and Telegraph, the secret bombings of Cambodia, and, of course, the Watergate affair, laid open the operations of the power elite to public scrutiny. Beneath the avalanche of scandals—sordid details of the sinister, corrupt, and morally bankrupt methods of the nation's leaders—lay a less spectacular exposé: the cast of characters that paraded before the television audience during the Watergate hearings was almost exclusively male. Only the minor roles of secretaries and the nonspeaking parts of loyal wives were played by women. Off-stage, bleak comic relief was provided by another wife in her telephone conversations, and the only fatality of the scandal was also a woman, a wife who died in an air crash while dutifully serving her spouse's corrupt interests. Perhaps women could take solace in the fact that their sex was so meagerly and peripherally implicated in this dirty business. Surely, however, it betokened one measure of sexual inequality: the denial of woman's inalienable right to be represented among the powerful practitioners of venality. Yet women were barred from the heroic roles in the Watergate affair as well as from the cast of heavies. It seemed that during the Senate hearings nary a woman could be found in the nation's capital to perform as a courtly senator, a counsel, or his trusted assistant. With the exception of one beleaguered senator of Japanese descent, the principals of the drama were all Caucasian as well as male. Racial minorities were even further removed from the scene of public power than were women. Although black Americans had marched on Washington thousands strong and then set the city ablaze with their bitterness a few years before, the complexion of the political establishment remained unchanged. Despite the militancy of blacks and women in the 1960s, the year 1973 dramatically underlined the age-old affront to the majority of the nation's citizens, that their color and their sex were not yet admitted to the ranks that ruled America.

Masses of Americans were outsiders not only to the cloisters of the powerful but also to the private life-styles of the American mainstream, including the middle-class distribution of sex roles. Many women, because of race and background, were denied access both to the velvet cage of bourgeois domesticity and the more comfortable posts of the female labor force. Those communities and subcultures that antagonized middle American standards of gender differences were heavily populated with the poor, the uneducated, and the cultural outcasts of every color. None of these groups, however, had evaded the snares of sexual inequality. Although the pattern of sexual discrimination might vary from class to class, the ubiquitous prerogatives of sexism penetrated to the very marrow of American society. Life at the bottom of the American system compounded the assaults on women, who became victims of racial, class, and sexual exploitation. The privacy of this segment of the population was not held as sacred as the homes of the middle class and, accordingly, its male-female relations have been subjected to the scrutiny of twentieth-century social scientists and public policy-makers, many of whom scarcely disguised their ethnocentrism. Beneath these often warped interpretations, however, distinctive configurations of sex roles can be discerned, patterns through which the careful observer can penetrate to the very core of womanhood, its ultimate contradictions as exposed in the extreme circumstances of the American poor and lower class.

The outcasts and fugitives from middle America shared certain basic alterations in the sociology of sex. First of all, women of the lower class, and especially those of racial minorities, were of necessity more prone to enter the work force. As late as 1930, 57 percent of the gainfully employed women in America were black or foreign-born, and right up through the 1970s poverty remained the strongest incentive for women to enter the work force.[1] This inducement to work was aggravated by the precarious family structure among the poor. Female-headed households accounted for 40 percent of the families living below the poverty line in 1971, as opposed to 10 percent among all American families.[2] This disruption of the traditional family unit, it must be noted, might operate as a cause as well as an effect of poverty; the absence of a male, with his superior earning power, could in itself reduce a family to poverty. Furthermore, the fatherless family was a product of the higher mortality rate among the poor as well as the result of desertion, divorce, separation, or illegitimacy. In other words, widowhood was a major cause of both poverty and woman's entrance into the job market.

The distinctive sexual division of roles beneath the middle-class strata of the American population, however, was more than a series of adjustments to poverty. The subcultures of the lower class also harbored unique domestic values and kinship organizations, which transformed to one degree or another the parameters of womanhood. Both the white working class and the black poor, for example, tended to rely on kinship support well beyond the nuclear household, taking in extended relatives, pooling financial resources in emergencies, and relying on kinsmen for routine companionship. These wider and stronger kinship ties often undercut the intensity of conjugal relations. Among the white working class of Protestant Anglo-Saxon background, women turned most frequently to their mothers and sisters for emotional sustenance. Working-class Italian-Americans in city neighborhoods also relied on relatives of the same sex rather than spouses for this personal support, as did the rural white women of Appalachia. Of the husbandless women in one public housing project, whose residents came from various races and backgrounds, fully one-fourth lived in households with an additional adult female. Among the black poor, the grandmother often headed a husbandless household. Thus, the poor and lower-class women of America often found special solace in their distinctive system of family organization, one that was anathema to the devotees of Dr. Spock.[3]

The neighborhood as well as the extended family served to broaden the personal contacts of women on the periphery of middle America. For example, Gerald Suttles observed in the near West Side of Chicago that black, Puerto Rican, Italian, and Mexican-American neighborhoods uniformly conducted an active social life in the streets. This phenomenon, as described by Suttles, illustrates a pattern of heterosexual interaction that again contradicts touted middle-class values.

The married women talk about household duties, family sickness, neighborhood scandals and their infants; the older men talk about their youth, pronounce judgments on local politics, and tell stories and joke about their peers. The young girls examine the latest work on clothing and pop tunes and tease each other about boys. The young boys follow the pattern of their fathers and converse about the exploits of their peers.[4]

In these slum neighborhoods, in short, social discourse was channeled into precise age and sex categories. This sex segregation was spacially represented in the Chicago streets: the adult women were assigned the stoop, their daughters the sidewalk nearby; young men congregated on the corner, and adult men took to clubs and taverns. Such male and female peer groups were also common among the rural poor of Appalachia, and elsewhere outside the bourgeois enclaves of domestic privacy and conjugal intimacy.

This precise sexual segregation set the stage for the inculcation of distinctive character traits in men and women. Studies of working-class attitudes toward the socialization of children reveal a differentiation between the parental demands on girls as opposed to boys that is slightly sharper than among the middle class. In particular, girls were expected to be especially polite and neat, while boys were called upon to display ambition and dependability.[5] The white working-class showed particular disdain for infractions against old-fashioned womanhood, such as a wife's joining the work force. In the Puerto Rican subculture the sex roles were drawn particularly tightly. Piri Thomas, for example, honored the woman who "respects me and does everything I ask," while his own role was to "support the family and make people respect the home." [6] The Italian Americans studied in Herbert Gans', The Urban Villagers, were equally attached to the standard of male dominance. The strong commitment to the practice of separating the spheres of the sexes typical of so many American sub-cultures often manifested itself in mutual distrust and male abuse, perhaps no harsher than among the middle class, but less subtle and less carefully disguised. Suttles recorded a conversation in an Italian-American tavern steeped in a derogatory conception of women. The men entertained themselves evaluating the physical attributes of the neighborhood women ("If my wife had tits like that I'd never get to work"). They then turned to a callous discourse on rape: "I heard some gal got raped up on Chicago Street," said Mike. "Yea, she's been up there ever since. Couldn't get laid anywhere else." The young male peer groups of the slums were notorious for predatory sexual escapades, boosting their egos by the conquest of women before they settled down with the wives whose fecundity established their virility.[7]

Within the institution of matrimony, the husband of the Anglo-Saxon and Italian working class, for example, kept his distance from his wife, except for sexual congress, which was likely to be brief, functional for the male and a duty for the wife. The care of the home and children was the sacrosanct domain of women. In general, among the working class the father remained even more detached from the process of child-rearing than did the middle-class male. The working class and poor mother performed her exclusive parental role without even the aid of father figures like Dr. Spock. Typically, she consulted only her own mother about the procedure of child care. Melvin Kohn's sophisticated analysis of class differences in the socialization of children demonstrated that working-class mothers eschewed the central concerns of developmental child psychology, the drawing forth of a child's individuality, independence, and distinctive personality. Working-class parents were more concerned with enforcing obedience and conformity to external authority, a priority that Kohn convincingly correlates with the exigencies of industrial labor, the regimented, uncreative and inflexible factory routines. The objectives of the mother in poverty were even more elementary, as described by one black woman: "Every morning the first thing I think about is what I can do to feed the kids." [8] Whatever the imperatives of child care, they fell squarely on the shoulders of females at all levels of the American social structure.

In summary, the women who lived beneath the border of the middle class experienced a distinctive set of roles and stereotypes, but they did not escape the insidious influence of sexual discrimination. It would be pointless and arbitrary to rank the relative degradation of female roles in the middle, working, and poverty classes. Sex segregation, for example, may have saved lower-class woman from the enervating false promises of conjugal intimacy; but it also left a legacy of mutual suspicion and misunderstanding between male and female. Outside the middle class, women might be spared the debilitating and self-defeating attempt to abide by the tenets of Dr. Spock; yet the regimen of rearing the children of the lower class was no less exhausting, no less frustrating, and remained the particular onus of the female. It was the ordeal of poverty, or the discomforts of a meager income in affluent America, that exacerbated the burdens of these women, and these difficulties were shared with the men in the same economic predicament.

Whatever unique traditions and social forms women might live by outside the boundaries of middle-America, these were threatened by agents and institutions of the middle class. Only one model of femininity emanated from American popular culture and through ubiquitous agents like the television set, insinuated itself into the homes of poor and lower class women. That alien image might be interpreted by lower-class audiences as a distraction, an object of ridicule, or an indictment of nonconformity. Yet for many young women in the ethnic neighborhood it was also seductive, and unleashed the forces of assimilation. At times the threat to non-conformity in sex roles was more concrete and inescapable; the deracination of rural women from their culture by the devastation of the local economy, or the dismantling of the neighborhood peer groups by slum clearance, and removal to the social wasteland of high-rise housing projects. At any rate, the United States was no more hospitable to geniune pluralism in sex role preferences than it was in political affairs.

The brutal irony of this cultural imperialism was that the economic system did not provide all Americans with the financial wherewithal to live in accord with the values which it ceaselessly promulgated. The black woman was placed in a completely untenable position; she was bombarded with fair white role models which she could not possibly emulate even with the aid of bleaching and straightening potions. Maya Angelou's first fantasy growing up in the South was to "look like a movie star . . . like one of the sweet little white girls who were everybody's dream of what was right with the world." [9] Kenneth Clark found such aspirations manifested in a psychic disease which pervaded the slums, driving children to balk in tears and terror when asked to play with dolls made in their own dark image. The proud images projected by the black culture of the 1960s at least erased the most insurmountable obstacles to a black woman's achievement of a tenable self-image.

The female inhabitants of a black colony in white culture were prey to more sinister forces than this, however. Personal experience within the black universe could in itself provide women with many positive models that contradicted white femininity. Maya Angelou, for example, lived in awe of her grandmother, who "some called a good-looking woman" but who represented only "power and strength" to her granddaughter.[10] This approving vision was common to many black women who saw in their mothers "the abstract principle of power." [11] From the perspective of the white outsider, however, such resourceful, rugged women often betokened a perversion of femininity—the black matriarch. This indictment was emphatically served upon black women in 1965 by Daniel Patrick Moynihan in the U.S. government publication *The Negro Family: The Case for National Action.* Based on raw statistical evidence of "female-headed families," high participation of women in the work force, and slightly superior educational attainment, Moynihan concluded that black wives and mothers were guilty of emasculating the race. The strong black woman overstepped feminine propriety and thereby sapped the ego strength of her mate, incapacitating him to achieve middle-class status in America. In the matriarchy argument, the long history of ideological assaults on woman's identity reached its nadir. The black woman, denied by race and poverty all the comforts and privileges of middle-class femininity and forced by necessity to shoulder a large share in the financial support of her family, was sternly condemned for castrating the rightful breadwinner.

The stigma of matriarchy had haunted black women long before Daniel Moynihan launched his attack in the 1960s. In fact, the pioneer black sociologist E. Franklin Frazier employed this invidious terminology to describe the family structure of his race in the 1930s. The term from the first referred to domestic units that lacked an authoritative and legitimate father. In other words, it was conferred upon women by default whenever a husband was absent as a result of births out of wedlock, widowhood, divorce, separation, or desertion. Matriarchy was traced to the institution of slavery, which, since it outlawed marriage among blacks, left only one family tie intact, the biological link between mother and child. This presumed centrality of the female in the slave family hardly justified the term matriarchy with its intimations of power and dominance antithetical to the status of chattel. At the time when Frazier coined the term, it was even more inappropriate for families several generations removed from the slave plantation.

By the 1930s the majority of the black population of the United States had settled into stable families in the rural South. Remarkably, by 1930 this population had advanced from a stage when legal marriage was unknown among them to a situation in which almost 90 percent of all births were legitimate.[12] Exhaustive studies of the families of black tenant farmers made by Charles S. Johnson in the '30s clearly refuted the matriarchy theory. Two-thirds of the families he studied contained both a mother and a father, and the bulk of the remainder were headed by widows, not by the divorced or the deserted.[13] The bugbear of female usurpation of the male role had been effectively discredited.

This is not to say that the black families of the South conformed to the conventional white pattern. Such conformity would be nothing short of suicidal for struggling sharecroppers, who required agricultural labor from children and women alike. The wives of tenant farmers took to the cotton and tobacco fields as well as to the domestic production and processing of almost all basic necessities. White as well as black farm women throve on agricultural labor; one put it this way, "gimme the field every time and tobacco growing."[14] The farm partnership initiated women into all the instrumental functions of the household provider, a role that many would have to shoulder alone in their widowhood. The economic capabilities of the black woman were abundantly illustrated in this letter to the Department of Agriculture during the Depression. "I am a widow woman with seven head of children; and I live on my place with plenty of help. All are good workers and I want to farm." She requested government relief in the form of a mule, wagon, and feed and closed with businesslike bluntness: "Because I am a woman I wants to ask you all to please help me to make a crop this year and let me hear from you by return mail. Yours for business. Mosel Brinson." [15]

Farmer Brinson also illustrated the peculiar form motherhood took for black women in the rural South. To white and black sharecroppers alike, children were valuable farm laborers, set to simple household chores when two years old and occupied in the fields by the age of ten. Young children became surrogate mothers as well as assistant farmhands, caretakers for the younger siblings soon after they could walk. The consequent reduction of specifically maternal duties, like the woman's expanded work role, was an essential adjustment to tenant farming. It displays the strength and versatility of the black woman, her willingness to cooperate with her spouse, not matriarchal arrogation of power. [16]

At the same time, the sharecropping home economy also undercut patriarchy. The low valuation of the tenant farmer's property offered minimal economic sanctions to the male head of the household. Title to a leased lot was hardly an awesome rod of authority. Conversely, women with land to till, farming experience, and the labor power of their children could subsist without the assistance of a husband and father. Accordingly, women were relatively free to abrogate the marriage vow. One self-reliant female reported this practice to Charles Johnson: "Everybody don't get married and if I can't get the one I want I don't want to get married." Another independent farmer and mother chose to live with a man out of wedlock, reasoning, "He's nice all right, but I ain't thinking about marrying. Soon as you marry a man he starts mistreating you, and I'm not going to be mistreated no more." The usual incidence of wife-beating (and counterassaults as well) were reported among black sharecroppers, but the self-sufficient farm woman could evade such abuse by exiling her husband or remaining single. The fact that the majority of black tenant farmers lived in stable conjugal units on the other hand indicated the strength of the male-female bond, without enforcement by stringent cultural sanctions.[17]

The black culture of the rural South was also tolerant of illegitimacy. When Johnson asked one black mother to plot the lineage of her children, she responded: "No sir, they ain't all got the same father. Them three is, but the two darkest ones ain't. Ain't seen the daddy of the first ones since year 'fore last. He married and don't give no help. . . . We started going together when I was a girl and just kept it up. I ain't seen these others' daddy since before this last one was born." Despite this complex marital and child-bearing history, all the children of the household were treated alike, and all shared a father figure in their mother's current husband. The father's family as well as the mother's was likely to take in illegitimate children and provide them with a stable family life and respectability. The rural black family succeeded in both relaxing the standard of monogamous sexual relationship and providing for the offspring of technically illicit unions, another efficacious adaptation to social economic circumstances.[18]

In short, the black family of the early twentieth century situated in the rural South cannot be blanketly categorized by reference to either a resident matriarch or patriarch. Some form of cooperative teamwork of all ages and sexes, under conditions that often breed capable, well-rounded female personalities, is a more likely possibility. Such was the background of Fannie Lou Hammer, for example, one of twenty siblings in a tenant-farm household, employed in the cotton fields at age six. By the 1960s, after a lifetime of beatings, jails, and bombings, she still stalwartly championed the rights of black men and women before county sheriffs and the elite of the Democratic Party.[19]

While ex-slaves and their children were reconstructing family life in the South, token numbers of black men and women forged their way into the middle and upper-middle classes. By the turn of the century, black women could be found in the ranks of the mothers of civilization and social housekeepers. Black women's clubs were founded in order to "give sustenance to black men," to encourage the "social uplift of the race," and to disseminate advice on childrearing. The civilizing mission merged into social activism with the formation of the National Association of Colored Women and the NAACP. Notable black women of the era traveled a familiar path: Elizabeth Ross Haynes was a pioneer social worker; Mary Church Terrell, a suffragist and comrade of Anthony and Stanton; Ida B. Wells Barnett crusaded against lynching and other assaults upon her race, and, of course, Mary McLeod Bethune launched her career of service to her race.[20]

By 1920 black ideology was torn by the same contradictory images of womanhood as was white culture. W. E. B. Du Bois celebrated, on the one hand, the "black All-Mother of men. . . . more sweetly feminine, unswervedly loyal, more instinctively pure in body and soul" and, on the other hand, proclaimed with pride that black women were "independent and approaching economic freedom." Du Bois surveyed 80,000 black female farmers, 22,000 teachers, 60,000 servants, and 50,000 tradeswomen, and concluded, "We cannot imprison women again in the home or have them on the pain of death to be nurses and housekeepers. . . . We will pay women what they earn and insist on their working and earning." [21] In the short span of time since emancipation some black women had worked through the entire dialectic of American womanhood, from being Adam's Rib in a subsistence agricultural economy to leaping the bounds of the middle-class home under a banner of social motherhood, until by 1920 they stood ready to demand equality and independence.

The post-suffrage era had a disorienting effect on black and white women alike. World War I brought a substantial upsurge in the migration of the black population to the cities, which continued to accelerate thereafter. By 1940, 49 percent of the nation's blacks lived in cities; the proportion reached 73 percent by 1960.[22] The dislocation of urbanization disrupted the rural family pattern and multiplied the social indicators used by sociologists to designate the black "matriarchy." The disruptive effect of urban living had been demonstrated as early as the ante-bellum era. For example, in 1839, 30 percent of the thirty thousand free blacks of Philadelphia lived in one-parent households. (It must be noted, at the same time, that the incidence of broken homes was at times larger among the immigrant population of northern cities.) The proportion of single-parent households among blacks in Philadelphia, however, rose to 37 percent by 1848. In fact, the transition from slavery into "free" urban living seemed to sap the strength of the black family. In southern cities immediately after emancipation, 90 percent of black families were intact; within fifteen years this figure was reduced by 20 percent.[23] As the black population moved relentlessly toward the city in the twentieth century, the rates of family disruption continued to grow. The percentage of black families containing both a husband and wife declined from 67 percent in the 1910s to 62 percent in 1940 and 58 percent in the 1960s. During the peak years of black urbanization, between 1940 and 1968, the black illegitimacy rate rose from 17 to 27 percent of all births. The proponents of the matriarchy theory add one further index of family disarray among blacks, the growth of female participation in the labor force from 38 percent in 1938 to 58 percent in 1960, twenty percentage points larger than the rate of employment for white women.[24]

These statistics do not, however, add up to an indictment of black family structure as essentially and perversely matriarchal. Not only did the majority of black children live in two-parent households, but many of the remainder were securely cared for by widowed mothers and fathers. The proliferation of fatherless households among blacks, furthermore, cannot be understood without reference to the social conditions that breed them. In 1970 in New York City 13.6 percent of the white, 29.1 percent of the Puerto Rican, 32.4 percent of the black families were headed by a single female parent, a scale that paralleled and reflected the economic status of these groups. When the statistical breakdown of family disruption is calculated in terms of wealth and place of residence, the differential between white and nonwhite family structure is drastically reduced. Among urban families whose income amounted to less than $3,000 annually, 53 percent of the nonwhite families and 62 percent of the white were fatherless. When only those urban families who made more than $3,000 a year are compared, the black and white rates of female-headed households come within 4 percent of one another. Since black wage earners make considerably less than whites, even above the poverty line this narrow differential is remarkable and the purely racial designation of matriarchy is proven fallacious. In point of fact, well over 90 percent of the black families with merely subsistence income managed to hold the two-parent household together.[25]

Still, the fact remains that it is the black woman of America who is most likely to experience the worst of urban poverty, which brutally overtaxes her in the roles of wife and mother. While these beleaguered women do not represent the majority of black females, their plight demonstrates the full ignominy to which women can be subjected at the bottom of American hierarchy, a status so often conferred by the arbitrary fact of race. The condition of these poor black women, although so often the sole support of their children, can hardly be glorified by the title matriarch. As one black feminist aptly put it, "the dominion of the kitchen and the welfare apartment are hardly powerful vantage points." [26]

The black woman who grew up in the pit of America's ghettos was quickly introduced to the debilities of both her sex and her race. In fact, she was likely to experience sexual discrimination long before her racial identity was established by confrontation with the white world beyond her neighborhood. The girl's socialization to femininity in the slum was apt to be particularly odious. The children of the ghetto often experienced invidious sex stereotypes from the songs that accompanied their street games. One folk song of Watts went this way: "My mother died./ How did she die?/ She died cooking./ She died cooking./ My father died./ How did he die?/ He died drunk./ He died drunk." Such fatalism transcended gender differences, but the modes of human destruction were clearly sex-typed: A woman died working in her kitchen, a man in the drunken paralysis of defeat. The girl child of Watts was advised of the abuse she would suffer from the embittered black man in a series of obscene misogynist lyrics. One of the more subdued stanzas went like this: "I saw your mother flying through the air./ I hit her on the ass with a rotten pear./ I saw your mother down by the river./ I hit her in the ass with two pounds of liver." [27] The fatherless girl of the slums was also particularly prone to respond to these taunts with a general distrust of men. One resident of the St. Louis ghetto named Rachel determined when she was only six years old that she would never marry. Her mother's experience had taught her that "when the baby comes, they go with another girl." A ten-year-old girl named Kim simply declared, "men are no good."

Kim's husbandless mother had done her best to insulate her child from the ghetto experiences that engendered such cynicism. Yet she soon saw the cause was hopeless and surrendered her daughters to the education of the slum streets.[28] It was there, in the company of a female peer group, that the ghetto girl was socialized to her female role. This relative freedom from home confinement enabled ghetto adolescents to mimic masculine patterns of behavior. The teen-age girls of the Chicago ghetto formed independent street gangs, with such titles as the Enraptured Misses and Prima Donnas. The crime rate among black teen-age girls also came closer to rivaling the incidence of criminality among males than in any other segment of the population.[29] Yet the bulk of the activities of the girls' peer group were feminine—talk of fashions, shoplifting wardrobes, and enhancing their physical appearance. To black adolescents, fashionable femininity could become even more central to a woman's identity than customary. As one girl put it, "I might live in the project but they sure can't outdress me."[30]

The adolescent girl's contacts with the opposite sex also provided a very dubious source of self-respect. Observers of the male youth culture in the slums, such as sociologist Lee Rainwater, seldom heard women referred to by titles other than whore or bitch and they were seldom regarded as more than objects on which to test the young male's sexual prowess. According to Claude Brown's account of growing up in Harlem, his peers had further ambitions: "Around 1955, everybody wanted 'a slick bitch' . . . chicks who would help you work a Murphy and who would sell some cunt if you got uptight."[31] The implications of such usage of the women in the ghetto were capsulized by a black feminist: "While white females are sexual objects, black women are sexual laborers."[32] Accordingly, young women often looked with distrust upon the advances of black men and tried to postpone sexual intimacy and bargain with their favors. One teen-ager described the female's cautious approach to ghetto sex relations as follows: "After you and the boy have been going steady for a few months and you don't go to bed with him, everyone will laugh at you . . . eventually you will let him have his way." [33] Life on the ghetto streets could expose black women to an even less ceremonious sexual initiation, rape. Maya Angelou's early sexual experience illustrates the exacerbation of woman's vulnerability to sexual assault and frustration in the underworld of the poor. Angelou, raped when she was eight years old, summoned the courage to conduct a seduction as an adolescent. Her expectations of a "moonlight-on-the-prairie feeling" as promised in the movies were not fulfilled—"the time was spent in laborious gropings, pullings, yankings, and jerkings." [34]

Maya Angelou's sexual experience illustrated another predictable outcome of adolescent love-making; "Three weeks later, having thought very little of the strange and strangely empty night, I found myself pregnant." In 1970, 2 percent of all black women shared Angelou's experience by age fifteen, and half of them were mothers by the time they were eighteen. Early illegitimate childbirth often disrupted black adolescence only slightly. Ninety percent of illegitimate black children (as opposed to 7 percent among whites) were welcomed into existing families, most often the mother's parental home, enabling the young mother to return to her peer group and continue in school.[35] Childbirth was often a rite of passage for a teen-age girl and provided a somber pittance of self-esteem for the ghetto's victims. One young mother in St. Louis proclaimed: "I can make a baby. Now I'm somebody and have some responsibility." [36] Illegitimate motherhood, and the welfare check it guaranteed, could also become a weapon to be used against the black male's ego, as in the case of a young mother in St. Louis who lashed out at her unemployed brothers, saying, "They just ain't man enough to make babies." [37] Yet the young woman left to care and provide for a child without the assistance of a husband hardly found herself in an enviable and triumphant position.

The many ghetto women who grew up surrounded by the offspring of their older sisters were unlikely to dream of maternal bliss. One teen-age girl in this predicament was determined never to become a mother. "There's too many babies following me now. My best friends these babies but they follow you . . . and interrupt you with their cries." [38] The high birth rate among ghetto teen-agers testified more to ignorance regarding contraception than to a strong desire for motherhood. National surveys of the sexually active young women of the black ghetto revealed widespread ignorance of the risks of conception and rare use of even the most elementary birth control techniques.[39] Married black women often expressed great joy in child-rearing, but not for the reasons white psychologists applauded. One mother explained the value of pregnancy this way: "To me having a baby inside me is the only time I'm really alive. I know I can make something, do something, no matter what color my skin is and what names people call me." To others, childbearing signaled a glimmer of hope amid the gloom of poverty—"At least the baby has a chance." [40] Despite this primitive solace of childbirth and reproduction most black women knew full well that having a large family compounded the difficulties of survival in the ghetto. Accordingly, by 1965, 86 percent of black wives surveyed had used or expected to use birth control, and the black fertility rate was rapidly declining from its postwar peak of approximately four children per female.[41]

The child-rearing objectives articulated by black women were often simple and forthright, to cultivate the Christian virtues of honesty and kindness and to foster the capitalist ethic, hard work and achievement. The inculcation of these values, however, was rife with difficulties. Early in the career of many a mother she reluctantly surrendered the guidance of her children—"The time has come for the street to take them away and teach them what a poor nigger's life is." The ghetto mother could easily lose faith in the very values she preached. One who "screamed the Ten Commandments" at her children day in and day out admitted her words grew hollow as she saw the grasping vice-ridden elite in the ghetto: the police, the merchants, the politicians. The black parent had the unique socializing task of teaching children to be self-protective, cynical, and cautious in white America. Preparing black children to deal with whites was a delicate operation. "It's like with cars and knives, you have to teach your children to know what's dangerous and how to stay away from it. Or else they sure won't live long." [42] To cultivate a naïve sense of trust in the child by way of intimate maternal ties, à la Dr. Spock, would be foolhardy in either the slums or in white America, less than trustworthy situations. Furthermore, the ghetto mother was seldom granted the opportunity to devote herself leisurely to child nurture. The priority of simply feeding her young drove her out of the home and into the work force.

Forty-four percent of the black mothers of children under six were in the labor force in the 1960s, while two-thirds of the black women living under poverty were employed outside the home.[43] The status and wage that these women acquired in the work force, however, did not provide the makings of matriarchy. The sex segregation of the labor force combined with the stigma of race to insure that black women would be economically inferior to black men. In the 1930s, when women moved en masse into white-collar jobs, black women still had difficulty securing employment in the factory. The southern textile mills, which did admit black women, either put them to work in segregated quarters or relegated them to "scrubbing floors and cleaning lint and cotton from the machine. They had no hope of promotion to anything else, as the skilled operations were performed by white women." The other few industries that employed black women, peanut factories and stockyards, for example, also provided only loathsome chores and meager wages. As of the 1930s, clerical jobs were closed to black women, and in the retail sector of the labor force, dark faces were hidden in the back rooms, packaging goods. Domestic service was the sphere of work allocated to the bulk of black women.[44] When these job opportunities dwindled in the '40s and '50s, black females became cleaning women in public institutions and office buildings and were admitted to the factories that white women had deserted, such as in the garment industry. White-collar jobs, however, still remained largely beyond their reach. Thirty-four percent of American black workers were in white-collar jobs in the '60s as opposed to 63 percent of the white workers.[45] On the other hand, nearly half of the black females in the labor force were employed as household or service workers in 1969 (as opposed to 19 percent of white women workers).

The monetary valuation of the black woman's

work was far too low to challenge the economic position of even the exploited black man. As of 1970, the median wage of the black woman amounted to $4,674 annually, as opposed to $6,598 for the black male. Only 13 percent of black wives secured an income equal to or greater than the income of their husbands in 1970. This economic ranking of husband and wife was reflected in their relative power within the household. Attitude surveys in the 1960s revealed that the black husband and father exercised domestic dominance slightly superior to his white counterpart.[46] The working wife of the black man was a junior partner in economic and domestic affairs. Her income was essential, however, for the typical black family with two workers still earned on the average an income inferior to the salary of a single white male. Rather than competing with the male, black women went into the segregated female labor force and secured the small paychecks that provided a desperately needed supplement to family income, which could mean the difference between abject poverty and minimal subsistence. In fact, an estimated 42 percent of the nation's nonwhite families would have been classified as poor in the mid '60s if not for the income earned by wives. Thanks to the labor of nonwhite women this figure was reduced to 19 percent.[47] Students of poverty like Daniel Moynihan seemed to be suggesting that black women should withhold this crucial economic contribution and risk their families sinking into destitution.

If, in fact, the American labor market guaranteed a lucrative job to every male, of any color, Moynihan's advice might have been less than lethal. But in actuality, black men were hardly assured the wages that could support an entire family in comfort. Moreover, in the course of the 1960s, that era of rising expectations for black Americans, the gap between white and nonwhite economic status actually grew wider. The black woman became a scapegoat for institutionalized racism, and the bugbear of black matriarchy distracted attention from the structural inequities of the American economic system. Moreover, the matriarchy theorists were myopic, if not downright hypocritical. The welfare policies at all levels of government were not calculated to enhance black femininity, motherhood, and marital cohesion. The policy of granting welfare only to children with absent fathers made it practical for an unemployed or low income husband to remove himself from the home, and thus allow his wife to collect Aid to Dependent Children funds. Neither was the ADC practice of discontinuing payment when a man was discovered in the house of the husbandless mother conducive to manly pride. The "man in the house" rule (only recently declared unconstitutional but still enforced in some states) denied black children a father figure and black women adult male companionship. The pitifully low welfare payments, furthermore, insured that the black mother would go to work to help make ends meet. At this juncture the ADC limitations on the sum that a mother could earn without forfeiting her welfare check were enforced. This ingenious policy played nicely into the hands of employers in search of cheap female labor by supplying job applicants who could make but a meager wage to supplement government doles. At times the collusion between the private and public sector was overt. In Cairo, Illinois, for example, the welfare bureau simply failed to deliver payments when black women were needed to participate in the cotton harvest. Public and private forces of sexual discrimination closed in on the black woman and trapped her in the ultimate contradictions of the dual female role.[48]

Remarkably, poor black women often succeeded in beating white Americans at their own game. In general, the children of black mothers displayed an achievement ethic stronger than the white poor, and black college students had a lower dropout rate than whites.[49] It was by no means uncommon to find adolescent black girls who were intent upon resisting the allure of ghetto street life and applying themselves to educational attainment and career preparation. Joyce Ladner's sociological investigation of the slums turned up many young women who aspired to be "teachers, nurses, secretaries and other professional people." [50] Black women entered the professions of law and medicine at a slightly higher rate than did white women, but in numbers far below black men. Black professional and highly educated women, moreover, were amply supplied with confidence and self-esteem. Psychological tests revealed them to be uncontaminated by the "fear of success" that so plagued white women in their position.[51] The women, who had been denied for generations the option of withdrawing into a protected and passive female role, often developed the strength to surmount the formidable obstacles strewn in the path of the black and female.

The obstacles of sex were often overlooked or given tacit approval by the black liberation movement. The writers who led the campaign to create a black identity in the '60s, for example, were not above malicious sex scapegoating. Claude Brown went so far as to blame female voters—with "their brains between their legs"—for the low quality of political leadership in Harlem. "Experts" on black identity, such as the psychologists William Grier and Pierce Cobbs, expressed concern that black women "neglect their figures and they seem to give up competition for male interest." The tenets of Freudian psychology were hurled with a vengeance at black women: "In the world of women an abundance of feminine narcissism is not only a cheerful attitude but a vital necessity to emotional well-being." [52] Some of the most infamous insults to black women came from the militant male leaders: Eldridge Cleaver's political schemes paired Black Power with "Pussy Power"; and Stokely Carmichael described the ideal position of women in SNCC as "prone." The tradition of the militant black females, from Sojourner Truth to the 250,000 mothers who enrolled in the National Welfare Rights Organization in the late '60s and stormed the white establishment with demands for humane treatment, was all too often passed over cavalierly in a crusade to vindicate black manhood. The following is a modest but characteristic description of the sexual hierarchy of the black movement in the '60s: "The revolutionary vanguard has male leadership but the black woman has stepped beside her man, engaged in struggle and given him total faith and commitment." [53]

Some black women leaped to endorse this allocation of sex roles. The poet Lethonia Gee wrote lovingly: "Black woman has one heavy thought/ and it's about her man." [54] The black sociologist Joyce Ladner, who was impressed by "the degree of femininity" displayed by the young women of the ghetto, made this pronouncement about sex roles: "The traditional 'strong' black woman has probably outlived her usefulness because this role has been challenged by the black man, who has demanded that white society acknowledge his manhood and deal directly with him instead of using his woman—considered the weaker sex—as a buffer." [55] The popular artifacts of the self-assertive black culture of the 1960s placed the new model of femininity in even sharper relief. This poster epitomizes the new standard of black womanhood:

BLACK GOLD

(a large, formidable profile of a black woman in an Afro)

I AM THE BLACK WOMAN, MOTHER OF CIVILIZATION, QUEEN OF THE UNIVERSE. THROUGH ME THE BLACK MAN PRODUCES HIS NATION.

If he does not protect his woman he will not produce a good nation.

It is my duty to teach and train the young, who are the future of the nation.

I teach my children the language, history, and culture when they are very young.

I teach them to love and respect their father, who works hard so that they may have adequate food, clothing, and shelter.

I care and make our home comfortable for my husband.

I reflect his love to the children as the moon reflects the light from the sun to the earth.

I sit and talk with my husband to work out the daily problems and necessities of running a stable and peaceful household.

The best that I can give my nation is strong, healthy, intelligent children who will grow to be the leaders of tomorrow.

I'm always aware that the true worth of a nation is reflected through the respect and protection of the woman, so I carry myself in a civilized manner at all times, and teach my children to do the same.

I am the Black Woman.[56]

Point by point the expressive, supportive roles of the bourgeois stereotype of the 1950s were recounted for the edification of black men and women.

The final irony of the sudden appearance of such feminine ideals within black culture is that they were fast becoming unfashionable among white Americans. Should black women retreat from the work force into the home, they would meet legions of white wives and mothers going in the opposite direction. When the census takers made their rounds in 1972, 43 percent of all American women were in the job market. In the course of that year 52 percent of America's females would spend at least some time in the work force. Women continued to be the major source of labor force expansion; fully two-thirds of the new employees of the 1960s were females. Furthermore, the typical female worker was no longer marking time before and after her career as a mother. By 1969, 48.6 percent of the women with children ages six to seventeen were in the work force, and 28.5 percent of the mothers of preschoolers were employed outside the home. As more young wives and mothers went to work, the age scale of female employment began to resemble the male pattern. Women were more solidly integrated into the work force than ever before.[57]

There were also some signs that the women of the 1960s and '70s were securing jobs outside the female sector of the labor force. In 1970 the census bureau had some sticky problems in categorizing jobs by sex—the anomalies of 756 female telephone "linemen" and 138 male "midwives." Women had assaulted some male domains in force. They accounted for one-half of the new reporters and editors, 75 percent of the novice bus drivers, and swamped the market for bartenders. Simultaneously, a few men timidly approached female occupations, particularly elementary-school teaching, and librarianship, while a handful of brave souls entered the field of nursing as well.[58]

These occasional renegades from the sex segregated labor force, however, accounted for only a tiny proportion of the job corps. The mammoth gains in female employment occurred in the most familiar place, as 3.8 million women took up clerical jobs, thus raising the proportion of women so employed from 30 to 35 percent in the space of a decade. On the other hand, the increase of women in the professions amounted only to 2 percent, despite the rapid growth in the number of college-educated women over the decade. Overall, the line of demarcation between the male and female work spheres grew slightly sharper in the 1960s.[59]

Consequently, the wage differential between male and female workers also grew larger. The millions of women entering the clerical and sales occupation with wages under $2 an hour counter-balanced any advances of more experienced and highly qualified female workers. In 1955 the earnings of full-time female workers amounted to 64 percent of the income of male workers; in 1970 women were making a paltry 57 percent of what men were. Even after the enactment of legislation prohibiting sexual discrimination in wages, in the period between 1968 and 1971 there was no appreciable increase in women's wages relative to men's. Female income was actually highest among professional people, but even here women's earnings were less than half of men's, a scandalous 48 percent. A large part of this inequity stemmed from the low level positions women obtained within the professions: public defenders rather than corporate lawyers, public health doctors rather than private physicians, elementary-school teachers rather than principals. Still, an estimated 20 percent of the income imbalance between male and female professionals was outright discrimination, unequal pay for equal work.[60]

By the 1970s the systematic discrimination against women clearly belied the trumpeted ideal of technological society, the meritocracy. By the arbitrary dictates of sex, women were removed to a secondary status system, a very squat pyramid in which only 1.1 percent of female workers earned more than $15,000 a year, while 45 percent of them made less than $5,000 annually.[61] Sexual discrimination also cut across the racial hierarchy of economic rewards. The median income of white and nonwhite men amounted to $9,373 and $6,598 respectively. Women of all races were amassed at the bottom of the economic ladder, with white women earning about $900 more than nonwhite females annually.[62] The aspiration of black women to achieve economic equity with white females was hardly an extravagant ambition.

Typically, however, a woman's economic status was still determined by her husband. Her wages usually accounted for less than one-fourth of the income in most two-worker households. For increasing numbers of families, nevertheless, the wife's income had become the measure of affluence in the 1960s. The highest level of female employment occurred in families with incomes between $12,000 and $15,000 a year. Highly educated women, who could command relatively large wages, for females, were particularly prone to reenter the work force in later life. By age forty-five, more than 80 percent of all women with five or more years of college education were gainfully employed and providing an ample increment of luxury for their families.[63] Most female participation in the labor force, however, was not the result of a desire for an extra fillip of affluence among these select segments of the population. Sixty-five percent of all working women and 80 percent of non-white women joined the labor force because they were either the sole support of themselves and their children or because their spouses made less than $7,000 a year.[64]

Still, the female labor market seemed to operate on the assumption that women worked only for pin money, perpetuating blanket sex discrimination and causing special hardships for poor families as well as countless widows, divorcées, and single women. This consequence of the sex segregated wage scale was dramatically illustrated in the plight of black women in the 1960s. While the number of male-headed black families living beneath the poverty level was cut in half in that decade, female-headed families, which grew in number over the decade, remained mired in poverty. Forty-seven percent of all poverty families were female-headed in 1969, an increase of almost 26 percent over the last ten years.[65] The specter of becoming the sole provider for one's self and children haunted women of all races as the divorce rate continued to skyrocket. The promise of alimony was a very weak reed for the divorced woman to lean upon. The typical child-support payments awarded by the courts were not only insubstantial, but also very difficult to collect.[66] By 1970, one in every ten American families was headed by a female, and nearly half of these were poor.[67] Protest against sex discrimination in the labor force was not trivial reformism for the middle class; it assailed a major source of poverty in America.

The typical employed woman, furthermore, worked overtime in the home with no pay whatsoever. Researchers in the 1970s calculated that a working mother with two small children devoted forty-two hours a week to housework. The overall domestic labor of women, evaluated at $8,600 annually, would increase the gross national product by 38 percent if they were remunerated. Working women could expect only eleven hours of assistance from their husbands in a typical week. Thus, it becomes clear why ⅓ to ½ of America's working women were employed outside the home only part-time. The unemployed wife and mother was hardly a laggard either. According to a conservative estimate, the typical mother of two spent sixty-seven hours per week engaged in household chores. The more liberal calculations of Chase Manhattan Bank estimated this workweek at

99.6 hours. Whether a woman worked in the home or outside of it, and most likely she did both, her labors were seldom evaluated according to male standards.

Woman's work was still rewarded with the honorific rhetoric of the feminine mystique. The advertisers of the late '60s alluded to the multiple burdens of the working wife in the usual glamorous and evasive manner. Pond's advertisements played on the theme "She's busy yet she's beautiful." This image was projected by such personages as a dress designer, who simultaneously mothered three children and served as a hostess for her famous husband. An actress, wife, and mother proclaimed in another ad, "I'm often tired but I never show it." [68] The *Ladies' Home Journal,* unable to ignore female participation in the labor force in the 1970s, nestled a regular column on the working woman in between its customarily elaborate advice on housekeeping, maternal care, and sexual accomplishment. The women who shouldered the double burdens of homemaker and worker and struggled to live up to this multi-faceted ideal were indeed likely to be tired, and a quaff of Geritol and a bit of.male flattery were hardly adequate supplements to their low salaries.

One might expect that by 1970 women recognized this double bind and determined to escape it by remaining single and applying themselves wholeheartedly to work. Highly trained single women, it turned out, did secure a level of economic success that rivaled men.[69] It was clear that the single state had acquired unprecedented stature and significance in the 1960s and '70s. As of 1970 there were thirty-seven million single adults in the United States, more than a twofold increase in fifteen years. In addition, the majority of single persons lived in independent households, apart from their parents, another sharp break with tradition.[70] Market researchers and magazine tycoons were among the first to comprehend the significance of this demographic phenomenon. In 1973 a group of shrewd entrepreneurs announced the forthcoming publication of *Single,* a magazine addressed to "one out of every three adults—the *largest undetected* market in America." Ladies' magazines had also begun to court the market of singles—*Cosmopolitan* in its racy style and the *Ladies' Home Journal* in its wholesome fashion with articles on such themes as "Saucepans and the Single Girl." Single women had at least achieved notice and fashionable status as an important category in the consumer market.

The expansion of the single population, however, was not the result of a widespread repudiation of marriage. It was, first of all, a delayed consequence of the postwar baby boom, which had deposited a heavy concentration of population in the traditionally single age group, eighteen to twenty. A slight tendency to delay marriage, raising the median age at which women married to twenty-one, also replenished the ranks of the single. By their early thirties, however, only 6 percent of the female population remained unmarried. The skyrocketing divorce rate also provided only a temporary increase in the ranks of the single. Ninety percent of the women who divorced before age thirty would remarry, most of them within a few short years. Thus, despite the swelling ranks of the single population, marriage was as popular as ever. In fact, the marriage rate increased a few percentage points each year through 1973.[71]

The single state, for all the glamour, sexiness, and hedonism surrounding it in the media, did not waylay women from matrimony for very long. Apparently the social life of the single bar and the swinger's apartment was not enduringly satisfying, and the typical job in the female labor force did not inspire lifelong dedication. The most congenial environment for the single person was the college community. Yet if college attendance declines, as is expected, in the '70s, the marriage rate may climb even higher. So women rushed to the altar as enthusiastically as ever, only a bit tardily, and in so doing turned away from all the daring values of singles culture, reverting to nineteenth-century feminine fantasies. More than 80 percent of the brides of 1971 donned the frills and lace of a wedding gown and embraced the ritual of a traditional ceremony. The pragmatic agents of the consumer economy welcomed the bride as well as the single women: The wedding business added $7,000,000,000 to the economy annually.[72]

The young married women of the '70s did, however, flaunt one central ideal of the feminine tradition. For the first time in history young women surveyed by the Census Bureau in 1971 aspired, on the average, to bear fewer than three children. The plummeting birth rate of the 1960s seemed destined to reach an all-time low. The dramatic confirmation came in 1972 when, based on the current birth rate, demographers projected that the mothers of the '70s would bear on the average 2.08 children, a jot below the replacement rate. If such a level of fertility could be sustained for seventy years, the American population would stabilize.[73] The achievement of zero population growth was still a precarious goal, but more probable than ever before. The predilections of women and economic expertise concurred in the opinion that unchecked fertility was profligacy. In 1972 the presidential commission on population growth, headed by John D. Rockefeller 3rd, carefully pointed out that per capita income would be 15 percent higher in the year 2000 if the typical woman bore two rather than three children.[74] The *Ladies' Home Journal* set Sylvia Porter to calculating the prohibitive cost of having a baby, a fact made patently obvious by soaring inflation. Such convincing arguments against the large family combined with the availability of oral contraceptives and the Supreme Court decision on abortion to provide women with both the incentive and the power to moderate their fertility. They acted decisively: In New York State in 1971 abortions actually exceeded live births.

With her maternity in check, woman's role was no longer so starkly different from man's. She could complete childbearing by her mid-twenties and enter the work force soon thereafter, putting in almost as much time as her husband over a lifetime. Simple clichés about woman's unique place could no longer justify discrimination between the sexes. The combination of woman's role in the work force with her residual home responsibilities, however, was still hopelessly cumbersome. Her dual performance entailed an excessive burden in the home and commanded an inferior wage in the job market. The mediation between these two roles functioned as an economic expedient, the best arrangement whereby to maximize income and at the same time provide domestic comfort for the prudently smaller family. Woman's place was being swallowed up by the voracious forces of advanced capitalism as the economic man was paired with the economic woman. The latter remained an unperfected economic creature, however, still dependent on a husband for much of her status and support, still handicapped by femininity in the job market. The discomforts of this position were heightened in the 1960s by an 80 percent increase in the divorce rate. A woman faced about a fifty-fifty chance that her marriage would be dissolved, leaving her an economic cripple. The status of women in the 1970s was built not only on an exhausting collection of conflicting roles, but on a precarious economic foundation as well.

This complicated arrangement of sex roles provoked a great deal of thought about alternative family styles. The '70s gave rise to proposals for revised marital contracts, communal households, even polyandry and group marriage.[75] A program for "open marriage" sold hundreds of thousands of copies in short order. All these schemes promised to grant women a more equitable marital role; all repudiated the prescriptions for femininity that pervaded the 1950s. The general malaise among domesticated women, which Betty Friedan originally called "the problem that has no name," was now confirmed by statistics on mental illness. Devoted mothers whose children had left home flooded psychiatrists' offices and mental institutions. While the incidence of psychic disorder was highest among single men, the married woman was almost as prone to mental illness, at a rate far above the single woman. Put another way, the healthiest and happiest wedded Americans seemed to be husbands married to discontented and neurotic wives.[76] Obviously, the marital relationships that provided such lopsided benefits to the two sexes needed reform. The favored remedy of the critics of the '60s and '70s was by one minor modification of the family or another to enlarge the wife's opportunities for self-fulfillment outside the home.

This new ethic was most apparent in the aspirations of educated women, as illustrated by a comparison of attitude surveys conducted by Mirra Komarovsky in 1943 and 1971. Fifty percent of the women attending a prestigious eastern college in 1943 indicated that they intended to retire permanently from the labor force after they became mothers. In 1971 only 18 percent of the women attending the same college planned to do the same. The majority of the women of the '70s looked forward to returning to work after their children were grown: 62 percent of them chose an option preferred by only 30 percent of the alumnae of the '40s. These highly educated women of the 1970s were prepared to assume dual roles and an interrupted career pattern, apparently oblivious to or unconcerned about the likelihood that they would receive considerably lower salaries than their husbands who remained continuously in the work force. Only 20 percent of the respondents intended to devote themselves wholeheartedly to a career, exactly the same percentage as in the 1943 survey.[77]

Komarovsky also discovered that the college women of the 1970s had, by and large, discarded that demeaning practice of their counterparts in the '50s, that of "playing dumb" to please potential mates. While intellectual equality was now regarded as a valuable aspect of the heterosexual relationship, college women were still reluctant, however, to apply their intelligence to career goals. Few of even the self-acknowledged liberated women were contemplating a precise program of professional or intellectual achievement. A survey of the career plans of 1971 college graduates revealed that despite a slight elevation in the ambitions of females (whose grades as a group were superior to males), men still outreached women in professional and academic aspirations by a margin of three to one.[78] A suggestive and partial explanation for this poor showing of women has been offered by psychologist Matina Horner.

During the late 1960s, Horner had uncovered a deep-seated resistance to worldly achievement on the part of women, which she called "fear of success." More than 80 percent of the college women Horner studied exhibited this disturbing symptom, which at times took on horrifying manifestations. For example, when one young woman was asked to complete a narrative about the subsequent career of a medical student named Anne who found herself at the top of the class, she responded as follows: "Anne starts proclaiming her surprise and joy. Her fellow classmates are so disgusted with her behavior that they jump on her in a body and beat her. She is maimed for life." Most of the women whom Horner subjected to this test, in dramatic contrast to the men, reacted negatively, if not with such a vehement sense of self-destruction. Overall, these women felt that career achievement jeopardized their femininity and marital prospects.[79] Whatever the flaws in Horner's experiments she had touched upon a sore spot in the career development of woman, and one that was a logical outgrowth of feminine conditioning, from her maternal role model as an infant to the retiring heroines of children's literature, and the adult images of the languid sexy female. This systematic stereotyping remains largely undisturbed today and continues to seduce the girl children of America into their dual and secondary adult roles.

Husbands continue to show a vested interest in the feminine stereotype as well. Men polled at an ivy league college in the '70s overwhelmingly endorsed the inferior and peripheral economic role of women. While only 24 percent of the sample expected their prospective wives to remain permanently stationed in the home, 48 percent preferred that they remain there until the children were grown. Only 16 percent of them would recommend that wives remain at work for their entire married life, and a paltry 7 percent of this intellectual and social elite had any intention of sharing home as well as work roles with their wives. One up-to-date ivy leaguer provided a complete scenario for the convoluted inequality of the wife of the near future:

> I believe that it is a good thing for mothers to return to full time work when the children are grown, provided the work is important and worthwhile. Otherwise housewives get hung up with tranquilizers because they have no outlet for their abilities. A woman should want her husband's success more than he should want hers. Her work shouldn't interfere with or hurt his in any way.

While the beatification of homemaking and motherhood gave way to nasty condescension toward the housewife, the roles she was offered outside the home were not invested with dignity or significance comparable to a man's work. The unfortunate wives of men like this would be expected to do double duty for half the honors, in the shadow of a self-important mate. Such revised but hardly liberating presumptions about woman's place undoubtedly lurk in the minds of many men in the 1970s.[80]

Yet the demand for egalitarian intimacy between husbands and wives was made more imperative than ever. Deep communion between mates was the cause célèbre of the most popular volume on marital reform, *Open Marriage* by Nina O'Neill and George O'Neill. This program for absolute trust, uninhibited communication, and mutual personal growth came complete with instructions for practice sessions in marital openness, schemes to develop sensitivity to the other, and ritualistic steps toward perfect intimacy. Modern couples scampered to encounter groups and sensitivity sessions in pursuit of the same maximization of heterosexual intimacy. Advertisers endorsed this subordination of domestic routine to marital companionship in their own crude fashion: "A woman's place is next to her husband not by her sink." [81]

Ideally, open marriage allowed for the independent identities, interests, friendship, and love affairs of the husband and wife. Yet there was no doubt that the personal bond and emotional support of the married couple would transcend all other human ties and undermine their strength. The communes of the '60s and '70s provided a more sympathetic environment than did "open marriage" for those men and women who valued a wider circle of integral human contact. By most accounts, however, these collective living arrangements were fragile and incomplete alternatives to marriage. Disruptive vestiges of the nuclear family, and pernicious sex roles as well, accompanied the modern communards to their new homes, which rarely rested on an autonomous and self-supporting economic base. Wracked by internal tensions and external pressure, the typical collective had a very short life, provided salutary but brief relief for a few eccentrics from the linear, enclosed relationship of heterosexual coupling.[82] As long as the American workplace proved to be a ruthless and alienating environment and society remained amorphous and impersonal, men and women would turn to the private sphere in search of salve for their discomfort. The simplest recourse was to the family, which women entered with their age-old liabilities, the excessive demands and inferior rewards of their traditional sphere.

Like the mystique of conjugal intimacy, the cult of maternity was in some disarray by the 1970s. The theoretical underpinnings of the maternal obsession encouraged by Dr. Spock were undercut by experiments in the institutional care of young children. The iconoclastic opinions of one such experimenter, child psychologist Bettye Caldwell, were emblazoned across the front page of the Los Angeles *Times* in 1971. Dr. Caldwell had concluded from her experience with day care that a child's mental growth was accelerated and his or her emotional development unharmed by removal from the mother. In fact, Caldwell dared to confess that she would accept a six-month-old infant into public group care without trepidation. Concurrently, sociologists and psychologists were reassessing the presumed connection between working mother and juvenile delinquency and found no direct correlation between the two.[83] Yet the old guard was not easily converted. President Richard Nixon vetoed day-care legislation with an invocation of the old saws: Institutional child care would "diminish both parental authority and parental involvement with children, particularly in the decisive early years when social attitudes and conscience and religious and moral principles are first inculcated."

Nixon's authority to speak on the origins of "moral principles" may have been diminished of late, but more legitimate experts also continue to buoy up the principle of maternal nurture. The women's page of *The New York Times* consulted four child psychologists on this issue and all concurred that children under three were better off at home with their mothers. Their cautionary refrain was familiar: "Day care can result in permanent damage to an infant's emotional development." The feasibility of day care for older children was also cause for controversy. Dr. Juliet Kestenberg discouraged it on the grounds that "a child can sense the tension in a working mother and it breeds anxiety. . . . A mother usually drops off her child at a day-care center on the way to work, often in a rush. That evening, very tired, she picks up the child and has to dash home for grocery shopping, dinner, and housework. What benefit can this pressure have for the child?" One might well ask what benefit this exhausting routine of multiple roles could have for a mother, but neither these child psychologists nor the editors of the women's page were concerned about reforming women's roles. The title of the article said it all, in the familiar guilt-inducing way: "Day Care: It's Fine for Mother, but What about the Child?" [84] Most of the debates about child-care were stymied between the poles of traditional motherhood and makeshift day care, incognizant of either paternal or societal responsibility for the rearing of America's young.

While the experts argued the relative benefits of maternal and institutional child care, however, both government and private industry were setting up a few day-care centers. Their motivation was rarely the welfare of either the mother or the child but rather sound economic policy. The KLH Corporation, for example, was at the vanguard of the day-care movement. Company literature was quite explicit about the goals of their child-care facilities. The availability of free child care enabled mothers to enter the labor force and to stay there for cheap wages; day care "helps prevent competition for workers that pushes up wage rates, promotes inflation and causes production bottlenecks."[85] Smaller firms relied on the government to provide these profit-enhancing facilities. For example, the garment manufacturers of New York's Chinatown gave their female employees (the direct descendants of the immigrant sweatshop operatives of nineteenth century) time off to protest government cutbacks in day-care funds. When the benefits of public day care to the employers of poor, nonwhite women are kept in mind, the appearance of support for these measures in illiberal quarters becomes intelligible. Why else would conservative southern senators be such staunch supporters of federal day-care legislation? Public day-care regulations are calculated to secure female employees willing to work for low wages. A low ceiling on the maximum income a mother may make and still receive free day care insures that many women will remain in the ranks of the working poor. In addition, unemployed mothers are often allowed the use of day-care facilities only for a few months, until they have secured employment at the appropriate low wage. Middle-class women, on the other hand, are expected to boost the economy by the direct purchase of child care. *Barron's* magazine summoned the ambitious entrepreneurs to invest in private day-care services, tempting them with the promise of a $7,500,000,000 market.[86] A long and hazardous wait is in store for mothers, nonetheless, if they are to rely on the benevolence of government, employers, and businessmen for assistance; in 1970 only 6 percent of the children of working mothers were placed in day-care centers.[87] Thus the supple threads of sexism wove through all female roles, drawing women of all classes into their dual burdens and inferior status.

Since the roles of women in the home and in the work force had become so muddled, the creators of mass culture were at a loss as to how to construct a simple evocative image of femininity. An evasive tactic was in order: Rather than presenting the ideal woman as either a mother or a worker, or an unwieldy combination of the two, she was projected as transcendent sexiness. By the mid '60s the beatific mother and the wide-eyed housewife were taking a back seat to the sinewy, streamlined seductress. On the glossy pages of popular magazines, models of femininity were posed in sensuous array. In 1965 a perfume ad in the *Ladies' Home Journal* surrounded a woman with no less than seven men and was accompanied by the caption "dashingly different on every man in your life." Another torrid vamp warned "If you don't give him 007 . . . I will." [88] These paragons of sexiness made a sales pitch for an appropriate series of products. The prime advertising spaces of the *Ladies' Home Journal,* once reserved for baby and homemaking products, were filled with full-page ads for cosmetics, perfumes, and explicitly sex-linked commodities such as the deodorizers of the female genitals. Eye makeup alone had become a $48,000,000 market by the 1970s. Not only was the female stereotype more aggressively sexual than ever before, but it also objectified men who were themselves embalmed in body enhancing products: cologne, deodorants, and hair sprays. Males and females doubled as pursuers and objects in the popular game and lucrative business of sexual voyeurism. *Playboy* "bunnies" met their match in the *Cosmopolitan* centerfold. *Playboy* magazine itself was mimicked by the publication of *Playgirl* in 1973, though the latter was a long way from achieving the circulation of fourteen million achieved by the master salesman of female sex objects, Hugh Hefner. Nonetheless, the boundaries between male and female seemed to be becoming more muted in matters of sex and work alike.

In fact, the sex researchers of the '60s and '70s were granting a special preeminence to woman. This at least was the implication of the laboratory investigations of William Masters and Virginia Johnson. Their work lent more authoritative and widely publicized support to the fact that all female orgasms center in the clitoris. Among the more novel findings of the Masters and Johnson research was the demonstration of the capacity of the female to experience more intense and more numerous orgasms than the male. This clinical evidence was frequently interpreted as a proclamation of the sexual insatiability of women. One daring psychologist, Mary Jane Sherfy, went so far as to suggest that the female animal was driven by an unquenchable sexual desire.

Her lusts were so overpowering, in fact, that the development of human civilization was retarded five thousand years while her sexuality was painstakingly brought under control.[89] Those familiar with the long and ingenious history of feminine stereotypes might be suspicious that this reading of biology was yet another Trojan horse, an apparently generous gift to women in which was hidden an arsenal of prescriptions for sexual inequality. The theory of the sexual insatiability of women could be construed as yet another invidious focus on the biological differences between the sexes calculated to divert females into secondary and primitive pursuits, this time the single-minded pursuit of orgasms.

Such an interpretation of the sexual obsession of the 1970s may be a bit paranoid but it is not entirely unfounded. The pervasiveness and profitability of the sexy female imagery in American popular culture must be viewed with suspicion. Women's magazines were all too ready to present instructions in every issue on how to maximize sexual pleasure. The *Ladies' Home Journal*'s enthusiasm for the sex craze of the '70s extended to establishing a regular column on the issue and even to the recounting of "Everything You Always Wanted to Know About Your Pet's Sex Life." Dr. David Reuben's similarly titled encyclopedia of human sexuality sold eight million copies in the same year. Meanwhile, the most popular novels of the era were penned by Jacqueline Susann, an author whose ability to mold the sexual sensibilities of women into a fast-paced, all-absorbing vicarious experience recalls the sentimental finesse of Harriet Beecher Stowe. At the very least this cultural obsession with female sexuality distracted women from the contemplation of the practical contradictions of their condition in the 1970s.

The popular literature of the '70s honored as cultural heroines women renowned primarily for their erotic exploits. The sex crazed culture elevated the prostitute to a glamorous position, in the person of Xavaria Hollander. Her paean to the delights of a life devoted to selling the female body, *The Happy Hooker,* sold four million copies in the space of a year. A career in the same field but without pay was recommended by the best seller *The Sensuous Woman.* The author, who chose to remain anonymous, directed the reader to build her life around sex: to choose her place of employment according to the fringe benefits of sexual contacts it offered; to decorate and redecorate her bedroom to enhance her love life; to routinely spend countless hours arranging her appearance and setting up social situations for the conquest of lovers. The author of *The Sensuous Woman* assumed that her readers were in one of two vulnerable positions: the pit of the female labor force (i.e., secretaries) or the wasteland of the suburban home. Sexual adventure was calculated to enliven the monotony of these women's lives and served to deflect their consciousness from the concrete problems of their lowly social and economic position.[90] Barbara Seaman, on the other hand, addressed her treatise on female sexuality, *Free and Female,* to independent and successful professional women. Seaman was, in fact, something of a sexual snob, proclaiming that this class of women had the best and most frequent orgasms. The orgasm was a major source of woman's liberation in Seaman's view: "Once an individual has experienced transcendent sex, even once, it seems to change her (or him) for a lifetime, making her (or him) more spontaneous, more open, more confident, more loving, more purposeful and more peaceful." The orgasm, an "almost mystical experience of renewal . . . giving meaning and immortality," appeared as one of the proudest accomplishments of these emancipated women, and every act that could possibly engender it, including breast-feeding and childbirth, was a sacred event of womanhood.[91]

Despite the vigor of the cult of female orgasm, female sexuality was still clothed in mystery in many quarters in the 1970s. A woman's gynecologist was still apt to be the source of ignorance and misinformation. Two-thirds of the gynecological textbooks published after 1967 failed to mention the findings of Masters and Johnson and continued to assert that women's sexual desires were weaker than men's. Some of these "experts" still repeated the old clichés of sexual politics: "An important feature of the sex drive is the man's urge to dominate the woman and subjugate her to his will. In the woman acquiesence to the masterful takes a high place." [92] The sexual revolution had not eliminated violent sexual attacks upon women. One study conducted at a midwestern college in 1967 disclosed that 23 percent of the males interviewed admitted to attempting to rape women they dated, while one-half of the women reported they had been the victims of sexual attacks by all-American college men.[93] In the 1970s a rising incidence of rape (perhaps attributable in part to the diminishing reluctance of women to report this crime) testified to the fact that female sexual experience often proved the occasion of painful degradation rather than "transcendent" joy. Furthermore, the actual increase in sexual behavior and freedom, as measured by statistics on premarital sexual experience, was hardly as dramatic as the cult of sexuality would suggest. The celebration of sexual liberation could, in fact, operate as another annoying and dehumanizing constriction on a young woman's behavior, now making virginity a cause for scorn and self-rebuke, prompting at times a grim submission to popular pressure and male desires. In summary, the cult of sexuality yielded an updated mystique of female fulfillment, an orgy of voyeurism, and pressure to conform to a new standard of womanhood. The actual resurrection of the body was often lost sight of, perhaps impeded, in the process.

The possible impact of the sexual standards of the '60s and '70s upon the quality of a woman's life is recounted in Ingrid Bengis' *Combat in the Erogenous Zone.* By her mid-twenties, the author had ricocheted from one feminine image to another and was emotionally exhausted: "I can't become the person each decade newly assumes I ought to be. I cannot be the completely feminine woman of the '50s, the emancipated sexually free woman of the '60s, and the militant, anti-sexist woman of the '70s." As Bengis recounted her personal history, however, it becomes clear that it was the pursuit of the ideal of sexual freedom that entrapped her and propelled her through "one experiment after another in alternative lovestyles." She admitted that flight from affair to affair, with men and women both, had been an "ersatz progress," impelled by a force "over which we have no control." Yet, she remained enthralled by the false promises of fulfillment through romantic sexuality, committed to a continual quest for "authenticity in search of sex and love which reflects that authenticity, and reflects the kind of purity which is reserved for essentials, even when those essentials prove to be less than pleasant." *Combat in the Erogenous Zone* is more than anything else the biography of a sex life and, consequently, a one-dimensional personal statement.[94]

Exhausted by this feminine odyssey, convinced that divisive combat was innate to sexual relations, Ingrid Bengis took refuge in some of the most shopworn theories of sexual differences. "There are times when I wonder whether nature isn't really the one to hold responsible. It seems a lot easier to blame nature than to blame men (although blaming society runs a close second), and I conclude that the real trouble derives from the fact that man and woman are vitally different not in those ways that provide an interesting variety, but in ways that make of sexuality a veritable war zone." These "natural" differences between the sexes included the familiar elements of the soap-opera mentality, which decreed that men were poorly endowed with the capacity for lasting love and nurture. To explain the superior emotional needs and sensibilities of women, Bengis took refuge in the oldest catchall of the female stereotype, maternity: "The need for growth and gestation seems to be extremely powerful and perhaps even innate." [95]

Unlike the nineteenth-century cult of motherhood, however, Bengis' typology of feminine nature did not foster an expansive humanism. Mired in the private universe of sexuality, Bengis, and the class and generation of women she presumed to speak for, moved "ever inward" toward introspection and self-fulfillment. Political and social action was suspect. For example, Bengis chose to deplore the "combat in the erogenous zone" rather than the destruction of life in the Indochina War. "If bodies are being killed all over the world because of politics rather than love, spirits are being smashed right next door, in apartment houses and shacks and on the street because of love rather than politics . . . love that can't—no matter how hard we try—be reinterpreted to fit any political mold, not even the mold of female oppression." [96] Thus, Bengis shied away from politics even as an avenue of escape from the sexual combat that she so bitterly decried. This heightened sexual consciousness could privatize and isolate women like never before and leave them to wallow in the ruins of a personal war.

Fortunately, not all women were mired in the mystique of sexual romance as the contradictions of the multiple female role sharpened in the 1960s. The political reawakening of women began with a subdued rumbling of discontent among upper-middle-class women. President Kennedy's Commission on the Status of Women, set up in 1961, proved one focus of rising discontent. The original purpose of the commission, to determine why the talents of educated women were under-utilized in the economy, was by no means feminist. The women set to grapple with this narrow problem, however, soon uncovered problems of another order. First, the disclosure of blatant discrimination against women in the professions raised a question of sexual equality rather than simple economic utility. Second, the commission members discovered the peculiar professional handicaps of the married women, the difficulties of balancing their home and work roles. The problem of the dual roles for educated women was also central to the spring issue of *Daedalus* published in 1964, which was devoted to women's issues and included the path-break-ing essay by Alice Rossi, "Equality of the Sexes: An Immodest Proposal."

It was at this conspicuous moment that murmur-ings of discontent were also heard in the cloisters of suburbia, later to be trumpeted in a best seller, Betty Friedan's *The Feminine Mystique.* Slowly the prob-lems of women began to take on an autonomous sig-nificance, consequential enough to demand a revival of organized feminism. Women did not acquiesce in the discriminatory adjustment of their kaleidoscopic roles for very long and, once again, womanhood was under siege. All these concerns came together in a Washington, D.C., hotel where in 1966 concerned women were assembled for a meeting of the National Conference of Commissions on the Status of Women. In Betty Friedan's room the National Organization for Women was quietly founded.[97]

From the start, NOW displayed the strengths and the weaknesses of the habitat in which it had ger-minated. NOW's leaders were in an opportune posi-tion to exploit the American ethic of equality of oppor-tunity. By the 1960s it was clear that contrary to the old sayings about woman's place, women were in the work force to stay and entitled to the same rights that men enjoyed there. Americans could not argue with the simple justice of equal pay for equal work. The governmental experience of NOW's founders in the Presidential Commission also placed them in an op-portune situation to enact their forthright demands. They were there to see to it that a clause forbidding sexual discrimination was included in the Civil Rights Act of 1964, and NOW was intent upon enforcing it despite the congressmen who thought the sex clause was something of a joke. The energy and efficiency of the National Organization for Women has brought untold benefits to thousands of women who have taken advantage of their legal rights and won millions of dollars in equity payments.

NOW, whose membership exceeded thirty thousand in 1973, had considerably broadened its programs: championing the rights of the poor, the nonwhite, and the Lesbian, as well as the middle-class middle-American woman and demanding abortion, day care, and political power as well as equal pay for women. Yet the organization's chief goals remain the piece by piece legislative alleviation of the most glaring sexual contradictions to the American dream of equality of achievement. The climb to equality so-defined is a steep and treacherous one, which requires that a woman be placed beside a male equivalent at each position along the immensely complicated occupational hierarchy of America. Feminism as espoused by groups like NOW summons each and every woman to the rugged status-climbing long required of men by the rags to riches myth. Such an assault upon the pinnacle of American politics is a particularly gargantuan feat. Women have hardly scratched the surface of the American political elite, capturing in the half century since suffrage only two cabinet posts, four governorships, and 2 percent of the seats in the United States Congress. Feminists can contemplate another fearsome struggle to penetrate the corporate establishment, with women now constituting around 2 percent of the nation's executive elite. The media of communication, the labor unions, and the educational elite also are formidable bastions of male supremacy.[98]

With supreme dedication and stamina, some women undoubtedly will succeed in infiltrating the ruling class, but the possible casualties of the struggle bear consideration. The cost to individual women of scraping and grappling to reach the top and the high price of staying there, as well as the quality of the prize itself, demand careful assessment. What is the inherent value of power within a corporation that creates useless or pernicious products, or a political party that sacrifices the common good to garner votes and campaign funds, or a profession that merely breeds esoteric information, unnecessary services, or vested interests? To say that the mere presence of women will automatically humanize the power elite is naïvely to embrace the old stereotypes. This is not to say that women should disdain power, but only that they should reconsider both the purposes to which it is put and the justice of consolidating it in the hands of a few persons of either sex before they set out on the campaign to help rule America. As they rebound from the "feminine mystique," some feminists uncritically attach themselves to its polar opposite, the imperative of male "achievement."

A similar myopia lurks in the unqualified demand of equal pay for "equal" work. The NOW constituency fails to question the basic assumption of competitive capitalism and the contemporary meritocracy, that all human labor can be neatly classified, its value ranked, and a man or a woman's just share of the fruits of the economy thereby be determined. This principle has provoked and justified the subjugation of masses of women in the past and could easily continue to do so. There is no guarantee that the elevation of talented, ambitious, and privileged women to high income levels will erase the inequities that all women suffer. In fact, it could have an opposite effect. Black women, intimately aware of the limited number of lucrative jobs available in the American occupational system, are quick to see the possible economic gains of white women as their probable losses. The unassailed assumption that the wealth of America will be held in family units compounds the potential of inequality, within the female sex, allowing the successful woman to pool her salary with an affluent man, while unsuccessful women are subject to poverty compounded by broken marriages. This development was already apparent in statistics on family income in the 1960s. Over the decade the economic differential between the middle and lower classes grew dramatically larger, just as middle-class wives entered the work force and while increasing numbers of poor mothers were left husbandless.[99] The advantages of middle-class women within the American meritocracy may herald an exacerbation of the mal-distribution of wealth and the continuing oppression of lower-class women, unless the structural underpinnings of sexual inequality, the free labor market, and the family are somehow revised.

Fortunately the tide of feminism in the 1960s emanated from a number of sources, many of them less prone to these oversights than the National Organization of Women: the civil rights movement, the youth culture, the new left. The political and social environment in which the feminism of younger women was kindled highlighted the issues of race, class, and alternative life-styles. The women who lent their whole-hearted support to these movements, however, confronted some particularly grating exhibitions of misogyny. In the new left, women were routinely delegated the most menial tasks, like leafleting, mimeographing, and generally serving as the secretaries of the revolution. Simultaneously, they were expected to be sexually accommodating "chicks," "prone" in SNCC, saying "yes to men who say no" during the anti-draft offensive. When women raised the issue of sexual oppression before male-dominated groups or formed a women's caucus within them, they were often greeted with condescension toward their "trivial" "personal" demands. A woman who raised the issue of sex on the podium of the 1967 New Politics Convention in Chicago was patted on the head by a male leader and called a "little girl." That woman was Shulamith Firestone, whose political maturity would soon be demonstrated as a theorist for an autonomous movement for the holistic advancement of the female sex, women's liberation.[100]

The women's liberation movement grew up wherever small groups of women jointly identified and articulated the sexual barriers that blocked their paths. Once the long suppressed question of woman's place was raised, an avalanche of complaints, aggravations, demands, and programmatic manifestos spurted forth. Contagious, seemingly spontaneous combustions of women's protest erupted throughout America, especially in the supportive habitat of the college campus. Despite the decentralization of the younger phalanx of the new feminism, a characteristic ambience suffused the movement, one inextricably tied to its social-historical origins. In keeping with both the amorphousness of student culture and the new left's suspicion of elitism, women's liberation groups eschewed the rigid organizational structure of NOW, disdained hierarchy, and never erected an explicit national organizational network. Organized into small groups, which aimed to maximize and equalize the participation of all members, women's liberation proceeded to delve into the ubiquitous restraints and commonplace inhumanities visited upon the female sex. The consciousness-raising group was designed first to express the complaints of individual women, to articulate the sexual oppression that all women shared, and then to identify its broader social causes. Ideally this process would strengthen individual women and bind them together for an assault on their common problems. Both the participatory organizational structure and the politics of the personal bespoke the origins of women's liberation in the youth rebellion of the 1960s. The women's movement merged these techniques with the age-old channels of supportive female communication, and transformed "woman's talk" into a mode of resistance and liberation.

The movement had its peculiar weaknesses as well as its strengths. The small group could detain its members in personal therapy and undermine their political and social effectiveness. The consciousness-raising sessions could become obsessed with the narrow issue of male-female relations, dishearteningly reminiscent of woman's "expressive function" and catch women in the familiar trap of the personal. The women's liberation rap session and some of its propagators came dangerously close to being captured by the snare of sexual stereotyping, elevating the symptoms of female confinement to feminine virtues. Both Kate Millett and Germaine Greer encouraged the belief that women were, by historical accident if not by nature, morally superior to men, the agents of love and peace rather than violence and aggression. The women's liberation movement was not able to escape the wiles of contemporary culture, and consequently its spokesmen verged occasionally toward the tempting obsession with free sexuality as a cure-all for female oppression. Germaine Greer, for example, would wage revolution in the bedroom and stake women's liberation on the act of transforming the penis from a weapon into a piece of human flesh. Some Lesbians within the movement also climbed out on the vulnerable limb of a sexual panacea, construing sexual relations between women not merely as a liberation of sexual behavior and enrichment of women's experience, but as a new chapter in sexual romanticism, portending in and of itself a Utopian equality in sexual relations. Each of these seductive byways of the women's liberation movement sapped the energies required for a concerted attack upon the integral and formidable system of sexual inequality in America.

As long as women's liberation eschewed organizational precision and strategic assaults outside the sphere of personal relations as masculine, the formless spirit of the movement was also prey to cavalier treatment by the mass media. Women's liberation was given definition by unsympathetic and often mercenary agencies of popular culture, attuned to the spectacular and trivial manifestations of feminism, or prone to construct an artificial national leadership from the most photogenic and femininely captivating women they could associate with the cause. Until feminists exercised firmer control over popular channels of communication, they were subject to the whims of fad and fashion and in danger of becoming passé at any moment. Those feminists who mimicked the techniques of the established media were easily ensnared in its limitations and contradictions. *MS.* magazine, for example, not only catered to a mainstream, upper-middle-class audience, but adopted a pragmatic advertising policy that gave an honored status to the excessive consuming habits of its affluent readers. *MS.* was so successful in this sphere that it has formed its own marketing corporation, which offers to advise manufacturers of the tastes of its readers, as well as the etiquette of nonsexist advertising. Such a smooth symbiosis with agencies that have so often manipulated and degraded women suggests that the editorial offices of a mass circulation magazine may not be the most congenial forum in which to develop challenging feminist policy. In fact, while *MS.* serves as an efficient and relatively far-reaching communications network for feminist sympathizers, it seldom issues a proclamation that would startle a reader of the *Ladies' Home Journal* and rarely questions the moderate feminism of NOW.

While one wing of women's liberation did battle with the American culture industry, another fought for autonomy and power within the American left. The bitter break of feminists from radical organizations was only one of the many setbacks and fragmentations that befell the student left in the late 1960s. As these splintered groups and interests attempt to rebuild American socialism in the 1970s, feminists stand uneasily to the side, clinging to their hard-won independence while deliberating about strategic alliances with other radicals or returning to organizations whose leadership is male. Left-wing feminism has been both enriched and complicated by the rejuvenation of Marxist theory, whose doctrines, which were not designed with the sexual division of labor clearly in mind, have occasioned the proposition that the women's movement is a petty bourgeois distraction from the struggles of the proletariat. Practice as well as theory was at stake in the feminist-socialist debates, as such programs as the Equal Rights Amendment, trade union organizing, and domestic reform all came under questioning. These debates pivot around one basic agreement, however: that sex roles must be related to larger social parameters and the hoped-for future of woman is irrevocably tied to the dialectics of history. By challenging the hegemony of capitalism as it encroaches from economic relations to social decisions and into private lives, the feminist-socialists secure a vantage point from which to assault all the serpentine snares of sexism.

Consequently, the feminist of the 1970s confronts American society with a substantially more sophisticated theory and broader programs than her foremothers. As early as 1966 the British new leftist Juliet Mitchell had assaulted the poverty of previous Marxist writing regarding the all-important social-historical category of sex. Mitchell's seminal article and subsequent book, *Woman's Estate,* dissected the structure and delineated the functions of womanhood and formulated a strategy for redistributing the onerous duties of the second sex. The publication in 1971 of Shulamith Firestone's *The Dialectic of Sex* molded social theory, history and psychology into a provocative treatise on sex and society. With a daring thrust, Firestone shattered a variety of icons, including romantic love, maternity, and childhood, and illuminated more Utopian goals for a socialist-feminist revolution. Both Mitchell and Firestone, whose writings served as a take-off point for further critical analysis of the feminist left, displayed acute awareness of the societal uses of sex roles and total freedom from the mystique of motherhood and domesticity.

This creative debate continued through 1974, infused with Marxist analysis, enlivened by provocative

European feminists such as Mariarosa Dalla Costa and Selma James, and painstakingly elaborated in the American radical press. Prompted by feminists, socialist theorists began at last to seriously examine the basic dichotomy of modern society between public and private life, man's world and woman's place. Such clarity regarding the social roots of sexism is duplicated on the level of cultural analysis by the pristine feminist cry for an androgynous humanity. Carolyn Heilbrun has devoted a volume to this ideal, which has been poignantly described by Barbara Deming: "I think the world has been split in half for much too long—between masculine and feminine. . . . And I would like to argue that perhaps our most crucial task at this point of history—a task for women and men—is not to celebrate these so-called differences between our natures but to question boldly, by word and act, whether they properly exist at all, or whether they do not violently distort us, whether they do not split our common humanity." [101]

The stubborn, poisonous haze of sexual differences, the omnipresent assumption that the soul of humankind must be divided into male and female, showed most hopeful signs of clearing by the 1970s. But the task of mediating between the enlightened consciousness of a few men and women and the murky confusion of contemporary culture seemed more arduous than ever. The anti-feminist backlash was under way in every quarter, among fearful men and timid women. In 1973 the anti-feminists took the offensive, represented by such audacious spokesmen as Stephen Goldberg, whose *The Inevitability of Patriarchy* defended the sexual status quo with extraordinary snideness and a minimum of the analytic intelligence which he claimed was a feature of maleness. The reflex reaction to feminism was at times almost inane. Such was George Gilder's jeremiad *Sexual Suicide.* Gilder invoked the old cliché that "the differences between the sexes are the single most important fact of human society." Unabashedly, he lumped feminism, gay liberation, sexology, and pornography together, and declared them suicidal on the grounds of a hackneyed Freudian theory. To Gilder, the simple reform of equal pay for equal work portended the annihilation of civilization. "Under such conditions, the men will bolt and this development, an entirely feasible one, would probably require the simultaneous emergence of a police state to supervise the undisciplined men and a child care state to manage the child. Thus would the costs of sexual equality be passed on to the public in vastly increased taxes. The present sexual constitution is cheaper." [102] This bizarre scenario, envisioning suicidal sexual warfare, a police state, and increased taxes with equal fear and trembling, exposes American sexism backed up against the wall and jibbering incoherently. Although the likes of George Gilder do not represent a worthy opposition to feminism, they illustrate the obstinacy of the dogma of gender differences and signal the fierceness of the continuing battle for sexual equality.

Today's and tomorrow's feminists must contend with more powerful and less shadowy enemies than the anti-feminist ideologues. They will face off against a whole economic and social system and a historical course that may veer in entirely unexpected directions. The position of woman at present, inhabiting two spheres and performing a dual role, gives her a certain advantage. As women become more tightly integrated into all facets of American life, at the nexus of social order in the home and simultaneously central to the economy in the female labor force, their collective power to shape the future course of history expands dramatically. Yet this status remains uncertain and at any point may be jeopardized by the changing demands of the labor market and the precarious predicament of the entire economy. If such a crisis occurs, woman, still the second sex, will be especially vulnerable to the forces of retrenchment and reaction. In any event the strength of women can grow only out of persistent vigilance and solid organization. The fundamental test of feminism in the 1970s, a time that seems to be characterized by cynical capitulation to the blandishments of the status quo, will be to remain steadfast in the fight, to keep criticism alive, and to maintain constant pressure upon every word, act, and institution that conspires to construct a new cage for womankind. No class, race, or constituency can be neglected; every opportunity for alliances, every woman's issue must be utilized. Concerted demands by women for equal economic rewards, beyond what the present beleaguered structure of capitalism can accommodate, pose a particularly menacing threat to the American system at this point in time. Such pressure challenges the obstinate assumption of man's history since the days of Plymouth, that the status and comfort of each and every American is to be determined by a ferocious struggle to obtain a superior portion of the world's goods, then to be horded within the male-headed family. The Utopian possibility that a feminist challenge can overtax this system of distributing wealth, with its legacy of inequality and joyless labor, must be kept alive in a multi-faceted and organized battle against the tyranny of manhood and womanhood in America.

INTRODUCTION

GENERAL REFERENCES

Ester Boserup, *Woman's Role in Economic Development* (London, 1970).

William Goode, *The Family* (Englewood Cliffs, N.J., 1964).

Ann Gordon, Mari Jo Buhle, and Nancy Schrom, "Women in American Society: A Historical Contribution," *Radical America,* Vol. V, No. 4 (July–August 1971).

Harriet Holter, *Sex Differences and Social Structure* (Oslo, 1970).

Eleanor Macoby, ed., *The Development of Sex Differences* (Standford, 1966).

Margaret Mead, *Sex and Temperament* (New York, 1963).

Juliet Mitchell, *Woman's Estate* (New York, 1972).

John Money and Anke A. Ehrhardt, *Man and Woman, Boy and Girl* (Baltimore, 1973).

Sherry B. Ortner "Is Female to Male as Nature Is to Culture?" *Feminist Studies,* Fall 1972.

Sheila Rowbotham, *Women, Resistance and Revolution* (New York, 1973).

Eli Zaretsky, "Capitalism, The Family and Personal Life," *Socialist Revolution,* Vol. 3, Nos. 1–3 (1973).

ADAM'S RIB

[1] William Secker, *A Wedding Ring, Fit for the Finger* (Boston, 1750).*

[2] Keith V. Thomas, "Women and the Civil War Sects," *Past and Present,* No. 13 (1958), p. 44.

[3] Peter Laslett, *The World We Have Lost* (New York, 1965), pp. 81–106.

[4] Wesley Frank Craven, *White, Red and Black* (Charlottesville, Va., 1971), pp. 1–38, *passim.*

[5] Berthold Fernow, ed., *The Records of New Amsterdam,* Vol. 1 (New York, 1897), p. 162.

* Seventeenth and eighteenth-century publications are from the Charles Evans American Bibliography, microprints edited by Clifford Kenyon Shipton.

NOTES

[6] Robert Bremner, ed., *Children and Youth in America: A Documentary History* (Cambridge, Mass., 1970), p. 16.

[7] Julia Cherry Spruill, *Women's Life and Work in the Southern Colonies* (New York, 1969), p. 9.

[8] John Demos, *A Little Commonwealth, Family Life in Plymouth Colony* (New York, 1970), p. 61.

[9] Edith Abbott, *Women in Industry: A Study in American Economic History* (New York, 1909), p. 12.

[10] Spruill, *op. cit.,* p. 11.

[11] Sumner Chilton Powell, *Puritan Village: The Formation of a New England Town* (Middletown, Conn., 1963), Chapter VIII, pp. 116–132.

[12] Josephine C. Frost, ed., *Records of the Town of Jamaica, Long Island, New York 1656–1751* (Brooklyn, 1919), Vol. 1, p. 1.

[13] *Collections of the Massachusetts Historical Society* (Boston, 1843), Vol. VIII of the Third Series, "A Coppie of the Liberties of the Massachusetts Colonie in New England," p. 229, hereafter referred to as the Massachusetts "Body of Liberties."

[14] Kenneth Lockridge, *A New England Town: The First Hundred Years* (New York, 1970), p. 144; Frost, *op. cit.,* p. 438.

[15] Secker, *op. cit.,* p. 13.

[16] "Body of Liberties," *op. cit.,* p. 229.

[17] Susie Ames, ed., *County Court Records of Accomach-Northampton, Virginia* (Washington, D.C., 1954), p. 63.

[18] *Early Records of the Town of Providence* (Providence, 1892), Vol. XIV, pp. 61–62; Vol. III, pp. 172–174.

[19] Demos, *op. cit.,* p. 86.

[20] Fernow, *op. cit.,* Vol. 1, pp. 296–297; Vol. 7, p. 186.

[21] Spruill, *op. cit.,* p. 78.

[22] Elizabeth Anthony Dexter, *Colonial Women of Affairs: Women in Business and the Professions Before 1776* (Boston, 1931), Chapter III, *passim;* Abbott, *op. cit.,* p. 12.

[23] Charles Edward Ironside, *The Family in Colonial New York: A Sociological Study* (Ph.D. Thesis, Columbia University, 1942), Chapter III.

[24] Eve Merriam, *Growing Up Female in America: Ten Lives* (New York, 1971), p. 297.

[25] Alice Morse Earle, *Margaret Winthrop* (New York, 1896), p. 229.

[26] Ames, *op. cit.,* p. 15.

[27] R. M. Downs, ed., *America Begins: Early American Writing* (New York, 1950), pp. 232–264.

[28] *Early Records of the Town of Providence, op. cit.,* Vol. IX, pp. 5–6.

[29] Abbott, *op. cit.,* p. 1.

[30] Fernow, *op. cit.,* Vol. 7, p. 74.

[31] Benjamin Wadsworth, *The Well-Ordered Family* (Boston, 1712), p. 29.

[32] Cotton Mather, *Ornaments for the Daughters of Zion* (Cambridge, 1692), p. 38.

[33] Secker, *op. cit.,* p. 22.

[34] Spruill, pp. 3–7.

[35] Fernow, *op. cit.,* Vol. VII, pp. 37–38.

[36] Cotton Mather, *Bonifacius (Essays to Do Good)* (Gainesville, Fla., 1967, original Boston, 1710), p. 69.

[37] *Worcester Historical Society, Collections* (Worcester, 1882), Vol. 10, p. 325.

[38] Edmund S. Morgan, *The Puritan Family* (New York, 1966), Chapter II, *passim.*

[39] Demos, *op. cit.,* p. 83.

[40] Fernow, *op. cit.,* p. 60.

[41] Lyman Chalkey, ed., *Chronicles of the Scotch-Irish Settlement in Virginia, Extracted From the Original Court Records of Augusta County, 1745–1800* (Baltimore, 1965), Vol. 1, p. 162.

[42] Augusta County Records, pp. 81–91.

[43] Mather, *Ornaments, op. cit.,* p. 79.

[44] Wadsworth, *op. cit.,* pp. 38–39.

[45] Mather, *Ornaments, op. cit.,* p. 7.

[46] Bremner, *op. cit.,* p. 37.

[47] Mather, *Ornaments, op. cit.,* p. 9.

[48] *Ibid.,* p. 74.

[49] *Ibid.,* "The Virtuous Wife."

[50] *Early Records of the Town of Providence,* Vol. VI, pp. 109–111.

[51] William Cairns, ed., *Selections from Early American Writers, 1607–1800* (New York, 1915), p. 249.

[52] Ironside, *op. cit.,* p. 44.

[53] Fernow, *op. cit.,* Vol. 1, pp. 238–239.

[54] Ames, *op. cit.,* p. 20.

[55] Edmund S. Morgan, "The Puritans and Sex" in Michael Gordon, ed., *The American Family in Social-Historical Perspective* (New York, 1973), p. 285.

[56] *Ibid.,* p. 288.

[57] Ames, *op. cit.,* pp. 19–20.

[58] Franklin P. Rice, ed., *Worcester Historical Society Collections* (Worcester: Worcester Historical Society, 1883), Vol. 5, p. 80.

[59] Morgan, *op. cit.*, p. 284.

[60] Wadsworth, *op. cit.*, p. 24.

[61] *Ibid.*, p. 27.

[62] *Ibid.*, p. 25.

[63] Secker, *op. cit.*, p. 16.

[64] Wadsworth, *op. cit.*, p. 36; Mather, *Ornaments, op. cit.*, p. 79; Secker, *op. cit.*, p. 16.

[65] Mather, *Ornaments, op. cit.*, p. 79; Wadsworth, *op. cit.*, p. 26.

[66] Wadsworth, *op. cit.*, pp. 28–32.

[67] Cairns, *op. cit.*, p. 58.

[68] *Ibid.*, p. 162.

[69] Spruill, *op. cit.*, pp. 45–46.

[70] William H. Grabill, et al., *The Fertility of American Women* (New York, 1958), p. 5.

[71] *Early Records of the Town of Providence*, Vol. III, pp. 112–117.

[72] Demos, *op. cit.*, p. 66.

[73] Cotton Mather, *Elizabeth on Her Holy Retirement* (Boston, 1710), pp. 3, 5, 18.

[74] Wadsworth, *op. cit.*, p. 45.

[75] Mather, *Elizabeth on Her Holy Retirement, op. cit.*, p. 5.

[76] *Ibid.*, p. 31.

[77] Mather, *Ornaments, op. cit.*, p. 96.

[78] Isaac Ambrose, *The Well-Ordered Family* (Boston, 1762), p. 10.

[79] Wadsworth, *op. cit.*, pp. 43–46.

[80] Fernow, *op. cit.*, Vol. 1, p. 131.

[81] *Early Records of the Town of Providence*, Vol. VI, p. 61.

[82] Cairns, *op. cit.*, p. 132.

[83] Earle, *op. cit.*, p. 327.

[84] Mather, *Ornaments, op. cit.*, p. 43.

[85] *Ibid.*, p. 3.

[86] Wadsworth, *op. cit.*, pp. 2–3.

[87] *Ibid.*

[88] Dexter, *op. cit.*, p. 100.

[89] Chalkey, *op. cit.*, p. 27.

[90] *Early Records of the Town of Providence*, Vol. III, pp. 30–32.

[91] *Ibid.*, Vol. III, p. 6; Vol. X, p. 23.

[92] Frost, *op. cit.*, Vol. 1, p. 186.

[93] Thomas, *op. cit.*, p. 54.

[94] Earle, *op. cit.*, pp. 266–267.

[95] Morgan, *op. cit.*, p. 44.

[96] Cairns, *op. cit.*, p. 147.

[97] Nancy F. Cott, ed., *Root of Bitterness* (New York, 1972), pp. 31–46.

[98] Rufus M. Jones, *The Quakers in the American Colonies* (New York, 1962), pp. 84–89.

[99] Cott, *op. cit.*, p. 38.

[100] Fernow, *op. cit.*, Vol. IV, pp. 3, 32.

[101] Cott, *op. cit.*, pp. 47–58.

[102] Chalkey, *op. cit.*, p. 64.

[103] Spruill, *op. cit.*, p. 333.

[104] Ames, *op. cit.*, p. 85.

[105] Cott, *op. cit.*, p. 48; Chadwick Hansen, *Witchcraft at Salem* (New York, 1969), p. 35.

[106] Paul Boyer and Stephen Nissenbaum, eds., *Salem Village Witchcraft: A Documentary Record of Local Conflict in Colonial New England* (Belmont, Calif., 1972), Part III, pp. 137–179, *passim.*

[107] *Ibid.*, pp. 181–225, *passim.*

[108] John Demos, "Underlying Themes in the Witchcraft of Seventeenth Century New England," *American Historical Review,* Vol. LXXV, No. 5 (June 1970), pp. 1311–1326, *passim.*

[109] Hansen, *op. cit.*, p. 55.

[110] Cott, *op. cit.*, p. 67.

[111] Boyer and Nissenbaum, *op. cit.*, pp. 202–225, *passim.*

CHANGING ROLES, NEW RISKS

[1] Charles Francis Adams, *Familiar Letters of John Adams and His Wife Abigail Adams, During the Revolution. With a Memoir of Mrs. Adams* (Boston, 1875), p. 149.

[2] Sidney Herbert Ditzion, *Marriage, Morals and Sex in America: A History of Ideas* (New York, 1953), p. 42.

[3] James T. Lemon and Gary Nash, "The Distribution of Wealth in Eighteenth-Century America: A Century of Change in Chester County, Pennsylvania, 1693–1802," in Gary B. Nash, ed., *Class and Society in Early America* (Englewood Cliffs, N.J., 1970), p. 166–188.

[4] Colin Forster and G. S. L. Tucker, *Economic Opportunity and White American Fertility Ratios, 1800–1860* (New Haven, 1972), p. 13–16.

5 Benjamin Bell, *The Character of a Virtuous Woman* (Windsor, N.H., 1794), p. 14.

6 John Cosens Ogden, *The Female Guide* (Concord, N.H., 1793), pp. 3–13.

7 Elizabeth Anthony Dexter, *Colonial Women of Affairs*, 2nd ed. (Boston, 1931), pp. 119–121.

8 *Worcester Society of Antiquity, Collections* (Worcester, Mass., 1898), Vol. 8, p. 56.

9 Adams, *op. cit.*, pp. 8, 152.

10 R. M. Tryon, *Household Manufactures in the United States, 1640–1860* (New York; reprint, 1966), p. 55.

11 *Ibid.*, p. 248.

12 Dexter, *op. cit.*, pp. 7, 31–32.

13 Charles Edward Ironside, *The Family in Colonial New York: A Sociological Study* (Ph.D. Thesis, Columbia University, 1942), p. 36.

14 S. R. Stearns, *Abridged Journal,* manuscript, the Arthur and Elizabeth Schlesinger Library for the Study of Women's History, Radcliffe College, Cambridge, Mass., Vol. II, 1810–1812, p. 4, Monday, October 17, 1810. Hereafter referred to as Schlesinger Library.

15 Dixon Wecter and Lazer Ziff, eds., *Benjamin Franklin: Autobiography and Selected Writings* (New York, 1969), p. 64.

16 Dexter, *op. cit.*, pp. 18–25.

17 Dexter, *op. cit.*, pp. 73, 81, 88.

18 Carl Bridenbaugh, *Cities in Wilderness: The First Century of Urban Life in America, 1625–1742* (New York, 1955), p. 72.

19 David H. Flaherty, "Law and the Enforcement of Morals in Early America, in *Perspectives in American History*, Vol. V (1971), p. 240.

20 Raymond A. Mohl, *Poverty in New York, 1783–1825* (New York, 1971), p. 31.

21 Wecter and Ziff, *op. cit.*, p. 179.

22 George F. Dow, ed., *Holyoke Diaries, 1789–1856* (Salem, Mass., 1911).

23 Martha C. Codman, ed., *The Journal of Mrs. John Amory and Letters from Her Father Rufus Greene* (Boston, 1923), p. 8.

24 *Eunice Callender Diaries, 1808–1824,* manuscript, Schlesinger Library.

24a Bernard Bailyn and Lotte Bailyn, *Massachusetts Shipping*

1697–1714: A Statistical Study (Cambridge, Mass., 1959), pp. 56–73.

[25] Bernard Farber, *Guardians of Virtue; Salem Families in 1800* (New York, 1972), p. 126.

[26] Julia Cherry Spruill, *Women's Life and Work in the Southern Colonies* (Chapel Hill, N.C., 1969), p. 127.

[27] Ironside, *op. cit.,* p. 36.

[28] Codman, *op. cit.,* p. 8.

[29] Samuel Woodworth, ed., *Ladies' Literary Cabinet,* Vol. 1, No. 1 (April 1819), p. 1.

[30] John Gregory, *A Father's Legacy to His Daughter* (Philadelphia, 1775).

[31] Edith Abbott, *Women in Industry: A Study in American Economic History* (New York, 1919), p. 265–266.

[32] *Worcester Society of Antiquity, Collections,* Vol. 10, p. 232.

[33] Mohl, *op. cit.,* p. 25.

[34] Farber, *op. cit.,* pp. 144–145, 183.

[35] Abbott, *op. cit.,* p. 32.

[36] Mohl, *op. cit.,* pp. 44, 85.

[37] *Worcester Society of Antiquity, Collections,* Vol. 10, p. 109–110.

[38] Mohl, *op. cit.,* p. 95.

[39] Abbott, *op. cit.,* p. 22.

[40] *Ibid.,* pp. 40, 50–51.

[41] *Ibid.,* pp. 71–72.

[42] *Ibid.,* pp. 268–269.

[43] *Ibid.,* pp. 46, 85, 275.

[44] *Ibid.,* p. 55.

[45] Hannah Josephson, *The Golden Threads, New England's Mill Girls and Magnates* (New York, 1949).

[46] William Kendrick, *The Whole Duty of Woman* (Philadelphia, 1788), p. 5; Robert Dodeley, *The Oeconomy of Human Life* (Philadelphia, 1751).

[47] Gregory, *op. cit.,* pp. 6–7.

[48] Dodeley, *op. cit.,* pp. 45–46.

[49] *The Lady's Pocket Library,* (Philadelphia, 1792), pp. 5–6.

[50] Dodeley, *op. cit.,* p. 46.

[51] Pierre Joseph Boudier de Villement, *The Ladies' Friend, Being a Treatise on the Virtues* (Philadelphia, 1771), p. 2.

[52] Amos Chase, *On Female Excellence* (Litchfield, 1792), p. 7.

[53] Villement, *op. cit.,* p. 5.

[54] James Bowdoin, *A Paraphrase on Part of the Economy of Human Life* (Boston, 1759), pp. 14, 15, 16.

[55] Gregory, *op. cit.*, pp. 31–32.

[56] Antoine Leonard, *Essays on the Character of Women* (Philadelphia, 1774).

[57] Edward Ward, *Female Policy Detected, or the Arts of Designing Women* (Boston, 1786).

[58] Leonard de Vrier and Peter Fryer, eds., *Venus Unmasked or an Inquiry into the Nature and Origin of the Passion of Love* (London, 1967), p. 60.

[59] Susanna Rowson, *Mentoria or the Young Ladies' Friend*, Vol. II (Philadelphia, 1794), p. 11.

[60] *Ibid.*, p. 32.

[61] James Fordyce, *The Character and Conduct of the Female Sex* (Boston, 1781), p. 20.

[62] Bowdoin, *op. cit.*, p. 32.

[63] Thomas Gisborne, *An Inquiry into the Duties of the Female Sex* (Philadelphia, 1798), p. 2.

[64] George Strebeck, *A Sermon on the Character of the Virtuous Woman* (New York, 1800), p. 19.

[65] Leonard, *op. cit.*, p. 7.

[66] *Ibid.*, p. 7.

[67] Farber, *op. cit.*, pp. 147–148.

[68] Ethel Armes, ed., *Nancy Shippen, Her Journal Book, The International Romances of a Young Lady of Fashion of Colonial Philadelphia with Letters to Her and About Her* (Philadelphia, 1935), pp. 40–41, 101.

[69] *Ibid.*, pp. 221–222.

[70] Woodworth, *op. cit.*, p. 5.

[71] Kendrick, *op. cit.*, p. 54.

[72] *Ibid.*, p. 55.

[73] Ogden, *op. cit.*, p. 34.

[74] Mason Locke Weems, *The Lover's Almanac, No. 1* (Alexandria, Va., 1798).

[75] Ironside, *op. cit.*, p. 58.

[76] Dexter, *op. cit.*, p. 18.

[77] Philip J. Greven, Jr., *Four Generations: Population, Land and Family in Colonial Andover, Massachusetts* (Ithaca, 1970), pp. 175–250; Daniel Scott Smith, "Parental Power and Marriage Patterns: An Analysis of Historical Trends in Hingham, Mas-

sachusetts, 1630–1880," pp. 419–428, *Journal of Marriage and the Family* (August 1973).

[78] Bridenbaugh, *op. cit.,* p. 340.

[79] Greven, *op. cit.,* Part III.

[80] Daniel S. Smith, "The Demographic History of Colonial New England," in Michael Gordon, ed., *The American Family in Social-Historical Perspective* (New York, 1973), pp. 397–411; Susan L. Norton, "Population Growth in Colonial America: A Study of Ipswich, Mass., *Population Studies* (Nov. 1971), pp. 433–452; Robert V. Wells, "Family Size and Fertility Control in Eighteenth Century America: A Study of Quaker Families," *Population Studies* (1971), pp. 173–182.

[81] Reverend Thomas Humphrey, *Marriage as an Honorable Estate* (Boston, 1752), p. 3.

[82] Edward Ward, *New Proverbs on the Tricks of Women* (Boston, 1787), p. 7.

[83] Wecter and Ziff, *op. cit.,* pp. 184–186.

[84] Ditzion, *op. cit.,* pp. 53–57.

[85] Anonymous, *Reflections on Courtship and Marriage* (London, 1779), p. 22.

[86] Anne K. Nelsen and Hart M. Nelsen, "Family Articles in Frontier Newspapers: An Examination of One Aspect of Turner's Frontier Thesis," *Journal of Marriage and Family,* Vol. 32, No. 4 (November, 1969), pp. 644–649.

[87] Benjamin Rush, *Thoughts on Female Education* (Philadelphia, 1787), p. 5.

[88] Strebeck, *op. cit.,* p. 20.

[89] *The Maternal Physician. A Treatise on the Management of Infants, from Their Birth until Two Years Old.* By an American Matron (New York, 1972, reprint of original published at Philadelphia, 1811), p. 8.

[90] Woodworth, *op. cit.,* Vol. V, No. 1, p. 5.

[91] James Armstrong Neal, *An Essay on the Education and Genius of the Female Sex* (Philadelphia, 1795), pp. 9, 17, 18.

[92] *Ibid.,* p. 29.

[93] Keith Melder, "Ladies Bountiful: Organized Women's Benevolence in Early 19th Century America," *New York History,* Vol. XLVIII, No. 3, (July 1967), pp. 231–254.

[94] S. R. Stearns, *op. cit.*

[95] *Eunice Callender Diaries, 1808–1824,* Vol. II, *op. cit.,* p. 2.

[96] Catherine Marie Sedgwick, *Diaries,* 28th December 1854, Mss., Massachusetts Historical Society.

[97] Mrs. Juliana Frances Turner, *Harp of the Beechwoods* (Montrose, Pa., 1822), p. 51.

[98] Nelsen and Nelsen, *op. cit.,* p. 647.

MOTHERS OF CIVILIZATION

[1] Owen P. White, *A Frontier Mother* (New York, 1929), p. 101; C. Richard King, ed., *A Victorian Lady on the Texas Frontier: The Journal of Ann Raney Coleman* (Norman, Okla., 1971), p. 84.

[2] William Forrest Sprague, *Women and the West: A Short Social History* (New York, reprint 1972, originally published in Boston, 1940), pp. 54–55; Eliza Woodson Farnham, *Life in a Prairie Land* (New York, reprint 1972, originally published 1846), p. 254.

[3] Sprague, *ibid.,* pp. 31, 105; Nancy F. Cott, ed., *Root of Bitterness: Documents in the Social History of American Women* (New York, 1972), pp. 230–234; William W. Fowler, *Woman on the American Frontier* (New York, reprint 1970, originally published in Hartford, Conn., 1879), p. 171.

[4] Merle Curti, et al., *The Making of an American Community: A Case Study of Democracy in a Frontier County* (Stanford, Calif., 1959), pp. 409–415; White, *op. cit.,* p. 99; Katherine Clinton, "Pioneer Women in Chicago, 1833–1837," *Journal of the West* (April 1973).

[5] Fowler, *op. cit.,* p. 170.

[6] Ruth E. Finley, *The Lady of Godey's, Sarah Joseph Hale* (Philadelphia, 1931), p. 124; Michael Gordon and M. Chaples Bernstein, "Mate Choice and Domestic Life in the Nineteenth Century Marriage Manual," *Journal of Marriage and the Family,* Vol. 34 (November 1970), p. 670.

[7] Margaret Coxe, *Claims of the Country on American Females,* (Columbus, Ohio, 1842), p. 13.

[8] Catherine E. Beecher, *The Duty of American Women to Their Country* (New York, 1845), p. 210, *passim.*

[9] Henry C. Wright, *The Empire of the Mother over the Character and Destiny of the Race* (Boston, 1870), p. 4.

[10] Lydia Maria Child, *The Mother's Book,* 5th ed. (New York, 1849), pp. 161–162; Lydia H. Sigourney, *The Girls' Reading Book* (New York, 1837), p. 6; Catherine M. Sedgwick, *Means and Ends* (Boston, 1839), p. 16.

[11] Mrs. L. Maria Child, *The Girl's Own Book* (New York, 1833), pp. 78, 79.

[12] Peter Andrews, "Games People Played," *American Heritage Magazine* (June 1972), pp. 70–71.

[13] *Diary of Mary Jane Walker,* Vol. III, Schlesinger Library, Saturday, January 6th, 1849.

[14] Margaret Graves, *Girlhood and Womanhood* (Boston, 1844), p. 152.

[15] Catherine Maria Sedgwick, *Clarence* (Philadelphia, 1830), p. 163.

[16] Frances Parkes, *Domestic Duties,* 3rd ed. (New York, 1931), p. 356.

[17] *Ibid.;* Mrs. E. D. E. N. Southworth, *The Curse of Clifton* (Philadelphia, 1875, originally 1850).

[18] Marion Harland, *Alone* (New York, 1856), p. 81.

[19] Augusta Jane Evans, *Beulah* (New York, 1876, originally 1859), p. 500.

[20] Donald Mitchell, *Dream Life* (New York, 1907), p. 181.

[21] Timothy Shay Arthur, *Tales of Married Life* (Philadelphia, 1858), p. 99.

[22] *The Mothers' Assistant and Young Ladies' Friend,* Vol. XIII, No. 3, p. 77.

[23] Lydia Sigourney, *Letters to Young Ladies* (New York, 1838), p. 74.

[24] Ralph Waldo Emerson, *Works* (Boston, 1898), Vol. XI, p. 341.

[25] Farnham, *op. cit.,* pp. 127–128.

[26] Timothy Shay Arthur, *What Can a Woman Do?* (New York, 1858), p. 87.

[27] G. J. Barker-Benfield, "The Spermatic Economy: A Nineteenth-Century View of Sexuality," in Michael S. Gordon, ed., *The American Family in Social-Historical Perspective* (New York, 1973), pp. 336–372; Charles E. Rosenberg, "Sexuality, Class and Role in 19th Century America," *American Quarterly* (May 1973), pp. 131–153.

[28] William D. Sanger, *The History of Prostitution* (New York, 1858); Thomas L. Nichols, *Esoteric Anthropology,* 15th ed. (London, n.d.), p. 100.

[29] Nichols, *ibid.,* p. 42; Ann Douglas Wood, "The Fashionable Diseases: Women's Complaints and Their Treatment in 19th-Century America," *Journal of Interdisciplinary History,* Vol. IV, pp. 25–52 (Summer 1973).

[30] Robert Latou Dickinson and Laura Beam, *A Thousand Marriages: A Medical Study of Sex Adjustment* (Baltimore, 1931), p. 139; Thomas L. Nichols and Mary Gore Nichols, *Marriage: Its History, Character and Results,* 3rd rev. ed. (Cincinnati, 1855), p. 265.

[31] Wood, *op. cit.,* p. 29.

[32] Colin Forster and G. S. L. Tucker, *Economic Opportunity and White American Fertility Rates, 1800–1860* (New Haven, Conn., 1972); Susan E. Bloomberg, et al., "A Census Probe into Nineteenth-Century Family History in Southern Michigan, 1850–1900," *Journal of Social History,* Vol. V (Fall 1971), pp. 26–45; Richard Sennett, *Families Against the City: Middle-Class Homes of Industrial Chicago, 1872–1890* (Cambridge, Mass., 1970).

[33] William Alcott, *The Physiology of Marriage* (Boston, 1856); George Ellington, *The Women of New York* (New York, reprint 1972, originally published 1869), p. 396.

[34] Alcott, *ibid.,* pp. 146–147, 196.

[35] Dr. G. Ackerley, *On the Management of Children in Sickness and in Health,* 2nd ed. (New York, 1836), p. ii; Dr. William Dewees, *A Treatise on the Physical and Medical Treatment of Children,* 5th ed. (Philadelphia, 1833), pp. 64–65; Mrs. Lydia Sigourney, *Letters to Mothers,* 6th ed. (New York, 1846), p. vii.

[36] Finley, *op. cit.,* p. 128; Wright, *op. cit.,* p. 4.

[37] Dewees, *op. cit.,* p. 54; Richard Kissan, *The Nurse's Manual and Young Mother's Guide* (Hartford, 1834), p. 90.

[38] Heman Humphrey, *Domestic Education* (Amherst, Mass., 1840), p. 184; Sigourney, *Letters to Mothers, op. cit.,* p. 32.

[39] John Abbott, *The Child at Home* (New York, 1833), pp. 12–13, 213.

[40] Sigourney, *Letters to Mothers, op. cit.,* pp. 13–14.

[41] L. H. Sigourney, *The Faded Hope* (New York, 1853), pp. 224–225, 244.

[42] Caroline Cowles Richards, *Village Life in America* (New York, 1913), pp. 30–31; Anne Firor Scott, *The Southern Lady* (New York, 1970), pp. 24–25; Harold G. Merriam, ed. (Norman, Okla., 1969), *Way Out West,* pp. 172–173.

[43] Sarah Payson Willis, *Fern Leaves from Fanny's Portfolio* (Buffalo, N.Y., 1853), pp. 363, 384.

[44] *Diary of Eliza E. Rogers,* Schlesinger Library, Nov. 29, 1860, Jan. 27, 1861.

[45] Harvey Elkins, *Fifteen Years in the Senior Order of Shakers,* (Hanover, N.H., 1853), p. 6; *First Annual Report of the Oneida Association's Transactions to January 1st 1849* (Oneida, N. Y., 1849), pp. 49, 51.

[46] John Humphrey Noyes, *Male Continence* (Oneida, N.Y., 1872), p. 11; *The Witness* (Ithaca, N.Y.), Vol. VII (January 23, 1839), pp. 149–150.

[47] *First Annual Report, op. cit.,* p. 7.

[48] *The Witness,* Vol. VII (January 23, 1839), pp. 5–6; Elkins, *op. cit.,* p. 34.

[49] *Harbinger,* Vol. III, No. 16 (September 26, 1846), p. 253; Henry Sams, ed., *Autobiography of Brook Farm* (Englewood Cliffs, N.J., 1858), p. 36.

[50] Elizabeth Margaret Chandler, *Poetical Works* (Philadelphia, 1836), p. 64.

[51] Boston Female Anti-Slavery Society, *Eleventh Annual Report* (New York, 1844), pp. 39–40; Chandler, *op. cit.,* p. 8; Angelina Grimké, *Appeal to the Christian Women of the South* (New York, 1856), p. 23.

[52] Grimké, *ibid.,* p. 25.

[53] Nehemiah Adams, quoted in Annual Report of Boston Female Anti-Slavery Society (Boston, 1837), pp. 42–43; Catherine Beecher, *An Essay on Slavery and Abolitionism with reference to the Duty of American Females* (Boston, 1839), pp. 98–99, 136–7.

[54] Angelina Grimké, *Letters to Catherine Beecher in Reply to an Essay on Slavery and Abolitionism* (Boston, 1839), pp. 7, 103, 107.

[55] *Ibid.,* p. 10; Boston Female Anti-Slavery Society, *Annual Report* (Boston, 1837), pp. 42–43.

[56] *The Lily,* December 1, 1955, pp. 169–170; Letter from S. M. Grimké to E. B. Loring, February 10, 1956, *Child MSS,* New York Public Library.

[57] Reynolds Farley, *Growth of the Black Population* (Chicago, 1970), p. 2.

[58] Robert S. Starobin, "Privileged Bondsman and the Process of Accommodation: The Role of Houseservants and Drivers as Seen in Their Own Letters," *Journal of Social History,* Vol. 5, No. 1 (Fall 1971), pp. 55, 57–58.

[59] Robert H. Bremner, et al., *Children and Youth in America: A Documentary History,* Vol. 1 (Cambridge, Mass., 1970), p. 376; Mel Watkins and Jay Donald, *To Be a Black Woman: Portraits in Fact*

and *Fiction* (New York, 1970), p. 17; Starobin, *op. cit.*, p. 70.

[60] Gerda Lerner, *Black Women in White America* (New York, 1972), p. 35; Watkins and Donald, *ibid.*, p. 16.

[61] Mary Ashton Livermore, *My Story of the War* (Hartford, Conn., 1888), p. 647.

WORKERS, IMMIGRANTS, SOCIAL HOUSEKEEPERS

[1] *Ladies' Home Journal,* February 1890.

[2] Elizabeth Faulkner Baker, *Technology and Women's Work* (New York, 1964); Robert W. Smuts, *Women and Work in America* (New York, 1959), p. 17; Lucy Maynard Salmon, *Domestic Service* (New York, 1927 reprint of 1897 edition), p. 75, *passim.*

[3] William I. Thomas and Florian Znaniecki, *The Polish Peasant in Europe and America* (New York, 1958), Vol. I, pp. 775–776.

[4] Hannah Josephson, *The Golden Threads; New England's Mill Girls and Magnates* (New York, 1949), p. 202.

[5] Frank L. Mott, "Portrait of an American Mill Town: Demographic Response in Mid-Nineteenth Century Warren, Rhode Island," *Population Studies* (March 1972), p. 156.

[6] Baker, *op. cit.*, p. 77.

[7] Thomas and Znaniecki, *op. cit.*, p. 777; Grace Abbott, *The Immigrant and the Community* (New York, 1917), Chapter III, p. 55.

[8] Caroline Manning, *The Immigrant Woman and Her Job* (New York, 1970), p. 22.

[9] Elizabeth Beardsley Butler, *Woman and the Trades* (New York, 1969 reprint of 1909 edition), pp. 75–101; Manning, *op. cit.*, p. 107.

[10] Butler, *ibid.*, pp. 60–61, 210–211.

[11] Edith Abbott, *Women in Industry: A Study in American Economic History* (New York, 1919), p. 252.

[12] Butler, *op. cit.*, pp. 44–52, 84–92, 115–122, 212.

[13] *Ibid.*, pp. 96, 212.

[14] Manning, *op. cit.*, p. 98.

[15] Elizabeth Hasanovitz, *One of Them, Chapters from a Passionate Autobiography* (Boston, 1918), p. 272.

[16] Manning, *op. cit.*, pp. 98, 212.

[17] *Ibid.*, p. 118.

[18] Butler, *op. cit.*, p. 337.

[19] Carroll D. Wright, *The Working Girls of Boston* (New York, 1969 reprint of 1889 edition), p. 77.

[20] Hasanovitz, *op. cit.*, p. 272.

[21] Manning, *op. cit.*, p. 121.

[22] Wright, *op. cit.*, pp. 20–21.

[23] Butler, *op. cit.*, pp. 318–320.

[24] Manning, *op. cit.*, p. 36.

[24a] *Abstracts of the Reports of the Immigration Commission*, Senate Doc. 747 U.S. Government Printing Office, Washington, D.C., 1911, Vol. 7, pp. 414–417.

[25] Smuts, *op. cit.*, p. 19.

[26] Bulter, *op. cit.*, p. 345.

[27] Rose Cohen, *Out of the Shadow* (New York, 1918), p. 108.

[28] Daniel J. Walkowitz, "Working-Class Women in the Gilded Age: Factory, Community and Family Life Among Cohoes, New York, Cotton Workers," *Journal of Social History*, Vol. 5, No. 4 (Summer 1972), pp. 464–490.

[29] Mary (Kenney) O'Sullivan, Autobiography, Mss., Schlesinger Library, p. 6.

[30] Butler, *op. cit.*, p. 348.

[31] William J. Goode, *World Revolution and the Family Patterns* (New York, 1963), p. 16.

[32] Manning, *op. cit.*, p. 14.

[33] *Ibid.*, pp. 52–53.

[34] *Ibid.*, p. 61.

[35] Helen Campbell, *Prisoners of Poverty, Women Wage Workers: Their Trades and Their Lives* (New York, 1970, reprint of 1887 edition), pp. 18–29.

[36] Manning, *op. cit.*, p. 60.

[37] *Ibid.*, p. 34.

[38] Thomas and Znaniecki, *op. cit.*, Vol. 2, pp. 1661–1667.

[39] Virginia Yans McLaughlin, "Pattern of Work and Family Organization: Buffalo's Italians," *The Journal of Interdisciplinary History*, Vol. II, No. 2 (Autumn 1971), pp. 299–314, *passim.*

[40] Manning, *op. cit.*, p. 139.

[41] Thomas and Znaniecki, *op. cit.*, p. 730.

[42] Cohen, *op. cit.*, p. 155, *passim.*

[43] Margaret Von Staden, "My Story (The History of a Prostitute's Life in San Francisco)," Mss., Schlesinger Library, p. 2.

[44] The "Maimie" Papers, Schlesinger Library, April 1911, *passim.*

[45] Mary (Kenney) O'Sullivan, Mss., *Autobiography*, p. 141.

[46] Roy Lubove, *The Progressives and the Slums: Tenement House Reform in New York City, 1891–1917* (Pittsburgh, 1963), Chapter 4, pp. 91–92.

[47] Manning, *op. cit.*, p. 70.

[47a] Robert Coit Chapin, *The Standard of Living Among Workingmen's Families in New York City* (New York, 1909), pp. 249–250.

[48] Moses Rischin, "The Lower East Side," in Leonard Dinnerstein and Kenneth T. Jackson, eds., *American Vistas* (New York, 1971), Vol. 2, p. 44.

[49] Mary (Kenney) O'Sullivan, *Autobiography*, p. 8.

[50] William H. Grabill, et al., *The Fertility of American Women* (New York, 1958), p. 106.

[51] Emma Goldman, *Living My Life* (New York, 1931), pp. 185–186.

[52] Campbell, *op. cit.*, pp. 133–134.

[53] Jane Addams, *Twenty Years at Hull House* (New York, 1960), pp. 244–247.

[54] Von Staden, *op. cit.*, p. 5.

[55] *Ibid.*, pp. 102, 171.

[56] Thomas and Znaniecki, *op. cit.*, pp. 1800–1821, 1935.

[57] *Ibid.*, pp. 1800–1821.

[58] Cohen, *op. cit.*, p. 297.

[59] Thomas and Znaniecki, *op. cit.*, pp. 1800–1821, 2225.

[60] Hasanovitz, *op. cit.*, pp. 102–103.

[61] Cohen, *op. cit.*, pp. 125–126.

[62] Lewis (Lorwin) Levine, *The Women's Garment Workers* (New York, 1924), pp. 146–147.

[63] Leon Edel, ed., *The Diary of Alice James* (New York, 1934), p. 43.

[64] Charlotte Perkins Gilman, *The Living of Charlotte Perkins Gilman,* (New York, 1935), pp. 89, 96.

[65] Addams, *op. cit.*, pp. 21, 44.

[66] Mary Ashton Livermore, *My Story of the War* (Hartford, Conn., 1888), pp. 136, 355.

[67] Addams, *op. cit.*, p. 93.

[68] Jane Cunningham Croly, *The History of the Women's Club Movement* (New York, 1898), p. 14.

[69] William J. O'Neill, *Everyone Was Brave: A History of Feminism in America* (Chicago, 1971), p. 36.

[70] *Diaries and Notebooks of Leonora O'Reilly,* Schlesinger Library, Vol. 18, December 10–12, 1911.

[71] Mary Jones, *The Autobiography of Mother Jones* (Chicago, 1972).

[72] Goldman, *op. cit.,* p. 61.

[73] Eliza Burt Gamble, *The Sexes in Society and History* (originally published as *The Evolution of Woman,* 1894; revised edition, 1916), p. 17.

[74] William I. Thomas, *Sex and Society: Studies in the Social Psychology of Sex* (Boston, 1907); Lester Ward, *Dynamic Sociology* (New York, 1968, reprint of 1883 edition), p. 615.

[75] Livermore, *op. cit.,* pp. 188, 477.

[76] Addams, *op. cit.,* p. 57.

[77] *Ibid.,* p. 59.

[78] *Ibid.,* pp. 93, 94, 98.

[79] Allen Davis, *Spearheads for Reform: The Social Settlements and the Progressive Movement, 1890–1914* (New York, 1967), p. 12,

[80] Mary Ritter Beard, *Women's Work in Municipalities* (New York, 1915); from "Introduction" by Clinton Rogers Woodruff, p. x.

[81] Croly, *op. cit.,* p. 112.

[82] Sophonisba Breckinridge, *Women in the Twentieth Century: A Study in Their Political, Social and Economic Activities* (New York, 1933), pp. 11–42.

[83] *Ibid.*

[84] Barbara M. Cross, ed., *The Educated Woman in America* (New York, 1965), pp. 30–45.

[85] Breckinridge, *op. cit.,* pp. 187, 305–321; Beard, *op. cit.* Cynthia Fuchs Epstein, *Woman's Place* (Berkeley, Calif., 1971), pp. 7, 8.

[86] Addams, *op. cit.,* p. 76.

[87] Dorothy Rose Blumberg, *Florence Kelley: The Making of a Social Pioneer* (New York, 1966); quoted in Gladys Boone, *The Women's Trade Union League in Great Britain and America* (New York, 1942), p. 99.

[88] Elizabeth Kemper Adams, *Women Professional Workers* (New York, 1921), pp. 174, 438.

[89] Richard Jensen, "Family, Career and Reform: Women Leaders of the Progressive Era," in Michael Gordon, ed., *The American Family in Social-Historical Perspective* (New York, 1973), pp. 267–280.

[90] Adams, *op. cit.,* p. 23.

[91] Florence L. Cross Kitchelt, Mss. Journal, Schlesinger Library, p. 3.

[92] Blumberg, *op. cit.,* p. 131.

[93] O'Sullivan, *op. cit.,* pp. 181, 182–183.

[94] Adams, *op. cit.,* pp. 31, 32.

[95] Julia Ward Howe, ed., *Sex and Education. A Reply to Dr. E. H. Clarke's "Sex in Education"* (New York, 1972, reprint of 1874 edition), pp. 55, 56; Carroll-Smith Rosenberg and Charles Rosenberg, "The Female Animal: Medical and Biological Views of Woman and Her Role in Nineteenth-Century America," *Journal of American History* (Fall 1973), pp. 332–357.

[96] Charlotte Perkins Gilman, "The Home," in William J. O'Neill, ed., *The Woman Movement: Feminism in Europe and America* (London, 1969), pp. 129, 131; Charlotte Perkins Gilman, *The Man-Made World or Our Androcentric Culture* (New York, 1970, reprint of 1911 edition), p. 131.

[97] Beard, *op. cit.,* p. 35.

[98] *Ladies' Home Journal,* September 1890, p. 10.

[99] *Ladies' Home Journal,* December 1899; March 1910.

[100] Mari Joe Buhle, "Women and the Socialist Party, 1901–1914," *Radical America,* Vol. IV, No. 2 (February 1970), pp. 36–55.

[101] August Bebel, *Women Under Socialism* (New York, 1971); from "Introduction" by Daniel De Leon, p. xviii.

[102] Buhle, *op. cit.,* p. 53.

[103] Aileen S. Kraditor, *Up from the Pedestal: Selected Writings in the History of American Feminism* (Chicago, 1968), p. 263; Gilman, "The Home," *op. cit.,* pp. 122–123.

[104] Livermore, *op. cit.,* p. 436.

[105] Beard, *op. cit.,* pp. 46–47.

THE SEXY SALESLADY

[1] Jane Addams, *The Second Twenty Years at Hull House* (New York, 1930), pp. 110, 120.

[2] William Henry Chafe, *The American Woman: Her Changing Social, Economic, and Political Roles, 1920–1970* (New York, 1972), pp. 25–47; J. Stanley Lemons, *The Woman Citizen* (Urbana, Ill., 1973).

[3] Chafe, *ibid.;* Breckinridge, *ibid.*

[4] Addams, *op. cit.,* pp. 192–198.

[5] Robert Lynd and Helen Merrell Lynd, *Middletown—A Study in Contemporary American Culture* (New York, 1956), p. 88.

[6] Otis Pease, *The Responsibilities of American Advertising* (New Haven, Conn., 1958), p. 23.

[7] *Ibid.,* p. 41.

[8] Breckinridge, *op. cit.,* p. 55.

[9] Samuel D. Schmalhauser and V. T. Calverton, eds., *Woman's Coming of Age: A Symposium* (New York, 1931), pp. 34, 343–353; Suzanne La Follette, *Concerning Women* (New York, 1926), p. 9.

[10] Charlotte Perkins Gilman, *The Living of Charlotte Perkins Gilman* (New York, 1935), pp. 318–319.

[11] Mable Dodge Luhan, *Intimate Memoirs,* Vol. II (New York, 1935), pp. 31, 34, 236.

[12] *Ibid.,* Vol. III (1936), pp. 146, 216, 482.

[13] Nathan G. Hale, *Freud and the Americans* (New York, 1971), p. 476.

[14] Lynd and Lynd, *op. cit.,* p. 242.

[15] *The Consumers' League of Connecticut,* pamphlet, Schlesinger Library.

[16] Frances R. Donovan, *The Saleslady* (Chicago, 1929), p. 96.

[17] Havelock Ellis, *The Psychology of Sex: A Manual for Students* (New York, 1960).

[18] Hale, *op. cit.,* p. 338.

[19] Robert Latou Dickinson and Lura Beam, *A Thousand Marriages: A Medical Study of Sex Adjustment* (Baltimore, 1932), p. 129; G. Stanley Hall, *Adolescence: Its Psychology,* Vol. II (New York, 1922), p. 109.

[20] Dickinson and Beam, *ibid.,* pp. 214, 216.

[21] Norman Himes, *Medical History of Contraception* (New York, 1963), p. 340.

[22] V. T. Calverton, *The Bankruptcy of Marriage* (New York, 1928).

[23] Schmalhauser and Calverton, *op. cit.,* p. 484.

[24] La Follette, *op. cit.,* pp. 73–74.

[25] Katharine B. Davis, *Factors in the Sex Life of Twenty-Two Hundred Women* (New York, 1929), p. 247.

[26] Calverton, *op. cit.,* as quoted on p. 101.

[27] Donovan, *op. cit.;* from "Introduction" by Robert Park, p. viii.

[28] *Ibid.,* p. 238.

[29] V. Calverton, "Are Women Monogamous?" in Schmalhauser and Calverton, *op. cit.,* pp. 475–488.

[30] Dr. G. V. Hamilton, "The Emotional Life of Modern Woman," in Schmalhauser and Calverton, *op. cit.,* pp. 207–229.

[31] Alfred C. Kinsey, et al., *Sexual Behavior in the Human Female* (Philadelphia, 1953), p. 349.

[32] *Ibid.*, p. 467.

[33] Dickinson and Beam, *op. cit.*, p. 100; Marie Robinson, *The Power of Sexual Surrender* (New York, 1959), p. 46.

[34] Robinson, *ibid.*, p. 33.

[35] Havelock Ellis, *Man and Woman: A Study of Human Secondary Sexual Characteristics* (New York, 1911), pp. 25–26.

[36] Hall, *op. cit.*, Vol. II, p. 391.

[37] Havelock Ellis, *The Task of Social Hygiene* (New York, 1927), introduction.

[38] Hall, *op. cit.*, Vol. I, p. 512.

[39] Havelock Ellis, "Women's Sexual Nature," in Schmalhauser and Calverton, *op. cit.*, p. 236.

[40] H. W. Frink, *Morbid, Fears and Compulsions* (New York, 1918), pp. 134–135, 136.

[41] Dickinson and Beam, *op. cit.*, p. 443.

[42] Helene Deutsch, *The Psychology of Women: A Psychoanalytic Interpretation* Vol. II (New York, 1945), pp. 7–9.

[43] Lundberg and Farnham, *op. cit.*, p. 149.

[44] Robinson, *op. cit.*, p. 70.

[45] Marie Bonaparte, *Female Sexuality* (New York, 1973), p. 55.

[46] Robinson, *op. cit.*, p. 69.

[47] Dickinson and Beam, *op. cit.*, p. 63.

[48] Kinsey, *op. cit.*, p. 171.

[49] Bonaparte, *op. cit.*, p. 85.

[50] Karen Horney, *Feminine Psychology* (New York, 1973); Clara M. Thompson, *On Women* (New York, 1964), p. 177.

[51] Gunther Stuhlman, ed., *The Diary of Anais Nin* (New York, 1969), Vol. III, p. 214.

[52] Mary McCarthy, *The Group* (New York, 1964), p. 44.

[53] Deutsch, *op. cit.*, pp. 102–103.

[54] *Ibid.*, p. 17.

[55] Bonaparte, *op. cit.*, p. 1.

[56] *Ibid.*, p. 54.

[57] Lundberg and Farnham, *op. cit.*, p. 275.

[58] Robinson, *op. cit.*, p. 34.

[59] *Ibid.*, p. 32.

[60] Deutsch, *op. cit.*, p. 105.

[61] *Ibid.*

[62] Bonaparte, *op. cit.,* p. 129.

[63] *Ibid.*

[64] Deutsch, *op. cit.,* p. 258.

[65] *Ibid.,* p. 107.

[66] Lundberg and Farnham, *op. cit.,* p. 278.

[67] Robinson, *op. cit.,* p. 36.

[68] Ellis, *Social Hygiene, op. cit.,* p. 65.

[69] Richard E. Gordon, et al., *The Split-Level Trap* (New York, 1961), p. 38.

[70] Gladys Groves, *Marriage and Family Life* (New York, 1942), p. 137.

[71] Caroline Latimer, *Girl & Woman: A Book for Mothers and Daughters* (New York, 1916), pp. 1–2.

[72] *Ibid.,* p. 255.

[73] Groves, *op. cit.,* p. 142.

[74] Robinson, *op. cit.,* p. 85.

[75] Lynd and Lynd, *op. cit.,* pp. 140–142.

[76] Phyllis Blanchard and Carlyn Manasses, *New Girls for Old* (New York, 1930), pp. 142–143.

[77] *Ladies' Home Journal,* August 1943.

[78] Groves, *op. cit.,* p. 145.

[79] Lynd and Lynd, *op. cit.,* pp. 263–264.

[80] George Lundberg, Mirra Komarovsky, Mary Alice McInerny, *Leisure: A Suburban Study* (New York, 1934), p. 182.

[81] Leo Handel, *Hollywood Looks at Its Audiences* (Urbana, Ill., 1950), p. 122.

[82] Blanchard and Manasses, *op. cit.,* p. 37.

[83] *Ibid.,* p. 37.

[84] Ben Lindsay as quoted in William Reich, *The Sexual Revolution* (New York, 1971), p. 93.

[85] Frances Donovan, *The Woman Who Waits* (Boston, 1920), p. 42.

[86] *Ibid.,* p. 213.

[87] *Ibid.,* p. 105.

[88] Davis, *op. cit.,* p. 190.

[89] Frances Donovan, *The Schoolma'am* (New York, 1938), pp. 35–36.

[90] Blanchard and Manasses, *op. cit.,* p. 174.

[91] Zelda Fitzgerald, *Save Me the Waltz* (London, 1953), p. 50.

[92] Pease, p. 35.

[93] *Ladies' Home Journal, passim.*

94 Mary Sidney Branch, *Women and Wealth* (Chicago, 1934), p. 107.

95 *Ibid.*

96 Warren Waite, *The Economics of Consumption* (New York, 1928), p. 196.

97 Isabel Ely Lord, *Getting Your Moneysworth* (New York, 1922), p. 3.

98 Lynd and Lynd, *op. cit.*, p. 196.

99 Eleanor Roosevelt, *It's Up to Woman* (New York, 1933), p. 248.

A KALEIDOSCOPE OF ROLES

1 William Henry Chafe, *The American Woman: Her Changing Social, Economic, and Political Roles, 1920–1970* (New York, 1972), p. 50.

2 Frances R. Donovan, *The Saleslady* (Chicago, 1929), p. 189.

3 Elizabeth Faulkner Baker, *Technology and Women's Work* (New York, 1964), p. 249.

4 Caroline Wormeley Latimer, *Girl and Woman* (New York, 1916), p. 263.

5 Ellen Key, *The Renaissance of Motherhood* (New York, 1904), p. 123.

6 Lorine Pruette, *Women and Leisure: A Study of Social Waste* (New York, 1924), p. xi.

7 Mary Ross, "The New State of Women in America," in *Woman's Coming of Age*, V. F. Calverton and S. D. Schmalhauser, eds. (New York, 1931), p. 546.

8 Valerie Kincade Oppenheimer, *The Female Labor Force in the United States: Demographic and Economic Factors Governing Its Growth and Changing Composition* (Berkeley, Calif., 1970), p. 6.

9 *Ibid.*, pp. 6–19.

10 Elizabeth G. Stern, *I Am a Woman and a Jew* (New York, 1926), pp. 25, 70.

11 *Ibid.*, pp. 73, 163.

12 *Ibid.*, pp. 200, 289.

13 Oppenheimer, *op. cit.*, pp. 143, 151.

14 Chafe, *op. cit.*, pp. 55–60.

15 Oppenheimer, *op. cit.*, pp. 10, 15, 177.

16 Pruette, *op. cit.*, p. 6.

17 Oppenheimer, *op. cit.*, p. 44.

[18] Mirra Komarovsky, *Unemployed Man and His Family* (New York, 1940), p. 49.

[19] Oppenheimer, *op. cit.*, pp. 127–130.

[20] Chafe, *op. cit.*, pp. 56–57.

[21] Joan Ellen Trey, "Women in the War Economy," *The Review of Radical Political Economies* (July 1972), pp. 40–57.

[22] *Ibid.*

[23] Chafe, *op. cit.*, p. 137.

[24] Dorothy Thompson, "Women and the Coming World," *Ladies' Home Journal* (October 1943), p. 6.

[25] Chafe, *op. cit.*, pp. 144–45, 165–73.

[26] Thompson, *Ladies' Home Journal, op. cit.*, p. 6.

[27] Theresa Wolfson, "Aprons and Overalls in War," *The Annals of the American Academy of Political and Social Science* (September, 1943), pp. 56–63.

[28] Chafe, *op. cit.*, p. 180.

[29] Oppenheimer, *op. cit.*, pp. 143–144, 175.

[30] *Ibid.*, pp. 70–75.

[31] Frances Donovan, *The Woman Who Waits* (Boston, 1920), p. 211.

[32] Frances Donovan, *The Schoolma'am* (New York, 1938), p. 348.

[33] Michael Korda, *Male Chauvinism: How It Works* (New York, 1972), p. 3.

[34] Oppenheimer, *op. cit.*, p. 104.

[35] Baker, *op. cit.*, p. 214.

[36] *Ibid.*, pp. 223–25, 234.

[37] *Ibid.*, p. 236.

[38] Elinor Langer, "Inside the New York Telephone Company," in *Woman at Work,* William O'Neill, ed. (Chicago, 1972), p. 315.

[39] *Ibid.*, p. 310.

[40] Oppenheimer, *op. cit.*, p. 104.

[41] *Ibid.*, p. 99.

[42] Caroline Bird, *Born Female* (New York, 1968), p. 64.

[43] *Ibid.*, pp. 63–64.

[44] Chafe, *op. cit.*, p. 61.

[45] Bird, *op. cit.*, pp. 62–63.

[46] Cynthia Fuchs Epstein, *Women's Place* (Berkeley, Calif., 1970), pp. 8, 10.

[47] Oppenheimer, *op. cit.*, pp. 20, 21.

[48] Chafe, *op. cit.*, p. 218.

[49] *Ibid.*, p. 63.

[50] Robert Lynd and Helen Merrell Lynd, *Middletown—A Study* in *Contemporary American Culture* (New York, 1929), pp. 27–29.
[51] *Ibid.*
[52] Chafe, *op. cit.*, p. 219.
[53] Donovan, *The Woman Who Waits, op. cit.*, p. 203.
[54] Donovan, *The Saleslady, op. cit.*, pp. 1–2.
[55] Langer, *op. cit.*, p. 338.
[56] Pruette, *op. cit.*, p. 123.
[57] Oppenheimer, *op. cit.*, pp. 42–52.
[58] *Ibid.*, p. 107.
[59] *Ladies' Home Journal,* February 1943, p. 35.
[60] Eric Barnuov, *The Image Empire* (Oxford, 1970), p. 18.
[61] Mary Burt Messer, *The Family in the Making* (New York, 1938), p. ix.
[62] Groves, *op. cit.*, p. 338.
[63] Paul Landis, *Your Marriage and Family Living* (New York, 1946), pp. 32–33.
[64] *Ladies' Home Journal,* February 1943, p. 35.
[65] Talcott Parsons and Robert Bales, *Family, Socialization and Interaction Process* (New York, 1955).
[66] Ernest R. Groves and Gladys H. Groves, *The Contemporary Family* (Chicago, 1947), p. 746.
[67] *Ibid.*, p. 397.
[68] Landis, *op. cit.*, pp. 123–124.
[69] Mirra Komarovsky, *Women in the Modern World* (Boston, 1953), pp. 77, 82.
[70] Landis, *op. cit.*, p. 137.
[71] Lynd and Lynd, *op. cit.*, p. 116.
[72] Helena Z. Lopata, *Occupational Housewife* (New York, 1971), p. 103.
[73] Ben J. Wattenberg and Richard M. Scammer, *The USA* (Garden City, N.Y., 1965), p. 76.
[74] George Lundberg, Mirra Komarovsky, Mary Alice McInerny, *Leisure: A Suburban Study* (New York, 1934), pp. 177, 178.
[75] John R. Seeley, R. Alexander Sim, and Elizabeth Loosley, *Crestwood Heights: A Study of the Culture of Suburban Life* (New York, 1956), p. 174.
[76] Lopata, *op. cit.*, p. 217.
[77] *Ibid.*, p. 51.
[78] Komarovsky, *Women in the Modern World, op. cit.*, pp. 108–109.

[79] Betty Friedan, *The Feminine Mystique* (New York, 1970), p. 203.
[80] Komarovsky, *Women in the Modern World, op. cit.,* pp. 7–8.
[81] Russell Lynes, *The Domesticated Americans* (New York, 1957, 1963), p. 271.
[82] Lopata, *op. cit.,* p. 207.
[83] John B. Watson, *Psychological Care of Infant and Child* (New York, 1928), pp. 5–6.
[84] Ellen Key, *The Century of the Child* (New York, 1909), p. 182.
[85] Watson, *op. cit.,* p. 44.
[86] L. Emmett Holt, M.D. *The Care and Feeding of Children: A Collection for the Use of Mothers and Children's Nurses* (New York, 1894).
[87] Key, *op. cit.,* pp. 101–102.
[88] Lynd and Lynd, *op. cit.,* p. 146.
[89] Mary McCarthy, *The Group* (New York, 1954), p. 360.
[90] Arnold Gesell and Frances L. Ilg, *Infant and Child in the Culture Today* (New York, 1943), pp. 56–57.
[91] Helene Deutsch, *The Psychology of Women, Vol. II* (New York, 1945), p. 292.
[92] Benjamin Spock, M.D., *Baby and Child Care* (New York, 1970), p. 3.
[93] *Ibid.,* p. 31.
[94] Gesell and Ilg, *op. cit.,* p. 56.
[95] Spock, *op. cit.,* p. 259.
[96] Spock, *op. cit.,* p. 564.
[97] Deutsch, *op. cit.,* p. 331.
[98] Ferdinand Lundberg and Marynia Farnham, *Modern Women: The Lost Sex* (New York, 1947), p. 256.
[99] Spock, *op. cit.,* pp. 321–322.
[100] Margaret Fowler Dunaway, *Diary,* Schlesinger Library, Vol. 8, March 4, 1953.
[101] *Ibid.,* September 28, 1936.
[102] *Ibid.,* February 7, 1958.
[103] *Ibid.,* November 12, 1928.
[104] *Ibid.,* August 15, 1960.
[105] Sylvia Plath, *The Bell Jar* (New York, 1971), p. 34.
[106] *Ibid.,* p. 282.
[107] A. Alvarez, *The Savage God* (Great Britain, 1974), p. 21.
[108] *Ibid.,* p. 101.
[109] *Ibid.,* p. 34.

THE CURRENT SNARES
OF SEXISM

[1] William Henry Chafe, *The American Women: Her Changing Social, Economic, and Political Role, 1920–1970* (New York, 1972), p. 57.

[2] *Consumer Income,* A United States Department of Commerce Publication, July 1972, p. 1.

[3] Robert B. Hill, *The Strengths of Black Families* (New York, 1972), pp. 5–6.

[4] Gerald D. Suttles, *The Social Order of the Slum* (Chicago, 1968), p. 74.

[5] Melvin Kohn, *Class and Conformity: A Study in Values* (Glenwood, Ill., 1969), p. 21.

[6] Gregory Armstrong, ed., *Life at the Bottom* (New York, 1971), p. 99.

[7] Suttles, *op. cit.,* pp. 85–87.

[8] Armstrong, *op. cit.,* p. 24.

[9] Maya Angelou, *I Know Why the Caged Bird Sings* (New York, 1969), p. 1.

[10] *Ibid.,* p. 38.

[11] Francis Beale, "Double Jeopardy: To be Black and Female," in *The Black Women,* Toni Cade, ed. (New York, 1970), p. 90.

[12] Jessie Bernard, *Marriage and Family Among Negroes* (Englewood Cliffs, New Jersey, 1966), pp. 2–5.

[13] Charles S. Johnson, *Shadow of the Plantation* (Chicago, 1934), p. 33.

[14] Margaret J. Hagood, *Mothers of the South: Portraiture of the White Tenant Farm Woman* (Chapel Hill, N.C., 1939), pp. 14–15.

[15] Gerda Lerner, *Black Women in White America* (New York, 1972), p. 399.

[16] Johnson, *op. cit.,* p. 116.

[17] *Ibid.,* p. 83.

[18] *Ibid.,* p. 70.

[19] Lerner, *op. cit.,* pp. 609–614.

[20] *Ibid.,* pp. 576, 585.

[21] Mel Watkins and Jay David, eds., *To be a Black Woman* (New York, 1970), pp. 219–235.

[22] Farley, *op. cit.,* p. 50.

[23] Theodore Hershberg, "Free Blacks in Ante-Bellum Philadelphia: A Study of Ex-Slaves, Free-Born and Socio-Economic Decline,"

Journal of Social History, Vol. 5 (1971–72), pp. 183–209; Elizabeth H. Pleck, "The Two-Parent Household: Black Family Structure in Late Nineteenth-Century Boston," Journal of Social History, Vol. 6 (Fall 1972), pp. 3–31.

²⁴ Farley, op. cit., pp. 145–147.
²⁵ Andrew Billingsley, Black Families—White American (New Jersey, 1968), p. 14.
²⁶ Kay Lindsey, "The Black Woman as Woman," in The Black Woman, op. cit., p. 89.
²⁷ Roger D. Abrahams, "Playing the Dozens," Journal of American Folklore (July 1962), pp. 209–220.
²⁸ Joyce A. Ladner, Tomorrow's Tomorrow: The Black Woman (Garden City, N.Y., 1971), pp. 55–57.
²⁹ Suttles, op. cit., p. 132.
³⁰ Ladner, op. cit., p. 118.
³¹ Armstrong, op. cit., p. 226.
³² Lindsey, op. cit., p. 88.
³³ Armstrong, op. cit., p. 108.
³⁴ Angelou, op. cit., p. 240.
³⁵ Hill, op. cit., p. 7.
³⁶ Ladner, op. cit., p. 123.
³⁷ Lee Rainwater, Behind the Ghetto Walls (Chicago, 1970), p. 206.
³⁸ Armstrong, op. cit., p. 105.
³⁹ Report of the Commission on Population Growth and the American Future (New York, 1972), p. 164.
⁴⁰ Lerner, op. cit., p. 314.
⁴¹ Farley, op. cit., pp. 85, 201.
⁴² Watkins and David, op. cit., pp. 88–89.
⁴³ Robert B. Hill, op. cit., pp. 10–17.
⁴⁴ Alice Henry, Women and the Labor Movement (New York, 1923), p. 204.
⁴⁵ Hill, op. cit., pp. 10–17.
⁴⁶ Ibid., pp. 18–19.
⁴⁷ Ibid., p. 12; Juanita Kreps, Sex in the Marketplace (Baltimore and London, 1971), p. 8.
⁴⁸ Frances Fox Piven and Richard A. Cloward, Regulating the Poor (New York, 1971), p. 141.
⁴⁹ Hill, op. cit., pp. 31–32.
⁵⁰ Ladner, op. cit., p. 85.
⁵¹ Cynthia Fuchs Epstein, "Positive Effects of the Multiple Negative: Explaining the Success of Black Professional Women,"

American Journal of Sociology, Vol. 78 (January 1973), p. 922.

52 Watkins and David, op. cit., p. 90.
53 Robert Staples, "The Myth of the Black Matriarchy," The Black Scholar (January–February), 1973, p. 16.
54 Lethonia Gee, "By Glistening, Dancing Seas," in Watkins and David., op. cit., p. 215.
55 Ladner, op. cit., p. 285.
56 Shulamith Firestone, Dialectics of Sex, (New York, 1970), p. 119.
57 Elizabeth Waldman, "Changes in the Labor Force Activity of Women," in Women in a Man-Made World, N. Glazer-Malbin and H. Y. Waehrer, eds. (Chicago, 1972), pp. 30–38.
58 The New York Times, February 11, 1973, p. 1.
59 Ibid.
60 Ibid., December 27, 1972, p. 34.
61 Ibid., January 7, 1973, p. 52.
62 Ibid., December 27, 1972, p. 34.
63 Glazer-Malbin and Waehrer, op. cit., pp. 34, 194–197.
64 The New York Times, January 18, 1973, p. 35.
65 Kreps, op. cit., p. 10.
66 Kirsten Amundsen, The Silenced Majority (Englewood Cliffs, N.J., 1971), pp. 26–28.
67 Kreps, op. cit., p. 10.
68 Ladies' Home Journal, March 1960.
69 Larry E. Suter and Herman P. Miller, "Income Differences Between Men and Career Women," in Glazer-Malbin and Waehrer, op. cit., p. 297.
70 The New York Times, October 15, 1972, p. 58.
71 Monthly Vital Statistics Report, Vol. 21, March 1973, p. 1. See also, Oppenheimer in American Journal of Sociology, January 1973, passim.
72 Marcia Seligson, The Eternal Bliss Machine (New York, 1973), pp. 1–2.
73 The New York Times, December 5, 1972.
74 Report on Population Growth, p. 46.
75 Herbert A. Otto, ed., The Family in Search of a Future (New York, 1970).
76 Walter Gove and Jeanette F. Tudor, "Adult Sex Roles and Mental Illness," American Journal of Sociology (January 1973), p. 828.
77 Mirra Komarovsky, "Cultural Contradictions and Sex Roles," American Journal of Sociology (January 1973), p. 883.

[78] Leonard L. Baird et al., *The Graduates, 1971* (Princeton, N.J., 1973), Chapter 6.

[79] Vivian Gornick, "Why Radcliffe Women Are Afraid of Sex," *The New York Times Magazine,* January 14, 1973, p. 54.

[80] Komarovsky, *op. cit.,* p. 881.

[81] *Ladies' Home Journal,* September 1970.

[82] Bennett Berger, Bruce M. Hackett, and R. Mervyn Millar, "Child-Rearing Practice in the Communal Family," *Family, Marriage and the Struggle of the Sexes,* Hans P. Dreitzel, ed. (New York, 1972), pp. 271–300.

[83] F. Ivan Nye, ed., *The Employed Mother in America* (Chicago, 1963).

[84] *The New York Times,* March 24, 1973, p. 38.

[85] Katherine Ellis and Rosalind Petchesky, "Children of the Corporate Dream: An Analysis of Day Care as a Political Issue," *Socialist Revolution* (November–December 1972), p. 14.

[86] Ellis and Petchesky, *ibid.,* pp. 22–23.

[87] *Ladies' Home Journal,* December 1965.

[88] Kreps, *op. cit.,* p. 5.

[89] Mary Jane Sherfey, "A Theory of Female Sexuality" in *Sisterhood is Powerful,* Robin Morgan, ed. (New York, 1970), pp. 220–229.

[90] "J" *Sensuous Woman* (New York, 1971), p. 11.

[91] Barbara Seaman, *Free and Female: The Sex Life of the Contemporary Woman* (New York, 1972), p. 191.

[92] Diana Scully and Pauline Bart, "A Funny Thing Happened on the Way to the Orifice: Women in Gynecology Textbooks," *American Journal of Sociology* (January 1973), p. 1048.

[93] Randal Collins, "A Conflict Theory of Sexual Stratification," in Dreitzel, *op. cit.,* p. 73.

[94] Ingrid Bengis, *Combat in the Erogenous Zone* (New York, 1972), p. xvii.

[95] *Ibid.,* p. 82.

[96] *Ibid.,* p. 208.

[97] Jo Freeman, "The Origins of the Women's Liberation Movemen," *American Journal of Sociology* (January 1973), pp. 798–799.

[98] Amundsen, *op. cit.,* pp. 68, 73, 76, 92.

[99] *Consumer Income,* July 1972, p. 1.

[100] Freeman, *op. cit.,* p. 801.

101 See Juliet Mitchell, *Woman's Estate* (New York, 1972); Shulamith Firestone, *The Dialectic of Sex* (New York, 1970); Sheila Rowbotham, *Woman's Consciousness Man's World* (Great Britain, 1973); *Radical American* (July–October, 1973); Barbara Deming, "Two Perspectives in the Women's Struggle," *Liberation,* June 1973, p. 33.

102 George Gilder, "Sexual Suicide," *Harpers,* July 1972, pp. 48–49.

Abolitionism, 180–184
Abortion:
    advertising, 163;
    colonial America, 58;
    commercial era, 121;
    19th century, 163;
    state laws against, 163;
    20th century, 215–216, 239,
      268, 401, 419
Abstinence, sexual, 121, 159,
    163–164, 235, 256, 258
Adams, Abigail, 85, 90
Adams, Elizabeth Kemper,
    237–238
Adams, John, 90
Adams, Nehemiah, 182
"Adam's Rib" quote from Bible,
    21
Addams, Jane, 218, 225,
    228–230, 232, 233, 235, 240,
    253, 255–256, 257, 292
ADC. *See* Aid to Dependent
    Children
Adipose tissue, 226
Adolescence, 149, 287–291;
    in black ghetto, 382–385
Adultery, 53, 161, 218, 293–295
    death penalty for, 53. *See*
    also Extramarital sex
Advertising, 295–302;
    MS. magazine, 425;
    before 1920, 241, 242, 259,
      295, 296;
    of 1920's, 259–260, 295,
      296–297, 299;
    post World War II, 298,
      301–302, 398, 406,
      410–411;
    sex-directed, 295–296, 411;
    sexual connotations of, 295,

      296–297, 298, 299,
      301–302, 410–411;
    statistics. 260
Aggressiveness, male, 6, 423
Agrarian subsistence economy:
    end of, 86–88, 91, 96, 105,
      120;
    woman in, 12–13, 21–22,
      29–32, 35.
    See also Colonial America
Aid to Dependent Children
    (ADC), 389
Albers, Aaltje, 29
Alcott, William, 163
Alcuin (Brown), 110
Almshouses, 101, 119
Alone (Harland), 152
Alvarez, Alfred, 359
Ambrose, Isaac, 59
American Association of Univer-
    sity Women, 231
American Federation of Labor
    (AFL), 222
American Socialist Party,
    243–244
Amory, Mrs. John, 97, 99
Anderson, Mary, 233
Andover, Mass., population im-
    plosion, 120
Angelou, Maya, 373, 384
Anglican Church, sexual hierar-
    chy in, 68–69
Anglo-Saxon working class,
    368, 370
Ante-bellum culture, 139–191,
    379;
    antislavery movement,
      180–184;
    birth rate, 141, 162;
    courtship and marriage,

Birth rate:
blackwomen, 186, 385–386;
colonial America, 57;
Depression years, 328, 334;
early 20th century, 215;
of immigrants, 57, 215;
late 18th century downturn,
120–121;
19th century, 141, 162–163;
of 1920's, 261, 328, 334;
of 1970's, 400;
post World War II, 298, 351;
of slaves, 186
Bishop, Bridget, 77
Black liberation movement,
390–391
Black women, 366–367,
372–393, 420–421;
employment, 367, 380,
386–390;
fertility, 186, 385–386;
ghetto girlhood, 381–385;
heads of household, 367,
368, 374, 380–381, 397;
and marriage, 374–375,
376–377;
in the middle class,
378–379;
motherhood, 374, 376, 377,
384–386;
racial discrimination
against, 387, 389;
sex discrimination against,
381–382, 387, 389–390;
in slavery, 30, 181, 185–190;
social activism of, 378–379,
391;
stereotypes, 373–374, 382.
391–393;
theory of matriarchy,
373–376, 379, 380–381, 389;

wages of, 387–388, 395–396
Blacks:
broken homes, 367, 368,
374, 379, 380–381, 389,
396–397;
family patterns, 375,
377–378, 380–381;
kinship traditions, 368;
in middle class, 378;
racial discrimination
against, 245, 366;
sexism among, 381–382,
383–384, 390–392;
transition from slavery into
free status, 379–380;
urban migration of, 379–380
Boarders, as women's income
source, 211, 212
Bok, Edward, 195
Bonaparte, Marie, 278, 279, 282,
284–285
Bosom, fashion standards for,
158, 299
Boston, Mass., 34, 73, 195;
Anne Hutchinson in, 71;
case of Ann Hibbens, 73–74,
76, 77;
emergence as city, 92;
employment discrimina-
tion, 203;
Female Anti-Slavery Soci-
ety, 181, 183;
female occupations, 92, 94,
203;
immigrant working women,
206;
merchant elite of, 97–98;
welfare cases, 101, 102, 128
Bottle-feeding, 346
Bow, Clara, 266
Bowdoin, James, 110

commercial era, 116–117, 124–126;
developmental approach of Gesell and Spock, 347–350, 351–352, 371;
industrial era, 210, 216–218, 237, 241–242;
institutional vs. maternal, 345, 407–409;
literature on, 124–125, 164–168, 241–242, 346–349;
maternal associations, 180;
for sexual roles, 148–150, 290, 352, 404–405;
in slavery, 186;
in slum conditions, 216–218, 381–382, 385–386;
20th century, 309, 337, 342–343, 344–352, 370–371;
20th century adolescence, 287–291;
in Utopian communities, 177–178;
varying role of love in, 168, 346, 349–350;
working class, 210, 216–218, 369, 370–371;
working mothers' problems, 210, 350.
See also Education; Girlhood
Child support, 51, 397
Childbirth, 57–59, 215–216, 285, 414;
death in, 58
Children's Bureau, 233
Chromosomes, sex, 3, 7
Church, sexual hierarchy of colonial era, 40–41, 68–69, 71

Cigar industry, 201–202, 203, 204
Cities:
antebellum period, 145–146;
birth rate, 162;
black migration to, 379;
child rearing in, 164–165, 216–218, 381–382, 385–386;
female merchants in, 92–93;
growth of, 92, 145;
social freedom of women fostered by, 118;
tenements, 214.
See also Ghettos; Slums
Citizenship rights, 248;
exclusion of women from, 64–66
Civil rights, women's quest for, 184, 246–249. See also Equal rights, quest for
Civil Rights Act of 1964, 418
Civil rights movement, 421
Civil War, 171, 190–191, 195, 225, 227
"Civilizing" role of women, 144, 147, 158, 165, 182–183, 195, 228–230, 233–234, 245, 378.
See also "Mother of Civilization"
Clarence (Sedgwick), 150–151
Clark, Kenneth, 373
Class conflict, 233–234, 243
Class society, 97–99;
emergence of, 87;
mid-18th century, 87;
19th century, 135, 195–196;
19th into 20th century, 233–234, 245. See also Lower class; Middle class; Upper classes

Cleaning women, 387
Cleaver, Eldridge, 39
Clerical work, 234, 314, 319–320,
    321–325, 333, 387, 394
Clitoral orgasm, 278, 280–281,
    411
Clitoris, 159–160, 161, 278, 279,
    284
Clothing, sex-related, 4, 45. *See
    also* Fashions
Cobbs, Pierce, 391
Cohen, Rose, 207–208, 209, 212,
    219, 221
Cohen, Sarah, 204
Cohoes, N. Y., cotton mills, 208
Coitus, 279, 285
Coitus interruptus, 121, 163
Coitus reservatus, 177
Cole, Anne, 76
Coleman, Anne, 140
College-educated women,
    403–404;
    job and pay discrimination
        against, 325, 332, 395,
        417;
    and marriage, 236, 332, 339;
    sexual freedom, 269–270,
        271;
    working wives, 330, 396, 403
College faculties, women on,
    233, 256, 327
College Settlement Association,
    228–229
Colleges:
    female enrollment, 339, 394;
    women excluded from, 69,
        71;
    women's, 228, 232
Colonial America, 12–13, 21–81;
    absence of sexual
        stereotypes, 62–64;
    birth rate, 57;

courtship and marriage,
    47–49, 52–56;
cultural affairs as male pre-
    rogative, 69–71;
daughters' status, 27, 28, 35,
    43;
economic contribution of
    women in, 29–36, 44, 62,
    86, 87;
family system, 24, 26, 27, 37,
    38–39, 41, 44, 60–61;
fashions, 46–47;
handling of servants, 38–39;
household economy of,
    29–32, 35, 37, 86;
household hierarchy,
    40–44, 54, 64;
immigrants' status, 24;
inheritance rights, 26–28;
land ownership, 22–23,
    24–29, 35;
land transfer rights, 26, 27;
motherhood, 38–39, 57–61;
need for women, 24, 29–30,
    31, 37–38;
political discrimination
    against women, 64–68;
property rights, 22–23,
    24–25, 26, 27, 31;
religious discrimination
    against women, 68–69,
    71–72;
sexual mores, 49–53;
single persons in, 34, 38,
    66–68;
social contributions of
    women, 32, 38–40;
social organization of, 22,
    37–38, 40–42, 64;
social status of women, 40,
    41–45;
welfare functions, 32, 39;

widows' status, 26, 27, 28, 35, 39, 41;
wives' status, 21–22, 26, 28–29, 40, 41–44, 52–53, 54–56;
women as traders, 33–35, 73;
women's work, 30–36
Combat in the Erogenous Zone (Bengis), 415–416
Commercial era, 86–135;
birth rate, 120–121;
class distinctions, 87, 97, 135;
daughters' status, 92, 93–94, 104, 105, 118–119;
decline of household economy, 86, 91, 96–97;
economic power in, 86–88;
economic role of women, 86–87, 88–95, 102–106, 109;
family unit shrinkage, 119–123, 128–129;
female occupations, 94–95, 99–100, 102–105;
female unemployment, 100, 102;
land ownership, 87–88;
lower-class women, 135;
marriage, 98, 112–116, 119, 122–124;
middle-class women, 128, 129–135;
motherhood, 116–117, 124–126;
political discrimination against women, 85–86;
property rights, 86–88;
rise of manufacturing, 86, 91, 96–97, 102–105;
sexual stereotyping, 107–109, 112–114, 126, 127;

social role and status of women, 106–135;
upper-class women of, 97–99, 106–118, 129, 134;
welfare functions, 100–102, 119–120, 128;
widows' status, 92, 94;
wives' function, 86, 113, 123–126;
wives' status, 86–87, 90–91, 93–94, 106, 113, 119, 123–124;
women as merchants, 89, 92–94, 96, 119, 135;
women's sentimentalism, 131–134;
women's status, 13, 112–113, 127–128;
women's volunteer charity work, 128–129, 131
Commission on the Status of Women, 417, 418
Common law, English, women's status in, 26
Commonwealth Edison Co., 321
Communal experiments, 25, 175–180, 402, 406–407
"Compensation neurosis," 276
Complex marriage, 176–177, 178
Conception, Victorian views of, 160, 164
Condom, 268
Consciousness-raising groups, 406, 423
Constitution of the United States, 85
Consumer, woman as, 14–15, 260, 295, 296, 297, 300–302, 329–331
Consumer economy, 258–261, 295–298, 300–303, 329–330, 400;

Consumers League, 254, 260,
   265
Continental Congress, 85
Contraception, 163, 215, 244,
   257, 268–269, 385, 401
Cosmetics, 297, 299, 411
Cosmopolitan magazine, 399,
   411
Cottage industry, 102–103
Cotton, John, 71
Cotton industry, 105, 208. *See
   also* Textile industry
Court action by women, 29, 43,
   66, 73–74
Courts, double standard for
   women, 66–67
Courtship and marriage, 47–49,
   123, 150–155, 171, 338–339.
   See also Husband hunting
Coxe, Margaret, 142, 145, 146
Coxe, Tench, 102, 104
Cukor, George, 294
Cultural affairs, colonial, male
   superiority in, 22, 69–71
Cummins, Maria, 143
Curse of Clifton, The (South-
   worth), 151, 152

Daedalus, 417–418
Dalla Costa, Mariarosa, 427
Data processing, 322, 326
Daughters:
   colonial era status of, 27, 28,
      35;
   commercial era, 92, 93–94,
      98, 104, 105, 118–119;
   court action against fathers,
      43;
   economic role, colonial era,
      29, 35–36;
   as industrial labor, 206–208,
      209;

inheritance rights of, 27, 28;
   upper class, 98;
   urban liberation of,
      118–119;
   in urban migration, 92;
   wages of, used by family,
      105, 206–208
Davis, Katherine B., 269, 292
Day care, 407–410, 419;
   federal legislation, 407, 409;
   wartime, 318
Debts of husbands, wives' re-
   fusal to honor, 29
Declaration of Independence,
   85, 184
Dedham, Mass., 26, 94, 103
Deed, cosigning by wife, 28
De Leon, Daniel, 244
Demand feeding, 347–348
De Mille, Cecil B., 266
Deming, Barbara, 427
Democratic Party, 254, 255
Demos, John, 37
Depression of 1930's, 297–298,
   300, 315–316, 328, 336
Desertion, by fathers, 367, 374;
   welfare rules as incentive to,
      389
Detroit, Mich., 162
Deutsch, Helene, 276, 282,
   284–285, 286, 298, 348, 351
Developmental child rearing,
   347–350, 351–352, 371
Dewson, Mary, 255
Dexter, Elizabeth, 114
Dexter, Timothy, 114
Dialectic of Sex, The (Firestone),
   426
Diaphragm, 268
Dickerson, Elizabeth, 50
Dickinson, Robert Latou, 268,
   272, 276, 278

Economic power (*cont.*):
  as male prerogative, 5, 26,
    35, 86–87, 91, 97–98, 133,
    145, 170, 234, 309;
  20th century, 234, 309
Economic role of women:
  black women, 375, 388;
  in colonial agrarian house-
    hold economy, 29–36, 44,
    62, 86, 87;
  in commercial economy,
    86–87, 88–95, 102–109;
  decrease in, 18th to 19th
    century, 91, 145, 170, 173;
  in industrial age family,
    206–213;
  in 20th century family, 309,
    328–331, 333, 387, 396,
    401–402, 405
Editors, women as, 394
Education:
  in antebellum period,
    149–150;
  in colonial America, 69–71;
  in commercial era, 117, 124,
    126–127, 129;
  role of women in, 38–39, 94,
    120, 124, 232–233, 234,
    320, 327, 395;
  of women, 69, 70–71,
    114–115, 124, 126–127,
    129, 149–150, 228, 232,
    236, 238, 240, 324
Ellis, Havelock, 267, 273, 274,
  275
Embryonic sexual development,
  3
Emerson, Ralph Waldo, 144
Employment, female:
  blacks, 367, 380, 386–390;
  colonial America, 34;

  commercial era, 94–95,
    99–100, 102–105,
    118–119;
  and day care, 318, 407–410;
  industrial age, 195, 196–212,
    220, 222–223, 241;
  mid-19th century, 197;
  of 1920's, 270, 307, 314, 321,
    324, 329, 331;
  post World War II, 313,
    318–334, 393–405, 409,
    417;
  poverty as incentive for,
    208–209, 316, 367, 388,
    396;
  promotion difficulties,
    201–203, 326, 333–334,
    387;
  sex appeal as job require-
    ment, 307, 320–321;
  sex discrimination, 13, 15,
    100, 104–105, 127–128,
    200, 201–203, 209,
    234–235, 248, 307–308,
    315, 318–322, 325–327,
    333–334, 395–397,
    417–419;
  statistics for 1890, 197, 200,
    208;
  statistics for 1900, 196, 313,
    314;
  statistics for 20th century,
    309–310, 313, 314, 315,
    317, 319–320, 327;
  statistics for 1920's, 196,
    207, 307;
  statistics for 1955, 313, 319;
  statistics for 1960, 319, 320,
    327;
  statistics for 1970's, 393,
    394;

sweatshop exploitation,
199, 202–206, 219, 222;
20th century, 307–334, 351,
386–390, 393–405, 409,
417;
types of work, 94–95,
99–100, 102–105,
197–198, 199, 200–203,
211–212, 232–233, 234,
307, 313–314, 316–317,
319–323, 387, 394;
wartime, 14, 241, 316–319;
white-collar assembly-line
work, 321–322;
working hours, 204, 209,
222, 316;
working mothers and wives,
15, 209–210, 236–238,
285, 308–313, 315–316,
317–319, 328–334,
350–351, 386, 388,
393–394, 396–398, 409.
See also Career women;
Professional women;
Wages
Engels, Frederick, 234
English immigrants, 23, 24, 68
Enlightenment, 124, 126, 127
"Equal pay for equal work"
principle, 316, 418–419, 420,
428
Equal rights, quest for, 246–249,
261, 417–429
Equal Rights Amendment, 426
Equality, sexual:
as dogma of dissenters, 68,
71, 72;
early champions of, 183;
examples of, for colonial
era, 21–22, 23, 36, 52–53,
63–64;

in Utopian societies, 175–180
"Equality of the Sexes: An Im-
modest Proposal" (Rossi), 418
Essays on the Character of
Women (Leonard), 110–111
Ethnic minorities, 316, 361, 371.
See also Immigrants; Irish im-
migrant women; Italian-
Americans; Puerto Ricans;
Slavic immigrant women
Evans, Augusta Jane, 143, 153
Executive positions, women in,
419
"Expressive function" of
women, 169, 337, 338,
339–340, 423
Extramarital sex, 402, 406;
colonial America, 49–52, 53;
1920's commonness of,
269–271;
Victorian era male practice,
161, 218–219. See also
Premarital sex

Factories:
emergence of, 91, 103–105;
female labor, 103–105, 196,
198–209, 220, 314, 387.
See also Manufacturing
Faded Hope, The (Sigourney),
170
Fair Soap Company, 259
Family, as institution:
among blacks, 374–375,
377–378, 380;
extended unit of lower
classes, 368;
19th century, 147, 336;
20th century, 335–337, 341,
345, 367, 368, 407, 421.
See also Family system

Female sexuality, 50, 52, 111,
172, 177, 262–264, 267–268,
271–273, 299–300, 303;
Freudian view of, 277–283,
285;
Masters and Johnson research, 411;
post World War II theory,
282–285, 411–414;
Victorian views of, 158–162,
164
Female stereotypes, 5, 13–14,
15, 274, 282, 412, 415, 416;
absence in colonial era,
62–64;
emergence of, 107–109,
112–114, 116, 126, 127;
familiar adjectives, 62, 108,
112, 113–114, 144, 152,
226, 274;
flapper, 256–257, 260, 261,
299;
manipulation for women's
ends, 172, 191, 245;
mid-19th century, 139, 143,
144, 151–153, 185;
Negro women, 373–374,
382, 391–393;
post World War II, 282–288,
352, 404–405, 410–411;
sex objects, 262–264, 266,
286, 299, 302–303, 383,
410–411
Feminine Mystique, The
(Friedan), 418
"Feminine mystique," 282, 313,
358, 398
Femininity, 4–6, 13, 144, 148,
243;
black women and, 373–374,
391–393;
criticisms of, 117–118, 148;

emergence of ideal,
106–109, 116, 135;
inconsequential in colonial
era, 46, 47, 62–63;
inculcation in girls,
148–149, 288, 290, 352,
404–405;
literature of, 106–108,
143–144;
motherhood as essence of,
164, 167, 286;
1920's standards, 256,
260–264, 266, 273;
1950's standards, 286, 352,
402;
1960–70's standards,
410–414;
subdued by frontier,
140–141;
womb as symbol of,
161–162
Feminism, 8, 14, 16, 309;
antebellum era, 183–185;
attacked by sex theorists,
273–277;
early 20th century, 243–249;
left-wing, 421–422, 425–427;
"New," 361, 418–427,
428–429;
of 1920's, 261, 273, 308;
opposition of 1970's to,
427–428;
socialism and, 243–245,
425–426
*Fern Leaves from Fanny's
Portfolio* (Willis), 172
Fertility. *See* Birth rate
Firestone, Shulamith, 422, 426
Fitzgerald, Zelda, 293–294
Flapper, 256–257, 260, 261, 277,
299
Flynn, Elizabeth Gurley, 244

single women, 197, 232,
235–236, 238;
suffrage movement, 196,
231, 232, 244, 245–246,
247–248;
upper-class women of, 196,
223, 224–231;
wage discrimination, 200,
201, 203, 205, 209, 222;
women and unions, 199,
221–223, 229, 230, 231;
women on strike, 199,
222–223, 230;
working daughters,
206–208, 209;
working wives and mothers,
15, 209–210, 222,
236–238.
See also Twentieth century
Industrialization, 102–105, 145
Inevitability of Patriarchy (Goldberg), 427
Infant care, 124–125, 166–168,
346, 347–348
Inheritance rights, women's,
colonial era, 26–28
"Instrumental" role of men, 337,
339
Intellect, women's:
colonial era references to,
44, 62, 70;
commercial era references
to, 107, 108, 110, 124, 126;
industrial age references to,
224, 237, 274, 275;
19th century references to,
161, 179, 183;
20th century references to,
338–339, 403–404
Intercourse:
abstention, 121, 159,
163–164, 258;

colonial era attitudes,
52–53, 54–55;
extramarital, *see* Extramarital sex; Premarital sex;
female role in, 272, 283, 284;
frequency, 159, 163, 164, 271;
positions, 272;
Victorian attitudes, 159–161;
working class habits, 370
International Business
Machines, 318
International Ladies' Garment
Workers' Union (ILGWU),
222–223
Intimate Memoirs (Luhan), 262
Intuition, female, doctrine of,
169, 179
Ipswich, Mass., 121
Irish immigrant women, 195,
199, 208
Italian-Americans, 208, 211, 368,
370

Jackson, Mary, 93, 94
Jacksonianism, 139, 147, 183
Jamaica, N. Y., 26, 27, 65, 68
James, Alice, 224
James, Henry, 224
James, Selma, 427
James, William, 224
Jobs. *See* Employment
Johnson, Charles S., 375,
376–377
Johnson, Virginia, 411, 414
Joint Congressional Union, 254
Jones, Anne, 93
Jones, Mary ("Mother Jones"),
226, 244
Journalists, 394
Judiciary:
a male field, 66;
women in, 232

Jung, Carl, 262
Juries, exclusion of women
  from, 66

Katherine Gibbs School, 314
Kay, Elizabeth, 35
Kelley, Florence, 229, 230, 234,
  237, 260
Kennedy, John F., 417
Kenney, Mary, 208, 213, 215. *See
  also* O'Sullivan, Mary Kenney
Kentucky, as frontier, 88
Kestenberg, Dr. Juliet, 408
Key, Ellen, 308, 346
Key-punch operators, 322, 326
Kinsey, Alfred C., 271, 272, 277,
  278
Kitchelt, Florence Cross,
  236–237
KLH Corporation, 409
Knight, Elizabeth, 76
Knights of Labor, 221
Kohn, Melvin, 371
Komarovsky, Mirra, 342, 403

Labia, 278, 279
Labor:
  agricultural sector, 102,
    197, 313, 375;
  cheap, women as, 102, 104,
    105, 198–209, 220,
    307–308, 325–326, 351,
    389, 409;
  discrimination against
    women, 100, 104–105,
    200, 201–203, 209,
    307–308, 315, 318–322,
    325–327, 333–334,
    395–397, 417–419;
  division of, 86 (*see also* Divi-
    sion of labor, by sex);

female, in colonial era,
  30–36;
female, in commercial era,
  94–95, 99–100, 102–105;
female, in industrial age,
  195, 196, 197–209, 220,
  222, 313–314;
immigrant women, 197,
  199–209, 313, 314, 367;
industrial sector, 102, 196,
  198, 215, 313, 314;
slave labor, 186;
tertiary (service, sales, clerical, etc.) sector, 313–315,
  319–320.
  See also Domestic service;
  Employment, female
Labor movement, 226, 247. *See
  also* Unions
Ladies' Home Journal, 195,
  240–242, 257, 264, 273,
  289–290, 294, 296, 300, 316,
  317, 318, 334, 335, 341, 345,
  398, 399, 401, 410, 412, 425
Ladies' Literary Cabinet, 126
Ladner, Joyce, 390, 391
Lady's Pocket Library, 107
La Follette, Suzanne, 261, 269
Land ownership:
  colonial America, 22–23,
    24–29, 87;
  commercial era, 87–88;
  male privilege, 25–26, 35;
  women's, 22–23, 24–25,
    26–28
Land supply, diminishing,
  87–88, 119, 120
Land transfer, 26, 27
Landis, Paul, 338, 339
Landless class, 88
Langer, Elinor, 323, 331

Lower-class women (*cont.*):
  role in families, 206–217,
    220–221, 370–372;
  sexual exploitation of, 216,
    218–219, 366;
  20th century, 361, 366–372,
    421. *See also* Black
    women
"Lower sort," class distinction,
    87, 117
Lucas, Eliza, 89
Luce, Clare Boothe, 294
Luhan, Mabel Dodge, 262–264,
    267, 293
Lundberg, Ferdinand, 282–283,
    285, 351
Lynd, Helen, 288, 340
Lynd, Robert, 288, 340

McCall's magazine, 341
McCarthy, Mary, 281, 347
McDowell, Mary, 223, 229, 230
Mademoiselle magazine, 358
Magazines:
  advertising, 241, 242, 299,
    410–411, 425;
  modern, and sex, 264–265,
    410–411, 412;
  teenage, 289–290;
  women's, 106–108, 142,
    143–144, 155, 164–165,
    185, 195, 240–242,
    264–265, 286, 294, 334,
    341, 344, 399, 410–411,
    412, 424–425
Male and Female (Ellis), 273, 275
Male and Female (movie), 266
Male continence, 177
Male role, 4–9, 139, 226, 303;
  in agrarian society, 13,
    21–22, 26, 30–31, 36,
    40–42, 44, 60;

in antebellum culture, 152,
    156–157, 164, 170;
  blacks, 382, 388, 391–392;
  in commercial era, 86–87,
    97–98, 104, 109, 126, 127;
  in industrial society, 13–14,
    220, 243, 309;
  "instrumental," 337, 339;
  20th century, 309, 333, 337,
    338, 340, 349, 352, 405–406;
  in working class, 220,
    369–370
"Man in the house" rule of wel-
    fare, 389
Mann, Mary, 171
Manufacturing, 313, 314;
  cheap female labor, 102,
    104, 105, 198–209, 220,
    387;
  household as major source
    of, 31–32, 90–91, 96–97,
    103;
  rise of commercial, 86, 91,
    96–97, 102–105
Marblehead, Mass., 100–101
Marriage:
  age at, 52, 119, 236, 313,
    328, 399;
  antebellum era, 150–155,
    158–162, 171;
  black, rural South, 374–375,
    376–377;
  as civil death of wife, 26;
  colonial America, 47–49,
    52–56;
  commercial era, 98,
    112–116, 119, 122–124;
  complex, of Oneidans,
    176–177, 178;
  conjugal intimacy as post-
    war ideal, 337–341, 406,
    407;

dissolution of, 52, 114–116
(*see also* Divorce);
industrial age, 197, 208–209,
221, 236, 237, 308–313;
infidelity, 53, 161, 218,
293–295;
love and sex in, 52–53,
54–56, 154, 158–161,
282–285;
1920's views of, 255,
269–270, 292;
outlawed for slaves, 186,
374;
postwar educational
courses for, 338;
professional women and,
197, 232, 235–236;
reform proposals of 1970's,
402–403, 406;
regarded essential for
women, 112–113, 148,
150, 153–154, 292–293,
335;
trial, 269;
20th century rate of,
399–400;
20th century stress on,
292–293, 332, 334–341;
upper class, 98, 340, 357;
working class, 208–209,
221, 370–371
Married Flirts (movie), 266
Marx, Karl, quoted, 10
Marxism, 234, 425, 426
Maryland, colonial:
exclusion of women from
Assembly, 64–65, 71;
family land allowances, 25;
women's manorial rights, 22
Masculinity, 4, 14, 144, 152, 243;
emergence of concept of,
108–109;

ill-defined concept in colonial America, 63–64;
inculcation in boys, 149,
290, 352
Masochism, 276, 282, 283–285,
299
Massachusetts Bay Colony, 23,
51, 72;
female employment, 34;
single persons in, 34, 38;
women's inheritance rights,
26, 27.
See also Puritans
Massachusetts Body of Liberties, 26, 27
Massachusetts State, domestic
servant statistics, 197
Masters, William, 411, 414
Masturbation, 164, 166, 268, 272,
278–279
Maternal associations, 180
Maternal Physician, The, 124–125
Maternity. *See* Motherhood
Mather, Cotton, 36, 42–43, 45,
54, 62, 69;
on motherhood, 58, 59;
*Ornaments of the Daugh-
ters of Zion,* 46–47
Matriarchy, black, theory of,
373–376, 379, 380–381, 389
Mechanization, 103, 104, 105,
322;
household, 242, 243, 258,
343–344
Medical profession, women in,
232, 390, 395
Medical schools, 327
Menstrual cycle, 274
Mental illness, 402. *See also*
Neuroticism
Merchants, women as. *See*
Traders

sex theory of, 284–285, 298;
in slavery, 186, 189, 374;
upper classes, 116–117;
Victorian Age, 162, 164;
working class, 210,
216–217, 370–371;
working mothers, 210,
236–238, 285, 309,
310–312, 317–318, 328,
333, 350–351, 386,
393–394, 408–410
Motion Picture Production Code
(1930's), 266
Mott, Lucretia, 184
Movie stars, 265–266
Movies, 217–218, 265–266, 290,
302–303, 334
Moynihan, Daniel Patrick,
373–374, 388
MS. magazine, 424–425
Muce, Ellen, 51
Muscular strength, 8–9, 62–63

Narcissism, 282, 283–284, 299,
351, 391
Nation, Carrie, 231
National American Woman's
Suffrage Association, 246, 254
National Association for the Advancement of Colored People
(NAACP), 378
National Association of Colored
Women, 378
National Biscuit Company, 202
National Organization for
Women (NOW), 418–419, 420,
421, 422, 425
National Welfare Rights Organization, 391
*Negro Family, The: The Case for
National Action,* 373

Negroes. *See* Black women;
Blacks
Neurasthenia, 224–225
Neuroticism, 224, 256, 276–277,
402
New Amsterdam, 23, 29;
court action by women, 29,
43, 73;
female traders of, 33, 34–35,
73
New England, colonial:
courtship and marriage,
47–48;
education in, 69;
female employment, 34;
immigrants, 24;
land distribution, 25–26, 28,
87;
sexual discrimination in
churches of, 68–69, 71–72;
single persons in, 34, 38;
witchcraft hysteria, 76–81;
women's status, 26, 27, 44
New England, post-colonial:
birth rate, 120–121;
early feminists, 183;
textile industry of, 103–104,
105, 198–200;
women's social sphere,
129–131, 173–174
New left, 421, 422, 425
New Netherlands, 24. *See also*
New Amsterdam
New Netherlands General Court
and Council, 38
New Politics Convention,
Chicago (1967), 422
New York City, 49, 101, 121;
charity work, 128;
early public welfare rolls,
100, 101–102;

New York City (cont.):
  18th into 19th century growth, 92;
  female-headed household statistics, 380;
  garment industry, 222–223, 409;
  prostitutes in, 95;
  shopping patterns studied, 300;
  society women, 98;
  tenements of 1890's, 214.
  See also Harlem
New York *Journal,* 91
New York *Post,* 49
New York State:
  abortions in, 401;
  Female Missionary Society, 128;
  "Genesee Fever," 88
New York Telephone Company, 323–324
New York Times, The, 321, 344, 408
Newport, R. I., 95, 114
Newspapers, women's appeal in, 134, 142
Nichols, Mary Gore, 161
Nin, Anais, 280–281, 293
Nineteenth Amendment, 246, 247, 248, 254
Nixon, Richard M., 407–408
North American Phalanx, 179
Northeastern cities:
  female merchants in, 92–93;
  growth of, 92;
  publishing centers, 142, 143;
  social freedom of women fostered, 118–119
Novels:
  of 1970's, 412–413;

sentimental, 143, 150–153, 172, 185, 189–190
NOW. *See* National Organization for Women
Noyes, John Humphrey, 176–177, 178
Nurse, Rebecca, 77–78
Nurses, 94, 394
Nursing, 57, 59, 164, 167, 242, 347, 414
Nurturance, female function of, 6–7, 13, 30–32, 113, 124–126, 145, 156–157, 166–169, 184, 226, 408

Oedipus complex, 345, 348
Office holding, 233, 419;
  exclusion of women from, 64–66, 68, 85, 247
Ogden, Rev. John, 88–89, 117
Oneida Community, 175–178
O'Neill, George, 406
O'Neill, Nina, 406
Open Marriage (O'Neill), 406
"Open marriage," 402
O'Reilly, Leonora, 223, 226, 292
Organizations, women's, 196, 231, 248, 254, 418–419;
  rise of, 223–232
Orgasm, female, 160, 267, 268, 272–273, 278–281, 283, 413–414;
  capacity for, 411–412, 413;
  clitoral, 278, 280–281, 411;
  vaginal, 278, 279, 280–281, 286, 303
Ornaments of the Daughters of Zion (Mather), 46–47
Orphan asylums, 119, 128
Osbourne, Sarah, 77
O'Sullivan, Jack, 213, 237

O'Sullivan, Mary Kenney, 213,
223, 237. See also Kenney,
Mary

Page, Anne, 93
Page, Margaret, 101
Parenthood:
  colonial America, 60–61, 70,
  126;
  commercial era, 118–119,
  126;
  control lessened, 118–119;
  19th century, 164;
  planning, 121, 269;
  20th century, 216–217, 242,
  341, 349, 352, 370;
  working class, 216–217,
  370.
  See also Motherhood
Park, Robert, 270
Parris, Elizabeth, 79
Parris, Samuel, 79
Parsons, Alice Beale, 275
Parsons, Talcott, 336–337
Passivity, female, 6, 144,
  282–283;
  emergence of ideal of,
  98–99, 107–109, 112–113
Patriarchal tradition, 40, 41–42,
  65, 105, 147, 220, 280
Peace organizations, 230, 246
Penis envy, 277–278, 280
Pennsylvania, colonial,
  women's land ownership, 25
Pennsylvania State, study of
  immigrant working women,
  201–202, 203–204, 205, 206,
  209–210
Perkins, Elizabeth, 92
Perkins, Frances, 255
Personality types, female vs.

male, 6, 8, 13–14, 107–109,
  113–114, 144, 152, 226,
  273–274, 286, 423
Philadelphia, Pa., 92, 93, 100,
  121, 379;
  female industrial labor, 205,
  208, 210;
  prostitutes in, 95–96;
  society women, 115–116;
  Young Ladies Academy,
  126–127
Philipse, Margaret Hardenbrook, 23
Pickford, Mary, 266
Pilgrims, 23, 25
Pinckney, Charles, 89
Pinckney, Eliza Lucas, 89
Pittsburgh, Pa., female factory
  labor, 201–202, 203–204, 206,
  207
Place, Sarah Stearns, 57
Planned Parenthood Clinics,
  269
Plath, Sylvia, 358–360
Playboy magazine, 411
Playgirl magazine, 411
Plymouth Plantation, 25, 57
Poets, women, 70, 134, 142, 181,
  358–360
Political parties:
  and women's goals, 254;
  women in, 243–244, 255, 420
Political power:
  antebellum era, 145, 170,
  181–182, 184;
  colonial America, 22, 64–68;
  early republic, 85–86;
  male supremacy, 5, 10, 22,
  64–68, 85–86, 145, 170,
  181–182, 184, 247, 248,
  255, 419;

Political power (cont.):
  women's ascendancy, 184,
    245–248, 253–254;
  women's "dovetailing with
    schemes of men,"
    253–255;
  women's reawakening of
    1960's, 417–427
Polyandry, 402
Poorhouses, 101, 128
Population growth:
  cities, 92;
  colonial America, 57, 58;
  postwar explosion, 351;
  of slaves, 186;
  slowdown, late 18th cen-
    tury, 120–122;
  zero, 400–401
  See also Birth rate
Populism, 247
Porter, Sylvia, 401
Post-industrial society, woman
  in, 11
Power of Sexual Surrender, The
  (Robinson), 286
Pregnancy, 57, 161, 164, 167,
  216
Premarital contracts, 28
Premarital sex:
  evidence of, in colonial
    America, 49–50;
  20th century, 270, 291–292,
    415
Presidential Commission on the
  Status of Women, 417, 418
Price She Paid, The (movie), 266
Printing industry, 143, 202–203
Prisons, 101, 119
Professional women, 197,
  232–233, 234–238, 256, 257,
  286, 316, 394;

blacks, 390;
  celibate careerism, 232,
    235–236, 256, 292;
  job and pay discrimination
    against, 320, 325, 327,
    395, 417.
  See also Career women
Progressivism, 234, 247
Property:
  preservation by matrimony,
    269;
  wives regarded as, 26, 152
Property rights, women's, 5, 184,
  247;
  colonial period, 22–23,
    24–25, 26, 27, 31;
  in family system, 26, 27;
  inferior to men's, 25–26, 35,
    86–87.
  See also Inheritance rights;
    Land ownership
Prostitution, 95–96, 159, 161,
  180, 218–219, 231
Providence, R. I., 67
Pruette, Lorine, 308, 332
Psychoanalysis, 277, 284–285
Psychology of sex, 266, 273–277,
  282–287
Psychology of Advertising, 295
Public health medicine, 234,
  309, 395
Publishing, 142–144;
  as a male prerogative, 69,
    70;
  women in, 394. See also Lit-
    erature, women's;
    Magazines; Novels
Puerto Ricans, 368, 369, 380
Puritans, 36, 44, 45, 46, 59;
  attitudes toward love and
    sex, 52–53, 54, 55;

sexual discrimination in churches of, 68–69, 71–72
"Pussy Power," 391
Putnam, Thomas, Jr., 78, 80
Putnam family, of Salem, 78, 80

Quakers, 68, 71–72, 121, 183
Queen of Sin (movie), 266

Racial discrimination, 245, 366, 381, 387, 389
Racial minorities, 316, 361, 365–366;
women of, 366–367. See also Black women; Blacks
Radcliffe Woman's Archives, 353
Rainwater, Lee, 383
Rape, 51, 370, 384, 414
Receptionists, 323
Reed, John, 263
Reform movements, female, 180–185, 196, 227–234, 235, 242, 243–247, 276;
black women in, 378;
decline after admission of women to vote, 253–255, 257;
maternal rhetoric of, 181, 185, 225–226, 230, 253. See also Feminism; Suffrage movement
Religious affairs, colonial era, 40–41, 64, 68–69, 71–72;
male superiority in, 22, 64, 68–69, 71–72;
women in, 23, 68, 71–72
Rembienski, Aleksandra, 198
Reproductive function, 7, 8, 23, 57, 122, 161–162, 164, 186, 239, 274, 284–285

Republican Party, 254
Retail industry, 307–308, 314, 387. See also Sales girls
Reuben, Dr. David, 412
Revolt of Modern Youth, The (Lindsay), 270
Reward of Virtue, The (movie), 292
Rhode Island, early textile industry, 103–104
Rhythm method of birth control, 163, 268
Richards, Caroline, 171
Ripley, Sarah, 93, 129–130. See also Stearns, Sarah Ripley
Roaring 20's:
adolescence, 287, 288–289, 290;
advertising, 259–260, 295, 296–297, 299;
career women, 256, 257;
emphasis on sex, 255–256, 261–266, 269, 287, 289–294;
flapper, 256–257, 260, 261, 277, 299;
low birth rate, 261, 328;
marriage, 256, 269–270, 292, 339–340;
motherhood, 261, 345–346;
movies, 265–266;
sexual freedom, 261–265, 269–271;
single women, 256, 292;
women's political situation, 253–255;
working women of, 270, 307, 314, 321, 324, 329, 331
Robinson, Dr. Marie, 272–273, 277, 278, 283, 285–286, 288

Robinson, John, 23
Rockefeller, John D., 3rd, 401
Rogers, Eliza, 173–174
Romantic love, 150–154, 171,
  269, 290, 299, 426
Roosevelt, Eleanor, 255, 300
Roosevelt, Franklin D., 255
Ross, Mary, 308–309
Rossi, Alice, 418
Rowlandson, Mary, 33
Rowson, Susanna, 111
Rush, Benjamin, 124
Ryan, Martha, 60

Sadism, 276
Salem, Mass., 25, 98, 121;
  witchcraft trials, 76–81
Sales girls, 307–308, 319–320,
  325, 326, 331, 333, 394–395
Sandys, Sir Edwin, 37, 38
Sanger, Margaret, 215, 244–245,
  262
Sanitary Commission, 225, 227,
  246
Save Me the Waltz (Zelda Fitz-
  gerald), 293
Schools, 120;
  coeducational high, 288–289;
  girls', 149. *See also* Educa-
    tion
Schuyler, Mrs. Philip, 32
Seaman, Barbara, 413
Secker, Rev. William, 36, 54, 123;
  "Adam's Rib" sermon of,
    21, 27
*Second Twenty Years at Hull
  House* (Addams), 253
Secretarial work, 234, 314, 323,
  326
Sedgwick, Catharine Maria, 134,
  148, 150

Segar, Catharine, 39
Seneca Falls, N. Y., women's
  rights convention, 184
Sensuous Woman, The, 413
Sentimental novels, 143,
  150–153, 172, 185, 189–190
Sentimentalism, 131–134,
  140–141
Serial monogamy, 269
Servants:
  handling of, in colonial era,
    38–39;
  in commercial era, 120;
  slaves, 186–187.
  See also Women servants
Service industries, 313, 319–320,
  387
Settlement houses, 196, 214,
  225, 229, 255
Seventeen magazine, 289
Sewell, Samuel, 48
Sex:
  in advertising, 295–297, 298,
    299, 301–302, 410–411;
  in movies, 265–266,
    302–303;
  20th century pre-occupa-
    tion with, 255–256,
    261–266, 269, 287, 289–
    303, 410–415
Sex drive, female, 52, 111, 172,
  262–264, 267, 285, 411–412;
  denials of, 159, 160–161,
    164, 268, 414.
  See also Female sexuality
Sex objects, women as, 15, 110,
  262–266, 286, 299, 302–303,
  383, 410–411
Sexual differences, 3–9,
  273–275, 286, 416, 427–428;
  behavioral, 6–7, 274;

biological, 3–4, 7–8, 226, 274, 277–278, 412; cultural, 4–9; embryonic, 3; espoused by Social Darwinism, 226; mental, 7, 274, 275; psychological, 273–275; undue attention to, 15–16, 109–112, 262. *See also* Personality types, female vs. male
Sexual mores: colonial America, 49–53; 1920's, 261–265, 269–271; 20th century, 293–295, 411, 412–415; upper class, commercial era, 111–112; Victorian era brothels, 218–219
Sexual stereotypes, 5, 13–14, 144, 152–153, 170, 226–227; absence in colonial America, 62–64; blacks, 373–374, 382, 391–393; emergence of, 107–109; established in 19th century, 126, 127, 139, 144, 185, 191; manipulation by women, 172, 191, 245; polarization diminished, 243; 20th century, 290, 299, 303, 352, 369–370, 371, 382, 391–393, 411; working class, 220, 369–370, 371. *See also* Female stereotypes

Sexual Suicide (Gilder), 428
Sexual theory: Freudian, 276–283, 285; Masters and Johnson, 411; 20th century, 262, 264, 267–268, 273–285, 411–412, 413–414; Victorian, 158–162, 164
Shakers, Society of, 175–176, 177–178
Sharecroppers, 375–377
Sheffield, Thomas, 61
Sherfy, Mary Jane, 411
Shippen, Nancy, 115–116
Shopping, 14, 300; late 18th century, 96–97
Short, Mercy, 80
Sigourney, Andrew, 170
Sigourney, Lydia Huntley, 134, 140, 148, 151, 165, 169, 170, 181
Silbey, Abigail, 48
Single magazine, 399
Single persons: career women, 232, 235–236, 292, 316; in colonial America, 34, 38, 47; 20th century women, 256, 292, 316, 398–400; women around 1900, 197, 232, 235–236, 238, 256; women discriminated against, 66–68
Sinners in Hell (movie), 266
Slater, Samuel, 103–104
Slavery, 30, 180–181, 185–190; marriage outlawed in, 186, 374
Slavic immigrant women, 201–202

colonial era status of, 21–22,
26, 28–29, 40, 41–44,
52–53, 54–56;
commercial era function of,
86, 113, 123–126, 127;
commercial era status of,
86–87, 90–91, 93–94, 106,
119, 123–124;
control of dowry, 28–29;
court action against hus-
bands, 43;
as husbands' property, 26,
152;
as husbands' status sym-
bols, 98, 106, 339–340,
356–357;
role in 1920's, 255, 293–294,
339–340;
sexual rights of, 52,
267–268;
20th century, 255, 283–284,
293–295, 308–313,
315–316, 317–319,
328–341, 388, 396–398,
401–406;
upper class, 98–99,
106–118, 340;
working wives, 15, 209–210,
222, 236–238, 308–313,
315–316, 317–319,
328–334, 350–351, 388,
393–394, 396–398
Wollstonecraft, Mary, 85, 276
Woman's Coming of Age
(Schmalhauser and Calver-
ton), 261, 269, 308
Woman's Estate (Mitchell), 426
Womb. *See* Uterus
Women, The (Luce), 294
Women and Economics (Gilman), 239

Women and Socialism (Bebel),
244
Women servants:
colonial era, 23, 25, 30;
commercial era, 99–100;
court action by, against
masters, 43;
emergence of paid domes-
tics, 99–100
illegitimate births, 49, 51;
indentured, 24, 34, 99, 120;
sexual abuse by masters,
50–51. *See also* Domestic
service
Women's Army Corps, 316
Women's Bureau, 233, 254, 317,
318, 329
Women's Christian Temperance
Union (WCTU), 231
Women's clubs, 196, 225, 227,
230, 231;
black, 378
Women's Garment Workers,
1909–10 strike of, 223
Women's liberation movement,
422–429
Women's rights movement:
antebellum era, 184–185;
early 20th century, 243–249;
1920's disintegration of,
254–255.
See also Women's
liberation movement
Women's Trade Union League
(WTUL), 223, 230, 233, 254
Worcester, Mass., 26, 51;
public welfare, 39, 89–90,
100, 101
Working hours, 204, 209, 222,
316
Working mothers and wives, 15,

Mary P. Ryan was born in
Prairie du Chien, Wisconsin.
She received her B.A. and M.A.
at the University of Wisconsin,
Madison, and her Ph.D. at the
University of California at
Santa Barbara. She taught at
Pitzer College and is now
assistant professor of history
at the State University
of New York at Binghamton.

ABOUT THE AUTHOR